THE DISCOVERY OF ANCIENT INDIA

for
Vijay

The Discovery of Ancient India

Early Archaeologists and the Beginnings of Archaeology

UPINDER SINGH

permanent black

Published by
PERMANENT BLACK
D-28 Oxford Apartments, 11, I.P. Extension,
Delhi 110092

First published in hardback 2004
First paperback printing 2005

Seventh Impression 2018

ISBN 81 – 7824 – 127 - 7

Printed and bound by Sapra Brothers, New Delhi 110 092

Contents

Illustrations

Abbreviations

ASR	*Archaeological Survey Reports*
IA	*The Indian Antiquary*
JASB	*Journal of the Asiatic Society of Bengal*
JBBRAS	*Journal of the Bombay Branch of the Royal Asiatic Society of Bengal*
JRAS	*Journal of the Royal Asiatic Society*
NAI	National Archives of India
Num. Chron.	*Numismatic Chronicle*
OIOC	The Oriental and India Office Collection of the British Library
PWD	Public Works Department
R&A	Revenue and Agriculture Department

References to archival sources indicate the name of the department, followed by the name of the specific branch of the concerned department, proceedings number and other details.

Acknowledgements

I am grateful to Professors Bridget and F.R. Allchin and the Ancient India and Iran Trust, Cambridge, for the grant of a Charles Wallace visiting fellowship in the summer of 1999, which enabled me to examine archival material in London and begin writing this book.

The staff of the National Archives of India, New Delhi, and the British Library, London, provided prompt assistance and advice on accessing archival sources. The Archaeological Survey of India, National Archives, National Library (Calcutta) and British Library were kind enough to provide material used to illustrate this book.

Tanika and Sumit Sarkar encouraged me to venture into the terrain of modern Indian history and were extremely generous with their time and advice.

I would like to thank Mudit Trivedi for valuable information on the Delhi Archaeological Society, and Jaya Kashyap for the tip on the connection between the two Coles.

I would also like to especially thank Nayanjot Lahiri for a constant, fruitful exchange of ideas throughout the research and writing of this book, and Rukun Advani for being such a meticulous and efficient editor and publisher.

Preface

Like many things in life, this book was the result of a chance encounter. The encounter was with a first edition of James Fergusson's *Archaeology in India with Especial Reference to the Works of Rajendralala Mitra* (1884). Fergusson had a brief stint in India as an indigo merchant but came to be better known as the author of a number of learned books on the history of architecture. Rajendralala Mitra was a distinguished Indian scholar who wrote extensively on various aspects of India's ancient past. Fergusson wrote *Archaeology in India* in the heat of the Ilbert Bill controversy, which erupted in 1883, when the British colonial government sought to introduce a bill that would allow Indian judges to try Europeans at the local level. Fergusson was quite frank about his aims:

> The real interest . . . of the volume—if any—will probably be found to reside, not in the analysis of the archaeological works of Babu Rajendralala Mitra, but in these days of discussions on Ilbert Bills, in the question as to whether the natives of India are to be treated as equal to Europeans in all respects. Under present circumstances it cannot fail to interest many to dissect the writings of one of the most prominent members of the native community, that we may lay bare and understand his motives and modes of action, and thus ascertain how far Europeans were justified in refusing to submit to the jurisdiction of natives in criminal actions.[1]

That a scholar of Fergusson's stature should have written such an undignified tract, openly proclaiming and justifying strong racial prejudice, fits with the political climate of 1883 in which racist sentiments, which might otherwise have remained dormant, exploded into the open, especially in Bengal.

While Fergusson's *Archaeology in India* made compelling reading, the copy casually handed to me in Delhi's Central Archaeological

[1] Fergusson (1884): vi.

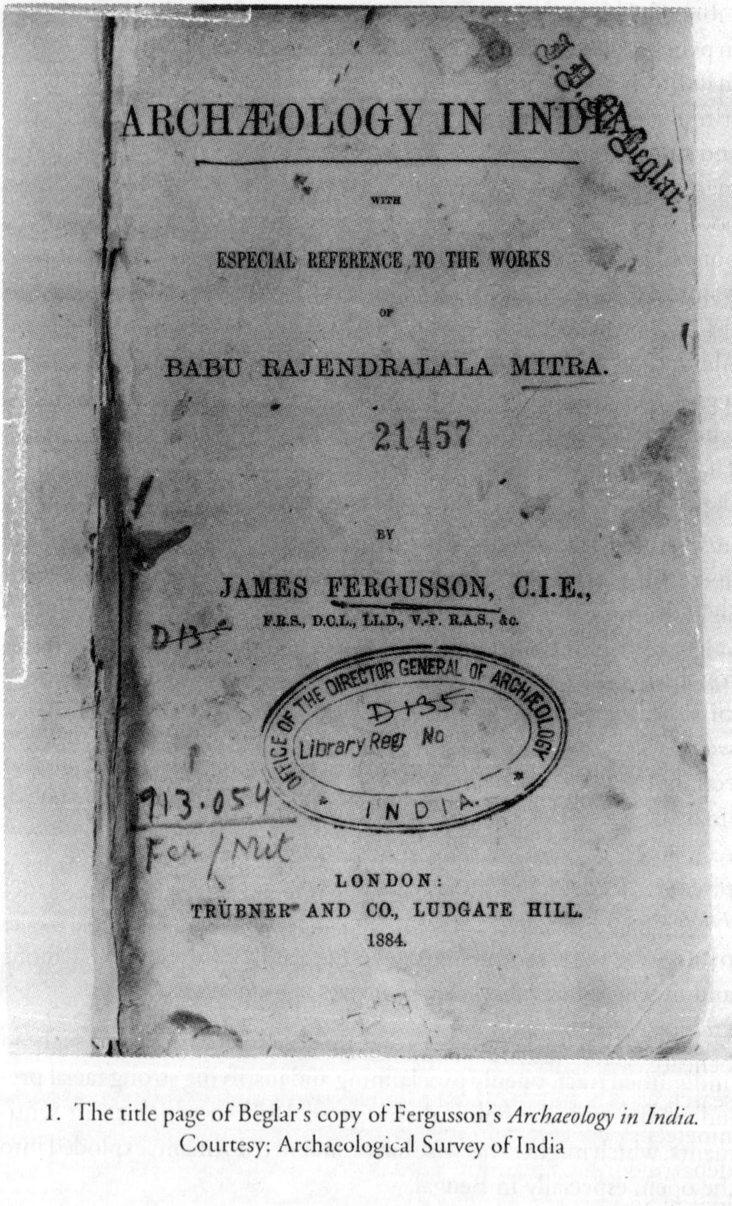

ARCHÆOLOGY IN INDIA

WITH

ESPECIAL REFERENCE TO THE WORKS

OF

BABU RAJENDRALALA MITRA.

21457

BY

JAMES FERGUSSON, C.I.E.,

F.R.S., D.C.L., LL.D., V.-P. R.A.S., &c.

LONDON:
TRÜBNER AND CO., LUDGATE HILL.
1884.

1. The title page of Beglar's copy of Fergusson's *Archaeology in India.* Courtesy: Archaeological Survey of India

Library had an added interest. The book had been profusely annotated in pencil in a small, neat hand by its original owner. At some later stage in its life, perhaps when it was re-bound, the edges of its pages had been trimmed. The result was that many of the comments were fragmentary and difficult to reconstruct. As I tried to decipher the writing in the margins and across pages, curiosity turned into acute suspense. Whose book was this? Who had pencilled in these remarks? Who had responded to Fergusson's violent polemic with such agitated, point-by-point rejoinders? The answer was on the title page, where the name 'J.D.M. Beglar' was stamped clearly and definitely. Beglar was one of Alexander Cunningham's assistants in the early years of the Archaeological Survey of India. He was one of a small group of archaeologists who had scoured city and village in northern and Central India in the 1870s and 1880s for historical sites and remains, documenting what they found. Beglar's pencilled notes got me interested in nineteenth-century archaeologists. A few forays into New Delhi's National Archives—my first exposure to the mesmerism of archival research—and there was no going back.

As I proceeded with my investigations, it became clear that they touched on larger issues which have been and remain a focus of discussion across many disciplines. Starting with Edward Said's seminal work, various exposés of Orientalism have revealed important connections between power and the construction of knowledge. Thus, the links between the colonial and Orientalist projects in India were direct, and indirect as well. An example of textual study politically inspired was the East India Company's sponsorship of a compendium of *Dharmashastra* precepts, a project linked to Warren Hastings' judicial plans. At a less direct and more general level—if we look at eighteenth- and nineteenth-century European writing on Indian history, art and architecture, and archaeology—the colonial bias is frequently visible beneath the veneer of disinterested scholarship. Archaeological research was an important part of the construction of India's past in the nineteenth century, and it eventually formed the focus of a separate department established in 1871 by the colonial state—the Archaeological Survey of India. There is no doubt that any discussion of nineteenth-century archaeological research in India must situate such research in the colonial context within which it was embedded.

And yet, while it is important to understand the colonial underpinnings of archaeological research in nineteenth-century India, such understanding has to form the base for further questions. These include: the interplay of the diverse ideas and methods of the many individuals who contributed to archaeological inquiry during this period; the institutional frameworks and constraints within which these people operated; the long-term validity and value of their discoveries and conclusions; the measures and policies adopted by the colonial government; and the attitude of India's princely states to archaeological research. A careful consideration of these questions reveals the complexities and conflicts that guided the development of archaeological research in nineteenth-century India. Another important question, which lies beyond issues relating to the construction and nature of archaeological knowledge, concerns what was actually happening to India's archaeological heritage—her artefacts, sites, and monuments—during these decades.

A large part of this book focuses unabashedly on individuals and their scholarly contributions. This is because of my conviction that individuals count and make a difference; they can make or break disciplines and institutions, more so at a time when these are in their fragile, embryonic stage. Therefore this book has much to say about the work of Alexander Cunningham (1814–93), the first director general of the Archaeological Survey. Although routinely referred to as the 'father of Indian archaeology', Cunningham's life and work have not been given the attention or importance they deserve. No one has written his biography, there is only one full-length book on him—Abu Imam's *Sir Alexander Cunningham and the Beginnings of Indian Archaeology.* A succinct account of Cunningham and his assistants can also be found in Dilip K. Chakrabarti's *A History of Indian Archaeology from the Beginning to 1947.*

Then, there are important architecture scholars such as James Burgess and James Fergusson, as well as less-known figures such as J.D.M. Beglar, A.C.L. Carlleyle, and H.H. Cole. And then of course while the nineteenth-century investigation of India's past was dominated by European scholars, it was not monopolized by them. There were, apart from traditional scholars—the *pandits* and *maulavis*—men such as Ṛam Raz, Rajendralala Mitra, and P.C. Mukharji. All these individuals played a part in the unearthing and interpretation of the material remains of India's ancient past, and their stories need to be told.

Upon his retirement from India in 1886, Alexander Cunningham divided his personal effects into two parts and despatched them on board two ships bound for England. One of these, the *Indus*, was wrecked on the Mullaittivu coral reef off the north-eastern coast of Sri Lanka. Cunningham's papers and notes, and many of his valuable antiquities, sank with it. For the researcher, the loss of these private papers is, to say the least, extremely unfortunate. Yet the published archaeological literature of the period is voluminous, and there is a fair amount of relevant archival material both in the National Archives of India and in the Oriental and India Office Collection of the British Library. Taken together, these offer valuable insights into Indian archaeology in the Cunningham era.

The early publications of the Archaeological Survey of India and the morass of Home Department and Revenue and Agriculture Department files reveal stories of individual initiatives, achievements, and failures. They also reveal behind-the-scenes discussions, debates and conflicts over a variety of issues that had an important bearing on Indian archaeology. There was a difference of opinion, for instance, on whether the archaeological enterprise should concentrate on field archaeology or architectural description. There was also a debate over the principles that should govern government policy *vis-à-vis* ancient artefacts, sites, and monuments, and the gradual realization that the documentation and description of sites and monuments must be supplemented by protection and conservation. There was the question of the extent to which 'natives' should be given a role in the archaeological enterprise. All these issues, and more, were deliberated upon in official circles, with an incessant governmental clamour for economy very audible in the background: the colonial state imposed strict financial constraints on what archaeology could do. On several occasions, these discussions brought into focus tensions between the head of the fledgling Archaeological Survey of India and the surveys of western and southern India, between the surveys and local governments, and between the colonial government and the princely states.

As for what was actually happening to artefacts, sites, and monuments, there is no doubt that the nineteenth century was an age of unprecedented archaeological discovery and documentation, a great part of it sponsored by the colonial government. Hundreds of sites were discovered and explored, and some excavated. Countless ancient antiquities and monuments were described, drawn, and photographed. The identification of a large number of place names mentioned in Indian, Chinese, and Greek texts created the basis of ancient Indian historical geography. Yet this century of archaeological discovery and documentation also saw the destruction of many sites by railway contractors, and by archaeologists themselves. Innumerable antiquities and architectural elements were dislocated from their original place, meaning and function to become items in private collections or objects of display in museums in India and abroad. It is not possible to reconstruct the life histories of all these myriad sites, monuments, and artefacts. It is, however, possible to take a few case histories and reflect on the complexities they reveal, and this is what I attempt.

The word 'discovery' in the title of this book may be misleading, but it is a handy term and a caveat should suffice. 'Discovery' suggests a swift, dramatic event, an unveiling of something completely lost or forgotten. But of course the past never exists fully constituted and formed; it is constituted and formed, interpreted and reinterpreted. Its discovery is therefore, theoretically, an endless process. Further, it is quite wrong to assume that indigenous, pre-colonial understandings of the ancient Indian past did not exist, or that Indians had developed a complete and collective amnesia about their history. At the same time, there is no doubt that colonialism introduced a new Western conceptual and analytical apparatus to the investigation of India's ancient past. This book deals with the archaeological aspects of this process of 'discovery'.

This is not, however, a comprehensive history of nineteenth-century Indian archaeology.[2] There are gaps and omissions in my narrative. For instance, many significant scholarly contributions have been mentioned in passing or only in specific contexts. Important developments in prehistory, most of which were achieved by individuals outside the ambit of the Archaeological Survey, have only briefly been

[2] There is already an excellent history of archaeology in colonial India: Chakrabarti (1988). Chakrabarti (2003) carries the narrative forward from 1947 to the present.

touched on. The aim of this book is to illuminate the history of Indian archaeology by drawing on published and archival material, selecting and discussing some of the important individual contributions, debates, and developments that marked those crucial decades during which archaeology emerged as a subject of academic inquiry in India.

CHAPTER 1

From Antiquarianism to Archaeology

In histories of European archaeology, the term 'antiquarianism' usually refers to the discovery, collection and description of antiquities, or to the amateur study of artefacts or monuments. In such study, artefacts and monuments are treated as ends in themselves. In early-nineteenth-century India, however, the word 'antiquarianism' had broader and more scholarly connotations. It was a time when strict disciplinary boundaries had not yet been drawn, allowing 'antiquarian' and 'antiquary' to be used as umbrella terms sheltering scholars who ranged over diverse areas—such as the study of ancient texts, languages, inscriptions, coins, antiquities, monuments, chronologies, and history. It was only in the second half of the nineteenth century that the term 'archaeology' came to the fore and began to assume a distinct identity within Orientalist discourse, denoting a branch of study concerned with the material remains of the past, with artefacts, sites, and monuments.

The formative phase in the history of antiquarian and archaeological research in India more or less coincided with the century of 'Company *raj*', the hundred years which stretched from the conquest of Bengal in the 1750s and 1760s to the Revolt of 1857. Changes in the nature and structure of colonial rule over this time, and the impact and responses these generated, had their ideological counterpart: there were visible shifts in the ideology of empire, in the many, complex intellectual strands that sought to justify and legitimize British rule in India.[1] This process of legitimization rested as much on interpretations of India's past as of its present.

[1] See Metcalf (1998).

The Surveyors

The expansion of the East India Company's Indian empire was accompanied by steadily intensifying initiatives and attempts to build up a body of knowledge about the country. The primary agents of these endeavours were the Company's civil and military officers. One of the important early contributors to the construction of geographical knowledge was James Rennell.[2] Rennell's survey of Bengal (1765–71) was the first regional cartography of the subcontinent. His maps of India and their accompanying memoirs were published in the 1780s and 1790s. Other landmarks in this mapping enterprise were William Lambton's triangulation survey south of the Krishna river, funded by the Madras government. In 1817, the Calcutta government took over responsibility for the triangulation, and this came to be known as the Great Trigonometrical Survey. The separate trigonometrical surveys which assumed this grand collective name were meant to provide the grid for the various topographical, cadastral, and revenue surveys that were also launched in this period.

The surveys really took off in the second half of the nineteenth century, especially after 1857, when the rule of the East India Company made way for that of the British crown.[3] Geological surveys were put on an organized footing in 1856; the first archaeological survey was launched in 1861, with the Archaeological Survey of India being established in 1871; the Indian Meteorological Department was set up in 1875; and by 1876 the basic triangulatory measurements of the Trigonometrical Survey of India were complete. By this time, a basic topographical survey of the country had also been almost accomplished. Geodetic observations began in the 1870s, and 1877 saw the beginnings of a systematic recording of tidal observations. Between 1875 and 1882 the Marine Surveys Department conducted the first phase of its surveys. The second phase followed in 1882–90, when the headquarters of the department moved from Calcutta to Bombay. The first general census was launched in 1871–2 and a second, more systematic and extensive one, was conducted in 1881. The establishment

[2] The East India Company's cartographic projects are discussed in detail by Edney (1999).

[3] Black (1891).

of the Archaeological Survey of India in 1871 was thus part of a wide range of surveys launched by the colonial government.

Early survey activities, of both the eighteenth and the early nineteenth centuries, were not as smooth and orderly as is sometimes thought. One reason was the initial lack of centralized coordination. The coordinating body, the Survey of India, which unified the trigonometrical, topographical, and revenue surveys, was established only in 1878, over a century after the earliest surveys had been launched. Uncoordinated statistical surveys of the eighteenth century were, similarly, placed on a systematic footing fairly late in the day—with W.W. Hunter, who was appointed director general of statistics in 1871. The nine volumes of the *Imperial Gazetteer of India*, published in 1881, were a consequence of this measure.

The idea of somewhat haphazard and amateur activity is reinforced if we look at the profiles of the men involved in survey work of various kinds during the eighteenth and early nineteenth centuries. Even among those who eventually applied themselves to fairly technical work, many had no special prior training in the area. They simply acquired their skills while on the job. This was the case, for instance, with the surveyor Reuben Burrow, who taught himself mathematics, astronomy, and surveying. Colonel Colin Mackenzie, the better-known surveyor (and collector) of the period, was also a self-taught and self-made man. A third name of significance is Francis Buchanan. The statistical surveys of the late eighteenth and early nineteenth centuries were especially significant from the archaeological point of view.[4]

Colin Mackenzie was a Scotsman who started his Indian career with the Madras infantry; shortly after, he was transferred to the Madras Engineers.[5] Between 1800 and 1810 Mackenzie was involved in a survey of Mysore and other parts of South India. In 1810, he became the first surveyor general of Madras. Between 1811 and 1814 he was sent off to serve in Java. Soon after his return to India, he was appointed the

[4] Cohn (1997: 80–1) points out that in the late-eighteenth and early-nineteenth centuries, the term 'statistical' did not have the connotations of collection, aggregation, and presentation of numerical data. It simply implied the collection of information considered necessary and useful to the state.

[5] See Edney (1999): 152 ff.

first surveyor general of India (in 1815), and continued in this post till his death in 1821.

Mackenzie had come to India out of an interest in Indian mathematics. After his arrival, this interest broadened and came to embrace ancient manuscripts, antiquities, and history. In these spheres, Mackenzie is known primarily as a collector. Over the many years of his travels as surveyor, principally in South India, he collected an enormous historical archive—the largest ever amassed by an individual before or since his time. Over his early career, military and engineering duties frequently tore him away from survey work; in the second phase of his career the demands of official survey work in some ways helped and in others hindered the 'parallel survey' or collection work he was conducting at his own initiative and expense. In spite of the constraints under which he operated, by the time he died Mackenzie's collection had swelled to include hundreds of manuscripts, drawings, copies of inscriptions, coins, transcripts of traditional histories, and antiquities.[6] While Mackenzie was himself the dynamic force behind this mammoth venture, he was assisted by a number of Indian assistants (including Brahmin pandits and a maulavi), principal among whom were C.V. Boria and Cavelly Venkata Lachmia.

Mackenzie did not systematize his collection nor use it in any large measure to construct a meta-text on India's history. No report or journal of his surveys ever appeared in print. His collection was catalogued several years after his death by H.H. Wilson, in 1828, but no part of it was ever actually published. Today, almost two centuries later, the 'Mackenzie Collection', preserved in the British Library, has assumed a different sort of significance—as a graphic, if not entirely typical, representation of the encounter between early colonial rule and India's past and traditions.[7]

Francis Buchanan, like Colin Mackenzie, was a Scot. Trained as a surgeon in Edinburgh, he joined the Bengal medical service (he assumed the name Hamilton some years after his retirement from India). In 1800, Buchanan was commissioned by Governor General Wellesley

[6] After Mackenzie's death, most of his oriental manuscripts eventually found their way to the Government Oriental Library in Madras, while the largest collection of the Mackenzie drawings currently forms part of the Oriental and India Office Library Collection of the British Library.

[7] See Dirks (1994) and Cohn (1997): Chap. 4.

to conduct a survey of Mysore. The area was not under the East India Company's direct rule, the survey set its sights on benefits that might accrue in the long run. The results of Buchanan's investigations were published in 1807, in three volumes.

In the same year, the Court of Directors appointed Buchanan to undertake another statistical survey, this time of the Bengal Presidency. Buchanan did a variety of things in the course of this survey: he compiled details of the occupational background of the inhabitants of various places, measured the temperatures of hot springs, collected botanical and geological specimens, measured distances and made detailed maps of the areas he traversed, and described the antiquities he saw and the sites he visited. The survey lasted seven years, and Buchanan submitted his report in 1816. A heavily edited and abridged version of the report, which left out a good deal of the information Buchanan had collected on antiquities and sites, was published in three volumes many years later, in 1838, by one Montgomery Martin. The detailed maps that Buchanan had compiled were never published, and the late publication of his report meant that his notices of important sites were left to others to announce. In fact, while Montgomery Martin's name was prominently displayed on the title page of the published version of the report, Francis Buchanan's was conspicuous by its absence.

The material collected and presented by Mackenzie and Buchanan is significant from several perspectives. It is part of the colonial enterprise and tells us about strategies of control. Neither Mackenzie nor Buchanan can be described as archaeologists; nevertheless, statistical surveys of this period generally contained a good deal of undigested historical and archaeological material, some of which was collected by surveyors at their own initiative (although they were given a very wide brief), and in Mackenzie's case at his own expense. Of particular importance, in such work, is the description of sites as they existed at the time of the surveys, often long before they were visited and described by archaeologists—by which time they often presented a very different appearance.[8] Buchanan's reports are, in this respect, even more significant than Mackenzie's. Buchanan was one of the first to recognize the importance of detailed plans and measurements of monuments and

[8] For a detailed account of the importance of Mackenzie's description of Amaravati and his interventions at the site, see Chapter 8.

sites. His report on the Bengal Presidency contains important information on sites such as Gaya, Rajgir, Bargaon, Kasia, and Gaur.

Apart from being collectors of historical material of very diverse kinds (inscriptions, texts, coins, oral traditions), Buchanan and Mackenzie can be described as amateur historians. Mackenzie wrote, for instance, on historical aspects of ancient remains in and around Amaravati and other ancient sites, on the history of the Jainas, and on aspects of political history. Buchanan, with stronger scholarly credentials, wrote on Indian religions. Anticipating the conclusions of much later research, he argued that the Buddha was a historical figure who lived in the sixth century BC.

The material Buchanan and Mackenzie collected in the course of their extensive travels and inquiries was full of archaeological and historical potential, but this potential was not fully utilized or followed up—neither by them nor by their immediate successors.[9]

The Antiquarians

Apart from this small circle of surveyors, various others contributed in a more direct and sustained way to the documentation of sites and monuments. The earliest notices and descriptions of Indian monuments, architecture, and sculpture are to be found in the writings of sixteenth- and seventeenth-century European travellers—Dutch, Italian, Portuguese, British, and French.[10] These writings display a dual interest—in temples such as those at Konarak and Ellora, and in the caves of western India such as Elephanta and Kanheri. While most such early accounts reveal the prejudice of the Western eye (for instance the account of the Dutch traveller van Linschoten), others

[9] There are some exceptions. The drawings in the Mackenzie Collection were used by James Fergusson (1868). Inscriptions and manuscripts from the Mackenzie Collection were also used by Dowson and H.H. Wilson in their writings on the political history of South India.

[10] For a detailed and comprehensive account of early European responses to Indian art and architecture, see Mitter (1977): Chaps. 1–3. Also see Chakrabarti (1988): 1–15. On the important impact of the discovery of Indian texts on Europe, see Schwab (1984) and Clarke (1997). Schwab and Clarke give details of the life and work of many of the European scholars involved in the Orientalist enterprise, only a few of whom have been discussed in this book (which deals primarily with British scholarship).

(notably Pietro della Valle) display a modicum of objectivity. This trickle of European descriptions of Indian monuments increased in the course of the eighteenth century, with the writings of Alexander Dalrymple, John Henry Grose, Thomas Coryat, Thomas Roe and various others.

The beginnings of systematic scholarly interest in ancient Indian monuments and sites can be located in the middle of the eighteenth century. The first precise descriptions of monuments were written at this time, particularly of the western caves and South Indian temples, by men such as Anquetil-Duperron,[11] Carsten Niebuhr, Le Gentil de Galasiere, and Pierre Sonnerat. An important addition to these descriptions of monuments was illustration: the late eighteenth century saw the publication of drawings by artists such as William Hodges, and this continued into the nineteenth century in the work of Thomas and William Daniels, and L. Langles.

The eighteenth century also saw the first forays into the historical geography of ancient India. Ancient Greek and Latin accounts, such as those of Pliny, Ptolemy, and the Periplus of the Erythraean Sea, served as reference points for attempts to identify ancient Indian sites. Antiquarians such as Jean Baptiste Bourguignon d'Anville, Joseph Tieffenthaler, Anquetil-Duperron, and Rennell were in the forefront of this enterprise, with Rennell's *Map of Hindoostan*, published in 1783, representing an important landmark.[12]

The spirit and enthusiasm of antiquarian scholarship in India was best represented by the Asiatic Society of Bengal, founded in 1784 by William Jones.[13] The society was more than the sum of the achievements and publications (impressive as these were) of its individual members. It was a meeting place for minds that shared similar interests. It stimulated, encouraged, and published the results of research on a great variety of related subjects.[14]

11 Anquetil-Duperron is best known for his translations of the *Zend-Avesta* and the Upanishads.

12 Rennell was the first to correctly identify ancient Pataliputra with modern Patna.

13 A detailed account of the early history of the Asiatic Society and the men associated with it is given in Kejariwal (1988). The Asiatic Society of Bengal was the first Asiatic Society. The Société Asiatique de Paris was founded many years later, in 1821, and the Royal Asiatic Society of Great Britain and Ireland in 1823.

14 Although the Asiatic Society is best remembered for its contribution and

The idea of setting up an institution devoted to the study of the East was simmering in Jones's mind even before he set foot on Indian soil in 1783 to take up a position as judge of the Supreme Court at Calcutta.[15] The 'Asiatick' Society was born on 15 January 1784 in the Grand Jury room of the Calcutta Supreme Court,[16] and the founder members included all the judges of the Supreme Court. The society had the approval of the East India Company's representatives in India. Jones's idea was to follow as closely as possible the pattern of the Royal Society of London, of which the king was 'patron'. The society therefore invited the governor general and his council to accept the title of 'patron', a request that was graciously accepted. However, Hastings declined presidentship of the society on the grounds that this was an honour that ought to go to William Jones.

The aims of the Asiatic Society were grand in their sweep. The title of William Jones's first address as president was: 'A Discourse on the Institution of a Society, for inquiring into the History, Civil and Natural, the Antiquities, Arts, Science, and Literature of Asia'. But Jones was not one to impose boundaries on the spirit of inquiry that the society was supposed to embody. He described the object of inquiry as 'Man and Nature'. The qualifications for membership were 'a love of knowledge and a zeal for the promotion of it'.

Jones's contribution to Indological or antiquarian studies had many facets. He was involved in a project, partly subsidized by the East India Company, to prepare a digest of Hindu and Muslim laws, an

---

impetus to antiquarian research, for a long time its energies were equally devoted to scientific investigations. These included the study of indigenous Indian science, but the society also played an important role in the promotion of Western science in India. See Baber (1998): 153 ff; and Pratik Chakrabarti (2004), *passim.*

[15] On Jones, see Kejariwal (1988): 30 ff; Cannon (1964); Mukherjee (1968); Majeed (1992).

[16] In the course of its long history, the society underwent various changes in name from the original Asiatick Society (1784–1825) to the Asiatic Society (1825–32), Asiatic Society of Bengal (1832–1935), and Royal Asiatic Society of Bengal (1936–51). Since 1951, it has been known as the Asiatic Society. Jones preferred to use the term 'Asiatic' rather than 'Oriental': '*Asiatick* appears both classical and proper, whether we consider the place or the object of the institution, and preferable to *Oriental,* which is in truth a word merely relative, and, though commonly used in Europe, conveys no very distinct idea' (Jones, 1788: xii).

enterprise that tied in with his professional concerns as a judge and the East India Company's interest in systematizing its judicial system. Jones was fascinated by questions of origins, dispersal, and connections—between human groups, languages, and cultures—and he saw language as the key to understanding these links. He maintained that Iran was the original point of dispersal of the various races of mankind. He was not the first to notice the affinities between Sanskrit and languages such as Greek and Latin, but he was the first to formulate the hypothesis that these languages were all descendants of a single parent language. His identification of 'Sandrocottus' in classical accounts with Chandragupta Maurya established an important chronological reference point in Indian history. And it was Jones who began the process of working out a uniform system of transliteration for Sanskrit words in the Roman script. Having stumbled upon a Bengali manuscript of Kalidasa's *Shakuntalam*, he proceeded to translate the play into English. Kalidasa was thus first introduced to the European public and the play became quite the rage in Europe, although some thought Jones was overdoing it by describing Kalidasa as the Indian Shakespeare.

Some of Jones's ideas seem somewhat bizarre today, but they seemed much less so in his time. For instance, his theory that Egyptian priests at some remote time in the past migrated and settled down in India, and that the Chinese were originally Hindus of Kshatriya caste, did not sound entirely outlandish to his contemporaries. Jones was closely involved in politics, first in England and then in India, and many of his writings, especially his work on the legal treatises, illustrate the close interface between scholarship and the colonial enterprise.[17] The fact that such an interface existed does not in any way diminish the significance of Jones's personal scholarly contribution and his occasionally exaggerated speculations, or the interest in things Indian that his writings generated in Europe, or the importance of the institution he created.

[17] Some of the connections are indirect, and more in the form of the implications of his research. Majeed (1992) points out that Jones's attempts to define an idiom in which cultures could be compared can to some extent be seen as a response to a need for such an idiom in the late eighteenth century. He also suggests that Jones's hymns to Hindu deities reflect an attempt to legitimize British rule in an Indian idiom.

The group of 'curious and learned men' who participated in the activities of the Asiatic Society in its earliest phase included Charles Wilkins, Francis Wilford, and Samuel Davis. The journal of the Asiatic Society—*Asiatick Researches,* founded in 1788—was the first of its kind in India.[18] Demand exceeded supply; a pirated edition soon hit the market in England, and French and German translations of some of the volumes were also soon in circulation. The importance of the contributions made by William Jones and the growing circle of scholars who came to be associated with the Asiatic Society lies in the beginnings they made and the initiatives they took, not necessarily in the accuracy or veracity of their conclusions. For the first time, there was now an institutional focus for efforts hitherto scattered and haphazard.

Over the years, the organization of the Asiatic Society gradually became more formal and systematic than it was during Jones's time. Land was obtained from the Government in 1805, and a new building for the society was built on it. A membership fee was introduced, and attempts were made to make the society's financial position less precarious. The museum of the Asiatic Society, established in 1814, was the first public museum to be set up in India. The collections of antiquities and natural history specimens that had been donated to the society over the years now found a home. A library was also established along with the museum.

During the years after Jones's death in 1794, the Asiatic Society survived some rough times. In the early nineteenth century, one of the leading figures associated with it was Henry Thomas Colebrooke, who went on to become its president in 1806. Colebrooke began his Indian career as assistant collector of revenue in Tirhut in 1786, and went on to work in the Court of Appeal in Calcutta. He also taught in the College of Fort William, where he was professor of Hindu Law and Sanskrit. His completion of the *Digest of Hindu Law* begun by Jones won him the approval of the governor general and considerably boosted his career. The first volume of his *Grammar of the Sanskrit Language* was published in 1805. Over the years, Colebrooke built a

[18] Twenty volumes of the *Asiatick Researches* were published between 1788 and 1839. This publication was ultimately superseded by the *Journal of the Asiatic Society of Bengal.*

strong international reputation as a distinguished Sanskrit scholar writing on a wide range of subjects, including the *Rig Veda*, Buddhism, Jainism, Indian astronomy, mathematics, social institutions, ancient monuments, and inscriptions.

This developing Indological tradition, involving most substantially the Western study of Sanskrit texts, was taken further by Horace Hayman Wilson. Wilson was associated with the Asiatic Society as its secretary between 1816 and 1832. His prodigious scholarly output included an English verse translation of Kalidasa's *Meghaduta* (1813) and a Sanskrit–English dictionary (1819) which he was commissioned to compile by the Court of Directors. Wilson wrote on a variety of subjects, including the history of Kashmir, the history of the Vaishnava, Shaiva, and Shakta sects, the *Puranas*, coins, inscriptions, and ancient Indian political history.

Nineteenth-century Orientalists tended to distinguish the Brahmanism of the ancient Sanskrit texts from the Hinduism of later times, between what another Sanskritist, Monier-Williams, described as the 'root' and the 'diseased outgrowth'. These scholars were prepared to invest a lifetime of research into the former, and were led to concede that the ancient texts of the East contained grains of wisdom as well as ideas that were lofty, profound, and inspiring.[19] Living Hinduism, in which they saw polytheism, idolatry, caste, and superstitions, was however another matter altogether. Over time, under the impact of utilitarian and evangelical critiques of Indian society, and as British rule in India became more firmly entrenched, the Western attitude towards Hinduism hardened.[20]

In the course of the nineteenth century Buddhism too was gradually textualized, defined, and made an object of Western academic inquiry.[21] This was the outcome of the discovery and study of texts in

[19] The problem, it seemed to them, was that these were offset by the less edifying features of ancient texts. 'I confess', Max Müller wrote in his Preface to the first volume of the Sacred Books of the East series, 'it has been for many years a problem to me, aye, and to a great extent is so still how the Sacred Books of the East should, by the side of so much that is fresh, natural, simple, beautiful, and true, contain so much that is not only unmeaning, artificial, and silly, but even hideous and repellent.'

[20] See P.J. Marshall, ed. (1970).

[21] See Almond (1988).

Sanskrit, Pali, Chinese and Mongolian. In India, Brian Houghton Hodgson amassed a large volume of Buddhist manuscripts in Nepal during his sojourn as British Resident there, and donated many of these to institutions in India (including to the Asiatic Society of Bengal) and Europe. The manuscripts he presented to libraries in Paris came to the notice of a French scholar, Eugene Burnouf, and formed an important basis for his influential book, *Introduction à l'histoire du Buddhisme indien*, published in 1844. Hodgson himself wrote on various aspects of Buddhism; many of his writings were published in the *Journal of the Asiatic Society of Bengal*. Around the same time, the first steps in the exploration of the language, literature, and traditions of Tibet were undertaken by William Moorcroft, and from there taken much further by the Hungarian scholar Alexander Csoma de Körös, who published a grammar and dictionary of the Tibetan language in 1830. Csoma de Körös was an honorary member of the Asiatic Society and served as its librarian for a few years.

In the 1830s, a new energy was infused into the Asiatic Society by James Prinsep.[22] Prinsep came to India at the age of twenty as assistant assay-master of the Calcutta mint. At the time, H.H. Wilson was assay master, and his interest in antiquarian studies communicated itself to Prinsep. In 1830 Prinsep was elected a member of the Asiatic Society. He soon took over the society journal, *Gleanings in Science*, from Major J.D. Herbert, and transformed it into *The Journal of the Asiatic Society*. When Wilson left for England in 1832, Prinsep succeeded him as secretary of the society. During his tenure the activities of the Asiatic Society started veering away from textual studies towards epigraphic, numismatic, and archaeological investigation. Prinsep also steered the Asiatic Society through continuing financial problems, which at this point of time coincided with an unsympathetic government attitude. This was Governor General Bentinck's tenure, and in the wake of the new educational policy which now favoured Western rather than indigenous learning, the government stopped funding the printing of ancient texts, a step that the Asiatic Society spoke up against—in vain.

Prinsep had a particular interest in ancient coins, not surprising in someone employed within a mint. The society's coin collection

[22] See Kejariwal (1988): 162 ff.

expanded enormously during his tenure. But the achievement for which Prinsep is best known is his decipherment of Ashokan Brahmi in 1837, an achievement that was really the culmination of efforts by a number of scholars, such as Charles Wilkins, Captain A. Troyer, W.H. Mill, and Revd. J. Stevenson. With the decipherment of this script, at one stroke, a mine of invaluable historical information became accessible to scholars. In the same year, George Turnour's identification of the 'Piyadassi' of the inscriptions with the Mauryan king Ashoka on the basis of the Pali chronicle the *Dipavamsa*, marked a major breakthrough in ancient Indian political history. Prinsep also had an important role to play in the decipherment of Kharoshthi, credit for which was shared by him and a number of other scholars such Christian Lassen, Charles Masson, Alexander Cunningham, and E. Norris.

Narratives of dynastic history now had to struggle to keep pace with the names of Indo-Greek, Kushana, Gupta, Valabhi, Vakataka, Kadamba, western Kshatrapa, and Rajput kings that were being revealed at unprecedented speed via coins and inscriptions. *The Journal of the Asiatic Society* began the important practice of publishing facsimiles of inscriptions. Prinsep appealed, in 1836, to the government for funds to restore and preserve the Bhitari pillar—this being the first time that the Asiatic Society interceded to preserve an ancient monument.[23]

Prinsep's early death in 1840 (he was only forty years old at the time) cut short a brief but brilliant career. His contribution to antiquarian studies was not limited to personal achievement. It also lay in the encouragement he gave to the research of others. Antiquarian research, in this period, had important elements of a cooperative endeavour, and Prinsep was always careful both to acknowledge his debt to other scholars, and to help these others in their researches. Among the many young scholars of the time, who were both influenced and inspired by Prinsep, was Alexander Cunningham, the subject of our next chapter.

The great discoveries and breakthroughs of these various European scholars could not have been made without the assistance of India's

[23] Kejariwal (1988): 101–2.

traditional scholars. Although a handful of Englishmen learnt Sanskrit and had some degree of access to ancient Sanskrit texts, pandits were essential to the antiquarian studies of this time. All the same, the Orientalist enterprise appears to a large extent as the discovery of India's past by European scholars, using the intellectual and interpretive apparatus of the West. In this scheme of things, the sort of assistance Indian pandits and maulavis provided could be dismissed as of the secretarial variety, not worthy of public acknowledgement. This was the reason why, while the names of European scholars were given public prominence, those of 'native' informants, crucial to the enterprise, were kept largely anonymous and are now forgotten. Among the early names that survive is Pandit Ramlochan, Jones's Sanskrit teacher, who played an important role in deciphering inscriptions. In subsequent decades, several pandits and maulavis played an important role in the preparation of catalogues of manuscripts and in the task of editing texts published in the Asiatic Society's *Bibliotheca Indica.* Some appeared as editors of texts. These included scholars such as Rajendralala Mitra, Iswarchandra Vidyasagara, Ramamaya Tarkaratna, Hara Chandra Vidyabhushana, and Visvanatha Sastri.[24]

The marginalization of traditional scholarship, and the dismissal of the very possibility that Indians might centrally contribute to the study of the past of their own country, were reflected in other ways as well. William Jones had set up the Asiatic Society as a meeting place for European minds, as an institution that would harness the intellectual energy and potential of Englishmen residing in a country—'every part of which abounds in objects of curious and useful speculation.'[25] The question of whether the doors of the society should be opened to 'learned natives' was deferred for the moment.

Till 1829 the Asiatic Society of Bengal remained a European club. Indians, off and on, made contributions to the society's journal, and were associated with its activities, but there were no Indian members. This pattern was broken in 1829 when, on the recommendation of H.H. Wilson, Prasanna Kumar Tagore, Dwarkanath Tagore, Russamay Dutt, and Rama Çomal Sen were elected members of the society. This was also the year when, in the wake of the collapse of Palmer

[24] For further details, see Chapter 9.

[25] Jones (1788).

and Co.—the financial agents of the society—a generous grant of Rs 20,000 by the king of Oudh and one of Rs 5,000 by his prime minister bailed the society out of financial crisis.[26] In subsequent years the Nawab Nazim of Bengal (in 1847), and a handful of Indian scholars, such as Sir Radhakanta Deva Bahadur (1855) and Professor Bapudeva Sastri (1868), were added to the list of the society's honorary members. Rama Comal Sen had started off as a clerk in the society's employ; in 1833 he was elevated to the position of 'Native Clerk', in effect functioning as treasurer. The number of Indian members gradually increased. But it took many decades for an Indian to be elected president of the society. This important event took place in 1885, when Rajendralala Mitra became the first Indian to hold the post.

The relationship between the Asiatic Society and the colonial government generally remained cordial. And, until it was closed down in 1854, the College at Fort William also had a close working relationship with the society. There were occasions when the government extended material support to the Asiatic Society, though such support was usually reluctantly and slowly given. In 1804 a plot of land on the corner of Park Street was granted free of cost to the society. The biggest windfall came in 1876, when the government offered the society the sum of Rs 1,50,000 as compensation in lieu of accommodation that had been promised it in the new building, which was also supposed to house the Indian Museum. In spite of occasional government subsidies, increasing financial needs combined with injudicious financial management and the folding up of two of the firms that handled its finances, and the Asiatic Society suffered from chronic financial difficulties.

Apart from the Asiatic Society of Bengal, there were other institutions that played a role in nineteenth-century Orientalist inquiry. The existence and activities of the College of Fort William in Calcutta (1800–54) and that of Fort St George in Madras (1812–54), although intended primarily to train newly recruited civil servants of the East India Company, resulted in a certain degree of interaction between Indian and British scholars and stimulated the study of Indian languages and literatures. These two colleges had distinctive personalities. Fort William focused on the Arabic, Persian, Hindustani, Bengali,

[26] *Centenary Review of the Asiatic Society* (1885): 71

and Sanskrit languages and literatures, and the College of Fort St George on South Indian vernaculars. This was also the period of the growth of the publishing industry in India and, in their heyday, the printing presses of both colleges produced an impressive number and range of publications.[27] Mention must also be made of the Literary Society of Bombay, founded in 1804 with the aim of 'promoting useful knowledge particularly such as is more immediately connected with India.' The Madras Literary Society, intended as a repository for the diverse researches of the East India Company's officers in Madras, complemented the College of Fort William; for many years the college and the society shared a library and a museum.[28]

Another less-known entity was the short-lived but energetic Delhi Archaeological Society, active between 1847 and 1854.[29] Henry Cope, editor of the *Delhi Gazette*, was its first secretary and, initially, the driving force behind the society's activities. The society eventually came to have some 120 members, including well-known British scholars such as Henry Elliot, E.C. Bayley, A. Sprenger, and Alexander Cunningham. It also had a number of Indian members, including distinguished notables and scholars of Delhi such as Nawab Zia-ud-din, Sayyid Ahmad Khan, and the 'pundits' of the Delhi College. Members of the society met and read papers in English, Urdu, and Persian on a variety of subjects, including but not restricted to, Delhi's ancient and medieval history. The society had a museum and a journal (of which only two volumes were published, in 1850 and 1852). Its most important achievement was the initiation of a mapping of Delhi's historical monuments and attempts to unravel its history by correlating references in Persian chronicles with archaeological remains. The society conducted excavations at Firuzabad in 1847 and repaired the Jantar Mantar observatory in 1852–3, using for the latter funds donated by the raja of Jaipur. The Delhi Archaeological Society

[27] On the College of Fort William, see Kopf (1969) and Das (1978). On the College of Fort St George and the distinctiveness of the 'Madras School of Orientalism', see Trautmann (2000), Blackburn (2003).

[28] The Asiatic Society of Madras was founded in 1812, and was reconstituted as the Madras Literary Society in 1829. The Bombay Literary Society became the Bombay Branch of the Royal Asiatic Society in 1829.

[29] I am indebted to an unpublished research paper by Mudit Trivedi for the information on the Delhi Archaeological Society which follows.

had cordial relations with the Asiatic Society of Bengal and the Literary Society of Madras, both of which helped build up its library by forwarding to it copies of its journals and other publications.

The Adventurers

If the early nineteenth century was an age of scholars poring over ancient texts and inscriptions and unravelling the tangled web of dynastic histories, it was just as much an age of a group of men who are perhaps best described as adventurers. This, not because the search for adventure was necessarily their driving force or goal (although it might well have been), but because when we look back at their lives it is the element of adventure that marks them out. These were men who pushed themselves beyond what seemed prudent or possible. Many of them were intelligence agents of the East India Company who negotiated parched deserts, formidable mountains, extremes of climate, and hostile and unpredictable tribes and chieftains in various disguises as part of the bitter, long-drawn-out Anglo-Russian game of oneupmanship that was being played out in Central Asia.[30] A few of them published accounts of their travels, although some of the most important discoveries were detailed in the secret despatches they sent to Company headquarters in Calcutta. Some of these men combined their political role with a scholarly one. Foremost among them were William Moorcroft, Alexander Burnes, and Charles Masson; to them may be added three Frenchmen—Chevalier Ventura, A. Court, and J.F. Allard—generals in the employ of Maharaja Ranjit Singh. The activities of these men were concentrated in the north-west, and they shared an interest in collecting coins and opening stupas, referred to at the time as 'topes' by Europeans. They were all in communication and interaction with the Asiatic Society and published accounts of their discoveries in its journal. In fact the Asiatic Society of Bengal played an important role in providing a scholarly meeting ground where traditional political rivalries were transcended.

William Moorcroft was a British veterinary surgeon, who had come to India in 1808 to become superintendent of the East India Company's stud.[31] It was ostensibly the search for a superior breed of horses that

[30] See Hopkirk (1991).

[31] Hopkirk (1991): 90 ff.

led Moorcroft to long journeys between 1820 and 1825, into Ladakh, Tibet and Central Asia. He was also concerned with expanding British trade opportunities in these areas, which entailed pre-empting and thwarting the Russians. Moorcroft and his companions were the first Englishmen to set foot in Leh, the first Europeans to see the colossal Buddha statues at Bamian, and the first to reach the banks of the Oxus. With so many important firsts to his credit, it is not surprising that Moorcroft carved out a name for himself as a great explorer. He was in contact with the Asiatic Society, sending across transcripts of inscriptions and texts to Calcutta. In 1825 the society received from him a letter giving a sketch of the Tibetan language and alphabet. Moorcroft died in 1825 in the course of his travels under mysterious circumstances, and was buried in an unmarked grave outside the walls of the town of Balkh. He never found the superior breed of horses which he had searched so long and hard in Central Asia. But he did succeed in inspiring the Hungarian Csoma de Körös into carrying forward his preliminary Tibetan studies—and in fact into dedicating his life to the study of the language and literature of that region.

Alexander Burnes came to India in 1821 as a sixteen-year-old cadet in the East India Company's Bombay Native Army. He swiftly mastered Hindustani and Persian and distinguished himself by his audacity and flamboyance. One of his most celebrated adventures was a successful journey 1000 miles up the Indus, ostensibly to deliver a gift of five exceptionally huge dray horses and a gilded stagecoach on behalf of William IV of England to Maharaja Ranjit Singh. The more pragmatic aim of Burnes's journey was to chart the navigability of the Indus up to Lahore. After completing this expedition Burnes journeyed into Afghanistan and Central Asia, publishing accounts of his travels. He played a leading role in what turned out to be the ill-conceived and ultimately disastrous British involvement in Afghan politics (the First Afghan War), which involved initially supporting Dost Mohammad and then suddenly shifting support to the unpopular puppet ruler Shah Shuja. As British Resident in Kabul, Burnes became one of the casualties of this policy: he was killed by an Afghan mob in 1841. Burnes is important in the history of antiquarian and archaeological study as one of the first to visit and describe the ruins of Harappa. He did the same for the important site of Manikyala, a village near Kabul, though he identified it incorrectly with ancient Taxila. Burnes documented many other stupa sites in the north-west (he thought stupas were royal tombs), and tried to identify several places mentioned in the Greek accounts of Alexander's invasion.

Charles Masson—his original name was James Lewis—was another man in the adventurer genre. Details of his background are few and obscure. Rumoured to be an American, Masson was actually an Englishman. His brief career in the East India Company's army came to an end after the siege of Bharatpur, when he deserted. Thereafter, for many years (1826–38), Masson travelled in the Punjab (he visited Harappa), Sind, Baluchistan, Afghanistan, and had many exciting adventures. He published an account of these journeys in three volumes. He was also soon drawn into the web of the East India Company's intelligence-gathering network: this won him an official pardon for his past desertion. The deal included an agreement that Masson would hand over all his present and future collections to the East India Company in return for the latter's financial support to his activities. From the viewpoint of antiquarian research, Masson's major claim to fame was his opening of a number of stupas in the north-west, and even more so his enormous coin collection, which came to include over 30,000 items amassed in the course of his travels.[32] Among his most sensational finds were hundreds of coins that he discovered at the site of Begram in Afghanistan. Masson's coins played an important role in the reconstruction of the political history of the north-western part of the subcontinent, particularly of the Indo-Greeks and the Kushanas. His memoirs on the antiquities and coins he discovered in Afghanistan were published in the *Journal of the Asiatic Society of Bengal.* Masson also contributed to the decipherment of the Kharoshthi script.

The end of the Napoleonic wars caused a diaspora of French army officers, many of whom thought nothing of travelling to distant lands in search of employment and fortune. In the 1820s some of these,

[32] The major part of Masson's coin collection found its way to the India Museum in London. The remainder was bought by Alexander Cunningham at a sale in London. (Imam, 1966: 25, fn. 5.)

namely J.F. Allard, J.B. Ventura and C. Court, found their way to the Punjab, where they became the nucleus of Maharaja Ranjit Singh's Fauj-i-Khas.[33] Allard had fought in Italy, Spain and France, and had participated in the Battle of Waterloo. Ventura was a colonel in the French infantry and seems to have taken part in Napoleon's Russian campaign. In India, Ventura played an important role in training the Sikh infantry, while Court trained the artillery. Allard eventually went on, in 1837, to become official Agent de France to Ranjit Singh's court.

During times of relative tranquillity, these French generals energetically collected antiquities and coins, many of which found their way to France. They were also inveterate stupa-openers: Ventura opened the largest stupa at Manikyala in 1830; Court opened a number of smaller stupas at Manikyala and made important coin finds. He also tried his hand at historical geography, attempting to identify places that lay on Alexander's march through Bactria. These generals were in communication with various learned bodies, such as the Société Asiatique and the French Academy in Paris: when Allard returned to India in 1836, he came armed with a series of instructions from the French Academy. These touched on the need for careful excavations of key sites, descriptions and drawings of monuments, and the preparation of lists of manuscripts.[34]

The French generals were also in regular communication with the Asiatic Society in Calcutta. With Prinsep and other antiquarians they shared a passion for collecting ancient coins. A selection of Ventura's coins was exhibited in the Asiatic Society in 1834; Court and Ventura were made honorary members of the Asiatic Society in 1835. Ventura came to Calcutta in 1837–8 bringing along with him some choice coins from his cabinet. He offered Prinsep any coin the latter fancied, but it seems there was none among them that Prinsep did not already possess.[35] Allard and Prinsep met and corresponded with each other. These communications and constant offers of numismatic gifts to Prinsep indicate an acknowledgement of the latter's scholarly

[33] For details, see Lafont (2002).

[34] Lafont (2002): 141–2.

[35] Imam (1966): 18, fn. 4. The entire set of coins was subsequently stolen from General Ventura's hotel room.

reputation and abilities. For his part, Prinsep prepared lists and published accounts of the French generals' coin collections and reported on their stupa-openings in the Asiatic Society's journal.

Early Archaeological Writings

In our overview of the early history of Indian archaeology, we need to distinguish between incidental references to archaeological data, specifically archaeological research and writings, and the beginnings of systematic and sustained archaeological inquiry. As has been pointed out, till about 1830 there were few writings that would qualify as 'archaeological' by present standards.[36] There were descriptions and drawings of ancient monuments, caves (Ajanta, Ellora, Bagh, etc.), and antiquities. There was the wealth of material zealously collected by surveyors such as Buchanan and Mackenzie, which for years on end lay more or less neglected and unutilized. But there were also the first handful of reports of field discoveries. These included Alexander Davidson's report to the Asiatic Society on the discovery of Roman coins at Nellore near Madras (1788), Jonathan Duncan's account of the discovery of Buddhist antiquities at Sarnath (1798), J. Babington's illustrated account of the megalithic graves of Malabar (1823), and Captain Robert Young's account of megalithic burials at Oopulgutt near Hyderabad (1827).[37]

Such notices and descriptions of sites gradually increased. P.T. Cautley's description of Behat near Saharanpur in Uttar Pradesh represents the earliest understanding of the basic stratigraphy of an ancient site.[38] The increasing notices of sites in different parts of the country were accompanied by the earliest accounts of excavations. These include A. F. Bellasis' description of his excavation of the site of Brahminabad in Sind, and the writings of Babington, Captain H. Congreave, and Captain Meadows Taylor on the megaliths of South India.[39]

[36] Chakrabarti (1988): 21.

[37] Davidson (1788); Duncan (1798); Babington (1832); Young (1827). Cited in Chakrabarti (1988).

[38] Cautley (1834a and 1834b).

[39] Bellasis (1857a and 1857b); Babington (1832); Congreave (1844–5); Meadows Taylor (1851, 1853). All cited in Chakrabarti (1988).

The increased momentum of archaeological investigation and inquiry after 1830 was fuelled by advances made in the study of ancient texts, inscriptions, and coins. The opening of stupas revealed important information about dynasties, such as the Indo-Greeks and the Kushanas, and eventually, about the history of Buddhism. The coins and sculptures discovered in the north-western part of the subcontinent remained an important focus of interest, and several attempts were made to identify places mentioned in classical Greek accounts.

Alexander Cunningham stands at the end of an important phase, to the period when archaeology in India ceased to be the exclusive and part-time preserve of surveyors, antiquarians, adventurers, dilletantes, and treasure-hunters. The study of the material relics of the past came now to be tamed, controlled, and bureaucratized. Many different sorts of men had dabbled in archaeology with varying degrees of success as a leisure-time pursuit, as a supplementary activity to their main vocation. Alexander Cunningham, in contrast, was the first full-time archaeologist in India.

CHAPTER 2

Alexander Cunningham: Engineer and Antiquarian

Alexander Cunningham arrived in Calcutta on 9 June 1833, a young man of nineteen years. That he arrived there at all was the result of chance and the generosity of friends. In British middle-class circles, a job in the colonies meant security and prospects, but to break into such a career required contacts and financial resources. Allan Cunningham, Alexander's father, had neither. Trained originally as a stonemason, he had swiftly established a reputation as poet and writer. In 1810 he moved out of Scotland to build his literary career in London. In 1814 he got a job as superintendent of works with a sculptor, Francis Chantrey.

Chantrey's studio was frequented by London's artistic and literary elite. Here, Allan Cunningham met Sir Walter Scott. Acquaintance soon turned into a friendship that had a great deal to do with the subsequent careers of two of Allan's sons. Walter Scott approached Lord Melville—then president of the Board of Control of the East India Company—and John Loch, an influential member of the board, and secured a Company cadetship each for Alexander and Joseph Davey Cunningham.

Ultimately, three of Allan Cunningham's five sons made their way to India. Joseph Davey held a number of positions in the Bengal Presidency, on the Sikh frontier, and in the Bhopal state. He fell from favour soon after the publication of his *History of the Sikhs* in 1849, the book being perceived as too sympathetic to the Sikhs. Francis, the youngest son, served in the Madras army and subsequently devoted himself to a literary career. Alexander started off with the Bengal

Engineers and and went on to a distinguished career as an archaeologist.[1]

Cunningham's Career: A Sketch

Alexander Cunningham was schooled at Christ's Hospital, an establishment noted for discipline and emphasis on classical learning. After going through the East India Company's Military Seminary at Addiscombe, he did a six-month stint at the Royal Engineers' Estate at Chatham. From here it was straight on to India as a lieutenant with the Bengal Engineers. He rose swiftly through the ranks. Between 1836 and 1840, he served as aide-de-camp to the governor general, Lord Auckland. In 1840 he married Alicia Maria Whish, the daughter of a Bengal civil servant. This was also the year in which he took over as executive engineer in the princely state of Oudh.

The 1840s saw the East India Company involved in a number of major military campaigns. Cunningham served in several of these as engineer and soldier. The first was the 1842–3 campaign in Bundelkhand for the capture of the rebel raja of Jaitpur. Then in 1843–4 Cunningham fought with the army of Gwalior at the battle of Punniar, where, in an audaciously successful manoeuvre, he turned the captured guns of the enemy against them. In 1845–6 he was with the army of the Sutlej and was selected by Lord Hardinge as political officer to accompany troops taking charge of Kangra. In 1848–9 he fought with the army of the Punjab in the battles of Chillianwala and Gujarat. Now he was promoted to the rank of brevet major.

For Cunningham these were not only years of military activity; they were also years of travel to remote and exciting places and provided him many opportunities for combining official duties with his growing interest in antiquarian investigation. In 1839 he was sent by Auckland through the hills from Simla to Ladakh and Kashmir, on what seems to have been an exploratory mission. In 1846 he was deputed, along with P.A. Vans Agnew, to arrange the boundary between the Ladakh territories of Kashmir and China. This was followed by a

[1] There was a fairly large representation of Scots in India and other colonial services; this was part of the larger process of assimilation of Scotland into the British empire in Europe. See Bayly (1989): 81–6.

second mission to Ladakh in 1847. This time Cunningham was accompanied by Lieutenant H. Strachey and the botanist Thomas Thompson.

The 1850s were quieter times during which the balance of Cunningham's activities began to more clearly and definitely tilt towards archaeological preoccupations. During 1850–1 he was executive engineer of Gwalior state.[2] During these years he explored many ancient places in the Bhilsa district of Central India, along with Lieutenant Maisey. Cunningham went on to spend over three years as executive engineer of Multan. In 1856 he was sent as chief engineer to Burma, where he worked two years.[3] In 1858 he returned to India as chief engineer of the North-Western Provinces.

After obtaining the regimental rank of colonel at the end of 1861, Cunningham resigned from military service at the age of forty-seven to take up appointment as archaeological surveyor, a designation given him by Viceroy Canning. He occupied this post from December 1861 to February 1866, when he returned to England. Four years later, in late 1870, Cunningham returned to India. He had accepted Lord Mayo's offer of the post of director general of the newly formed Archaeological Survey of India. He was to hold this position till 1885, for a period of over fourteen years. Cunningham was made a Companion of the Order of the Star of India (C.S.I.) in 1871, and Knight Commander of the Order of the Indian Empire (K.C.I.E.) after his retirement from the Archaeological Survey of India.

Cunningham and Prinsep

A close intense friendship developed between James Prinsep and Alexander Cunningham soon after the latter's arrival in India. Cunningham submitted his first paper to the Asiatic Society in 1834. He had definite views on membership of the society, which he expressed in a letter to Prinsep:

[2] Imam (1966: 12, fn 4) has pointed out that the only remnants of Cunningham's engineering career are the stone bridge he built over the river Morar in Gwalior and the memorial he designed for his friend Vans Agnew in Multan.

[3] Here, on the instructions of Major Phayre, Commissioner of Pegu, he maintained a daily register of the rise and fall of the Irawadi river (Cunningham, 1860).

> With respect to my becoming a member of the Asiatic Society—it is an honour which in my opinion ought not to be *asked for* but conferred upon those who pursue the Arts and Sciences for their own sake—If you think that I am worthy of becoming a member after my expressing this opinion—I shall feel obliged by your proposing me—but not otherwise—. . .[4]

Cunningham's name was proposed for membership of the Asiatic Society by Prinsep in 1836.

Until Prinsep's departure from India in 1838 and his death two years later, he and Cunningham were in constant contact. Cunningham describes this close association, which began at a time when Prinsep was an established scholar and Cunningham a young man in his early twenties, still trying to find his feet in antiquarian circles.

> During a great part of the years 1836 and 1837, the most active period of his career, I was in almost daily intercourse with him. With our mutual tastes and pursuits this soon ripened into the most intimate friendship. I thus had the privilege of sharing in all his discoveries during their progress. The matured results will be found in the pages of the Bengal Asiatic Society's Journal; but the germs of his discoveries are related in his letters to me, sometimes almost in the same words as he afterwards made use of in the journal, but generally in the more familiar language of friendly correspondence.[5]

The two collaborated closely in their numismatic studies and Prinsep acknowledged this collaboration warmly: 'Henceforward my readers should understand, and they will soon perceive the fact, that my coin essays are joint productions, and that I have an auxiliary at my elbow, far better acquainted with the contents of, I may say, all the collections of coins in India, than I have leisure to become.'[6] Extracts from Prinsep's letters to Cunningham, quoted in the latter's Introduction to the first volume of his *Archaeological Survey Reports,* bring out the feverish energy, excitement, and passion that characterized Prinsep's scholarship and his ability to communicate these to others.

[4] Letter from Alexander Cunningham to James Prinsep, dated Benares, 24 January 1836, European Manuscripts, C351, OIOC.

[5] Cunningham (1871b): vii.

[6] Prinsep (1836): 652.

> The quickness of his perception was indeed wonderful, so that many of his discoveries may be said literally to have flashed upon him; or, as he himself describes in a letter to me, 'like inspiration, or lightning, or Louisa's eyes, the light at once broke upon me.' But the great point in Prinsep's character was his ardent enthusiasm, which charmed and melted all who came in contact with him. Even at this distance of time, when a whole generation has passed away, I feel that his letters still possess the same power of winning my warmest sympathy in all his discoveries, and that his joyous and generous disposition still communicates the same contagious enthusiasm and the same strong desire to assist in further achievements.[7]

Cunningham's relationship with the Asiatic Society survived Prinsep's death. He was elected an honorary member of the society in 1868, and over the years served on many of its committees. He published extensively in the society's journal; his reports as archaeological surveyor in the 1860s were also published in its pages.

Cunningham was also a member of the shortlived Delhi Archaeological Society which, as we saw, took a number of important initiatives to reconstruct the history of Delhi and its monuments. Cunningham was elected a member of this society in May 1848 and gifted to it a number of coins from his personal collection. Passing through Delhi in the summer of 1848 he read to the society a paper titled 'Some Account of the Rebellion of Seif-oo-din Kutlugh Khan, in the reign of Nasir-oo-deen Mohummud Ghorie of Delhi, in A.D. 1255–1257.' His paper on the Grecian coins of India was published in the society's journal.[8] Cunningham's connections with the Delhi Archaeological Society may help explain the fact that, when he started his career as archaeological surveyor in 1861, a survey of Delhi's ruins was one of his priorities.

Cunningham's early writings—those of the 1830s and 1840s—include geographic, ethnographic, numismatic, and architectural

[7] Cunningham (1871b): xvii. The words cited are from a letter from Prinsep to Cunningham, dated 27 January 1838. In his letter, Prinsep wrote the name 'Louisa' in Ashokan Brahmi (as Lu-i-ja).

[8] Cunningham (1850). All information regarding Cunningham's connections with the society is based on Mudit Trivedi's unpublished paper on the Delhi Archaeological Society.

studies. During these years he evidently acquired a knowledge of Sanskrit. This was also the time when he articulated, for the first time, a specific project of archaeological investigation based on following the trail of the seventh-century Chinese pilgrim Xuan Zang (Hsuan Tsang).[9] Cunningham's writings of these two decades represent a formative phase in his scholarly career, for many of the preoccupations that were to distinguish his later work came now to take clear shape.

A good reason for looking at Cunningham's work chronologically is to chart the development of his experience, thought and approach towards archaeological and historical study. This enables us to identify elements of continuity and change within his ideas and writings, and to test the assertion that there was no essential change in Cunningham's archaeological method and approach over his long career.[10] Whether this was so remains to be seen, but if it was, it may be partly because Cunningham started off at the very outset with clear and diverse interests and goals.

Early Numismatic Writings

Cunningham's scholarly career was launched by an article on a numismatic subject and his debut was heralded by Prinsep. In 1834 his paper on certain Roman coins found in the Manikyala stupa was published in the Asiatic Society's journal. In this paper Cunningham corrected Prinsep's estimate of the age of Roman coins found in that stupa and questioned the latter's estimate of the stupa's age. Cunningham also had remarks on Masson's collection of coins, 'but I must defer them until I know whether those that I have already made are acceptable or not. I hope you will pardon the liberty I take not only in addressing you [i.e. Prinsep], but in differing from you in opinion.'[11] Prinsep's response to this tentativeness was given in a note which he prefixed to Cunningham's article: 'We compliment our young friend upon the

[9] The earlier Hsuan Tsang is now spelt Xuan Zang; however, spellings of place-names mentioned by pilgrims have not been changed here and are given as they occur in nineteenth-century translations of travelogues. The title of Xuan Zang's travel account is *Da Tang xi yu ji* (*Si-yu-ki*).

[10] Imam (1966): 203; Chakrabarti (1988): 59.

[11] Cunningham (1834).

success with which he has commenced his numismatic studies, and shall always be happy to profit by his criticisms.'

During the 1840s Cunningham wrote on the coins of the Indo-Bactrians and Indo-Scythians,[12] and on the coinage of Kashmir, with Bactrian coins attracting most of his attention. As he described individual coins, Cunningham discovered the names of unknown Indo-Bactrian kings and tried to unravel their genealogies. He cautioned coin collectors against the prevalence of forgeries of ancient Bactrian coins. He described ancient Bactrian gems and seals. He suggested that several of the monograms found on Greek coins of Ariana and India represented cities where mints were located.[13] With great ingenuity he connected, even if somewhat unconvincingly, motifs on certain Indian and Sassanian coins with the scene of a hero overcoming a lion depicted on a silver plate found at Badakshan. Apart from Bactrian coins, Cunningham wrote of certain 'Indo-Scythian' coins (he was referring to Kushana coinage), highlighting the evidence of Buddhist emblems on the coins of the king Kanishka.[14]

Cunningham had collected over 1000 coins when he visited Kashmir in September 1839, mostly from Bij-Bihara, one of the oldest towns in the region. Introducing his account of the ancient coinage of Kashmir, he boasted that the series he was describing was larger in number and extended over a much longer period (fifteen centuries) than any yet known.[15] His history of Kashmiri coins was framed within the context of the political history of the region, from the beginning of the Christian era down to the Mughal conquest in the sixteenth century.

Cunningham was, in short, one of the foremost coin collectors of his time. Many of the coins he described in his articles were part of his personal collection, which expanded steadily with his discoveries and purchases.[16] He continued to write on numismatics till the end of his

[12] He included the Shakas, Kushanas and White Huns in this category.

[13] The term Ariana was frequently used by scholars of this period to refer to the region between India and Iran, i.e. the area in and around modern Afghanistan.

[14] Cunningham (1840a, 1840b, 1842, 1840c, 1841b, 1841c).

[15] Cunningham (1843–4).

[16] In 1860, the Asiatic Society's journal carried a list of valuable coins being offered for sale or exchange by Cunningham. According to Imam (1966: 232),

life.[17] Meanwhile, the reconstruction of Indo-Bactrian genealogies soon moved far ahead of Cunningham's views. All the same, even though many or even most of his conclusions are no longer valid, Cunningham's contribution to nineteenth-century numismatic studies remains important.

The Journey to the Sources of Punjab's Rivers

The pages of the early volumes of the *Journal of the Asiatic Society of Bengal* are crowded with accounts of journeys by various European travellers, recording a wide range of impressions and information. Although charged with individual initiative and interest, this flurry of activity had official backing. The East India Company was keen to chart unfamiliar terrain, the expansion of geographical knowledge being vital for the realization of its economic and political ambitions in India.

Cunningham's *Abstract Journal* was published within the *Journal of the Asiatic Society of Bengal* in 1841.[18] One of his many accounts, it describes a journey lasting a little over three months, in 1839, which took Cunningham and his companion, Lieutenant Broome, on a reconnaisance assignment through Lahul, Chamba, and Kashmir. Compared to writings in the descriptive travelogue genre, which were quite the rage at the time among officials of the East India Company, Cunningham's accounts are crisp, precise, and methodical, while being marked by notices and descriptions of antiquities and ancient monuments. The journal format of Cunningham's early writings lent itself well to the brisk cataloguing of information. This style of documentation and description is a precursor of his later archaeological reports.[19]

Cunningham and Broome's travels added significantly to the Company's information about the geography of the mountainous stretches

---

during his retirement in England many years later, Cunningham carried on a flourishing business selling coins, particularly to the British Museum.

[17] For an account of these later writings, see Chapter 4.

[18] Cunningham (1841a).

[19] There is, however, a difference in that the archaeological reports say little about the journeys themselves, simply presenting their results.

of Punjab and Kashmir. Between them, the two officers surveyed either the whole or sections of the courses of the Spiti, Tirthan, Beas, Chakki, Nyi, Budhil, Ravi, Chandra, Bhaga, Chandrabhaga, Tohi, Shopian, and Yunam rivers.[20] The arduousness of the journeys was offset by a sense of achievement. 'From Tandee on the Chundra Bhaga river, where I parted with Lieut. Broome, I continued my way along the right bank of the river, with the proud consciousness that I was the first European who had ever visited that part of the Chundra Bhaga.'[21] Cunningham's *Abstract Journal* details topography, roads, bridges, and views. It describes mountain passes and river crossings. It gives estimates of the population of districts and revenue yields. It describes the livelihood of the people, their crops, their items of trade. Cunningham's account of his journey to the source of Punjab's rivers also displays his interest in recording details about temples and images, and collecting traditional histories. At Chambapura, he obtained a long list of the rajas of Chamba from the current raja's pandit. At Rajaori, he obtained a manuscript of a traditional history of the area, some *farṃans* issued by Aurangzeb and Nadir Shah, and a copy of the grant of the Rajaori territory by Bahadur Shah.

The *Abstract Journal* also touched on the identification of ancient places, which was to be an issue of abiding interest for Cunningham. In the early nineteenth century, several scholars shared this interest: the difference was that, for Cunningham, the identification of ancient places was not an armchair exercise. It involved following a trail, not only on a map but also on the ground. After leaving Jammu, Cunningham tells us that he crossed the Chenab ten miles below Aknoor, 'near where Taimoor had crossed it'. He goes on to quote the relevant sections of Arrian's account, which suggest that it must have been between the Tohi and the Chenab that Alexander pitched his camp, at about the same season of the year. Cunningham is led to propose an identification of the Tohi with Arrian's Tutapus.

These early accounts display several features of Cunningham's later archaeological writings—a focus on identifying ancient routes and

[20] While I have in several cases retained the nineenth-century spellings (or misspellings) of place and river names, I have given modern versions for some of the more incongruous early names.

[21] Cunningham (1841a): 105.

places, a sensitivity to the importance of topography, a concern for searching out manuscripts of historical value, an attentiveness towards documenting architectural and antiquarian remains (including inscriptions), and an interest in the way of life of people within the places he visited.

More Journeys to Remote Places: Ladakh

Gulab Singh, the Dogra ruler of Jammu, had invaded Lhasan territory in 1841 and the East India Company feared a repeat performance would adversely affect the import of shawl wool into British territory as well as disrupt trade between the hill states and Tibet. Such an eventuality might also damage relations between British India and China. Against the background of increasing hostilities between Dogras and Tibetans, the colonial government decided to send two commissioners to the frontier to remove 'the most common cause of all disputes in the East'—an unsettled boundary. In August 1846 Alexander Cunningham and Vans Agnew were sent on a delicate mission to the Ladakh–Tibet border, to demarcate the boundary between British territory and that of Gulab Singh's domain.[22]

The two commissioners left Simla on 2 August 1846 and proceeded north through Mandi, Kullu, and Lahul, through the Bara Lacha Pass on to the Tshomoriri (or Tso Morari: 'tso' being Tibetan for 'lake'). In the course of the journey, Cunningham mapped the British boundary from the Lahul–Zanskar border to the Chinese frontier. A letter from the governor general to the Chinese governor of Lhasa was successfully despatched through an emissary.

Cunningham's account of this mission included a description of the journey, recording miscellaneous details such as distances and heights, temperature, landscapes, routes, roads, streams, and passes. He corroborated or corrected details mentioned in the accounts of earlier travellers to the region. In line with military concerns, he made suggestions about road construction at Bajaora and recommended Pachind as an ideal location for establishing a British cantonment.

[22] For details of these missions, see Cunningham (1848c, 1854a). For Cunningham's account of the boundary between Gulab Singh's territory and that of the British, accompanied by a map of Rukchu and Lahul, see Cunningham (1848e).

But there is much more. There is a graphic description of the method of crossing rivers on inflated buffalo skins. The method of extracting iron from ores, practised at Kuman near the Ohl river, is described. The local tradition connecting Manali village and the legendary sage Vasishtha is recounted. The appearance, attire, livelihood, and migratory habits of the nomads of Rukchin are described. And at Yunam lake, inspired by the silent grandeur of the landscape, Cunningham breaks into verse, one of several compositions found scattered through his early writings.

Eternal silence reigneth there
Upon his snow-girt throne;
And the unsyllabled dull air
Sleeps echoless and lone . . .[23]

Early in 1847, the raja of Bisahar reported that certain Chinese officials despatched by the governor of Lhasa had arrived at Gara. Cunningham was sent off again as commissioner to the same area. The object of the second commission was to establish the boundary between Ladakh and Tibet on the basis of discussion with Chinese officials. This time, Cunningham was accompanied by Captain Henry Strachey and Dr Thomas Thomson. Strachey had already established his reputation as an intrepid traveller by a successful trip to Manasarovar in the previous year, and Thomson was a well-known botanist.[24]

Apart from the political goal of establishing a boundary between British and Chinese territory, Cunningham and his two colleagues were instructed to try increasing the Company's geographical knowledge. The mission was equipped with portable magnetic and meteorological instruments to record temperature, moisture, as well as magnetic dip, declination and intensity. Cunningham was directed to pursue his own antiquarian investigations as well.

It was just as well that Cunningham and his colleagues had been given such a wide mandate. The political objectives of the mission could not be realized, because neither the Chinese boundary commisioners nor Maharaja Gulab Singh's representatives showed up. Cunningham, Strachey, and Thomson were therefore free to concentrate on

[23] Cunningham (1848c): 216–17.

[24] For details of this expedition, see Cunningham (1848b).

their own spheres of interest. Much of their time and attention was devoted to making meteorological observations.

The route Cunningham chose for this mission (along the Indus, to Khalets, the Dras river, and onwards) was in fact geared towards the dual objectives of gathering geographical and historical information. One of his greatest ambitions during this second expedition to the Tibet border was to locate Aornos, the mountain stronghold where Alexander had met such fierce resistance and won a very difficult battle. He found the Aornos of the Greek historians in the hill fortress of Rani-ghat or Rani-garh, immediately above the small village of Nogram, about sixteen miles north by west from Ohind. Cunningham made a number of other identifications of places mentioned in classical, Chinese, and Indian sources, and correctly identified the location of the most ancient capital of Kashmir at Pandrethan.

The Temples of Kashmir

Another of Cunningham's major aims during his second expedition to the Tibet border was to examine the ancient temples of Kashmir. The full results of his investigations were incorporated in *An Essay on the Arian Order of Architecture, as Exhibited in the Temples of Kashmir*, published in in 1848.[25] This was Cunningham's first piece of writing on architecture and the first comprehensive survey ever published of the details and stylistic features of the temples of Kashmir.

Cunningham's description of the various shrines (mostly Brahmanical, a few Buddhist) was accompanied by several drawings of plans, sections, and elevations. In his discussion of the chronology of the temples, Cunningham relied on textual evidence where available (e.g. the *Rajatarangini*), as well as the architectural features of the buildings. He suggested that the Shankaracharya temple was built by Jalauka, son of Ashoka, and was the oldest temple in Kashmir. The essay also compared the architectural conventions of ancient Greece and ancient India. For the Indian part, Cunningham drew occasionally on Ram Raz's *An Essay on the Architecture of the Hindus.*[26]

Cunningham argued that Kashmiri architecture constituted a distinctive style, different and superior to that prevailing in other parts

[25] Cunningham (1848d).

[26] For more on Ram Raz, see Chapter 9.

of India. He went on to identify its characteristic features—the lofty pyramidal roofs of the temples, the trefoiled doorways covered by pyramidal pediments, and the great width of the intercolumnations (the distance between two columns). He suggested that the last of these features—an intercolumnation of four diameters—was referred to by the ancient Greeks as the 'Araiostyle'. It is after this term, and also because the Kashmir style of architecture was the style of the Arians or Aryas of Kashmir, that Cunningham chose to describe the style of Kashmiri architecture as belonging to the 'Arian Order'.

Cunningham was emphatic in noting a Greek influence on the Kashmir temples. He referred to the strong resemblance between Kashmiri colonnades, with their fluted pillars, and the classical peristyles of the Greeks. He argued that the proportions of the width and height of the capital in relation to the shaft in the Kashmir temples matched the rules of all classical orders except the Corinthian. He also identified certain similarities between Kashmiri and Greek (particularly Doric) mouldings. He suggested that Kashmiri and Grecian architecture had something else in common—a stereotyped style, displaying little change over the centuries. Cunningham asserted that all these similarities could not be mere coincidences; they pointed to a borrowing, probably via the Bactrian Greeks. At the same time, he conceded that the temples of Kashmir betrayed other, 'Hindu', sources of influence.

In Cunningham's opinion it was the Greek influence that made the temples of this region aesthetically pleasing:

> The architectural remains of Kashmir are perhaps the most remarkable of the existing monuments of India, as they exhibit undoubted traces of the influence of Grecian art. The Hindu temple is generally a sort of architectural pasty, a huge collection of ornamental fritters huddled together either with or without keeping; while the Jain temple is usually a vast forest of pillars, made to look as unlike one another as possible, by some paltry differences in their petty details. On the other hand, the Kashmirian fanes are distinguished by the graceful elegance of their outlines, by the massive boldness of their parts, and by the happy propriety of their decorations. They cannot indeed vie with the severe simplicity of the Parthenon, nor with the luxuriant gracefulness of the monument of Lysiscrates: but they possess great beauty; different indeed, yet quite their own.[27]

[27] Cunningham (1848d): 241.

Some of Cunningham's conclusions, particularly his estimate of the age of certain shrines, came in for criticism from his contemporaries. For instance, the third century BC date he assigned to the Shankaracharya temple was held as untenable by Bühler and Fergusson (though Fergusson himself was way off the mark in assigning it to the seventeenth century). More recent writings on the subject have confirmed some of Cunningham's hypotheses and dismissed others. The existence of a distinctive Kashmiri style of architecture is acknowledged. Stylistic change, if not entirely absent, as Cunningham maintained, is seen as very minimal. The foreign influence on the architecture of this region is also recognized, although the nature of the influences that are identified (including those from Iran and Central Asia, apart from the Graeco-Roman) are far more diverse than those suggested by Cunningham.[28] There is, on the other hand, at least in some recent architectural writing, a greater concession of the 'Indianness' of the idiom and style of the temples of Kashmir than we find in Cunningham.

On the Trail of Chinese Pilgrims

In 1836 the publication of a book in Paris created ripples of excitement in antiquarian circles. The book was *Foe Koue Ki ou Relation des Royaumes Bouddhiques* by Remusat, Klaproth and Landresse. This work, which brought to light the contents of the travelogue of the Chinese pilgrim Fa Xian (Fa Hsien/Fa Hian/Fa-Hien) who visited India in the early fifth century, offered important material for the study of ancient Indian historical geography. The first to take up the challenge was H.H. Wilson, who proposed identifications of a large number of sites mentioned in Fa Xian's account.[29] Cunningham quickly joined the fray. His special qualification and advantage over others was his intimate knowledge of the geography of India, acquired over years of military duty.

Cunningham proposed his first identification—that of Fa Xian's Seng-kia-shi with Samkassa (Sankisa)—in a letter to Colonel W.H. Sykes. Sykes had served with the Bombay government for many years before becoming a director of the East India Company in 1840. He

[28] Harle (1986): 191; Huntington (1985): 353.

[29] Wilson (1839).

had established a scholarly reputation for himself on the basis of a large number of publications on various subjects, ranging from the classification of birds to Indian antiquities. In 1842 Sykes had published a long paper in the *Journal of the Asiatic Society*, which included, among other things, a tirade against the Brahmins and a contemptuous indictment of Indian sources of history. Sykes here paid glowing tribute to the beacon of light 'from the literature of that remarkable people—the Chinese' (he was referring to Fa Xian's account) that, thankfully, existed to illuminate the Indian past. He gleefully sought to demonstrate that the Brahmins, who gave themselves such airs and graces, might well have been foreigners to this land; that the Pali language was older than Sanskrit; and that in the remote past Buddhism and not Brahmanism had reigned supreme in India. All these conclusions gave cause for hope that 'by proper means, applied in a cautious, kindly and forbearing spirit', it was possible 'to raise the intellectual standard of the Hindus, improve their moral and social condition, and assist to promote their eternal welfare.'[30]

Cunningham's letter to Sykes was published in the *Journal of the Royal Asiatic Society* in 1843.[31] Remusat and Wilson had already made some general suggestions about the possible whereabouts of Fa Xian's Seng-kia-shi, but Cunningham was the first to suggest a specific location—Sankisa village on the north bank of the Kali-nadi.[32] Cunningham documented the details of the site, its ruins and antiquities, including the elephant capital found there. On the basis of his identification of Seng-kia-shi, Cunningham also determined the length of the ancient *yeu-yan* (the measure of distance used by the Chinese pilgrims), or *yojana*, as fractionally more than seven English miles.

Cunningham was not content identifying the places on Fa Xian's route. What great discoveries might be made, he thought, if someone were to follow the Chinese pilgrim's route from point to point, seek

30 Sykes (1841): 450.

31 Cunningham (1843).

32 Sankisa is in modern Farukhabad district, Uttar Pradesh. Actually, the place lay on the route not only of Fa Xian but of Xuan Zang as well. When Cunningham wrote about the site many years later in the first volume of his *Archaeological Survey Reports*, he discussed the references to Sankisa in the accounts of both these Chinese pilgrims.

out all the Buddhist ruins, and open all the 'topes' that lay on the way. Furthermore, such a project would have political gains to offer. It

> would be an undertaking of vast importance to the Indian government politically, and to the British public religiously. To the first body it would show that India had generally been divided into numerous petty chiefships, which had invariably been the case upon every successful invasion; while, whenever she had been under one ruler, she had always repelled foreign conquest with determined resolution. To the other body, it would show that Brahmanism, instead of being an unchanged and unchangeable religion which had subsisted for ages, was of comparatively modern origin, and had been *constantly* receiving additions and alterations; facts which prove that the establishment of the Christian religion in India must ultimately succeed.[33]

This may look like proof of hidden political and evangelical agendas behind Cunningham's archaeological investigations, the revelations of an unguarded moment by a young man in the course of personal correspondence.[34] But there is a more plausible explanation. At this time Sykes was an influential member of the Court of Directors of the East India Company, and the sentiments in Cunningham's letter, as also its subsequent publication, can be seen as part of an attempt to elicit backing for a project which had taken shape in Cunningham's mind, and which was never to leave him.

The travels of Fa Xian (AD 404–14) were very limited in scope compared with those of Xuan Zang (AD 630–44). Fa Xian had moved from the north-west into the Ganga valley, down to the eastern seaport of Tamralipti. He had then taken the sea route to Simhala (Sri Lanka), going from there to South East Asia, from where he then headed back to China. Xuan Zang, on the other hand, had taken the land route to get to Sri Lanka, and had travelled down the length of peninsular India and back. An account of the life and travels of Xuan Zang was published in French by Stanislas Julien in 1853. A complete French translation of the travelogue appeared in 1857–8, when Julien's two-volume work was published, but the scholarly world was already well aware of some of its details and its importance.

[33] Cunningham (1843): 246–7.

[34] We find no hint of such agendas elsewhere in Cunningham's voluminous writings.

During the 1840s, Cunningham identified a large number of places mentioned by Xuan Zang. In fact his 'Verification of the Itinerary of the Chinese Pilgrim, Hwan Thsang . . .', goes over 141 places in Xuan Zang's itinerary.[35] Identifications of some of these sites had already been proposed by Landresse, Lassen, and Vivien de St Martin. Cunningham made specific suggestions pertaining to the identification of almost a hundred sites. In some cases he went further by connecting these places with those mentioned in Western classical accounts. For instance, Xuan Zang's Fei-she-li (which Landresse had identified with Vaishali), was correctly located by Cunningham as modern Bassar (Basarh), about twenty miles north of Patna, and he went on to identify the people who lived here with the Passalae mentioned by Ptolemy and Pliny. Further, in a rejoinder to those sceptical of the value of Xuan Zang's account, Cunningham offered a spirited defence of its utility and accuracy.[36]

Cunningham's interest in the route of the two Chinese pilgrims was thus clearly manifest in his earliest writings: he had already expressed the desirability of tracing Fa Xian's route in his letter to Sykes. Now it was only a small step towards his idea of following the trail of both Fa Xian and Xuan Zang. In 1848 Cunningham forcefully articulated this idea.[37]

An important part of his well-crafted proposal was an aggressive argument for a shift from a text-based study of India's ancient past to one based on archaeology: 'The discovery and publication of all the existing remains of architecture and sculpture, with coins and inscriptions, would throw more light on the ancient history of India, both public and domestic, than the printing of all the rubbish contained in the 18 Puranas.'[38] According to Cunningham, clear proof of the deceptiveness of the ancient Sanskrit sources, such as the epics, the *Puranas*, and the *Dharmashastras*, was their silence about Buddhism. A study and publication of all the existing remains of Buddhism

[35] Cunningham (1848a).

[36] Cunningham (1848f).

[37] Cunningham (1848g).

[38] Ibid.: 535. It may have been because of a need to make his case forcefully that Cunningham was so dismissive of textual sources. His later writings are more mellow. See, for instance, Cunningham (1871b).

(architecture, sculpture, coins, inscriptions) would significantly adding to information about the history of India. These investigations could not be postponed. 'It is a duty which the Government owe to the country. The remains of architecture and sculpture are daily deteriorating, and inscriptions are broken or defaced; the sooner therefore that steps are taken for their preservation, the more numerous and consequently the more valuable these remains will be.'[39]

Cunningham's proposal was specific. As Pliny had followed the route of Alexander in his 'Eastern Geography', an enquirer into Indian archaeology should follow in the footsteps of the Chinese pilgrims. The project would require at least two people, one of these a good draftsman: 'But the one to whose judgement the selection of objects for preservation is to be confided should have a knowledge of the ancient history of India. He should be conversant with the sculptured forms and religious practices of the present day, and with the discoveries made by Prinsep and others in Indian Palaeography and Numismatology; without such a head to guide the selection of objects worthy of preservation the labour of the most perfect draftsman would be thrown away.'[40]

Cunningham was essentially putting forward a project for archaeological documentation, but he also touched on the issue of preservation. Perhaps modesty prevented him proposing himself for the job, but it is quite clear that that is in fact what he had in mind. What is most important is that he was suggesting a new route to India's ancient past—an archaeological rather than literary one.

Ladakh: Physical, Statistical, and Historical

During the time that he was executive engineer in Gwalior state, Cunningham made various experiments on the strength of different varieties of wood and stone. The result was a monograph on the stone and timber of the Gwalior area.[41] In this small book Cunningham identified the sources of raw materials used in that area, discussed indigenous terms for various kinds of stone, and listed the names of mountain

[39] Ibid.
[40] Cunningham (1848g): 536.
[41] Cunningham (1853).

ranges in Indian and classical sources. The very next year (1854) saw the publication of another two books by him—one on Ladakh, the other on the 'topes' of Central India.[42] These works represent the first major syntheses of Cunningham's early years of exploration and study.

Cunningham was not, of course, the first European to visit or write about Ladakh. In the early eighteenth century this mysterious mountain paradise had attracted Jesuit priests such as Hippolyte Desideri and Francesco Orazio della Penna de Billi. Warren Hastings had sent two missions to Tibet—one under George Bogle and the second under Captain Turner (who was not allowed to enter Lhasa, but nevertheless left an interesting account of his mission). Among the celebrated nineteenth-century travellers was William Moorcroft, who spent two years in Ladakh (1820–2) disguised as a horse merchant. There was also Dr Henderson, who arrived in Leh in 1834 poorly disguised as a Muslim named Ishmail Khan and soon found himself languishing in a Ladakhi prison.

But Cunningham's *Ladák, Physical, Statistical, and Historical* was the first detailed descriptive account of this area and its people. The book was illustrated with beautiful sketches and paintings. Some of the landscape paintings were made by one Colonel Bates; several others, including portraits, seem to have been made by Cunningham himself. Among the major achievements here were Cunningham's identification of Ladakh (or Khà-chan) with the Akhassa Regio of Ptolemy, and the Kie-chha of Fa Xian.[43]

Of direct utility to the East India Company was his detailed account of the geography of Ladakh and neighbouring areas, with special attention to the mountains and rivers, lakes and springs. The most important part of the book, from a geographical point of view, was its detailed map of the area. Made by John Walker, geographer to the East India Company, and compiled on the basis of earlier maps—including those made by Cunningham, Strachey, and de Vigne—the map was drawn on a scale of 1 inch: 1 mile. Apart from topographical details, it also indicated the routes traversed by Cunningham, Strachey,

[42] Cunningham (1854a, 1854b).

[43] The latter identification was later questioned by many. Legge identified it with Skardo in Baltistan, A. Stein with Kashgar in Turkistan, and Gergan and Hassnain with Kashgar in the Chitral valley.

and Thomson.[44] The book described the seven principal routes of the region (some of which Cunningham had travelled), as well as the less-frequented and more difficult paths. The principal mountain passes, roads, and bridges were detailed. The snowline on several mountain ranges of the Punjab was determined. The length of the course and the minimum discharge of the rivers of the Punjab were described and this data was compared with that for the Ganga. The floodings of the Indus and Sutlej were discussed, and several observations made on temperature, magnetic and meteorological data, and the causes of prevailing day and night wind conditions. Cunningham's discovery of fresh-water fossil shells in sandy-clay formations above the level of Ladakh's salt-water lakes indicated that these were once fresh and much larger. His discussion of the climate of the area was accompanied by observations on the palaeo-environment which, he suggested, must have been marked by milder climatic conditions.

Geography, landscape and climate formed only part—although an important part—of Cunningham's concerns. Of equal significance was a discussion of the way of life of the Ladakhi people. Their animals and wool-manufacture are carefully described.[45] Details about agricultural operations, trade, resources, government expenses are given. Attire, food and drink, amusements, buildings (palaces, monasteries, ordinary homes), social customs and ceremonies are described. In 1847, Cunningham had made a census of most of the villages along his route through Ladakh. Now he presents the data he collected, including an estimate of the total population and population density of the region. The book also has an important linguistic component: it discusses the vocabulary of the Tibetan language, and compares it with the dialects of the Dards, Afghans, and Kashmiris, those of the Hindu 'races' of the Himalayas, and of the Indo-Tibetans of Kanawar.

[44] The map was published separately in *JASB*, 34 (1865).

[45] Cunningham tells us that he bought twenty Purik sheep at the rate of one rupee each and brought the flock down to Simla. From here, they were sent to England by the governor-general. The Court of Directors presented them to Prince Albert. After being put on display by him in the Zoological Gardens, the sheep were distributed to various people interested in sheep breeding. (Cunningham, 1854a: 213). In Plate VIII, Cunningham gives us a sketch of this variety of Ladakhi sheep.

Cunningham cites evidence that the Tibetan people and their language were once spread over a much greater area.

Ladák also contains incursions into racial ethnography. Racial affiliations and the origins and migrations of people were subjects of interest not only to Cunningham but also to a number of nineteenth-century European scholars. All this was very much in tune with the larger colonial classificatory enterprise, in which all aspects of the lives of natives, including their bodies, had to be meticulously measured, described, and put in their place. (The anthropometric enterprise was taken to greater heights several decades later by H.H. Risley.) Cunningham speculates on the origins of the Botis or Bhotiyas of Ladakh and concludes they were an offshoot of the Mongolian race. His discussion of the racial affiliations of the people is accompanied by a detailed presentation of data relating to their physical characteristics. There is also a tabulation of the height of men, women, and landlords (!), with break-ups according to religion, and a discussion on longevity among the Ladakhis. We also see Cunningham's brief fling with craniometry, based on three Ladakhi skulls he somehow acquired: he dilates on the relationship between cranial capacity and race—a catch-all category into which he collapses religion as well.

Ladák was the first work to give a connected account of the history and religion of Ladakh. While he was in the region, Cunningham had had a copy of the existing traditional history of the area transcribed for him in the original Tibetan, and an Urdu abstract of the account prepared by a munshi. He used these, as well as other sources, to construct a history of Ladakh. One of the impotant sources he quotes in detail on Zorawar Singh's invasion of Ladakh is an eyewitness account dictated to him by Mehta Basti Ram, one of the principal officers involved in the Dogra expedition of 1834–9.[46] Cunningham's discussion of the religion of Ladakh begins with an account of the pre-Buddhist Bon religion and goes on to examine the history and features of Tibetan Buddhism. Ladakh gave him an exposure to living Buddhism; later, he used this as a key to ancient religious practice.

Its comprehensive, detailed treatment of a region of the subcontinent gives *Ladák* a special place in Cunningham's corpus of writings.

[46] Cunningham (1854a): 333–46.

We see here the results of investigations into a remarkable range of subjects—scientific, geographical, anthropological, historical, religious, ethnographic, and linguistic. It was this kind of range, and an eye for detail of all kinds, that remained the hallmark of this man and his work.

The Bhilsa Topes

In 1849, at the recommendation of Captain J.D. Cunningham (Alexander Cunningham's brother), the political agent at Bhopal, the Court of Directors directed Captain F.C. Maisey to prepare an illustrated report on the Buddhist site of Sanchi. In January 1851 Maisey was joined by Alexander Cunningham, and, over the next two months or so, the two opened a number of stupas within a seven-mile radius of Sanchi. The results of these explorations were published in Cunningham's book, *The Bhilsa Topes*.[47] This was his second major work of synthesis and was published in the same year as his book on Ladakh.

One of the general features of nineteenth-century Western interpretations of Eastern religions was 'textualization': certain texts were identified as reflecting the original essence and tenets of these religions, before they came to be diluted and corrupted in later times. This newly unfolding Western understanding of ancient Buddhism was based on the slow but steady discovery and translation of a stream of Buddhist texts in a variety of languages—Pali, Sanskrit, Chinese, Mongolian, and Tibetan. By the 1850s a number of works on the history and doctrines of Buddhism had been published by textual scholars such as Christian Lassen, Eugene Burnouf and Spence Hardy.[48] In *The Bhilsa Topes* Cunningham drew heavily on earlier researchers, namely Turnour and Hodgson, and to a lesser extent on Burnouf, de Körös, Prinsep and Wilson. At the same time, he emphasized the importance of non-textual sources for the history of Buddhism and recognized the importance of archaeological evidence for historicizing the Buddhism

[47] The term 'tope' came from the word then in use for tumuli or mounds in Afghanistan. It was only gradually replaced by the more correct term stupa (from which tope was evidently derived).

[48] The publication of Pali texts received a fresh impetus some years later with the founding of the Pali Text Society by T.W. Rhys Davids in 1881.

of the texts. In this sense it could be argued that *The Bhilsa Topes* was the first detailed examination of the history of Indian Buddhism which incorporated archaeological evidence from Buddhist sites in a substantial manner.

In the early decades of the nineteenth century, there was considerable confusion and debate among Western scholars on a number of issues—the place of origin of Buddhism, the historicity and dates of Gautama Buddha, whether or not Buddhism had a history before Gautama, and the relationship between Buddhism and the other philosophical doctrines and religions of India.[49] The 1850s represent a watershed in Western interpretations of Buddhism, when many of these confusions were more or less sorted out (though a few lingered). The Buddha was now generally accepted as a historical figure and placed in the sixth or fifth century BC, although the *precise* dates of his life remained (and still do) a subject of debate. There was general agreement among Western scholars that the Buddhist doctrine was essentially pessimistic and atheistic, while there continued a lack of consensus on specific aspects of this doctrine, particularly the nature of Buddhist nirvana.

Cunningham's *Bhilsa Topes* epitomizes both the confusion of the pre-1850s phase of the European understanding of Buddhism as well as the resolution of certain basic issues. In line with the writings of earlier decades, Cunningham displayed a penchant for identifying cross-cultural similarities, for instance between the stupas of Buddhist India and the 'Druidical colonnades' of Britain, between the Buddhist veneration of trees and the English reverence for the oak. He saw connections between the Buddha and Western gods such as Hermes, Buddwas, and Woden. Of the many Buddhas recognized in the tradition, he realized that one of them—the Sakya-muni—was a historical figure who lived approximately between 623 and 543 BC. He thought it possible to outline the life history of this individual by pealing away the miraculous elements and the exaggerations in which the texts abounded. But Cunningham also thought that there was a more ancient Buddhism, as old as the Vedas, which had travelled to many parts of the world, elements of which were absorbed by the historical Buddha into his doctrine. His more useful insights include his

[49] See Almond (1988).

recognition of the significance of the reference in the *Mahaparinabbana Sutta* to an earlier practice of building tumuli over the funerary remains of kings, indicating the pre-Buddhist ancestry of the stupa. To this we can add his hypothesis that some of the Buddhas who found a place in the Buddhist pantheon were probably pre-Buddhist heroes or saints whose worship was incorporated into the new faith.

Cunningham thought that the earliest texts of the Buddhists were in Pali and Sanskrit—the *Sutta* and *Vinaya Pitakas* in Pali and the more esoteric *Abhidhamma* in Sanskrit. He recognized the similarities and differences between Buddhism and other Indian philosophical systems such as Sankhya. Unlike many of his contemporaries, he did not see Buddhism as an atheistic faith. Following Hodgson, he distinguished between the multitude of Manushi Buddhas and the celestial Adi Buddha who, according to him, had the status of a self-existent Supreme Being and was a creator god. But Cunningham's primary interest was not in Buddhist doctrines. There is no detailed exegesis of Buddhist doctrines in *The Bhilsa Topes*, and nothing on questions such as the nature of the Buddhist nirvana that were, at the time, exercising the minds of many Western interpreters of Buddhism.

Cunningham's central focus was on the history of Buddhism in India—its rise, spread, and decline. His discussion of this history was framed within a detailed account of the political history of ancient India. *The Bhilsa Topes* touched on a large number of important issues—the life of the Buddha; a synopsis of the Buddha's doctrines; the social impact of his teachings; factors that attracted women to the order; the Buddhist councils; monastic rules; aspects of chronology; schisms; Buddhism in Ashoka's time; the subsequent history of the religion, including its decline; the description, classification, and significance of stupas; the building of stupas and the ceremonies associated with this; the location of the eight original relic stupas, and the meaning of Buddhist symbols. While Cunningham was aware of the existence of different Buddhist sects, changes in the complexion of the religion, and the theistic and the tantric elements that became associated with it in later phases, he says little about all these things.

There is much in Cunningham's *The Bhilsa Topes* that is not acceptable today: for instance his understanding of Aryan ('Arian' as he spelt it) as a racial term. There is also his long, confused account of the dichotomy between the brahmanas and 'Swastikas', the latter, according to him, being an atheistic school that denied the doctrine of the transmigration of souls, and derived their name from their symbol, the mystic cross. There is his allusion, laced with occidental prejudice, to the characteristics of Eastern people: 'The fatalist doctrine of eternal annihilation, and consequent escape from future punishment, will always be popular amongst people of weaker minds and strong passions; and as these have ever been the prevailing characteristics of mankind in the East, the Atheistical principles of the *Swastikas* were received by the bulk of the people with very great favour.'[50] At the same time, Cunningham was quick to point out that Eastern religions were not the only ones replete with miraculous elements and superhuman feats: 'the miraculous incidents narrated by devout Buddhists are not more wonderful than those which are recorded and believed of the Virgin Mary, and scores of Roman Catholic saints, as well as of the Arabian Mohammad.'[51] More unusual by the standards of his time was what Cunningham had to say about the similarities between Greek and Indian thought, specifically between the ideas of Anaxagoras and the Sankhya system, and between those of Pythagoras and the Buddha. He saw coincidences too strong to be accidental and thought Buddhism must have travelled in ancient times to Greece. The very suggestion of such a possibility at a time when any cultural similarity was invariably interpreted by Western scholars as a reflection of Indian borrowing, is striking.

The writings of many nineteenth-century European scholars of Buddhism were marked by a selective admiration of the personality of the Buddha alongside the deprecation of modern Buddhism as a corrupt form of a once-pure faith. The Buddha was frequently portrayed in scholarly as well as more popular literature as a heroic social reformer who stood forth valiantly against the evils of Brahmanism. Cunningham's interpretation of Buddhism broadly matches this widely prevalent perspective. *The Bhilsa Topes* indicates that Cunningham's lifelong fascination with Buddhism was based at least in part on a strong admiration of the founder of the faith, even if this admiration stemmed from an exaggerated view of the Buddha as a radical

[50] Cunningham (1854b): 19.

[51] Ibid.: 22.

religious and social reformer. The Sakya-muni was 'one of the chief benefactors of his country.' This 'wonderful man' was not only the founder of a new religious system but a social reformer who challenged 'the most powerful and arrogant priesthood in the world', preaching the abolition of caste and the perfect equality of all mankind. He was a patriot who incited people to resist the abduction of their women by powerful men and who introduced to India a code of 'pure and practical morality'.[52]

Cunningham was one of the first scholars to emphasize Buddhism's appeal for women. The Buddha's *dhamma* offered hope in this life and the next 'to the young widow, the neglected wife, and the cast-off mistress'. It offered women a respectable escape from 'the daily indignities to which they were subjected by grasping relatives, treacherous husbands, and faithless lords'. In fact the very success of Buddhism can be attributed to the admission of women, 'who, even in the East, have always possessed much secret, though not apparent influence over mankind.'[53] Cunningham recognized the significance of the large number of female donors mentioned in the votive inscriptions at Sanchi.

This admiration for the Buddha and his teaching is clearly revealed in the contrasts Cunningham makes between the purity of the Buddhist dhamma and 'the corrupt state of Brahmanism'.[54] It also comes out clearly in the comparisons he makes between Muhammad and the Buddha.

> The former propagated his religion by the merciless edge of the sword; the latter by the persuasive voice of the missionary. The sanguinary career of the Islamite was lighted by the lurid flames of burning cities; the peaceful progress of the Buddhist was illuminated by the cheerful faces of the sick in monastic hospitals, and by the happy smiles of travellers reposing in *Dharmsâlas* by the roadsides. The one was the personification of bodily activity and material enjoyment; the other was the genius of corporeal abstinence, and intellectual contemplation.[55]

[52] Ibid.: 51, 53.
[53] Cunningham (1854b): 60.
[54] Ibid.: 53.
[55] Ibid.: 53–4.

As in most sympathetic Western interpreters of Buddhism, Cunningham's enthusiasm for Buddhism was not without limit. Buddhism was only the best of all non-Christian religions.[56] Although Buddhism scored well when compared with Brahmanism and Islam, it was not quite up to the mark when compared with Christianity.

The most important part of *The Bhilsa Topes* is the description of the discoveries made by Cunningham and Maisey in the course of opening over twenty-seven stupas at Sanchi, Sonari, Satdhara, Bhojpur, and Andher. Their *modus operandi* was to make careful measurements and then open a vertical shaft down the exact centre of the stupa. Cunningham claimed that they adopted this method because it caused less damage to the structure than the more indiscriminate openings by earlier excavators.[57] Perhaps the more pressing reason was that they found that this method invariably led them to the relic boxes enshrined in the stupas in a very short space of time. The operation generally took no more than two or three hours.

Some of the stupas Cunningham and Maisey opened in this manner had already been disturbed by villagers or by amateur archaeologists. Some yielded very little, but all the sites ultimately yielded relic caskets. The most sensational discoveries were made at Sanchi. Stupa No. 1 at Sanchi yielded nothing, but Stupa No. 2 contained the relics of ten monks associated in Buddhist tradition with the missions sent out by Ashoka to the Hemavata country. Stupa No. 3 contained the relics of two monks well known from the texts—Sariputta and Mahamoggalana. Subsequently, relics of these same two monks were discovered by Cunningham and Maisey in Stupa No. 2 at Satdhara. Here was important evidence indicating the historicity of monks who had a prominent place in the Buddhist tradition. The relic boxes, caskets, and the relics themselves found in the course of the opening of stupas at Sanchi, Sonari, Satdhara, Bhojpur, and Andher are carefully described and illustrated in *The Bhilsa Topes.*

Cunningham identified Sanchi with the Sha-chi of Fa Xian's account. His discussion of the site included a detailed description of the site, the stupas, and the sculptures, accompanied by a number of

[56] See Almond (1988).

[57] Cunningham (1854b): 269.

sketches. He also identified a number of embankments in the area. Some of the inscriptions at Sanchi had already been published by Prinsep in the Asiatic Society's journal, but Cunningham's was a more comprehensive cataloguing of their text and translation. The discussion of the inscriptions included an assessment of their age, and of the age of the monuments they were associated with. This assessment was based on the palaeography of the inscriptions and also on clues given in the contents, for example the name of the Satavahana king Satakarni in one of them.

Among the important details in Cunningham's account of Sanchi are his descriptions of the pillars he saw there. The pillar lying to the south of Stupa No. 1 had an inscription which Cunningham had great difficulty reading (the text was obliterated in various places), but of which he nevertheless gave a text and translation. He recognized it as an Ashokan inscription and also figured out the basic purport of the inscription.[58] The capital of the pillar, which Cunningham found lying nearby, was crowned by four addorsed lions, the abacus above the inverted lotus was ornamented with the carving of pairs of *hamsas* or geese. The boldness of line and the accuracy of the delineation of the feet of the lions of the capital (four large front claws and one small hind claw) convinced Cunningham that the lions had been sculpted by a Greek artist. More unusual were the remains of a broken pillar lying to the north of the Great Stupa, originally crowned by a capital consisting of a larger-than-life-size dhoti-clad human figure. Cunningham suggested that this represented the Mauryan emperor Ashoka.[59]

Cunningham was aware of the spectacular nature of the archaeological evidence they had unearthed and described. 'In illustration of the ancient history of India, the bas-reliefs and inscriptions of the Bhilsa Topes are almost equal in importance to the more splendid discoveries made by the enterprising and energetic Layard in the

[58] In later years this inscription came to be known as one of Ashoka's schism edicts. Cunningham also devoted much space to explaining why H.H. Wilson's scepticism of the identification of the Priyadarsi of the inscriptions and the Mauryan king Ashoka was unfounded.

[59] Cunningham (1854b): 197. Later research assigned this pillar a later date. It is generally held to belong to the Gupta period. And the figure surmounting the pillar is indentified not as Ashoka but as the *bodhisattva* Vajrapani. Nevertheless, pillars of this kind remain very rare.

Fig. 14 Lion Capital, Sanchi, Gupta Period

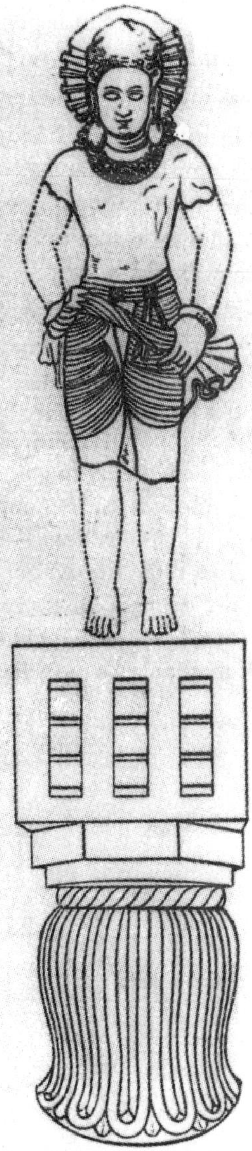

Fig. 15 Vajrapāṇi Capital, Sanchi, Gupta Period

2. Sketch of the Sanchi pillar capitals.
Courtesy: Archaeological Survey of India

mounds of the Euphrates.'[60] *The Bhilsa Topes* is, for all these reasons, an important and indispensible reference work for the archaeology of early Buddhist monastic centres. As is the case with Cunningham's archaeological reports in general, what makes his descriptions particularly important is the fact that while some of the sites have yielded much new information resulting from more recent excavation, much of what Cunningham described has disappeared. His accounts thus form an important part of the documentation of sites as they existed in the mid-nineteenth century.

The Bhilsa Topes closes with a poem composed by Cunningham which evokes his excitement and triumph at his discoveries at Sanchi:

Nought but the Topes themselves remain to mock
Time's ceaseless efforts; yet they proudly stand
    Silent and lasting up their parent rock,
    And still as cities under magic's wand;
    Till curious Saxons, from a distant land,
Unlock'd the treasures of two thousand years;
And the lone scene is peopled;—here a band
Of music wakes the echoes; there the cheers
Of multitudes, alive with human hopes and fears.

[60] Cunningham (1854b): viii.

CHAPTER 3

The First Archaeological Survey

During his years as a military engineer, Cunningham went where the army sent him. The geographical scope of his investigations was thus predetermined, and military duties frequently impinged on his archaeological interests. But as archaeological surveyor, and later as director general of the Archaeological Survey of India, he had a free hand in choosing his field of operations. His retirement from military service in 1861 and his new appointment now gave him the freedom to devote himself to archaeological exploration. All this had a great deal to do with Charles John Canning.

Lord Canning, as he is better known, happened to be the governor general during the Revolt of 1857. In the aftermath of the revolt, once rule over the Indian colony was transferred from the East India Company to the British crown, Canning became India's first viceroy. His regime (1856–62) saw policy shifts and initiatives as well — attempts to forge an alliance with the Indian princes, administrative changes reflected in the Indian Councils Act of 1861, and legislative and financial reform. Yet 1857 is generally presented as the high point of Canning's career, the subsequent years being a sort of anti-climax marked by poor calculation, vacillation, lack of firmness. Seen from the point of view of the history of Indian archaeology, however, Canning is important inasmuch as he swiftly sanctioned Cunningham's first archaeological survey in 1861.

The Background

The launch of the first archaeological survey was the result of several impulses and pressures, some direct, others indirect. By this time, several decades of loosely coordinated antiquarian and archaeological inquiry had built up a certain momentum. The Asiatic Society had since 1784 provided a meeting ground for a large variety of antiquarian and archaeological investigations, and many important discoveries had been announced in the pages of its journal. But at no point of time had the Asiatic Society lobbied for a government-sponsored archaeological survey. Perhaps the society prided itself on being a loose association of spirited, independent individuals, and was sceptical of the bureaucratization of scholarly investigations. This might explain why the parent of all Asiatic societies played only an indirect role in the initiation of an archaeological survey in India.

A more direct role was played by the Royal Asiatic Society of Great Britain and Ireland. The Royal Asiatic Society was founded in 1823 with the aim of sensitizing Europe to the contribution of Asia to the world's cultural heritage and to explore connections between ancient Greek and Indian philosophical traditions. From time to time, the society petitioned the home government on matters of antiquarian and archaeological interest, urging it to sponsor and promote the investigation of Indian antiquities.

By this time the British interest in Eastern antiquities had a down-to-earth utilitarian aspect as well, reflected in the emergence of a movement for the revival of industrial design. Prominent spokesmen of the movement were Owen Jones, Mathew Digby Wyatt, Gottfried Semper, Richard Redgrave, and Henry Cole.[1] These men identified Eastern ornamental design as a potential source of interesting motifs and ideas which could be utilized to infuse new life into British manufactures. Under the patronage of Prince Albert and the leadership of Henry Hardy Cole, the resuscitated Society of Arts played a key role in this movement. From 1847 the society organized a number of annual exhibitions of British manufactures and decorative art. The improvement of industrial design, geared towards the boosting of British manufactures in the international market, also became an important item on the agenda of the British government. In 1852 a new Department of Practical Art (later named the Department of Science and Art) was established. Functioning under the control of the Board of Trade, the goal of this new government department was to promote British industrial design.

In the middle of the nineteenth century, a number of extremely successful international exhibitions were held in Europe. The first of these

[1] For details, see Mitter (1977): Chap. V.

was the 'Great Exhibition of the Industry of All Nations' held in the Crystal Palace, London, in 1851. The exhibition, which aimed at improving design by bringing together artefacts from all parts of the world, had a section on Indian raw materials and crafts. Indian crafts and antiquities found a place in later exhibitions as well. The exhibits at the Paris Exhibition of 1867, for instance, included photographs and pieces of ancient sculpture from the ancient Buddhist site of Amaravati.

The major constraint on government sponsorship of archaeological projects in British India was financial, stemming from a reluctance to spend on matters not considered strictly essential to the practical interests of colonial rule. When it came to the initiation of new projects, apart from the governor general, the attitude of the Court of Directors (in the pre-1857 days) and the secretary of state (in the post-1857 phase) was crucial. The background to the first government-sponsored archaeological survey in colonial India consisted of a few sporadic and desultory initiatives. In 1844, in response to recommendations made by the Royal Asiatic Society, the Court of Directors directed the Government of India to take steps towards the preservation of the Ajanta caves and to have copies of their paintings made. The directors further requested that they be provided with a set of drawings illustrating the various aspects and phases of Indian culture as represented in architecture, artefacts, costumes, etc. The Government of India responded by setting aside a small sum of money for the repair of monuments. In 1847, the Bombay government proposed a long-term project for preparing drawings of the principal objects of antiquarian interest in western India. The proposal was vetoed by the Court of Directors, who suggested that an antiquaries' commission to document Indian antiquities be established instead. The viceroy, Lord Hardinge, was of the opinion that any long-term project should be preceded by preliminary spadework done by officers deputed specially for the job.

Subsequently, several appointments were made. In 1847, Major Markam Kittoe was appointed Archaeological Enquirer to the North-Western Provinces. In 1848, apparently at the instigation of James Fergusson and the Royal Asiatic Society, the Bombay government set up the Bombay Cave Temple Commission. At the commission's insistence, the caves of Ajanta, Aurangabad, and Elephanta were cleared of accumulated earth and debris. Lieutenant Brett was deputed to make impressions of the inscriptions in the caves of western India. At about the same time, Captain Robert Gill of the Madras Army was sent to make oil copies of the paintings in the Ajanta caves.[2] In Central India, Captain F.C. Maisey of the Bengal Native Infantry was appointed to draw the antiquities at Kalinjar and Sanchi in 1849.

During these years, a few important initiatives were also taken towards photographing Indian antiquities and monuments, largely at the behest of the Court of Directors. Certain officers were released for a short period from their regular duties and sent off on specific photographic assignments. William Armstrong Fallon was commissioned by the Bombay government in 1851 to make drawings of the Elephanta sculptures and to draw and measure the caves. In February 1855 Captain T. Biggs of the Bombay Artillery was appointed photographer to the Bombay Presidency. He went on to produce a number of views of Bijapur, Dharwar, and Mysore. In November 1855 Biggs was replaced by William Pigou of the Bombay Medical Service. Pigou produced a number of photographs of the temples and inscriptions of Dharwar and Mysore. In 1856 Captain Linnaeus Tripe of the 12th Madras Native Infantry was appointed official photographer in the Madras Presidency. He went on to photograph several temples in the far south, at places such as Madurai, Tiruchirapalli, and Tanjavur.[3]

With the outbreak of the Revolt of 1857 many things, other than antiquarian and archaeological projects, suffered dislocation. With the subsequent restructuring of colonial rule via the transfer of the Indian empire from Company to crown, the colonial state launched a vigorous and concerted data-collection drive. In the numerous surveys sanctioned in this period we can identify officers who played a key role in initiating and implementing these projects. In the case of the archaeological survey, the crucial initiative came from Alexander Cunningham.

[2] Major Gill spent about a decade of his life on this project, carefully producing a number of large-size copies of the Ajanta frescoes. The results of his effort were almost totally wiped out when the copies on display at the Crystal Palace at Sydenham perished in the great fire that engulfed it in 1866. Only five copies, safe in the stores of the India Office, remained.

[3] On these photographers, see Falconer (2000).

Cunningham had been in Burma during the upheaval of 1857. He returned in 1858 to take up duties as chief engineer of the North-Western Provinces. This was also, by the way, the year when the second volume of Julien's translation of Xuan Zang's account was published. Perhaps this had something to do with the timing of the proposal that Cunningham put before the viceroy. The proposal was similar in terms of its general goals to that which Cunningham had proposed as a young officer in the 1840s—following the footsteps of Chinese pilgrims—although his emphasis had shifted from Fa Xian to Xuan Zang. By this time, he was a senior and seasoned military officer and had an established reputation as a scholar as well. The last time round, in 1848, Cunningham had aired his ideas before the antiquarian community in an academic journal; this time he placed a specific project squarely before the viceroy.

The Proposal

In November 1861 Colonel Alexander Cunningham submitted a memorandum to Canning: it had an unmistakable tone of urgency.

> During the one hundred years of British dominion in India the Government has done little or nothing towards the preservation of its ancient monuments, which, in the almost total absence of any written history, form the only reliable sources of information as to the early condition of the country. Some of these monuments have already endured for ages, and are likely to last for ages still to come; but there are many others which are daily suffering from the effects of time, and which must soon disappear altogether, unless preserved by the accurate drawings and faithful descriptions of the archaeologist.[4]

Cunningham emphasized that all efforts in this direction had so far been the result of private efforts by individuals, and were for this reason 'desultory and unconnected and frequently incomplete'. Now that the energies of the government need no longer be exhausted in the task of extending and consolidating of empire, it was time it instituted 'a careful and systematic investigation of all the existing monuments of ancient India.' Cunningham proposed an archaeological investigation

[4] Quoted in Cunningham (1871b): Preface.

of upper India which would follow the tracks of Xuan Zang. He listed the principal places in the North-Western Provinces and Bihar he thought he could explore and examine in the course of two cold seasons' (i.e. winters') work, and identified other parts of the country that merited similar attention. As for the *modus operandi*:

> I would attach to the description of each place a general survey of the site, showing clearly the positions of all the existing remains, with a ground plan of every building or ruin of special note, accompanied by drawings and sections of all objects of interest. It would be desirable also to have photographic views of many of the remains, both of architecture and sculpture; but to obtain these it would be necessary to have the services of a photographer. Careful facsimiles of all inscriptions would of course be made, ancient coins would also be collected on each site, and all the local traditions would be noted down and compared. The description of each place with all its accompanying drawings and illustrations would be complete in itself, and the whole, when finished, would furnish a detailed and accurate account of the archaeological remains of Upper India.[5]

Cunningham's proposal was well timed. It was a good moment to project the Government of India as a cultured and enlightened regime. The era of enthusiastic official promotion of the study of ancient texts had long waned.[6] The scorn for indigenous literature and learning had been expressed forcefully by Macaulay in his famous Minute of 1835, and the colonial state's subsequent promotion of the English language and Western learning had long-term implications. Not only were the indigenous languages and literatures now seen as incapable of equipping India for the challenges of the future, many were sceptical of their value for the study of India's ancient past as well. A good case could therefore be made for a historical study that was based not on the garbled traditions of dubious historical value, as embodied in ancient Indian texts, but on archaeological data—which could be presented as much more susceptible to scientific, empirical inquiry.

If Cunningham had pleaded his case well, the viceroy, in his response, argued it even more passionately:

[5] Ibid.: vii

[6] There were a few notable exceptions to this, such as the support offered by the Marquis of Salisbury while he was secretary of state for India, towards Max Müller's Sacred Books of the East series.

> It will not be to our credit, as an enlightened ruling power, if we continue to allow such fields of investigation, as the remains of the old Buddhist capital in Behar, the vast ruins of Kanouj, the plains round Delhi, studded with ruins more thickly than even the Campagna of Rome, and many others, to remain without more examination than they have hitherto received. Every thing that has hitherto been done in this way has been done by private persons, imperfectly and without system. It is impossible not to feel that there are European Governments, which, if they had held our rule in India, would not have allowed this to be said.[7]

More commendable than the sentiments Canning expressed was the swiftness with which he translated idea into action. Alexander Cunningham ('who has, more than any officer on this side of India, made the antiquities of the country his study') was immediately appointed archaeological surveyor to the Government of India, to implement the archaeological investigation he had proposed. His survey was to focus on the documentation of ancient remains. Apart from the salary to be payed to Cunningham (Rs 450 per month with a field allowance of Rs 350), no provision was made for any additional establishment. It was a one-man show which, as Canning pointed out frankly, would cost very little, and would not commit the government to any future or unforeseen expense. Repair and conservation did not form part of the survey's concerns. Alexander Cunningham retired from the army in November 1861 with the rank of Major General at the age of 47, to take up his new job. The appointment was initially intended for two years.[8] This is how the first comprehensive government-sponsored archaeological survey in India happened.

[7] The governor general's Minute on the Antiquities of Upper India, dated 22 January 1862. Quoted in Cunningham (1871b): Preface.

[8] According to Imam (1966: 232 & n.), the terms of appointment allowed Cunningham a share of the antiquities discovered by him. Imam bases this conclusion on the following statement made in Canning's Minute: 'It would be somewhat premature to determine how the results of Colonel Cunningham's labours should be dealt with; but whilst the Government would of course retain a proprietary right in them for its own purposes, I recommend that the interests of Colonel Cunningham should be considered in the terms upon which they may be furnished to the public.' In my opinion, Canning was referring to the publication of the results of Cunningham's work, not to the disposal of antiquities discovered by him. S. Roy (1953: 10, n. 8) asserts that Cunningham was given a share in

Bihar and the North-Western Provinces 1861–2

A major part of the results of Cunningham's archaeological investigations is to be found in twenty-three volumes of Archaeological Survey reports.[9] Of these, the first two volumes contain an account of four seasons of explorations by him as archaeological surveyor between 1861 and 1865. The fieldwork was conducted each winter, and the reports written up during the summer and monsoon months. The four reports were submitted to the government and copies printed for official circulation. They were subsequently published (minus the maps and sketches) as supplements in the *Journal of the Asiatic Society of Bengal.* After Cunningham took over as the director general of the newly established Archaeological Survey Department in 1871, all four reports were published in two volumes for a wider audience. Maps and drawings were included, and a long Introduction inserted at the behest of the Government of India.[10]

The Introduction to the first volume is interesting from several points of view. Among other things, it indicates the scholarly lineage that Cunningham saw himself as part of.[11] Cunningham gives a detailed account of the many men who contributed to understanding India's ancient past, starting with Sir William Jones and the founding of the Asiatic Society in 1784, down to his own explorations and publications. He discusses the contributions of Charles Wilkins, Samuel Davis, Francis Wilford, Henry Colebrooke, Francis Buchanan,

---

antiquities as part of the terms of his appointment, but does not indicate his source of information on this point. I have not found any document that indicates that this was part of the deal. On the other hand, there is no doubt that Cunningham amassed a large collection of antiquities of diverse kinds during his stay in India, many of which must have been obtained by him in the course of his archaeological surveys.

[9] Volume 24 consists of an index to the reports, prepared by Vincent Smith.

[10] During his years as archaeological surveyor, Cunningham also published a few articles on inscriptions, coins, and antiquities in the *Journal of the Asiatic Society of Bengal.*

[11] Although the Introduction precedes the Reports for 1861–5, it was written many years later, after Cunningham was appointed director general of the Archaeological Survey of India.

H.H. Wilson, William Erskine, Colonel Sykes, Colin Mackenzie, and James Prinsep; he singles out Buchanan and Prinsep for special praise. Among Prinsep's successors, he discusses James Fergusson, Markham Kittoe, Edward Thomas, Sir Walter Elliot, Colonel Meadows Taylor, Dr Stevenson, and Dr Bhau Daji. The fact that an Indian figures in this list is significant, given the general European tendency of the time to ignore or minimize contributions made by 'natives' in the recovery of their past. What is also notable in Cunningham's Introduction is the tone of warm and generous recognition of work by others, even those with whom he had differences of approach and opinion.

Cunningham described the early phase of archaeological research in India, the years between William Jones and James Prinsep (1784–1834) as a period of Closet or Scholastic Archaeologists. He was clearly using the term 'archaeology' as synonymous with history.[12] Most of the time, in fact, Cunningham worked with a very broad and flexible understanding of archaeology, one which could include a large number of approaches to the study of the past, not all of them, strictly speaking, archaeological. The post-Prinsep era, according to Cunningham, saw the coming to the fore of 'field archaeologists' and 'travelling antiquarians'.[13] In 1843 Cunningham had recklessly dismissed 'the rubbish contained in the eighteen *Puranas.*' Now, he gave a more appreciative assessment of textual scholars and the texts they had painstakingly studied. He distinguished the textual and archaeological approaches but ended on a note of humility.

> In closing this review of the progress of Indian archaeology, in which the chief share has been achieved by men who were not professed scholars, I beg it to be distinctly understood that we field archaeologists make no claim to more than ordinary scholarship, and that if we have been successful in many of our archaeological researches, we can truly ascribe our

[12] Take the following statement: 'From the foundation of the Asiatic Society by Sir William Jones in 1784 down to 1834, a period of just half a century, our archaeological researches had been chiefly literary, and, with a few notable exceptions, had been confined to translations of books and inscriptions' (Cunningham, 1871b: xviii).

[13] The term 'field archaeologist' is supposed to have been first used by Prinsep, who himself did not fit into this category. Cunningham was referring to contemporaries such as Ventura, Court, Masson, and himself.

> success in great measure to the hitherto difficult path having been smoothed by the labours of our great Sanskrit scholars, whose translations have placed within our reach nearly all the chief works of Indian learning. If we have sometimes been able to perceive what had escaped the notice of our more learned contemporaries, it has been owing to the lift that we got from them; for as the old scholiast says, *Pygmoei gigantum humeros, &c.*, 'even pygmies on the shoulders of giants can see farther than the giants themselves'.[14]

The empirical spirit and aims of Cunningham's own archaeological investigations are indicated by two epigraphs in the title page of every one of the twenty-three volumes of the *Archaeological Survey Reports*. The first was from Canning's Minute:

> What is aimed at is an accurate description, illustrated by plans, measurements, drawings or photographs, and by copies of inscriptions, of such remains as most deserve notice, with the history of them so far as it may be traceable, and a record of the traditions that are preserved regarding them.

The second was from James Prinsep:

> What the learned world demand of us in India is to be quite certain of our data, to place the monumental record before them exactly as it now exists, and to interpret it faithfully and literally.

Cunningham began his operations as archaeological surveyor in the manner he had proposed in his memorandum to Canning. He travelled with the accounts of Fa Xian and Xuan Zang in his hands, scouring the landscape for places they mentioned. At the same time, not all the sites explored by him on this and later tours were on the itinerary of the Chinese pilgrims. Twenty-five sites are described in his first report.[15] Beginning his explorations in Gaya, Cunningham surveyed places of historical interest in Bihar, Tirhut, and Champaran. He went on to explore several sites in Gorakhpur, Azimgarh, and Jaunpur before heading to Benaras, where he closed his work for the season. The sequence of discussion in this, as in the later reports, was based on the order in which he visited the sites.

[14] Cunningham (1871b): XLII.
[15] Ibid.: 1–130.

Cunningham's report for 1861–2 contains some of the earliest careful and detailed descriptions of several important sites in eastern India, including a concise account of Bodh Gaya. Because it had been repaired and renovated so many times over the centuries, the Bodh Gaya temple was difficult to date. Cunningham thought that there was a strong probability it had been built in about AD 500 by Amara Simha, author of the *Amarakosha*.[16] Cunningham described the site of Rajgir and traced the fortification wall of Rajagriha, the ancient capital of the kingdom of Magadha. He supplemented his description of Bargaon—ancient Nalanda—with a sketch of its ruins. He described the caves in the Barabar–Nagarjuni hills, citing evidence of their successive Buddhist, brahmanical, and Muslim occupation.

Among the major identifications of places offered by Cunningham in this Report were the identification of ancient Pava (the capital of the Mallas and the last halting place before the Buddha reached Kushinagara) and Kushinagara (the place of the Buddha's *parinibbana*). He identified Pava with Padarona/Padaravana village, twelve miles to the west of the River Gandak, twenty-seven miles north-north-west of Lauriya Navandgarh. Some twelve miles away from Padarona, thirty-five miles due east of Gorakhpur, was Kasia village, which Cunningham identified as the site of ancient Kushinagara. He identified several spots mentioned by the Chinese pilgrims at Rajgir (ancient Rajagriha), Baragaon (Bargaon, i.e. Nalanda), Basarh (Vaishali), and Kasia (Kushinagara).

In the course of his 1861–2 explorations, Cunningham made a number of small excavations at Rajgir. He sank a 41-ft deep shaft down to the foundations of the brick structure known as Jarasandha-ki-baithak, and continued a trench which had been begun many years ago at the base till it met the shaft from above. He found nothing that could throw light on the function of the building. Beneath the foundations of a structure next to it, however, he found eighty-four seals in medieval Nagari characters. A shaft dug near the Maniar Math led to the discovery of three small figurines at a depth of 19 ft. Cunningham

[16] This was a contentious issue that Cunningham was to consider and reconsider for many years. The inscription of Amara Deva, on which he based his initial hypothesis about the age of the temple, was shown by Rajendralala Mitra to be a forgery.

mentions a Punjab sepoy with a servant making an excavation here at the same time. Excavating at another spot at Rajgir, Cunningham unearthed the remains of a room, some steps, and a passage. At Bargaon (Nalanda), excavations made at several places revealed various structural remains such as stupas and walls of buildings. Cunningham also opened a few of the mounds at Kasia. He established the remains of a stupa on Matha-Kuar-ka-kot at Kasia and ran a horizontal gallery through the centre of the structure at its base. Although he found nothing, he was convinced that there was a more ancient stupa at a deeper level.

Some of the season's important documentation and excavation work was connected with Ashokan pillars. Cunningham excavated all around the shaft of the Ashokan pillar at Bakhira village, adjacent to Basarh (ancient Vaishali). Ground water at 14 ft below the level of the courtyard prevented him reaching the base of the pillar. While the Vaishali pillar did not bear any Ashokan inscription, Cunningham reported some short inscriptions in 'shell-shaped' characters of the seventh–eighth centuries AD.[17] He also found various names of visitors inscribed on the shaft, including those of the surveyors Reuben Burrow and Colin Mackenzie. Documentation of local traditions was an intrinsic part of Cunningham's method of investigation. He informs us that the Basarh pillar was known locally as 'Bhim-sen-ka-lat' or 'Bhim-sen-ka-danda'. At Lauriya Araraj, Cunningham did not excavate, but was content to describe the Ashokan pillar here (again noting the graffiti left by Reuben Burrow in 1792). He made an eye-copy and an inked impression of the inscription. At Lauriya Navandgarh (i.e. Nandangarh), he identified the rows of earthen mounds as pre-Buddhist royal sepulchral mounds. Cunningham described these stupas and excavated a few. He made a careful eye-copy and ink impression of the Ashokan inscription, and also noted the text of the medieval epigraph of the time of Aurangzeb inscribed on the same pillar. Reuben Burrow had been here as well, as had certain other individuals whose names Cunningham found carved on the pillar. Cunningham tells us that the erection of the Lauriya Navandgarh pillar was

[17] The 'shankhalipi' was an ornate derivation of the Brahmi script, used mainly for signatures. It was used (again mostly for signatures) in many parts of India except the far south between the fourth and eighth centuries AD.

ascribed by locals to 'Bhim Mari', and that it was currently being worshipped as a lingam. At Bhitari, he excavated around the Gupta pillar which bore an inscription of the time of the emperor Skandagupta, and made an eye-copy and impression of the inscription.

One of the many important early historical sites he explored in 1861–2 was Sarnath, the place of the Buddha's *Dharmachakrapravartana* ('the turning of the wheel of law', i.e. his first sermon). Cunningham's description of Sarnath is particularly important as it gives an account of several excavations at the place, including those he had conducted in 1835–6. His operations had been fairly intensive, of longer duration that any of the excavations he subsequently undertook. Work had begun on 18 January 1835 and had continued for fourteen months. Cunningham informs us that the cost of opening the Dhamekh stupa had been shared among James Prinsep, Captain Thoresby, Major Grant, and himself. The work was slow because it involved removing, one by one, large pieces of stone secured to each other by a considerable number of iron cramps. Due to the difficulty of the task, Cunningham had to hire quarrymen from Chunar to do the job. A vertical shaft and a horizontal gallery were excavated through the body of the stupa, and an additional gallery was run through the brickwork of the foundation. He concluded that the gigantic stone stupa (the completion of which he dated to the sixth century) was built over an older brick stupa (perhaps Ashokan) of more modest proportions.

While Cunningham had been disappointed in not finding relics in the Dhamekh stupa, he did find a stone slab inscribed with a standard Buddhist formulaic inscription. He also uncovered fairly extensive structural remains of a monastery, a shrine, and several sculptures and bas-reliefs. There was distinct evidence of burning and hasty abandonment of the site. Cunningham removed some of the best sculptural pieces he had found at Sarnath and presented them to the Asiatic Society. He reported without comment that several of the remaining statues which he had collected and left lying on the ground were subsequently taken away by one Mr Davidson and thrown into the Barna river under the bridge to check the cutting away of the bed between the arches.[18] Cunningham's activities at Sarnath had been

[18] Cunningham (1871b): 123.

abruptly brought to an end by his being ordered to proceed to Calcutta. It was fortunate that he had drawn plans of the structures he had excavated while the 1835–6 excavations were in progress, because nothing of what had been then unearthed remained at the time of writing the report for 1861–2.

Apart from the important details of his own excavations at Sarnath, Cunningham also gives an account of Major Kittoe's activities at the site (conducted at government expense), in 1851–2. Kittoe died before he got round to compiling his account of his excavations at Sarnath, and this makes Cunningham's reconstruction of these—based on correspondence between Kittoe and himself—particularly significant. A summary of subsequent excavations at the site by E. Thomas and Professor FitzEdward Hall is also given. Cunningham's account of Sarnath is thus extremely important for the history of explorations and excavations at Sarnath, as also for the history of its spoliation.

The North-Western Provinces 1862–3

The scope of Cunningham's explorations during the winter months of 1862–3 lay well to the west of the areas he had surveyed the previous year. He concentrated on Delhi, Mathura, and Khalsi and on the ancient sites lying to the north of the Yamuna in the Gangetic Doab, Oudh, and Rohilkhand. From Mathura to Shravasti, he followed Xuan Zang's route, occasionally making minor detours. He established the location of the important early historical cities of Ahichchhatra, Kaushambi, and Shravasti, in addition to suggesting other identifications. Twenty-six sites are described in Cunningham's second report.[19] But the season's work began at Delhi, which did not form part of the itinerary of the Chinese pilgrims.

Cunningham's report on Delhi stands as an important account of the city's history. Although Cunningham moves with facility through the city's medieval history and monuments, what is more significant is the material he marshalls on Delhi's ancient past. This includes an account of various traditions connected with the city in different periods, ranging from references in the epics and *Puranas*, Rajput legends

[19] Cunningham (1871c).

and the records of *bhats* (traditional genealogists), to those recounted in medieval Persian chronicles. Cunningham did not leave his preoccupation with historical geography behind; he proposed the plausible identification of Ptolemy's Indabara with Indraprastha and the unlikely identification of Daidala with Dilli.

Cunningham's account of the ancient ('Hindu') remains of Delhi was based on monuments, inscriptions, and literature—written and oral. It included a description and history of the ancient pillars in Delhi. He described the Delhi-Topra and Delhi-Meerut pillars, the text of the major and minor inscriptions on their surface, and the history of the pillars in medieval and modern times. He described the iron pillar ('one of the most curious monuments in India') that stood in the courtyard of the Jami Masjid at Mehrauli, settling the debate about its metallic composition.[20] Cunningham read the name of the king on the Mehrauli pillar inscription incorrectly as Bhava.[21] He traced an inscription of Anangapala Tomara on the iron pillar and discussed the connection between the Tomara and Chauhan Rajputs with Delhi. He identified and mapped the circuit of the walls and the gates of the Rajput forts of Lal Kot and Qila Rai Pithora.

Cunningham described the medieval settlements and forts of Delhi. His treatment of specific monuments was cursory, and his excuse for this was that some of these had already been adequately described, while he intended to deal with others in a separate work on medieval architecture (which he ultimately never wrote). He did, however, discuss the Qutb complex, giving detailed and conclusive refutation of arguments and evidence that had been proferred by Sir Sayyid Ahmed Khan to support the idea that the Qutb Minar was originally a Hindu monument. Cunningham's discussion of the Jami Masjid is also important, as he brought out the history of the masjid as it had

[20] Till then, there had been confusion about the metal out of which the pillar was made. Like some others, Cunningham had thought it was made of some sort of 'mixed metal' similar to bronze. However, he had a small piece from the lower part of the pillar analysed, and this revealed that the material was pure malleable iron of 7.66 specific gravity (Cunningham 1871b: 170). This is one of the earliest instances of metallurgical analysis of archaeological material in India.

[21] Prinsep read the name as 'Dhava'. The correct reading of the name of the king on the Mehrauli iron pillar is Chandra.

been built and then modified during the times of Qutb-ud-din Aibak, Iltutmish, and Ala-ud-din Khilji.

From Delhi Cunningham moved on to Mathura, which lay on the route of the Chinese pilgrims. Here he documented the layers of religious accretion—Buddhist, Hindu, Muslim—evident in the archaeological remains. He described the prolific sculptural remains of Mathura. A curious piece identified by Prinsep as a statue of the satyr Silenus suggested to him the possibility of the presence of a small body of Greek sculptors at Mathura. In fact, Greek influence was 'the only way in which I can account for the very superior execution of many of the earliest specimens of Indian art, but also for many of their ornamental details, such as the fluting of the pillars in the Western Panjab architecture, and the honeysuckle and astragal ornaments of Aśoka's monoliths, all of which are of undoubted Greek origin.'[22]

At Khalsi (Kalsi), near Dehradun, Cunningham was convinced that he had found the capital of the ancient kingdom of Srughna referred to by Xuan Zang. He described the rock which bore the edicts of Ashoka (these had been discovered by a Mr Forrest in the early 1860s), and made an eye-copy and impression of the inscriptions. He reported certain fragments of Buddhist railings in the vicinity and identified a number of places mentioned in the Chinese pilgrims' accounts.

One of the important early historical sites surveyed and described by Cunningham in 1862–3 was Ramnagar, which he identified with Ahichchhatra, the ancient capital of north Panchala. His excavations at Ramnagar yielded moulded bricks and a few sculptures. A more dramatic discovery was the discovery of a relic casket when he sank a shaft vertically down the centre of a stupa and continued an old gallery made some thirty years earlier by some British officers. Further excavations at the site revealed remains of a Buddhist shrine, monastery and sculptural fragments.

The second major ancient site identified and investigated in this season's work was Kosam, a village on the Yamuna, some thirty miles north of Allahabad, the site of ancient Kaushambi. This identification had been suggested to Cunningham by E.C. Bayley; his first glimpse of the extensive ruins at the place convinced him it was correct.

[22] Cunningham (1871b): 243.

Cunningham excavated around the Ashokan pillar at Kosam to a depth of 7 ft 4 in, without reaching the end of the polished portion. He cited the medieval inscription of the time of Akbar on this pillar and recorded local traditions that referred to it as 'Ram-ki-chharhi' or 'Bhim-sen-ka-danda'.

The third major early historical site explored during 1862–3 was Sahet-Mahet, which he identified with ancient Shravasti. He excavated the Jogini-baria mound and identified it as the site of the Jetavana monastery. He traced a number of structural remains, including walls and wells. The opening of a brick stupa yielded no relics, but a major discovery was a colossal Buddha figure with a donative inscription of about the first century AD. This bore the name of Shravasti and clinched the identification of the place with this celebrated city of ancient India.[23]

Cunningham made several excavations on the mounds at Sankisa, a site which he had discovered in 1842, but with no significant results. The report for 1862–3 also contains a discussion of the ancient history of Kanauj, Ayodhya, and Allahabad. Cunningham's discussion of Allahabad (ancient Prayaga) contains useful material on the history of the city, including an account of the history of the Ashokan pillar in the Allahabad fort.

Towards the end of the report there is an interesting instance of Cunningham indulging in dendrochronology. In the vicinity of Ayodhya, at a village known as Hatila or Asokpur, the central mound bore the ruins of a Shaiva temple known as the Asoknath Mahadeo. The ruined brick walls of the temple had been lifted up by the roots of a huge *pipal* tree and the matted roots had almost completely covered the stone lingam. This gigantic tree had been cut down by the *tahsildar* of the neighbouring village in 1862. Cunningham counted 849 annual growth rings in the trunk of the cut tree, and on this basis concluded that the tree must have been planted in 1013, which fitted in well with other evidence that indicated that this was about the time when the temple was built.[24]

[23] This (along with Cunningham's other correct identifications of Kushinagara, Kaushambi, and Sankisa) was questioned by Vincent Smith.

[24] Cunningham (1871b): 328–9.

The Punjab 1863–4

Cunningham's explorations of 1863–4 were concentrated in the north-western part of the subcontinent. The report of this tour, as well as that of the succeeding year, was published several years later in the second volume of the Archaeological Survey Reports series.[25] Cunningham documented details of thirty-two sites in the Punjab. The most interesting subject of inquiry for him in this region was the identification of people and places mentioned in classical accounts of Alexander's invasion, but the Chinese pilgrims' accounts were not left behind. 'With their journals (i.e. the Classical and Chinese authors) in our hands we may venture to visit the ruined cities of the Panjab with the certainty that our time will not be wasted in fruitless research.'[26] He divided discussion on the Punjab into two parts—ethnology and antiquities. The discussion of ethnology used the terms race, tribe, and ethnic group interchangeably, and was based on a threefold racial classification—early Turanians or aborigines, Aryas or Brahmanical Hindus, and later Turanians or Indo-Scythians. 'Turanian' was fashionable in scholarly circles of the time and was used as a catch-all term to refer to sundry groups considered non-Aryan. Burdened as it was with nineteenth-century confusions and misconceptions on ethnography, Cunningham's discussion of the ethnology of the Punjab is of historiographical rather than intrinsic value. At the same time, there are certain points of additional interest, such as his attempt to delineate the political history of Central Asian immigrant groups such as the Yueh Chi, Shakas and Parthians, and his attempt to identify the tribal origins of place names.

From a historical point of view, the most important identification proposed in this report was that of the ancient city of Taxila or Takshashila, which Cunningham identified with the ruins near Shah-dheri. Like some others, he had earlier identified Taxila with Manikyala. He established the correct identification of the ancient city by putting together details in classical and Chinese accounts. Cunningham's is

[25] Cunningham (1871c). Among the places outside the Punjab that were surveyed during this season were Pehoa, ancient Prithudaka. Cunningham published a paper on the Pehoa inscription. Cunningham, 1864b.

[26] Cunningham (1871c): 82. Cunningham drew on Vivien St Martin's discussion of Xuan Zang's geography and Lassen's memoir on the ancient geography of the Punjab.

the first detailed and systematic description of Taxila. His description of the ruins on its various mounds—Bhir, Hathial, Sirkap, Kacha-kot, Babar Khana, and Sirsukh—was accompanied by a plan showing the positions of the mounds and ruins. Cunningham conducted a few small excavations at Taxila. He excavated a tower on the crest of the north ridge on the Hathial mound down to a depth of 26 ft, and found only regular courses of large, rough blocks. To the west of this tower, he traced the remains of a large enclosure. He cleared the remains of a large temple at Sirkap.

By the time John Marshall began his excavations in Taxila in 1920, some of the remains cited by Cunningham in his report for 1863–4 had vanished—two stupas (which had yielded an inscribed vase and a copper plate inscription), and two large buildings which seem to have been important shrines. Marshall therefore gives a synopsis of Cunningham's description of these.[27] Here, once again, Cunningham's report contains a valuable account of remains that were soon to disappear.[28] The correct location of ancient Taxila made possible the identification of a number of other places in its vicinity.

The important Buddhist site of Manikyala had been described by Elphinstone and explored by the French generals Ventura and Court. Cunningham's report for 1863–4 described the remains here, providing a map of the ruins. He described the great stupa, giving detailed measurements. On the basis of coin finds he identified two structural phases in its construction—one in the early centuries AD, the other in the eighth century. Linking certain elements of the local legend of Rasalu and the Buddhist legend of the Buddha offering his body to appease the hunger of seven tiger cubs, Cunningham identified one of the stupas at Manikyala with the stupa-of-the-body-offering (marking the spot where the Buddha is supposed to have offered his body to assuage the hunger of the tiger cubs). Excavations at several places at the site revealed remains of a monastery and shrines. The opening of a stupa on the Sonala Pind mound took several days, but Cunningham was rewarded with a crystal relic box. Generally, however, Cunningham took no more than a few hours to wrap up an excavation.

Many of the stupas in the Punjab area had been opened earlier by

[27] Marshall (1951): 7, 9–10.

[28] Cunningham published two papers on inscriptions from Taxila. Cunningham (1863, 1864a).

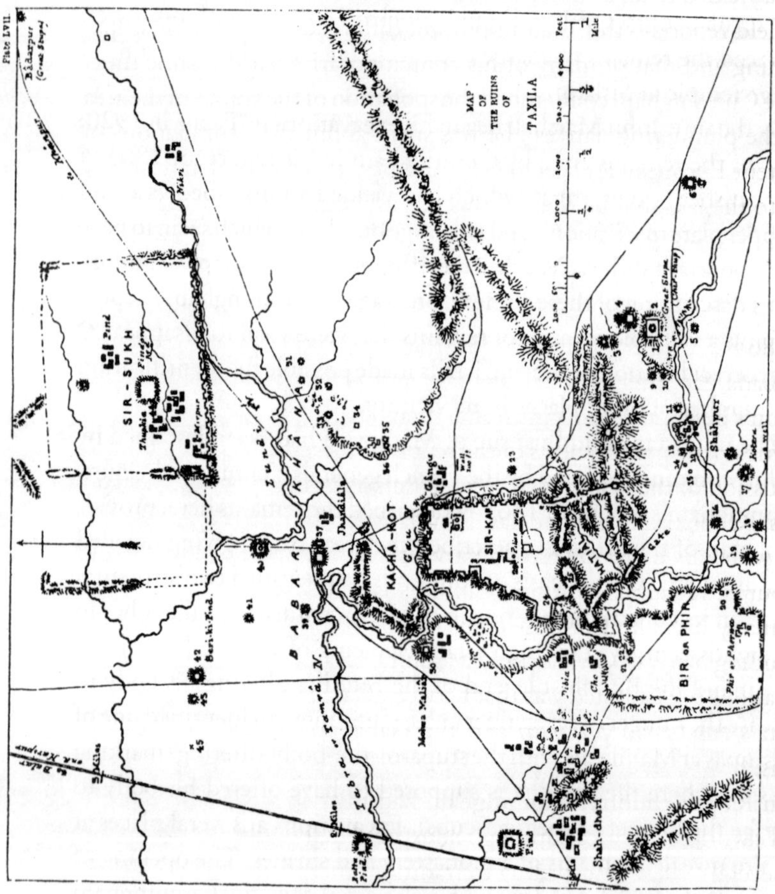

3. Cunningham's map of the Taxila ruins. Cunningham (1871c), Plate LVII.

Ventura and Court, the French generals at Ranjit Singh's court. However, their investigations largely focused on the opening of the stupas for the sake of relics and coins, and they did not as a matter of course publish complete details of their operations and discoveries. Cunningham was not uninterested in finding relics and coins, but, whether a stupa yielded relics or not, he was careful to describe the operations in his field reports—this is an important difference between his stupa-opening and that of many of his contemporaries. At the same time, while Cunningham condemned the spoliation of the stupas of the area by 'the plundering natives', he was silent about the depradations of amateur European archaeologists. And he seemed completely oblivious to the fact that he himself was not innocent of this crime.

Rajputana and Malwa 1864–5

In 1864–5 Cunningham surveyed the area between the Jamuna and Narbada, covering parts of Rajputana and Malwa. His account of this season's explorations begins in Bairat and ends at Mahoba.[29] One of the most important aspects of the report of these explorations was his discussion of the histories of various Rajput clans, such as the Chauhans, Kachhavahas, Chandelas, Pratiharas, and Tomaras on the basis of a wide range of sources—literary, epigraphic, numismatic, bardic accounts, and local traditions. Cunningham also directed attention to the many Naga kings whose coins had been found at various places, including Narwar, Gwalior, and Mathura. One of the important identifications he suggested was that between Ganapatinaga of Samudragupta's Allahabad *prashasti* and the Ganapati or Ganendra of the coins.[30]

In Rajput country, Cunningham had many occasions to refer to Tod's work on the area, although he expressed disagreement with Tod on several issues.[31] According to tradition, there were once 108 temples at Jhalra Patan or Chandravati on the banks of the Chandrabhaga

[29] Cunningham (1871c): 242–459.

[30] The correlation of numismatic and Pauranic evidence regarding the Naga kings was elaborated on in Cunningham (1865).

[31] The two volumes of James Tod's magnum opus, *Annals and Antiquities of Rajasthan* had been published in London between 1829 and 1832.

river. One of the temples had been described by Fergusson and by Tod. Cunningham described the other remains at the site. The temples of Chandravati were destroyed some years later by railway contractors who used the exquisite sculpted stones for ballast.[32] Cunningham's comprehensive description of the Chandravati became even more important in the light of its subsequent destruction.

Cunningham gave a ground plan and view of the Buddhist caves at Kholvi (about thirty miles north-west of Augar). Here he put forward one of his earliest general observations on stupa architecture—a chronology of stupas based on the relationship between the height and diameter of the structure.[33] The mechanical formula on which this thesis was built perhaps tied in with Cunningham's engineering background. A tendency towards increasing height was certainly one of the aspects of the history of stupa architecture, but other stylistic features, many of which were peculiar to different regions, also have to be taken into account.

As he moved from one place to another, Cunningham reconstructed the history of settlements and the traditions connected with them. In addition to medieval chronicles, such as those of Ferishta, he referred to the Rajasthani epic, the *Prithviraja-Raso*. He also consulted histories compiled by the bhats, manuscripts or copies of which he assiduously collected. Cunningham was by no means a credulous collector of information: he was often disconcerted by their contradictory statements. The lists of the Chandela kings given in the accounts of the traditional annalists differed so much 'that my confidence in authenticity of all bardic chronicles is completely shaken.'[34] In spite of this, the documenting of traditional histories remained one of the constant features of Cunningham's surveys and reports. This seems to have stemmed from a conviction that, whether reliable or not, the traditional histories of a place formed an integral part of its past and therefore must be recorded.

Another important constant feature of Cunningham's surveys was the recording of popular oral traditions. This was the case at Sarangpur, supposedly the birthplace of the queen Rupmati. Cunningham observed that although the songs ascribed to Rupmati were still sung all

[32] For an account of this incident, see Chapter 7.

[33] Cunningham (1871c): 286–8.

[34] Ibid.: 448–9.

over Malwa, he had never been able to find any written collection of them. He did, however, manage to transcribe some of the songs from the recital of musicians, and he gives a sample of one of the verses with his own translation.

Among the many places Cunningham described in the account of his 1864–5 explorations, Gwalior received particular attention. There is a detailed description of the city, its fort, temples, palaces, sculptures, and inscriptions. The report also contains a list of forty-six inscriptions (ranging from the third to the nineteenth century) that Cunningham had collected for the illustration of Gwalior's history.

Other major sites described by Cunningham in this report were Mahoba and Khajuraho. Cunningham identified Khajuraho with the Chi-chi-to or Jajhoti of Xuan Zang. His detailed description of the temples and ruins of Khajuraho was accompanied by a map. His assessment of the age of the temples was based on inscriptions and on masons' marks. Cunningham's reaction to the eroticism of Khajuraho sculpture was one of controlled disapproval. While describing the Kaṇdariya Mahadeo temple, Cunningham referred to the three broad belts of sculpture running around the temple. 'All of these are highly indecent, and most of them are disgustingly obscene, but the remainder of the sculptures are the ordinary representations of the Hindu gods and goddesses, in different positions and under various forms.'[35] Again, while discussing the rows of sculptures above the plinth of the Chhatr-ko-patr temple, he observed: 'There are, however, no large obscene subjects as on the other, but many of the smaller figures are very indelicate.'[36] He disapproved, but he was not overwhelmed, and his reaction to the eroticism of some of the sculpture did not prevent him from recognizing the aesthetic beauty of the temples.

The Suspension of the Archaeological Survey

At the end of four seasons' work between 1861 and 1865, Cunningham had made good progress. He had systematically surveyed and documented over 166 sites in various parts of northern India. He had confirmed through excavation the identification of many important ancient cities. Epigraphic and numismatic evidence had been firmly

[35] Ibid.: 420.

[36] Cunningham (1871c): 422.

harnessed towards the reconstruction of the political history of North India. A good deal of information on the local history of the surveyed places had been collected.

These important beginnings were cut short in 1865 (already two years more than the initially sanctioned period), when the government of Lord Lawrence decided that it did not want to finance the project any more.

> With reference to the decision of the Government of India, that no further provision shall be made for my Archaeological researches, I beg to inform you that I propose to leave Calcutta by the steamer of the 9 February, by which time the whole of the proof-sheets of the Report now submitted, will have been corrected, and my work in India brought to a close.[37]

Cunningham left for England in early 1866. The first government-sponsored archaeological survey was brought to an abrupt end, just as it seemed to be taking off.

[37] Letter dated 5 January 1866 from Cunningham to the Secretary of the PWD, PWD/Civil Works/Miscellaneous, March 1866, No. 6, Part A, OIOC. It may be noted that S. Gopal (1965: 61–2) describes John Lawrence as one of the weakest of the viceroys, and his tenure (1864–9) as one lacking in perspective and initiative.

CHAPTER 4

Director General of the Archaeological Survey of India

Alexander Cunningham's explorations of 1861–5 had made an important beginning towards the description and documentation of historical sites and monuments in India, but much more remained to be done. The surveys had concentrated on North India and parts of Central India, but even here many gaps remained, while South India had not been touched at all. Some six years later, in 1871, the idea of a government-sponsored archaeological survey was revived, and a separate Archaeological Department was created. Archaeological investigations in India were for the first time given a firm organizational basis.

During the years after the suspension of Cunningham's first archaeological survey, the imperial government had issued a number of directives to local governments at the behest of Sir Stafford Northcote, the newly appointed secretary of state. These urged the collection of photographs, the compilation of lists and descriptions of monuments and remains, and the preparation of plaster casts of some of India's best artistic specimens.[1] A Government Resolution of 24 February 1868, forwarded to all local governments and administrations, asked for the inclusion of a separate chapter on archaeology in their annual administrative reports. This was to give an account of the condition of all works of art mentioned in the lists that were to be prepared. Local governments were to be responsible for small-scale repairs of historical monuments, while larger-scale operations were to be referred to the Public Works Department.[2]

[1] Government of India Circular No. 57-4030-40 A, dated 29 August 1878, and Secretary of State's Public Despatch No. 165, dated 9 December 1867, cited in Home/Public, 30 July 1870, Nos. 204–16, Part A, NAI. Also see Public Proceedings, November 1872, No. 44, Part A, OIOC.

[2] Ibid.

In 1868 H.H. Cole of the Royal Engineers, an employee of the Public Works Department, was appointed archaeological surveyor in the North-Western Provinces. His 1868–9 surveys of the temples of Kashmir and Mathura and Brindaban led to a compilation of a number of photographs which were subsequently published by the India Office.[3] In 1868 the Calcutta-based scholar Rajendralala Mitra submitted to the lieutenant governor of Bengal a proposal for an archaeological survey of Orissa. The lieutenant governor recommended the proposal and the Government of India sanctioned it. The results of the survey were published some years later at government expense in two volumes as *The Antiquities of Orissa.*

In the course of the Paris Exhibition of 1867, various European princes had signed a 'Convention for Promoting Universally, Reproductions of Works of Art for the Benefit of Museums of All Countries.'[4] For some time thereafter, casts of sculptures and architectural elements became highly desired commodities. The Council of Education of the Science and Art Department in England urged the Government of India to have such casts made and agreed to share the costs. The Schools of Art of Bombay, Madras, and Bengal were roped in to help train modellers. Casts were subsequently made of the temples at Ambernath, Cuttack, and Sanchi.

In spite of these sorts of initiatives, the overall results of government directives and initiatives of these years were not particularly encouraging. An important lack during these years was overall direction and coordination. Most of the photographs obtained by local officials were of poor quality and the negatives were not always available. As for the lists of monuments and antiquities, these depended a great deal on the interest and initiative of officials: many of the lists forwarded to the Government of India were incomplete or lacking in adequate detail. Some of the provinces—e.g. Oudh and British Burma—sent no reports at all. The casting process was fairly successful, but far more important tasks needed urgent attention.

[3] Cole created some consternation in official circles by styling himself Superintendent of the Archaeological Survey, and also by his penchant for proposing expensive publications that the Government of India had no desire to subsidize.

[4] The signatories included the royal representatives of Britain, Prussia, Hesse, Saxony, France, Belgium, Russia, Sweden, Norway, Italy, Austria, and Denmark.

A New Initiative

In 1869 Lord Mayo succeeded John Lawrence as viceroy and, in the same year, the Duke of Argyll was appointed secretary of state for India. Mayo's tenure was cut short by his assassination in the Andaman Islands in 1872, but his brief period in office was marked by important initiatives, especially in financial decentralization. From the point of view of archaeology, the presence of a strong viceroy and a strong secretary of state was a fortuitous coincidence, especially since the latter had definite ideas about the need to give archaeological research in India a more systematic form and direction. In a despatch dated 11 January 1870 the Duke of Argyll, while appreciating early archaeological endeavours, said:

> It appears to me, however, that the time has now arrived for directing these researches in a somewhat more systematic and deliberate manner than was attempted at the outset . . . Now, therefore, that the field is, to a certain extent, mapped out, and the course which future researches may profitably take is sufficiently indicated, it might be advisable, in the first place, to prosecute operations gradually, beginning with certain selected areas from which the most valuable results may be most easily obtained. And, in the next place, I should recommend the supervision of the whole being concentrated in one department of your Government, if that be practicable, and not left, without control, to the management of different chiefs, under different local governments . . .[5]

The secretary of state also recommended certain other changes in approach. The home government did not wish to invest any more funds in the making of casts. Plans and photographs needed to be taken and chosen with greater care and negatives should in all cases be obtained. The cataloguing and describing of works of art should be pursued more methodically. The secretary of state suggested that antiquities should, as far as possible, not be removed from their original place. He especially emphasized the responsibility of government in preventing wanton destruction of these antiquities by its own officers. His despatch was accompanied by copies of a *Report on the Illustration of the Archaic Architecture of India* by Forbes Watson, with appendices by

[5] Despatch from the Secretary of State for India to the Government of India, Home/Public, 30 July 1870, No. 206, Part A, NAI.

James Fergusson, Alexander Cunningham, and Philip Meadows Taylor.[6] These enclosures embodied the opinions of men whose opinion had been specifically solicited by the home government.

Forbes Watson of the India Museum, London, urged a greater degree of professionalism in illustrating the architecture of India through photographs, drawings, plans, sections and other architectural drawings, as well as through moulds and casts. James Fergusson suggested a greater emphasis on photographic and descriptive records rather than on casting. Meadows Taylor and Alexander Cunningham looked beyond architecture. The former focused on the classification and distribution of prehistoric archaeological remains. Cunningham's memorandum was by far the most comprehensive in scope: it classified the archaeological remains of India into four main categories—architecture, sculpture, coins, and inscriptions—and discussed each separately. It also discussed the achievements and future course that archaeological research in India should take. Cunningham urged the employment of a larger staff for the job for a few years, lest the many objects that required documentation disappeared, as he had seen them do during his long career in India.

The secretary of state had recommended the supervision of archaeological research by a single government department. Mayo went one step further and mooted the creation of a small, separate department for the purpose. Events now moved at a rapid pace. The most important task was to find a person to head the new department. Cunningham seems to have been the choice of E.C. Bayley, secretary in the Home Department. Bayley had a special interest in the matter as he himself was a scholar closely associated with the Asiatic Society. Apart from Cunningham, among those whose candidature was considered for the post were J. Gibbs and Bhau Daji in Bombay, Rajendralala Mitra in Calcutta, Lieutenant-Colonel Pearse in Madras, Revd. Sherring in Benaras, and Major Stubbs in Amritsar—these being the handful of

[6] Home/Public, 30 July 1870, Nos. 204–16, Part A, NAI. Forbes Watson was 'Reporter on the Products of India' in the India Museum in London. Fergusson was (as we have seen in the earlier chapters) a well-known scholar of architecture. Meadows Taylor had worked in various capacities in the dominion of the Nizam of Hyderabad and simultaneously pursued his archaeological interests, with a special focus on prehistoric and megalithic remains.

men in India who were thought to have some sort of understanding of archaeology. Others, who fell into a second category by the criteria of eligibility, were Lieutenant Waterhouse, Captain Ayreton Pullon, G.W. Terry, and James Burgess at Madras, F.S. Growse in the North-Western Provinces, A.C.L. Carlleyle of the Agra Museum, and Baden-Powell in Lahore. Out of all these men, Bayley thought Major-General Cunningham the best qualified, and it was he whom he ultimately recommended for the job: 'His means are not very large, his health and that of his wife (which mainly induced them to leave India) are thoroughly re-established, and I believe that, if invited and allowed to work in the hills in the hot season, he would very probably accept the appointment on a staff allowance of, say, Rs 1,000 in addition to his pension, which I imagine would be a sufficient pecuniary inducement . . .'[7] In Bayley's opinion Cunningham would not only do the job well, he would be able to train a group of archaeologists in India. The Asiatic societies of Bombay and Calcutta could be called upon to help in the project. And, Bayley added persuasively, the cost of the whole enterprise would be moderate.

'Investigating, Describing, Protecting . . .'

The viceroy had reacted with enthusiasm to the secretary of state's suggestion that the Government of India take decisive measures to promote archaeological investigations. Now, he swiftly accepted Bayley's recommendation that Cunningham be requested to head the new Archaeological Department. For the first time in the history of British rule in India, government policy emphasized the connection between archaeological investigation and conservation and assumed responsibility for both.

> I believe that in the matter of archaeological research, the Government of India has done little or nothing, which is to us a source almost of shame. I think that the Government should at once divest itself of taking casts or of authorizing an indiscriminate system of photography.
>
> The duty of the Government is of a widely different and much larger and more important kind. I believe that the duty of investigating, describing, and protecting the ancient monuments of a country is one that

[7] E.C. Bayley's Notes in Home/Public, 30 July 1870, Nos. 204–16, Part A, NAI.

is recognized and acted on by every civilized nation in the world. India has done less in this direction than almost any other nation and considering the vast materials for the illustration of the history which lie unexplored in every part of Hindoostan, I am strongly of opinion that immediate steps should be taken for the creation under the Government of India of a machinery for discharging a duty, at once so obvious and so interesting . . .

. . . I think the time is come when a great and enlightened Government can no longer neglect contributing to the archaeological literature of the world, the result of systematic investigations into monuments and remains, which, perhaps, are unequalled in their historical and archaeological value . . .'[8]

Cunningham was in England at this time, working as director of the Delhi and London Bank. Bayley tested the waters by writing to him, informing him about the proposal to create an archaeological department, and expressing the hope that he would agree to head it. Bayley emphasized that the government wanted it clearly understood that if Cunningham accepted the job, they would expect him to submit and make public an annual report of his work.[9]

Cunningham accepted the appointment, but only after insisting that he be given double the salary he had been offered (Rs 2000 per month instead of Rs 1000), in addition to his pension. Despite its chronic stinginess, the Government of India accepted his terms. The post was with effect from Cunningham's embarkation to India, and was initially sanctioned for a period of five years. Cunningham left England by ship on 3 December 1870 and reached Bombay in February 1871. The original designation for the post—Central Agent for the Archaeological Survey—was soon replaced by that of Director General. The terms of the new arrangement were laid out in a Government Resolution of 2 February 1871.[10] Cunningham was given a series of specific instructions. He was to prepare a brief summary of the labours and results of former scholars. He was to prepare a general scheme of systematic inquiry for the guidance of a staff of assistants in present

[8] The Viceroy's Note, 30 July 1870 in ibid.

[9] Letter dated 29 July 1870, from E.C. Bayley to Alexander Cunningham, Home/Public, 30 July 1870, Nos. 204–16, Part A, NAI.

[10] Home/Public Proceedings, 18 February 1871, No. 28, Part A, OIOC.

and future researches. This scheme should clearly indicate what had already been done and what remained to be done. It was to give clear and detailed instructions about the nature of information and the manner of illustration required for the effective documentation of archaeological remains. Cunningham was also to map out the order and areas in which archaeological research should proceed so that as little time as possible was lost in travel. He was to submit a statement of the establishment and expenses his department would involve. The government also urged the employment, as far as possible, of natives in the work of photography, measurement, surveying buildings, directing excavations and deciphering inscriptions. Cunningham was to submit an annual report regarding the nature, amount, and general value and importance of the work done by his team. The government envisaged that the material collected in these annual reports should be eventually published.

Cunningham's Plan of Action

On taking over his new appointment as director general, Cunningham submitted for government consideration a sketch of his plan for the Archaeological Survey of India.[11] For the purposes of survey, India could be divided into five separate provinces of nearly equal size, named after the five principal seats of government—Punjab, the North-Western Provinces, Bengal, Bombay and Madras. Each of these could be further divided into three subdivisions, each small enough to be explored by a single party in a single season of five to six months. Cunningham had a rather optimistic estimate of the time-frame involved:

[11] Letter dated 7 February 1871 from Major-General Alexander Cunningham, Director of the Archaeological Survey of India to A.O. Hume, Officiating Secretary to the Government of India, Home/Public, 30 July 1870, Nos. 204–16, Part A, NAI. Archaeology was placed under the purview of the Public Branch of the Home Department. On 1 July 1879, with the constitution of the Home, Revenue and Agriculture Department, it was transferred to its Surveys Branch. On 6 July 1881, the Home, Revenue and Agriculture Department was bifurcated into the Home Department and the Revenue Department, and a new, independent Archaeology and the Conservation of Ancient Monuments Branch was created under the Home Department. On 13 April 1887, the Archaeology Branch was transferred to the Revenue and Agriculture Department. In 1895, the name of this branch was changed to the Archaeology and Epigraphy Branch.

> If five surveying parties could be organized, the whole of the *known* remains of India could most probably be examined within three years; or, if only three parties can be raised, the survey will extend to five years. I would myself undertake the exploration of one circle, and two other circles could be explored by two assistants, acting under my guidance and supervision. . . .
>
> . . . As well as I can judge at present, . . . not more than one-half of the archaeological remains of India are now known to us. As the operations of the survey proceed, it may be confidently expected that our enquiries and explorations will lead to fresh discoveries. The work to be done will thus grow under our hands, and the time required for the survey of the whole country will consequently be extended to ten or twelve years.[12]

An immediate problem was to identify and train assistants. Cunningham had made inquiries in both England and India about possible candidates, but most of those who seemed suitable already had better-paying jobs than employment in the Archaeological Survey could offer. Cunningham finally identified three who he thought should be associated with the newly formed survey. He was particularly impressed by the credentials of James Burgess. Burgess was an architect well versed in Indian languages. Cunningham had heard that he was likely to be appointed director of the Bombay School of Art, and thought that Burgess could simultaneously function as superintendent of the archaeological survey of the Bombay Presidency. He also identified Burgess as a good candidate for the post of director general of the survey upon his own retirement.[13] The two men whom Cunningham proposed as his own assistants were J.D. Beglar, assistant engineer in the Bengal Public Works Department, and A.C.L. Carlleyle, curator of the Riddell Museum at Agra.

Ultimately, the organization that Cunningham came to head was much smaller than the one proposed in his plan. Instead of five survey parties, there was only one. It consisted of a principal staff of three—Cunningham himself, and two assistants, Beglar and Carlleyle.[14] The establishment also included one draughtsman, two measurers, two

[12] Letter dated 7 February 1871 from Cunningham to A.O. Hume, op.cit.

[13] Ibid.

[14] H.B.W. Garrick took over charge from Beglar in 1880.

servants, and six temporary hands. The total annual commitment on the part of the Government of India on account of salaries, travel and contingency expenses was Rs 54,000. The activities of the Archaeological Department were largely confined to northern and central India. A separate Archaeological Survey of Western India was set up in 1873 under the direction of James Burgess. But the establishment of a similar organization for South India had to wait till 1881, when Burgess was given additional charge of the Archaeological Survey of Southern India.

Report for the Year 1871–2

The field surveys of the Archaeological Survey were remarkable in their regularity and range, if not so much in their depth. Their results were published in the volumes of Cunningham's *Archaeological Survey Reports.* Cunningham's report for the year 1871–2 embodies the results of the first season's work of the newly constituted survey.[15] Cunningham was director general and had a team, a rather small one, but a team nonetheless. Travelling on foot, horseback, elephant, camel, palanquin, and in later years increasingly by rail, the three-man Archaeological Survey scoured town and countryside for ancient sites and remains. The third volume of the *Archaeological Survey Reports* gives us an explicit synopsis of the 'Cunningham method' of archaeological exploration and documentation in the memorandum he prepared for his assistants. We also see Cunningham venturing further into the architectural sphere, offering a comprehensive chronological classification of ancient and medieval Indian styles of architecture.

Cunningham's Memorandum of Instructions to his assistants (his terms of appointment required him to prepare one) is an important document in the history of Indian archaeology. In it, the first director general of the Archaeological Survey gave a detailed, systematic exposition of his understanding of the scope of archaeological inquiry. Archaeology, he stated, was not concerned only with broken sculptures, old buildings and mounds of ruins. The study of architecture was similarly an important, but not the only, part of an enterprise

[15] Cunningham (1873a). Out of the twenty-four volumes in this series, some contain the reports of Cunningham's assistants, while Volume 24 consists of an index to the entire series prepared by Vincent Smith.

4. Alexander Cunningham, flanked by antiquities.
Courtesy: Archaeological Survey of India

which extended 'to all ancient remains whatever that will help to illustrate the manners and customs of former times.'[16]

According to Cunningham, reports on a particular place should always include detailed information on the following aspects: the various names of the place along with the origin or derivation; the date of its foundation, either historical or traditional or both; the extent of the settlement; a description of the main buildings, whether standing or in ruins; the history (either written or oral) and plan of the principal buildings, with a section of at least one typical of each style. He directed particular attention to inscriptions, including masons' marks, as a guide to the age of structures. He emphasized the need to carefully examine Jaina temples, a pertinent point given the prevailing confusion among scholars about the history and doctrines of Jainism.

While Cunningham's own interest tended towards the high tradition of sculpture, he was not oblivious to the importance of less spectacular remains. His memorandum speaks of the importance of noting the details of all sati pillars and monuments. It also directs attention to the numerous monuments of undressed stone, i.e. megaliths, in India (something that Cunningham personally did not seem to have been particularly interested in). The memorandum makes no reference to excavation. The main aim of the survey (it was, after all a *survey*) was clearly documentation and not excavation, for which resources were in any case rather inadequate.

Cunningham's memorandum is methodical but has a vibrant undercurrent. It refers with controlled enthusiasm to the aesthetic aspects of Indian sculpture and architecture—the 'splendid monoliths', the 'wonderful, rock-hewn caves', the 'singular beauty' of the ancient sculptures of the Yusufzai district and the fretted ceilings of Hindu temples, the 'gorgeous ornamentation of the glazed tiles . . .'[17] Cunningham also refers in passing to the possibility of ancient sculpture and architecture having something of value for contemporary architecture.

The most remarkable part of Cunningham's memorandum, however, lies in his inclusion of various features and details of contemporary village life within the scope of archaeological survey. Thus, he

[16] Cunningham (1873a): iv.

[17] Cunningham (1873a): vi–viii.

recommends the noting of details of the caste affiliations of village inhabitants, as part of an attempt to understand the distribution of races, 'a subject of great interest and importance for the illustration of Indian history'.[18] He mentions the significance of fragments of sculpture collected under trees and worshipped in older villages. He talks about the importance of carefully noting weights and measures prevalent in an area, and the names and shapes of agricultural implements, sugar and oil mills, and carts.

> In noting these few examples, I desire chiefly to direct attention to the many curious and old-fashioned things which still exist in several parts of India. Some of these may help to throw light on the scenes sculptured on old monuments; others may serve to illustrate passages in ancient authors; whilst all will be valuable for preserving a knowledge of things which in many places are now fast passing away, and will soon become obsolete and forgotten.[19]

The report for 1871–2 offered a chronological framework for the classification of Indian architectural styles. Cunningham described his classification as a provisional one that could be used till such time as a more mature understanding of Indian architectural styles was achieved. Although the classification purports to deal with the broader category of 'archaeological remains', as a matter of fact it deals primarily with architectural features and style, which are given the role of the prime index of the age of archaeological remains. It was based on a primary classification into two periods—'Hindu' (1000 BC to AD 1200) and 'Muhammadan' (AD 1200 to 1750). Cunningham's nomenclature of the phases of the Hindu period displayed considerable emphasis on foreign influence as well as a general focus on north India—not surprising for the time. Yet he went against prevailing opinion on the question of the antiquity of stone architecture in India, insisting that its origins lay in the period before contact with the Greeks.

The archaeological surveys were initiated by Beglar being sent to survey Delhi and Carlleyle to Agra, after which they were to proceed to Bundelkhand and Rajputana respectively. The assistants were sent

[18] Cunningham (1873a): xi.

[19] Ibid.: ix.

into the field armed with Cunningham's Memorandum of Instructions, a map on which places possessing objects of interest were connected with red lines, and copies of Cunningham's previous reports. Cunningham himself headed to the districts north of the Yamuna.

Mathura was one of the important sites discussed in the report for 1871–2. Cunningham had been here before, and in 1871 he spent several days exploring the area in and around the city. Once again he undertook the exercise of correlating the Mathura remains with references in Xuan Zang's account.[20] He discovered a large number of inscriptions which threw important light on dynastic history and chronology, and he excavated the Chaubara and Kankali Tila mounds.

The sculptural and structural remains unearthed by Cunningham on the Kankali Tila clearly indicated that this was the site of an important Jaina establishment between the first century BC and the first century AD. 'This is perhaps one of the most startling and important revelations', Cunningham observed, 'that has been made by recent researches in India.'[21] However, this evidence failed for a very long time to make any impact whatsoever on the ongoing debate on the antiquity and early history of Jainism, which scholars such as Albrecht Weber thought was a younger offshoot of Buddhism. Many years later, in the late 1880s, Bühler used the epigraphic evidence discovered by Cunningham to prove the antiquity and continuity of the early Jaina tradition. Bühler also used his influence with Burgess to have the Kankali Tila excavated once again. The mound was reopened in 1889 by Führer.[22]

Another important site explored by Cunningham in 1871–2 was Bitha (Bhita), ten miles south-south-west of Allahabad. It is in connection with Bitha that we find some of the earliest references in the Cunningham reports to ordinary artefacts, suggesting a change in perspective. Cunningham's description of Bitha refers to the discovery of numerous small, sharply pointed spikes of bone, the purpose of

[20] Recent writing tends to be quite dismissive of his exertions in this direction. M.C. Joshi says that such attempts made by Cunningham as well as Growse were a signal failure because both assumed that the Katra mound marked the centre of the ancient city, whereas the site of ancient Mathura is marked by an extensive elevation to the south-west of the town (Joshi, 1989: 170).

[21] Cunningham (1873a): 46.

[22] Folkert (1998): 103–12.

which he wasn't sure of, but which he found sufficiently interesting to describe and draw. He also refers to the 'commonest specimens of antiquity' at the site—a large number of stone stools or seats supported on four feet, some plain, mostly ornamental. Cunningham speculated that they may have been bathing stools. Among the notable ordinary objects were certain intriguing fragments of pottery. 'In the excavation which I made in the eastern face of the fort, I found pieces of pottery covered with a thin black glaze of metallic lustre. This kind of glazed pottery I have found in all the more ancient sites, and a more complete specimen of it was exhumed in one of the Bhilsa topes as the receptacle of the relics.'[23] These statements constitute some of the earliest references to pottery in Cunningham's reports. This is not the only place where he mentions what later came to be referred to as Northern Black Polished Ware. While commenting on these potsherds, Cunningham seemed to be on the verge of elaborating on the important connection between ancient pottery types and ancient sites, but he stopped short.

Another area in which Cunningham just missed making an important connection appears within his observation linking the antiquity of the settlement to the gradual gradient of the mound.[24] Cunningham would have been on the right track if he had linked the height, rather than the gradient of the mound, to the antiquity of the site. He did make such a connection the following year, but in too mechanical a manner.

Further east, Cunningham revisited the famous Buddhist site of Bodh Gaya. He had briefly described this in the report for 1861–2. Now he listed the inscriptions found there, gave a more detailed discussion of the temple, including a description of excavations carried out at the site by himself and (on his recommendation) by Major Mead. On the age of the Bodh Gaya temple, he voiced disagreement with Rajendralala Mitra, who gave the temple a very early date (about 200 BC) as well as with James Fergusson, who placed it as late as the fourteenth century AD. According to Cunningham, the temple that stood at Bodh Gaya was essentially the same that Xuan Zang saw in the seventh century; he believed it had been subsequently repaired but not rebuilt, as Fergusson imagined.

[23] Cunningham (1873a): 51.

[24] Ibid.: 52.

Cunningham's disquisition on the age of the Bodh Gaya temple led him on to two important general issues—the origins of stone sculpture and monumental stone architecture in India. Like many European scholars, for Cunningham too the story of Indian sculpture was one of decay from the high point—achieved via Greek contact—to 'the wooden inanities and bestial obscenities of the Brahmanical temples.'[25] But while Cunningham was convinced that the ancient Indians had learnt the art of *sculpture* from the Greeks, he was equally convinced that the art of stone *architecture* was known to them before the time of Alexander's invasion. The 'proof' that he cited for this came not from Bodh Gaya, but Rajgir.

Cunningham had approached the city of Rajgir from the north-east, determined to settle once and for all the question of the identification of the Sattapani cave, the place where the first Buddhist council had been held soon after the Buddha's death. He reiterated his identification of the Son-bhandar cave with the Sattapani cave.[26] Cunningham's argument for the pre-Mauryan antiquity of stone architecture was based on evidence from the Vaibhara cave and the stone structure known as Jarasandha-ki-baithak (which seems to have been a watch tower). The Vaibhara cave was a rough excavation, the lower portion of which was later lined with brick. According to Cunningham, this cave was undoubtedly the quarry from which the stones for Jarasandha-ki-baithak came. Therefore, he argued, the Baithak must be as old as the cave, i.e. it must go back to the time of the Buddha or even earlier.[27]

[25] Ibid.: 100.

[26] This identification was not accepted by subsequent investigators. John Marshall thought Sattapani was represented by a hall and not a cave. The Sattapani and Son Bhandar are generally located on opposite sides (western and eastern respectively) of the Vaibhara hill at Rajgir. An inscription in the Son Bhandar cave suggests it was excavated in the third or fourth century AD for Jaina ascetics (Kuraishi 1987: 19, 28).

[27] Actually, it is very difficult to ascertain the precise age of Jarasandha-ki-baithak in particular and other early remains (including caves and structures) at Rajgir. Archaeological investigations at this important site have been fairly limited, although they do indicate a Northern Black Polished Ware level and hint at an earlier occupation as well. The Rajgir fortifications went through several stages of construction in mud, brick and stone, and it is difficult to date them precisely.

Two other sites held the promise of Buddhist remains, and Cunningham excavated at both. At Kiyul (on the left bank of the Kiyul river), he discovered the remains of a Buddhist monastery and a steatite stupa-shaped relic casket. At Nongarh (on the western bank of the Kiyul river, six miles south-south-east of Jaynagar), he sank a shaft from the top of the brick mound and at 7 ft found a small chamber containing three small stupas of unburnt clay. Lower down, at about 8½ ft, there were eight clay stupas in a second chamber. He continued the shaft till 11½ ft with no further result. Beglar was entrusted with carrying on the excavation at the site, and he reported the interesting results of these further diggings at Nongarh.[28]

While Cunningham recognized the importance of epigraphic evidence from the beginning of his scholarly career, the emphasis on this aspect increases in his writings after 1871. From Volume 3 of the *Archaeological Survey Reports,* there is abundant and regular material on inscriptions—lists, facsimiles, translations, discussions. The report for 1871–2 gives lists of inscriptions found at Mathura, Bodh Gaya, Gaya, and other places. These are accompanied by translations or summaries and by a discussion of their bearing on dynastic history. On the basis of evidence in inscriptions and medieval literary sources, Cunningham constructed a genealogy of the Pala kings of Bihar and Bengal, and a more ambitious series of genealogical lists relating to the history of Magadha from the Shaishunagas to the Palas.

The Punjab and Yusufzai 1872–3

During the winter of 1872–3 Cunningham toured various parts of the north-west, including the Punjab and Yusufzai. He also visited

But it is indeed likely that the stone fortifications go back to a pre-Mauryan age, because Rajgir started losing its political importance after the transfer of the Magadhan capital to Pataliputra in the middle of the fifth century BC during the reign of Udayin. If this is so, then Cunningham's arguments are plausible, though not conclusive. Many years later, James Fergusson (1884: 12–13) ridiculed Cunningham's claim about the pre-Mauryan origins of Indian monumental stone architecture and asked whether he had ever substantiated his claim with any evidence. Whether the claim stands or not, Cunningham did in fact cite evidence for his hypothesis, which Fergusson seems to have been unaware of, or perhaps chose to ignore.

[28] See Chapter 5.

and described temple sites in Kangra. The results were embodied in Volume 5 of the *Archaeological Survey Reports*.[29] Cunningham described a number of Buddhist sculptures of the Indo-Scythian period in the Yusufzai area and elaborated on the Greek and Persian influence on Indian sculpture.

The main groups of ruins in the Yusufzai area included those at Shahbazgarhi, Sawal-dher, and Shahri Bahlol in the plains and Ranighat, Jamalgarhi, Takht-i-Bahi, and Kharkai in the hills. Cunningham described his own admittedly 'partial and hurried researches' and 'the more complete and deliberate explorations' that had been made under his instructions by the Sappers and Miners. Cunningham made a fresh copy of the Ashokan inscription at Shahbazgarhi and discussed its contents. Superficial excavations yielded the remains of a vihara in one place. The ruins of Takht-i-Bahi had previously been excavated and described by Dr Bellew, and also by Sergeant Wilcher who had supervised the excavations by the Sappers and Miners in early 1871. Cunningham quoted from Bellew's account. He made superficial excavations at several places and found numerous sculptural fragments and structural remains. He observed that the whole surface of the mound was thickly strewn with small pieces of stone and pottery fragments. The description of some of the potsherds (with a black shiny glaze both inside and outside) matches that of Northern Black Polished Ware.

It is in connection with certain circular pits, partially filled with debris (which Cunningham referred to as 'rubbish') on the top of the Shahri-Bahlol mound that Cunningham made one of his rare comments on occupational debris at a site. One of these pits had been cleared by Dr Bellew, and, from the description of the results of the venture, Cunningham guessed that this must have been a grain pit.

> . . . the most curious result revealed by Dr Bellew's excavation is the fact that the soil beneath the pit was an accumulation of rubbish to a depth of 27 feet. The mound was therefore not less than 45 feet in height when Buddhism was still flourishing in this district, or not later than AD 800. If the accumulation of rubbish be calculated at 1½ foot per century, which is the approximate rate ascertained by excavations at Multan, then the site of Shahri-Bahlol must have been occupied as early as 3000 years before AD 800, or about 2000 BC. The same date may be derived from the present

[29] Cunningham (1875).

> accumulation of 60 feet, if calculated at the same rate of 1½ foot per century.[30]

While the idea of stratigraphy was implicit in Cunningham's remarks, what was questionable was his belief that a uniform, mechanical formula could be used to ascertain the age of an archaeological deposit.

The Sappers and Miners under Lieutenant Crompton of the Royal Engineers had been excavating at Jamalgarhi as well. Cunningham had discovered the site in 1848; in 1872–3 he visited it twice. During the second trip, he conducted some partial excavations, exposing the evidence of a large stupa surrounded by a circle of shrines. Further clearance by the Sappers and Miners led to the exposure of a complete Buddhist complex, which he described in detail.

In the report for 1872–3 Cunningham reaffirmed his conviction of the correctness of his earlier identification of Shah-dheri with ancient Taxila. During his recent visit to the site he had excavated several Buddhist viharas, and had also found the bases and capitals of some Ionic columns of pure Greek design. In the course of his discussion, Cunningham emphasized the importance of epigraphic and numismatic evidence in ascertaining the date of ancient structures.

Cunningham had made some excavations around the base of the Manikyala stupa in 1863. He had subsequently requested Sir Donald McLeod, lieutenant governor of the Punjab, to have the lower part of the stupa uncovered and the ground around it cleared and levelled. This had been done, and when Cunningham returned to the site in 1872 he made a thorough examination of the site. The report for 1872–3 contains a detailed description of the stupa and a sketch of a section (based on the combined results of his and Court's 1830 excavations), clearly indicating the coins found at different levels. Cunningham also excavated a new site called 'Mahal', near the stupa, and discovered two huge Buddha heads made of sandstone.

In the Punjab plains, Cunningham visited a number of sites such as Harappa, Depalpur, Tulamba, and Multan, describing the sites and the antiquities they yielded. Coins were aplenty in this area as well. At Shorkot in the lower Chenab valley he encountered a huge mound ('loftiest of all the mounds that I have seen in the Panjab'). He gave a

[30] Ibid.: 37–8.

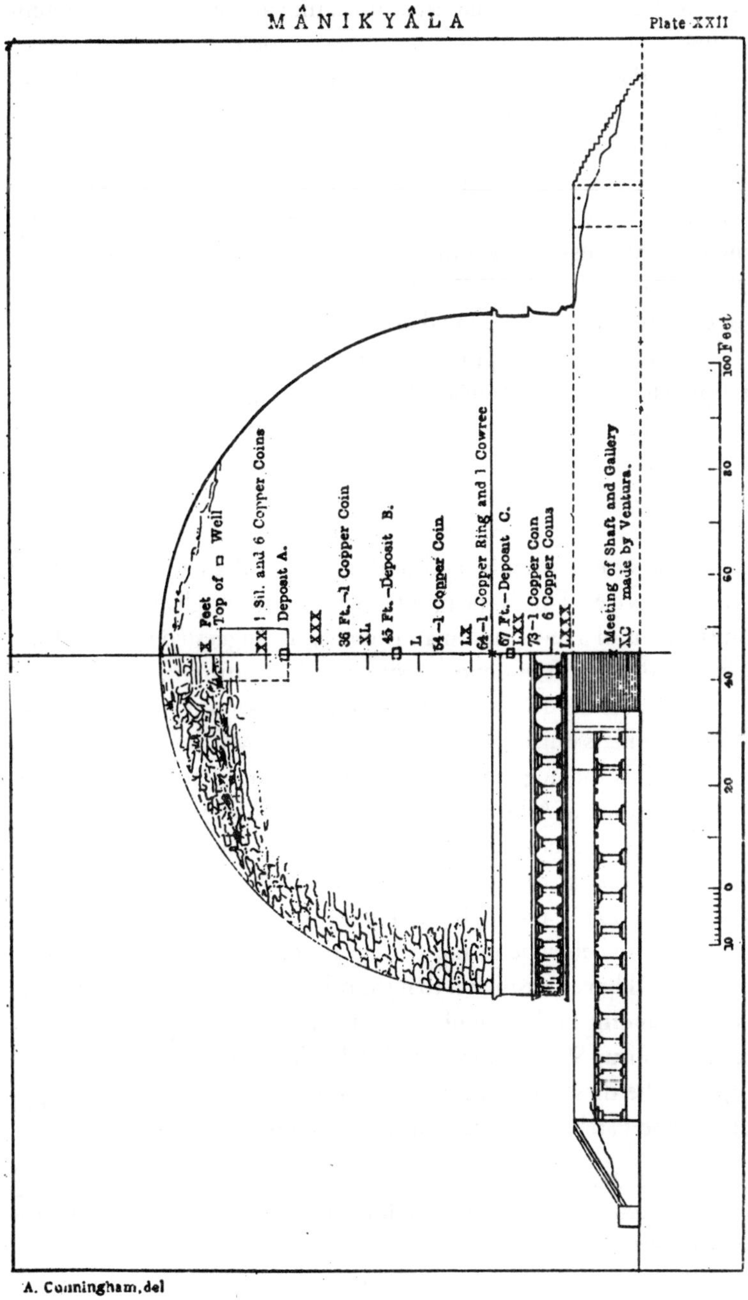

5. Section of the Manikyala stupa. Cunningham (1875), Plate XXII.

sketch of a section of the mound, indicating its gradient. He also illustrated various kinds of bricks—carved, moulded, and inscribed—found at the site. He recounted the medieval history and local traditions of Depalpur, Tulamba, Multan, Jalandhar, and Pathankot.

Cunningham's excavations at Multan are significant. This is the only place where a Cunningham report gives the stratigraphic sequence of a site, indicating the discoveries made at various depths, including details of brick dimensions. He sank several wells (i.e. shafts) down to natural soil at different places at the site, informing us that 'one of my objects in sinking these wells was to obtain some trustworthy data for fixing the approximate rate of accumulation of debris.'[31] Hoping to find evidence of ancient remains, he sank a shaft 36 ft down to natural soil outside the wall of the roofless temple of Prahladpuri. He gave the result of the findings in a tabular form, indicating the finds at various levels, including ash, brick size, and coins. The excavation seems to have been an exceptionally careful one. We are told that 'the earth was sifted carefully, and nothing larger than a pea could have escaped notice.' This is the point at which Cunningham erred when, on the basis of a few clues (mainly coins), he suggested the simplistic formula that 1½ ft of deposit represented a century.[32]

The report for 1872–3 contains some important material on the Ashokan pillars outside the main area toured by Cunningham in this season. This includes the text and translation of the short pilgrim records on the two Ashokan pillars in Delhi. More interesting are Cunningham's acute observations on the base of the Hissar pillar, first noticed as similar to the pillars at Allahabad and Delhi by Captain Brown in 1838. Cunningham thought that the pillar had originally been installed elsewhere, and had been brought here by Firuz Shah Tughluq. 'I have a suspicion that the other portion of the Hisar pillar is now standing at the neighbouring town of Fatehabad, where it was set up by Firuz Shah's eldest son, Fateh Khan, the founder of Fatehabad.'[33] The thesis that the portions of the pillars today standing at Hissar and Fatehabad once formed part of one and the same Ashokan

[31] Ibid.: 128.

[32] Ibid.: 126. This is the formula he had applied at Shahr-i-Bahlol as well. He does not mention it thereafter.

[33] Ibid.: 142.

pillar has been presented recently;[34] Cunningham had made this acute observation over a century earlier.

The most important discovery made by Cunningham in 1872–3 was one whose significance eluded him completely. The ruins of Harapa (i.e. Harappa) were noted by Cunningham as the most extensive of all the old sites along the banks of the Ravi. Charles Masson had been here in 1826 and had suggested its identification with Sangala, the capital of Porus, the king who had valiantly fought against Alexander in 326 BC. Five years later, in 1831, Alexander Burnes had visited the place and recognized it as an important site. Cunningham himself had been to Harappa in 1853 and 1856, when he traced the remains of a flight of steps on the eastern and western faces of the high mound to the north-west, and also the basement of a large square building. At that time the mounds seem to have been fairly intact. In 1872–3, when he returned to explore the mounds, he found them extensively disturbed by railway contractors. Cunningham proposed that Harappa could be identified with Xuan Zang's Po-fa-to or Po-fa-to-lo (which in his *Ancient Geography*, published in 1871, he had identified with Shorkot). Thousands of coins had been reported from Harappa, but the sorts of antiquities that interested Cunningham were not forthcoming. What he did find—stone implements, ancient pottery, and a seal—did intrigue him enough to illustrate them and to describe them.

> I made several excavations at Harapa, but the whole surface had been so completely cleared out by the Railway contractors that I found very little worth preserving. My chief discovery consisted of a number of stone implements for scraping wood or leather. Several specimens of these are given in the accompanying plate. Most of them have one edge more obtuse than the other, with a flat surface between; but a few have the two edges alike, with a single ridge between them. They are nearly all made of a dull cream coloured stone, but a few of these are nearly black in colour.
>
> My excavations also brought to light numerous specimens of ancient pottery, of which I have given some sketches in the accompanying plate. Fig. 22 appears to be a spoon or ladle.
>
> The most curious object discovered at Harapa is a seal, belonging to

[34] Falk (1995).

> Major Clark, which was found along with two small objects of chess pawns, made of a dark brown jasper. All these are shown in the accompanying plate. The seal is a smooth black stone without polish. On it is engraved very deeply a bull, without hump, looking to the right, with two stars under the neck. Above the bull there is an inscription in six characters, which are quite unknown to me. They are certainly not Indian letters; and as the bull which accompanies them is without a hump, I conclude that the seal is foreign to India.[35]

With all his archaeological experience and intuition, why did Cunningham not realize the enormous significance of what he had stumbled on at Harappa? Part of the reason seems to be his general preoccupation with things Buddhist. The fact that he thought Xuan Zang had been here probably spurred him on to excavate in the first place. He did find remains of structures, very tentatively labelled by him as a temple and a monastery, but there was nothing substantial or definitely Buddhist. This encounter with the unfamiliar did not lead, curiously, to further investigation or questioning. The Harappan seal, which Cunningham described and illustrated, was a vital clue. Its significance was lost when Cunningham decided it was a foreign object on the basis of the fact that the bull depicted on it was not the typical Indian humped variety. A few years later, Cunningham had changed his mind and reached the conclusion that the writing on the seal represented an early indigenous Indian script; in fact he suggested certain similarities between its characters and Ashokan Brahmi. But he was way off the mark when he dated the writing on the Harappan seal to circa 400 BC.[36] It would take another half century for the dramatic importance of the remains at Harappa to be realized.

[35] Cunningham (1875): 108.

[36] Cunningham (1877): ii–iii. 'With regard to the Indian Pâli alphabet, I have ventured to claim for it a local origin quite independent of all other alphabets. If my views be correct, the alphabetical characters of India must have passed through a pictoral stage of writing, similar to that of the early Egyptian hieroglyphics. It is true that no specimens of this kind of writing have yet been *found* in India, but it is quite possible that some may still exist, although they have hitherto escaped notice. I have myself published one early specimen of writing on a seal which was found in the Panjâb. The only difficulty about such a small and easily-transportable article as a seal is the possibility that it may have been imported from the west. But opposed to this objection is the strong fact that the cuneiform alphabets of the

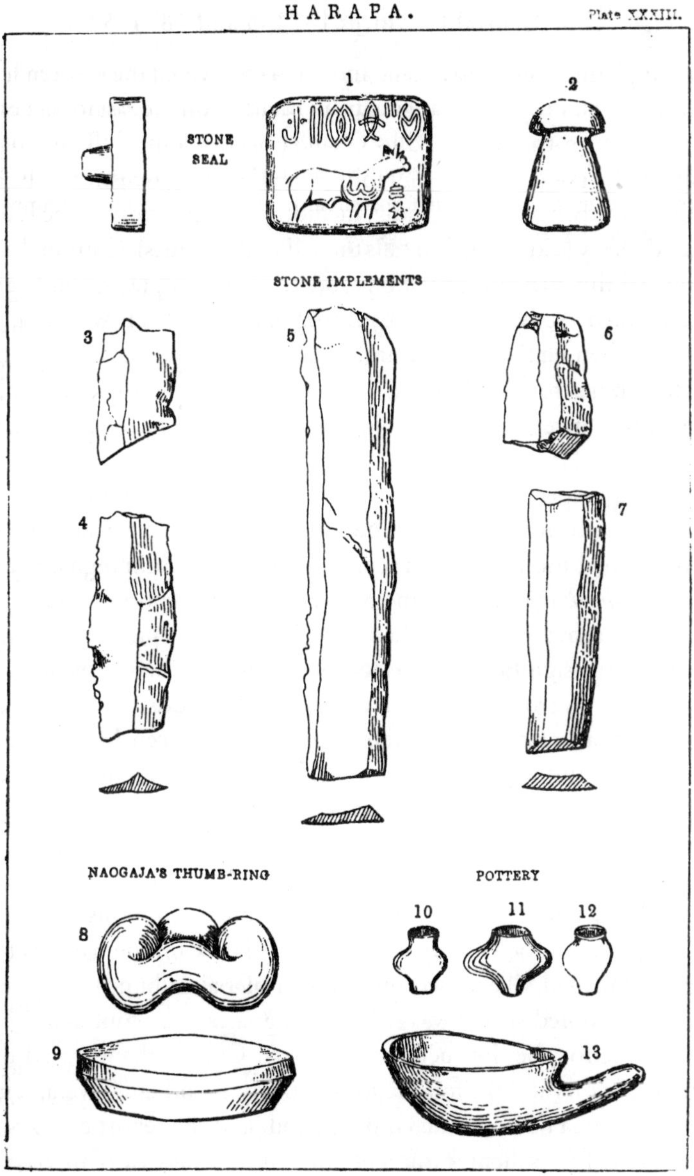

6. Cunningham's sketch of some of his discoveries at Harappa. Cunningham (1875), Plate XXXIII.

The Central Provinces 1873–4 and 1874–5

Cunningham's tours of 1873–4 and 1874–5 covered the western half of the Central Provinces, ranging from Bharhut on the east to Asir and Burhanpur on the west, and to Chanda on the south.[37] The report contained a good deal of epigraphic material and discussions on the political history of Central India, including a long history of the Kalachuri dynasty (Cunningham calls them the Kulachuris). Cunningham discussed the question of the initial date of the Gupta era, and concluded (incorrectly) that it probably began in AD 195. He was on surer ground when he fixed the beginning of the Kalachuri era in AD 249. In the reports for 1873–4 and 1874–5, the first photographs make their appearance in the Archaeological Survey Reports, many of them taken by Beglar.

The most spectacular discovery of 1873–4 was made at the start of the tour, with the discovery of the Bharhut stupa. The details of the stupa formed the subject of a separate volume by Cunningham, *The Stûpa of Bharhut*, published in 1879. Here, in the report written soon after the discovery, Cunningham gave a brief description of the site. He noted the significance of its location near the junction of two important routes from Allahabad and Benaras towards the south, and near the head of the pass of the Tons valley between Mahiyar and Jokhai. He conducted an excavation at Bharhut and was disappointed at finding no seals. He did, however, find a single bronze figure and a number of ordinary artefacts such as razors and nail-parers.

One of the important aspects of this report is Cunningham's account of the temples, sculptural remains and inscriptions found at several places in the vicinity of Bharhut. When Cunningham visited Tigowa (a small village two miles north of Bahuribund), only one small, flat-roofed shrine was still standing: a railway contractor was responsible for the destruction of the rest. Cunningham traced the entrance of one and the foundations of thirty-six others. Several temples in the area dated to the Gupta period, and the report contains a discussion of the salient features of the architectural style of this age.[38]

---

countries to the west of the Indus, which are now known to us, offer no affinities with the characters of the seal.'

[37] Cunningham (1879a).

[38] Ibid.: 42–4.

Cunningham also found the remains of a circular cloister of a tenth-century Chaunsat Yogini temple at Bhera Ghat, at the confluence of the Narmada and Banganga. He compared the Yogini temples here with those at Ranipur Jharial and Khajuraho, noting that all of them were hypaethral (roofless).

True to the instructions he had given his assistants, Cunningham described sati shrines and various assemblages of ancient sculptures in village shrines that he encountered. At Keljhar, a large village about halfway between Chanda and Markanda, Cunningham found and described two small 'cromlechs or dolmens'.[39] He paused to record local traditions connected with these shrines of the Kurumbar shepherds, citing Meadows Taylor on their function as shrines, not tombs, and noting their frequent appearance all over this part of Central India.

The report contains a description of the fort, temples and tombs of the Gond kings at Chanda. It includes detailed ethnographic accounts of the Gond and Sabara tribes, based on tribal traditions, Rajput bardic lore, and references in Sanskrit texts. Cunningham's views on migrations in ancient India were typical of the confused ideas current in his time:

> Here I fully agree with Dr Caldwell, that the Sudras were most probably the people with whom the Aryans came into contact in Northern India. But I think that he has unnecessarily hampered himself by supposing that the Dravidians entered from the north-west. On the contrary, I believe that they came from the west, and that they were the Accad or Accadians, a branch of the southern Turanians, who occupied Susania and the shores of the Persian Gulf and Indian Ocean including the Delta of the Indus. From these seats they were eventually driven out by the Aryans of Ariana and Persia, when they retired to Southern India, leaving only a remnant of the nation behind in the Brahui mountains, where they still exist.
>
> Under this supposition the Dravidians may have occupied the greater part of southern India about the same time that the Aryans took possession of the Punjâb and Aryavarta, while the whole of Northern India was held by another Turanian people, who had entered long before from the north-west. The latter I believe to have been a Medo-Scythian race. Such of them as submitted were allowed to join the Aryan nation as a separate

[39] The term cromlech was used at the time for megalithic structures consisting of three vertically placed stone slabs surmounted by a horizontal one, with one side open.

class under the name of Sudras; while the greater number retired to the east of the Karmanasa River, where they bade defiance to their enemies for several centuries.[40]

Bundelkhand and Malwa 1874–5 and 1876–7

During the winters of 1874–5 and 1876–7 Cunningham toured a total of twenty-three sites, a few in the Gangetic valley, but most of them in Bundelkhand and Malwa in Central India.[41] The report includes a corrected list of the Chandela kings with their probable dates and an account of Kalachuri and Chandela coins, the latter from Cunningham's own collection. In an Appendix on the Gupta era, Cunningham detailed the evidence, largely astronomical in nature, to support his hypothesis that this era began in AD 167 and marked the death of Skandagupta. Other scholars, such as James Fergusson, had already figured out correctly that the Gupta era began in AD 319–20. Cunningham's error in this matter meant that his assessment of the age of inscriptional and other evidence that used the Gupta era as a reference point was off the mark by close to two centuries.

The report begins with an account of three important sites in the Ganga valley—Kosam, Bitha (and neighbouring Deoriya), and Garhwa. All these had been visited and described before by Cunningham. Since his first visit to Kosam, Cunningham had visited the site twice and made some excavations close to the Jaina temple here. He had hoped to find remains of a Buddhist shrine; instead, he discovered a large cluster of Jaina sculptures, most of them broken, which he assigned to the eleventh or twelfth century. His announcement of a reward for any piece of ancient sculpture brought to him by villagers resulted in the discovery of a number of Buddhist sculptures, architectural fragments, and personal ornaments in the shape of Buddhist symbols.

Cunningham's thorough search of the villages neighbouring Bitha and Deoriya resulted in the discovery of several sculptures and inscriptions, some belonging to the Gupta period. He excavated the ramparts of the Bitha fort and at the site of an old temple, 'but without any useful

[40] Cunningham (1879a): 159–60.
[41] Cunningham (1880a).

result'. At Garhwa he spent several days clearing the jungle and exploring ruins. The results were the discovery of four donative inscriptions and several sculptural and architectural remains.

In Central India Cunningham revisited Khajuraho. His aim was to ascertain the correctness of Fergusson's suggestion that the Ghantai temple was a Jaina, not a Buddhist, shrine—which was what Cunningham thought it was. He cleared out the interior of the temple and excavated around the buildings. The Jaina sculptures that were unearthed confirmed Fergusson's opinion on the matter.

The report contains a long description of the site of Besnagar (ancient Vidisha), its mounds, and antiquities. Between 1875 and 1877 Cunningham visited the place twice and made a thorough survey of the ruins there, and in the villages around it, for several miles. He mapped the site and made excavations in some mounds, discovering the remains of structures and pillars. Of particular interest were two stone pillars ('perhaps the most curious and novel discoveries that I have ever made'), one which Cunningham thought was originally surmounted by a fan-palm capital that he found lying nearby, and another by a *makara* (crocodile) capital. The place where the former pillar stood had been occupied by a young fakir and the pillar had become an object of worship that regularly attacted pilgrims from afar. Its surface was covered with an opaque layer of vermilion, and to Cunningham's chagrin he was not allowed to ascertain whether this concealed an inscription. The result was that he missed out on the famous inscription of Heliodorus, which was discovered over three decades later.[42]

Between 1875 and 1877 Cunningham visited Sanchi twice and found fresh architectural fragments. He searched around the place where he had found the broken shaft of a Gupta pillar, digging out two other pieces of the shaft and a broken lion capital. In all, twenty-one new inscriptions were found. The text and translation of all these newly discovered records are given in the report. Cunningham also put

[42] Cunningham assigned the pillar to about AD 200–350 (the Gupta period according to his reckoning of the Gupta era). (Cunningham, 1880a: 42). He was wrong. The pillar belongs to the second century BC. The inscription on it indicates that it must have once been crowned by a *garuda* (the mythical bird which is the vehicle of the god Vishnu) capital, not a fan-palm. The inscribed letters on the pillar were first noted by H. Lake, engineer of the Gwalior durbar, in 1908.

forward, in the form of a table, his hypothesis regarding how the approximate age of bell-capitals could be ascertained from the relative proportions between their diameter and height.[43] He outlined and illustrated changes in the features of the pillars of Central India.

Cunningham described and illustrated the principal antiquities of Eran, on the left bank of the river Bina, sixteen miles above its junction with the Betwa (about fifty miles north-east of Bhilsa). This was the site of the ancient city of Erakaina. He discovered a large square stone with a long inscription of the time of Samudragupta. An image of the god Vishnu with a boar's head was found in the house of a Brahmin. The discoveries included a pillar of the time of Budhagupta, with a curious capital. Above the inverted lotus was the abacus and a square block. On the upper half of this, on each face, were carved two addorsed lions. This supported a male figure, about 5 ft high, with a radiating halo around his head. The figure was a double one, with two faces and no back. The report contains a photograph by Captain Waterhouse of this unusual pillar.

Tours in the Gangetic Provinces 1875–6 and 1877–8

The explorations during the seasons of 1875–6 and 1877–8, described in Volume 11 of the *Archaeological Survey Reports,* stretched across the Gangetic provinces, from Badaun to Bihar, and covered a total of thirty-six sites with remains ranging from the early historical to the medieval.[44] One of the important aspects of this report is the documentation of several ancient mounds in the Ganga valley.

Among the important sites Cunningham noted was Singror or Sringaverapura, on the north bank of the Ganga, twenty-two miles north-west of Allahabad. He found the whole mound a mass of brick, mostly large brick. He also obtained a substantial number of coins, ancient and medieval. He thus reported that this was 'undoubtedly a very old and important site.'[45] Sringaverapura is today recognized as an important early Northern Black Polished Ware site.

[43] Cunningham (1880a): 61.

[44] Cunningham (1880b). There is an overlap in the chronological sequence of the explorations described in volumes 9, 10, and 11.

[45] ibid.: 70.

Another early historical site visited and described by Cunningham in this report was Kampil or Kampilya, capital of ancient south Panchala and of King Drupada in the *Mahabharata*. Cunningham found the place strewn with square *kankar* blocks, some with mouldings and carvings. There were also several Jaina temples, some with inscribed images, but the priest would not allow him access.

Cunningham had visited Sankisa three times over the previous few years. In March 1876 he went there again with the express purpose of finding the remains of the Ashokan pillar, of which only the capital had been discovered. In less than a few hours' digging, he found a square brick base. He also found traces of a brick floor all around the basement of the pillar, at a depth of 4 ft beneath ground level. He swiftly made the following deduction: 'As the depth of the elephant capital below the ground-level is only 2½ feet, a rough approximation to the date of its fall may be made by taking 4 feet as the accumulation of soil in 2,000 years. This would give 1,125 years for the period of accumulation round the elephant, which deducted from AD 1875, leaves AD 750 as the approximate date of the fall of the pillar.'[46] He suggested that the enclosing wall of the monastery and the pillar may have been simultaneously thrown down by an earthquake.

Near Pakna Bihar, six miles east of Sankisa, Cunningham identified the site of a stupa and monastery of the Indo-Scythian period. He narrates how he obtained access to the place in order to excavate the site.

> At my first visit to Bihar, I found the zemindars very uncommunicative, but on my second visit, after some questioning, a man voluntarily informed me that in one of his fields on the mound numbers of pieces of stone had been seen when ploughing. I at once purchased the green wheat standing in the part of the field which he had pointed to . . . and began an excavation. At from 1 foot to 2 feet below the surface numberless fragments of stone of all sizes were exhumed, amongst them were bits of sculptured figures and carved stones.[47]

Cunningham revisited Sahet-Mahet (ancient Shravasti) in this season in order to excavate the Jetavana monastery. This seems to have

[46] Cunningham (1880b): 23. The rate of soil accumulation suggested here (1 ft = 500 years) is different from what he applied at Multan and Shahr-i-Bahlol (1 ½ ft = 100 years).

[47] Cunningham (1880b): 33.

been a very thorough operation: Cunningham spent eleven days examining the site. His report contains a map of the Jetavana, showing the location of all the ruined buildings he excavated. He cleared away as much of the jungle as possible, and although the clearing was only partial, he was sure he had missed no structure. Progress was hastened by his offering rewards for the discovery of ruins or statues to all his diggers. Excavations were made in twenty mounds, ten of which revealed the remains of temples, five of stupas, and five others of remains of dwelling houses or mounds previously dug up for bricks.

At Tandwa (referred to incorrectly as Tadwa in his earlier account), Cunningham spent five days making a complete survey of the ruins, which included a large brick stupa and the remains of what seemed to be a monastery. He also made excavations at two small mounds at Piprawa, which revealed a small temple enshrining a Shivalinga.[48]

Cunningham described the history of ancient Pataliputra, dipping into the accounts of the Chinese pilgrims. He discussed changes in the course of the Ganga in the area near Patna. He also identified the site of the Ashokan stupa with the ruins at Panch-Pahari. He excavated one of the Nirandpur mounds and found several walls consisting of large bricks laid in mud mortar, but none of the walls were continuous. At Ghosrawa, eight miles east of Nalanda, excavations revealed the remains of a temple and coins of a king named Vigraha (whom Cunningham identified as a Pala king).

In the previous season's report, Cunningham had described and discussed the temple at Deogarh. In the report for 1875–6 and 1877–8, he described the Bhitargaon temple, another important surviving specimen of Gupta temple architecture The Bhitargaon temple was important because of the arches in the shrine areas and porch. This showed that the use of the arch was known and used in Hindu architecture. Cunningham took along two masons from Kora-Jahanabad to repair one of its broken corners. This is one of the few references to repair activity in his reports. The detailed description (accompanied by plans and photographs) of this particular temple was accompanied by a more general discussion of the characteristics of the Gupta style of temple architecture.

[48] Piprawa (Piprahwa) was near Koron Dih, which was forty miles from Buila Tal and eighteen miles east of Basti. Recent excavations have indicated this to be the site of ancient Kapilavastu (although the issue is still hotly debated).

The report for 1875–6 and 1877–8 described the history and architecture of several medieval sites such as Badaun and Jaunpur. Cunningham cited Fergusson's *History of Indian Architecture* on several points, and expressed his disagreement with him on the question of the pillars of the masjids of Jaunpur. Unlike Fergusson, Cunningham thought that many of these were re-used Hindu pillars. He gave the text and translation of the Sanskrit inscriptions, evidently re-used blocks of old temples, found in the masjids of Jaunpur. Describing Sahsaram, the site of Sher Shah's tomb, Cunningham gave a disquisition on the features of Afghan tomb architecture.

Cunningham took time off from his description of sites and antiquities to give an eyewitness account of the Magh Amavasya fair held at Baksar Ghat and Gunir. He also gave two versions of an incident that had occurred here during the Revolt of 1857, when a small party of Englishmen escaping from Kanpur found their boat grounded. Cunningham gave the account of an Indian and an Englishman, both of whom had been participants in the incident.

Tour in the Punjab 1878–9

In 1878–9 Cunningham began his explorations in the north-west and wound his way eastwards into the Indo-Gangetic divide, beginning his tour at Manikyala and Shah-dheri, and ending at Thanesar. Thirty-five sites were discussed in the report of this season's work.[49] The tour yielded a large number of coins, many issued by the Indo-Greek kings. Several new identifications of places mentioned in classical and Chinese accounts were made.

Cunningham's description of Manikyala was accompanied by a map, a plan of one of the stupa-vihara complexes, and sketches of various antiquities, including the relic caskets. He also examined the country around Manikyala for many miles, identifying the remains of various Buddhist structures. On the basis of numismatic evidence Cunningham suggested that the site of Manikyala was first occupied during the period of the early Indo-Scythians.

Cunningham conducted some small excavations at Manikyala: he was not the only one so engaged. A zamindar was busy digging into a mound to the south of the stupa excavated many years earlier by Court,

[49] Cunningham (1882a).

in search of building material. Cunningham made a clearance all around the stupa and found a terracotta and a plaster figure in the monastery. Other mounds in the vicinity yielded the remains of sculptures, stupas, and monasteries. He found no relic caskets in the course of his exploration of these mounds, but he did obtain two soapstone relic caskets and the lower half of a relic casket from a coin dealer who could provide no information regarding their find-spots or contents. The report gives a sketch of these and some of the other artefacts obtained from Manikyala.

Cunningham's visit to Shah-dheri (Taxila) led to the discovery of the remains (mainly pillar fragments) of a second Greek temple in the heart of the city. Cunningham also found the remains of a very large vihara on the nearby Jhandial mound, to the north of the city. He gave an account of the Buddhist structures already lying exposed on the Meri hill to the east of the city. His discussion of the remains at Shah-dheri was accompanied by maps, plans, and sketches, including a description of ordinary, utilitarian objects he found at the site. These included the handle of an antimony rod, a door handle, the rim fragment of a dish, a goldsmith's hammer, and image fragments. Apart from these Cunningham described and illustrated a number of terracotta and clay seals, and coins. The discovery of single-die coins at Taxila, according to him, was evidence that coinage in India pre-dated the period of Greek contact. The discovery of the indigenous square copper coins of Taxila, along with those of Pantaleon and Agathocles in the same hoard at the site, in 1879, clinched the issue.

Thirty miles west of Rawalpindi and twenty-four miles south of Shah-dheri, Cunningham excavated a large mound outside Fatehganj town: 'I made numerous excavations, but although I found many walls, yet most of them ran at different angles and evidently had no connection with one another.'[50] During his long years of experience Cunningham had frequently encountered structural layers. But it is only when these layers represented a change in religious affiliation (e.g. a stupa surmounted by a temple or temple elements reconstituted into a mosque) that he remarked on them. It is difficult to believe that Cunningham did not realize that the walls he had excavated on the Fatehganj mound belonged to different structural phases. What is more

[50] Ibid.: 24.

likely is that the nondescript walls he unearthed did not interest him particularly.

One of the interesting aspects of the report for 1878–9, and something that brings out Cunningham's amazing ability to reach conclusions on the basis of very meagre evidence, occurs in his account of the town of Rokri, not far from Mianwali and Kafir Kot. Here, in 1868, floods in the Indus had exposed a section of two concrete circular walls, plaster sculptures, and concrete mouldings. The sculptures were collected and eventually reached the Lahore Museum. Subsequently, another round of floods in the Indus swept away the walls and every trace of the site. By the time Cunningham arrived at Rokri, only one triangular brick remained. Piecing together the fragments of evidence, including the solitary brick and the brief notice of the remains in the Punjab Government gazette, Cunningham concluded that the place had marked the site of a stupa, whose diameter must have been 24 ft and that of the enclosure 40 ft.[51]

Another place where Cunningham reconstructed, in similar ingenious fashion, the contours of a disappeared structure was at Sohdara, once the chief passage across the Chenab, five miles above Vazirabad. Here had once stood an octagonal brick tower known as the Pir Minar, ascribed to the Ghaznavid period. On the basis of an investigation of the site, the traces of the foundations, a measurement of some of the bricks of the *minar* that had been reused to build a house in the locality, and the account of the villagers, Cunningham was able to offer a description of the vanished monument.[52]

From the north-west, Cunningham travelled to Kurukshetra, of which he gave a detailed account. This included a compilation of an outline of the main events of the *Mahabharata* war, and the various literary references to Kurukshetra in ancient and medieval texts. Cunningham also put together a list of places of pilgrimage in the area on the basis of various sources including *sthala-mahatmyas.*

The report contained a detailed account of local traditions associated with the old town of Sirsawa on the Yamuna (ten miles north-west of Saharanpur and forty miles south-east of Ambala). This was supposed to be the birthplace of a popular folk hero named Guga

[51] Ibid.: 29–30.
[52] Ibid.: 43–4.

Chauhan. Cunningham put together the information he had gathered from a variety of sources from different places about this legendary figure. This included the text and his own translations of various popular songs sung in praise of Guga.

A significant aspect of the report for 1878–9 is Cunningham's identification of a number of medieval sites with an ancient past. One of the important identifications which straddled India's ancient and medieval past was Cunningham's identification of Topra, the place from where an Ashokan pillar had been removed in the fourteenth century by Sultan Firuz Shah Tughluq and installed in Firuzabad in Delhi.[53] An account of Firuz Shah's removal of the pillar was given by the medieval chronicler Shams Siraj Afif. Cunningham used this account to narrow his search down to two villages, both named Topra/Tobra, two miles apart, near the banks of the Rakshi river. On digging in the two mounds to the east of the Bara Topra village, he found fragments of large bricks. This proved the ancient credentials of the site. The presence of a pir's tomb at the place suggested to Cunningham that Topra lay on the marching route of medieval conquerors. In fact, the place was situated between Ambala and Sirsawa, and it was known that both Timur and Babur had marched by Sirsawa. Further, the Yamuna was nearby (Afif talks of the pillar being transported to Firuzabad on a barge down the river). All these points confirmed the identification.

The report for 1878–9 included genealogies of the rajas of Rajaori, Chamba, and Mandi. The account of the rajas of Mandi included the text and translation of the sati pillars of these rulers 'as they were explained to me by my old friend Wazir Gusaon, the astute minister of the Mandi State.'[54] In his account of the Kunets of the Simla hills, Cunningham makes one of his frequent forays into ethnography. He gives population estimates (including those compiled by himself in the course of his travels), and describes the history, language and customs of these communities.

The report closes with a separate section on the 'Autonomous Coins of Ancient India'. These were coins of oligarchies and cities found in various parts of northern and western India. They included

[53] Ibid.: 78.
[54] Ibid.: 123.

coins of Audambara, Aparanta, Kuninda, Yaudheya, Sibi, Ujjain, Eran, and Malava. The importance of these coins, Cunningham emphasized, was in far greater proportion to their numbers. All except one of the coins he discussed were part of his impressive personal collection.

Tour in Bihar and Bengal 1879–80

During 1879–80, Cunningham's operations moved eastwards into Bihar and north Bengal. The results were published in Volume 15 of the *Archaeological Survey Reports* series.[55] The report documented a total of thirty-five sites. Apart from incursions into political history and ethnography, it also brought out the relationship between settlement and change in the lower courses of the Ganga and Brahmaputra. For a good part of this tour, Cunningham was tracking down places mentioned by Xuan Zang, and so followed his route in certain segments.

Cunningham had already toured this area, and some of the sites, such as Bodh Gaya, Patna, and Kukrihar, were hurriedly revisited and mentioned in passing. In terms of excavation, not much was accomplished this season. The only place where Cunningham excavated somewhat systematically was at Sultanganj on the Ganga, not far from Bhagalpur, where he identified and excavated a brick stupa. He drew attention to the large number of stone seats or stools found at all ancient Buddhist sites and suggested that these may have functioned as primitive chairs for monks. He noted that they were currently being worshipped by local inhabitants as 'Goreyas' or spirits.

This volume contains a considerable amount of material on the medieval sites of Bengal. The buildings at Gaur and Hazrat Pandua were discussed in particular detail. The description of sites was accompanied by a discussion of various aspects of their history. In the last section of the report, Cunningham discussed the geographical units of Bengal and the political history—ancient and medieval—of the region, including genealogies of the Pala and Sena kings, expressing his disagreement with Rajendralala Mitra on certain points of political history and chronology.

[55] Cunningham (1882b).

Tours in North and South Bihar 1880–1

In the winter of 1880–1 Cunningham toured Bihar. The results were published in Volume 16 of the *Archaeological Survey Reports.*[56] The report included a discussion of the ancient course of the Gandak river. By this time, Beglar had made way for Cunningham's new assistant, H.B.W. Garrick, whose survey account is included in the report.[57]

Many of the sites described by Cunningham in the report for 1880–1 had been visited by him earlier. Bodh Gaya was visited twice this season—in November 1880 and February 1881. While clearing the area around the temple, Cunningham discovered a raised promenade outside the northern wall. Other important finds included the Vajrasana, coins and precious stones inside the temple. However, he described his activities at Bodh Gaya very briefly, as he wanted to reserve the details for a later publication dealing exclusively with this site.[58]

Cunningham's account of Besarh (Basarh, ancient Vaishali) supplemented the details he had given in Volume 1 of the *Archaeological Survey Reports.* He made some excavations across the ramparts, hoping to find some traces of the city walls, but in vain and reported the results without enthusiasm.

> I was disappointed, as the diggings disclosed only accumulations of broken bricks and rubbish, with a few uninteresting fragments of pottery. I found three clay whorls, one copper trenail, one clay pestle (*thapi*), three beads of bloodstone, jacinth, and crystal, one square copper coin cast in a mould, with an elephant, Bodhi tree and other symbols. The only object of any interest was a burnt clay inkstand, with a large Buddhist symbol, and a short inscription in Gupta characters.[59]

At the adjacent site of Bakhra, Cunningham described the Ashokan pillar and the surrounding remains. Excavations at the site yielded traces of a building and a small brick stupa.

The ancient remains at Dharawat, north of the Barabar hills, had

[56] Cunningham (1883a).

[57] The results of Garrick's explorations during his years as assistant are contained in volumes 16,19, and 23 of the *Archaeological Survey Reports.* Garrick's work has not been discussed in any detail within this book. For more on him, see Chakrabarti (1988): 92–4.

[58] The book, *Mahâbodhi*, was eventually published in 1892.

[59] Cunningham (1883a): 12.

been identified by Beglar with Xuan Zang's Gunamati monastery. Cunningham's excavations here revealed various walls and sculptures associated with a monastery. On the hill above the monastery he excavated a stupa which yielded a number of clay seals bearing Gupta characters. The discovery of a single punch-marked coin at the site was proof enough for Cunningham of its great antiquity.

During his tour in Tirhut, Cunningham had often heard of two brothers named Harwa and Barwa. His assistant Carlleyle had learnt of two mounds named after them near Nonaora, fourteen miles north-east of Motihara. The report for 1880–1 contains an account of the traditions connected with these two brothers of the Dusad caste (a caste associated with pig-rearing). At Husenpur-Kako, Cunningham visited the *dargah* of Bibi Kamalo and recorded local traditions about this woman. At another place named Andhara, a meteorite seemed to have recently fallen and become an object of worship. Cunningham's aim in visiting the place was to witness the rise of its worship.

He visited several ancient Brahmanical brick temples at Deo Markanda, Mahadeopur, and Deo Barnarak. He described Deo Markanda village as being situated on a mound 'which is thickly covered with broken bricks and pottery, the latter being chiefly glazed with a shining black.'[60] This reference suggests it was a Northern Black Polished Ware site. He described a very curious temple at Mahadeopur: it was twelve-sided up to 8 ft, above this circular, and further up square in shape. At Deo Barnarak Cunningham found an inscription on one of the temple pillars and dated it to the later half of the seventh century, suggesting that the temple itself was two or three centuries older. According to Cunningham, this was very important evidence as it proved the use of the arch in the fourth and fifth centuries.

The report contained notices of several inscriptions of the later Guptas and their contemporaries. Cunningham emphasized the importance of these inscriptions in reconstructing the political history of the 'dark period' between the death of Skandagupta and the rise of the Palas. The account of these centuries had hitherto been dependent on scattered inscriptional evidence and 'the untrustworthy chronicles of the Hindu bards'.[61]

[60] Ibid.: 59.
[61] Ibid.: 78.

Tour in the Central Provinces and Lower Gangetic Doab 1881–2

In 1881–2, Cunningham toured the Central Provinces and the lower Gangetic Doab. The results of this tour, which covered thirty-three sites, were published in Volume 17 of the *Archaeological Survey Reports*.[62] The main aim of this season's tour was to explore three major temple sites—Rajim, Arang, and Sirpur. The report included copies of ancient inscriptions found at these sites. Piecing together the information provided by a variety of sources—inscriptions, literary references, and local chronicles—Cunningham gave an account of the history of Dakshina Kosala.[63] The season's tour ended at Mathura, where Cunningham found a sculpture of Herakles strangling the Nemaean lion being used as a side of a watering trough for cattle. He rescued the piece and despatched it to the Indian Museum in Calcutta.

The longest description in the report for 1881–2 is that of Rajim, its landscape, temples, and inscriptions. Cunningham described the principal temple of Rajiva-lochana (which he assigned to the fifth century), the inscriptions, including pilgrims' records in the temples, and the various legends associated with the deity and the place recounted by local informants.

Cunningham described a number of other places in the area, their temples, sati pillars, and inscriptions. He noted the position of places *vis-à-vis* trade routes. He visited the famous temple of Boram-deo, mentioned in the *Gazetteer of the Central Provinces* as the most ancient building in the Chhattisgarh district. He pointed out that the reading of the date on an inscription in the temple was off the mark by close to a thousand years (Samvat 1608, not 160). He argued that the temple had not been built by the Gond kings, nor was it dedicated to the Gond deity Boram Deo. It was originally a temple dedicated to the god Vishnu, whose image was placed over the middle of the three entrances, and seems to have been taken over by the Gonds in the fourteenth century. The report discussed various aspects of the history of the Gond chieftains.

Cunningham offered certain important identifications of places in

[62] Cunningham (1884a).

[63] This corresponds roughly to the modern Raipur, Bilaspur, and Sambalpur districts of Madhya Pradesh and Orissa.

the Central Provinces. He identified ancient Shripura with modern Sirpur. He also put forward some tentative identifications for ancient Sharabhapura, suggesting either Arvi or Sambhalpur. He suggested several identifications of places mentioned in the accounts of Ptolemy and the Chinese pilgrims.

Among curious contemporary religious practices recorded by Cunningham in the report for 1881–2 was the worship of the tomb of an Englishwoman at a place called Murmari, twelve miles east of Bhandara and fifty miles east of Nagpur. An inscription (dated 1831 or 1851) on the tomb identified her as the wife of a Major Claye Watson. According to local informants, the husband had come to this place to build a bridge or a road, and the wife had died on her way from Raypur to Nagpur. The tomb was the object of worship by people of the neighbouring villages of Murmari.[64]

For Cunningham, archaeology frequently spilt out into ethnography, and this report was no exception. There are two long appendices to the report, the first one on the Savara tribe ('for which I had been collecting notes from several years'). The section on the Savaras is particularly interesting as it combines ethnographic observations made by Cunningham and others (such as Ball, Buchanan, and Dalton) with references to this important tribe in ancient literature and inscriptions.

The second appendix dealt with demon-worship in northern India, which Cunningham identified as one of the many non-Aryan elements that became an all-pervasive aspect of Indian culture. His account includes a selection of mantras associated with the worship of the demons (he included in this category the deified dead, spirits, ghosts, etc.), forms of propitiation and worship, and shrines associated with them. His information on all these was based on oral traditions. Cunningham gave the text and translation of a sampling of secret mantras, along with his comments on them.

Tour in Eastern Rajputana 1882–3

In 1882–3 Cunningham toured eastern Rajputana, from where he went on to Meerut, Gurgaon, and Delhi. The results of this tour form Volume 20 of his reports.[65] The main focus in this season's work was

[64] Cunningham (1884a): 1–2.

[65] Cunningham (1885a).

on medieval forts, mosques, and inscriptions. Visited and described were the forts at Tahangarh, Bayana, Kotila, and Indor. Some, such as Tahangarh, had been hitherto unnoticed. Others, such as the Vijaymandargarh fort of Bayana, were of pre-medieval antiquity. Older vestiges of temples, Sanskrit inscriptions, and sati pillars were noted where they occurred. Cunningham's description of structures and inscriptions in medieval forts is framed within a narrative of political history. The section on Bayana is fairly detailed and includes the facsimile, text and translation of several medieval inscriptions found here. Cunningham also visited the battlefield of Khanwa, the famous scene of Babur's victory over Rana Sangram Singh: 'Here I sought for, and found, the Baoli well which Babar built on the spot where he poured out all the wine in his camp, in fulfilment of a vow which he had long made, and regularly neglected, until the imminent danger of his position in front of an overwhelming force reminded him of his broken vows.'[66] Quoting profusely from Babur's memoirs and Erskine's *Life of Babar*, Cunningham's sharp eye observed that the date of the battle of Khanwa had been incorrectly recorded by both.[67]

Among the temple sites described by Cunningham was a large cluster of small stone temples of the later Gupta style at Paroli and Paravali, in the hills north of the Gwalior fort. Cunningham did not personally visit the old temple site of Dubkund but sent his draughtsman, Babu Jamna Shankar Bhatt, to supervise measurement of the shrine and to make copies of its inscriptions. Cunningham asserted that the ruins in this place were Jaina, not Buddhist (as a previous notice of the structures had suggested them to be). In his account of the Jaina ruins at Dubkund, Cunningham expanded on the theme of Brahmanical persecution of Buddhists and Jains, asserting that persecution was 'as rampant among the Hindu priesthood as amongst the most bigoted of Musalmans.'[68]

The discussion of eastern Rajputana contains an account of what Cunningham refers to as 'the principal races who have held these

[66] Ibid.: v.

[67] Ibid.: 97. Cunningham points out that Babur states that the battle took place on Saturday, the 13th of the 2nd Jamadi, A.H. 933. But the 13th was a Sunday in that year, and Saturday was the 12th. So the correct date of the battle must have been Saturday the 12th.

[68] Cunningham (1885a): 103.

countries for about three thousand years.' These included the Yaduvamshis and Nikumbhas of ancient times and the Khanzadahs and Meos of more recent times. Cunningham's history of the first two was based on various sources such as inscriptions and bardic histories. There is a longer discussion of the Mevs or Meos, their clan organization, customs, and traditions.

Mathura was a site Cunningham visited frequently to check on fresh discoveries of sculptures and inscriptions. The report for 1882–3 gave a brief outline of the political and religious history of the place. It also contained descriptions and photographs of some of the most interesting discoveries, including an inscribed colossal image of polished grey sandstone at Parkham which Cunningham thought belonged to the Mauryan period. He reasserted his identification of the Ḳatra mound as the site of the old city of Mathura and noted several sites in the vicinity of Mathura, some of which had yielded Buddhist remains.

Cunningham's explorations of 1882–3 ended at Delhi: 'I closed my tour by a visit to the ruins of Delhi in the hope that I might find something that had escaped my notice on previous visits. And I was not disappointed, as will be seen in the following pages.'[69] This fresh visit to Delhi enabled him to add a few more details to the different versions of the story linking Anangapala Tomara with the Mehrauli iron pillar. Occasionally citing Sayyid Ahmed Khan's *Asar-al-Sanadid*, he described various medieval structures, including those in the area south of Delhi such as those at Sohna, Bhondsi, and Gurgaon. In the Mehrauli area he noted the medieval tombs in and around Mahipalpur, Begampur, and the curious tower known as the Chor Minar, about three miles north of the Qutb Minar. Unnoticed structures were documented; others were carefully measured and their inscriptions recorded.

Bundelkhand and Rewa (1883–4), and Rewa, Bundelkhand, Malwa, and Gwalior (1884–5)

Cunningham's last archaeological tours were conducted in Central India. In 1883–4, he toured Bundelkhand and Rewa, and the following year he went over this area again, and also into Malwa and Gwalior.

[69] Ibid.: 139.

The results of these explorations are contained in Volume 21 of the *Archaeological Survey Reports,* the last in the series to be penned by Cunningham himself.[70] A few places en route to Central India were also discussed.

Among the most important sites discussed in this report were the great forts of Kalanjar and Ajaygarh. Other forts visited and described are Marpha, Kalpi, and Gurgi-Masaun. There is a very strong emphasis on inscriptions discovered at these and other places. The report gave the text (sometimes with translation) of some of these.

Cunningham revisited Khajuraho with the aim of searching for undiscovered temple ruins and some older remains. On the issue of the relative chronology of the temples, Cunningham suggested that the hypaethral Chaunsat Yogini temple was the oldest extant at Khajuraho. He reported that the pre-900 date of this temple was confirmed by two short inscriptions he found on the pedestals of two small statues. In order to fix the approximate dates of the Khajuraho temples, Cunningham copied all the masons' marks and pilgrims' records on the walls and pillars of the temples. The report contains a comprehensive account of the Khajuraho inscriptions, from the ninth to the twelfth century.

At Nachna-Kothara, Cunningham described (and illustrated through plan, elevation, and sketches of detail) the Parvati temple, which he ascribed on stylistic grounds to the Gupta period.[71] Other temple sites discussed in the report included Mahoba, Baijnath, Suriya, Madanpur, and Terahi. Cunningham's exploration along the course of the Kiyan or Ken river led to the discovery of a number of temples, sculptural remains, and inscriptions.

Cunningham's account of the waterfalls of the Tons river referred to a row of four sati stones on the high ground near the falls and two inscribed hero stones nearby. While describing a sati stone at Simra (a village three miles south of the Jokahi and Damoh road, fifteen miles west of Jokahi), Cunningham made a general observation about the location and orientation of sati monuments—that almost all of them

[70] Cunningham (1885b).

[71] Although known as the 'Parvati' temple, this shrine was probably originally dedicated to Shiva. Along with the Vishnu temple at Deogarh (although stylistically different from it in certain important respects), it represents the formative phase of the Hindu temple.

were placed on the western bank either of a stream or reservoir, and faced east.

The report for 1883–4 included a section on Ptolemy's map of north-west India, which gave a series of identifications, some previously suggested, others new. It also contained certain identifications connected with the epic tradition. Cunningham asserted that the Chitrakuta of the *Ramayana* was located in Bundelkhand, on the left bank of the Paisuni river, about five miles south-west of Karwi. He further suggested that the Godavari stream searched for by Lakshmana in the epic could be identified with the Gupta-Godavari which emerged from a cave in a hill a few miles south of Chitrakuta.

Cunningham's report brought the history of Central India up to date in the light of contemporaneous epigraphic discoveries. The section on the Chandela kingdom in the report for 1883–4 included a genealogical list of the Chandela Rajput kings that he had compiled from various sources. The report also contains a history of the Baghelas and Baghelkhand: citing inscriptions, local traditions, and medieval chronicles, Cunningham gave a genealogical list of the Baghela rulers.

Other Writings

During his years as director general of the Archaeological Survey of India (1871–85), given the rigorous routine of the annual field surveys, Cunningham's main publications consisted of the Archaeological Survey Reports. Apart from these he wrote a few papers, largely on numismatic subjects, especially Greek coins.[72] Four books, representing Cunningham's considered thoughts on very different issues, were also published during these years—*Ancient Geography of India* (1871), *Inscriptions of Aśoka* (1877), *The Stûpa of Bharhut* (1879), and the *Book of Indian Eras* (1883). The *Book of Indian Eras* discussed ancient Indian eras and methods of reckoning time, and contained a number of tables, most of them prepared by Cunningham for his own use many years previously, for calculating ancient Indian dates.

Cunningham's *Ancient Geography of India* put together in one place the results of several decades of investigations into India's historical geography.[73] The geography of India was divided into three

[72] See, for instance, Cunningham (1872, 1873b, 1883b, 1884b).

[73] Cunningham (1871a).

parts, 'each broadly named after the prevailing religious and political character of the period which it embraces', Brahmanical, Buddhist, and Muhammadan. The first phase corresponded to the Vedic age, the second stretched from the post-Vedic period up to the invasion of Mahmud of Ghazni, and the third from the Ghaznavid invasion till the Battle of Plassey. The subject of Cunningham's book was the second of these periods—the Buddhist or the Ancient. The main contribution of the book was the identification of a large number of place names based largely on references in Xuan Zang's travelogue and classical accounts; references in Indian texts were given secondary importance. Cunningham pointed out that the extent and completeness of Xuan Zang's fifteen-year-long travels in India, extending from Kabul and Kashmir to the mouths of the Ganga and the Indus, and from Nepal to Kanchipuram, had never been surpassed, not by Francis Buchanan-Hamilton, not by Jacquemont, and not even by himself.

In the field of historical geography, Cunningham counted as his major achievements the identifications of Aornos, Taxila, Sangala, Srughna, Ahichchhatra, Bairat, Sankisa, Shravasti, Kaushambi, Padmavati, Vaishali, and Nalanda. Other scholars such as Vivien de Saint-Martin, H.H. Wilson, and Christian Lassen had already tried their hand at this exercise, with considerable success, but Cunningham had a special advantage—the opportunity and ability to confirm or reject identifications on the basis of fieldwork.[74] He did get some things wrong, but he got many things right. Cunningham's *Ancient Geography of India* remains even now an important landmark and reference work on the historical geography of ancient India.

[74] The book included a number of useful maps, an account of the approximate chronology of Xuan Zang's travels, a discussion of Indian and Chinese measures of distance and a correction of Ptolemy's eastern longitudes. Cunningham's identifications were not accepted by all his contemporaries. One of the scholars who was particularly dismissive of his methods and conclusions (and also of Julien's translation of Xuan Zang's work) was Thomas Watters (1904–5). Among other things, Watters questioned Cunningham's identifications of major sites such as Kapilavastu, Kushinagara, Kaushambi and Vaishali. Another major critic was Vincent Smith, who argued tenaciously against several of Cunningham's identifications, many of which were conclusively confirmed by clinching evidence many years later.

Cunningham's *The Stûpa of Bharhut* gave a detailed description of the structural remains, sculptures, and inscriptions of the ancient Buddhist site he had discovered in November 1873.[75] The illustration of this important monument by means of a number of clear, well-produced photographs of the sculptures—instead of exclusively by means of sketches, as was the norm in those days—was one of the important features of the book. The plates in the book included a map of the site, plans and elevations of the stupa and other structures, drawings of the sculptures, and the text of the inscriptions.

A significant aspect of *The Stûpa of Bharhut* was the fact that it embodied the first attempt to interpret the relief sculptures of Bharhut. The sculptures were of a varied nature. Some of the narrative scenes depicted scenes from the life of the Buddha, including historical incidents connected with him. There were also a number of scenes from the *Jataka* stories, which Western scholars had become aware of through the textual sources.[76] While the sculptures of Sanchi and Bharhut had much in common, a significant difference was that many of the Bharhut sculptures had label inscriptions which helped explain their purport.

The fact that Cunningham was able to successfully interpret many of the scenes depicted in the Bharhut sculptures was in part the result of the large number of European publications on various aspects of Buddhism that had been produced in last few decades. In its references to these publications, *The Stûpa of Bharhut* also gives the most comprehensive list available in Cunningham's writings of the primary and secondary sources on which his understanding of Buddhism was based. Cunningham cited authorities such as Spence Hardy, Burnouf, Julien, Beal, Upham, Bigandet, Foucaux, Fausboll, and de Körös, whose writings had done much to enhance the Western understanding of Buddhism in the last few decades. For a list of the Jataka stories and their English translation, Cunningham relied most heavily on his friend, the Buddhist monk Subhuti. Subhuti's translations are quoted extensively in the book.

[75] Cunningham (1879b).

[76] Fausboll, ed. (1877–97); Rhys Davids (1880) and Cowell, gen. ed. (1895–1913).

Cunningham noted the similarities and discrepancies between the Jataka 'titles' in the Bharhut inscriptions and the textual references. He also noted similarities between the Jataka stories and those of the *Panchatantra* and *Katha-sarit-sagar*. Cunningham was aware that there was a Buddhist version of the Rama legend in the *Dasharatha Jataka*. He identified some of the Bharhut narrative reliefs as scenes from the story of Rama in exile, and concluded that the Rama legend was popular even in early Buddhist times. Other sculptures (especially those connected with monkeys) were, according to him, scences of pure humour. Then there were the plethora of ubiquitous *yakshas, yakshis, nagarajas, apsaras, devatas*, trees, animals, and ornamental designs and symbols. Using the inscriptional labels as a guide, Cunningham discussed the trees that the various Buddhas were associated with. He described the head-dresses, ornaments, and tattoos visible in the sculptures. He observed that the stupas in the Bharhut sculptures were often decorated with garlands, a practice still observed in Burma (the garlands in the latter case were made of muslin cloth). More rashly, he suggested that the trinity of Jagannatha, Subhadra and Balabhadra worshipped in Orissa must have been derived from the Buddhist *triratna* symbol.

The Stûpa of Bharhut gave the text and translation of sixty-six Bharhut inscriptions, occasionally citing Rajendralala Mitra and Childers on certain points of translation. On the basis of the palaeography of the inscriptions (Cunningham thought they all belonged to the Ashokan period) and the simplicity of the pillar capitals, Cunningham estimated that the Bharhut stupa must have been built between *c.* 250 and 200 BC. Later research has indicated that the construction of the Bharhut stupa extended over several stages, covering more than a century, from the third century BC to the first century BC, and that the inscriptions were inscribed over *c.* 125–75 BC. None of this diminishes the importance of Cunningham's discovery of the Bharhut stupa or of his pioneering work on it.[77]

[77] Guha-Thakurta (1998: 35) describes Cunningham's *The Stûpa of Bharhut* as 'an exemplar of colonial archaeology and its scholarly canon.' I am not convinced that nineteenth-century archaeology was uniform enough to be exemplified in any one text. I also think that Cunningham shared not in a reification (Guha-Thakurta, op. cit.: 38) but an idealization of India's Buddhist past. Guha-Thakurta's discussion of the historical tale woven by Rakhaldas Banerjee around

Cunningham had begun and ended his scholarly career with writings on numismatics, and his post-retirement work concentrated on this area. A number of papers written by him during these years appeared in the *Numismatic Chronicle*.[78] There were also two full-length books: *Coins of Ancient India: From the Earliest Times Down to the Seventh Century A.D.* (1891) and *Coins of Mediaeval India from the Seventh Century Down to the Muhammadan Conquests* (1894). One of his most important works published during this period was, however, on a different subject altogether—*Mahâbodhi* (1892) was a comprehensive account of the monuments, sculptures, and inscriptions associated with the Mahabodhi temple at Bodh Gaya.[79]

Cunningham's list of publications makes impressive reading, both in terms of number as well as diversity. His scholarly output is all the more remarkable when we recall the constraints of time under which it was produced. The initial writings belonged to the period in his life when a great deal of his time was taken up by his duties as an army officer. After his retirement from the army and his full-time employment as director general of the Archaeological Survey of India, there was the rigorous routine of the annual field surveys, year after year, every winter. In spite of his prodigious output, there were certain volumes Cunningham planned to write which he never got round to doing or completing. At several places in his *Archaeological Survey Reports*, he mentions a comprehensive work he proposed to write on the subject of Indian architecture: this never saw the light of day.

In 1872 Cunningham submitted for perusal to the government a set of thirty-six plates illustrating the 'coloured ornamentation of the

---

a Bharhut stone makes fascinating reading, but contrasting Banerjee's *Pashaner Katha* with Cunningham's account of Bharhut ('the very rigour of his archaeological project would throttle its poetic intentions') in order to prove a glaring contrast between the poetic and imaginative sensibilities of the two men is unfair. An academic work on archaeology cannot (and should not) read like a work of historical fiction, and vice versa.

[78] See Cunningham (1888a, 1888b, 1889, 1890, 1892b, 1893a, 1893b, 1894a).

[79] The late publication of this book was partly because of the fact that the photographic negatives were lost along with Cunningham's papers and antiquities, when the *Indus* sank off the coast of Sri Lanka. The collotypes for the Bodh Gaya volume had to be prepared from the photographic prints, which luckily were preserved.

Muhammadan architecture of India'. He proposed to add to the set photographs of buildings and an explanatory text, to compose a work on this subject.[80] He did actually prepare a monograph on mosaics and was also working on a volume on Indian trellis work. In 1878 he forwarded his monograph on Indian mosaics to the officiating secretary to the Government of India.[81] The manuscript, illustrated with forty-three coloured plates, was one for which he had been collecting material for many years. He explained that the subject of Indian mosaics was one that could not be dealt with in detail in the annual reports of the Archaeological Survey and the illustrations for a work on this subject were too intricate and elaborate to be done in India. Cunningham pointed out that the surviving specimens of mosaic work were few, and that this was a dying, if not dead, craft. His manuscript was forwarded by the Government of India to the secretary of state. The home government, however, rejected the proposal to finance its publication on the grounds that the drawings were not up to the mark and the project would involve an inordinate financial outlay.[82]

The Promotion of Epigraphic Research

The foundations of Indian epigraphic research had been laid in the early nineteenth century. Cunningham took particular care to locate and document epigraphic evidence in the course of his own explorations. His reports are replete with notices of inscriptions, and facsimiles, texts, and translations of these. At the same time, he was aware of the need to put epigraphic research on a more systematic footing.

In 1835 the French Orientalist Jacquet had proposed compiling a Corpus of Inscriptions which would be added to the Mackenzie collection. Jacquet died before he was able to see this project through. In

[80] Letter No. 144, dated Simla, 7 October 1872, from Cunningham to H.L. Dampier, Officiating Secretary to the Government of India, Home Proceedings/ Public, October 1872, No. 532, Part A, OIOC.

[81] Letter No. 203, dated Calcutta, 7 January 1878, from Cunningham to the Officiating Secretary to the Government of India, Home Proceedings/Public, February 1878, Nos. 76–8, Part A, OIOC.

[82] Home/Public, February 1878, Nos 76–8, Part A, Home/Public, September 1878, No. 10, Part A, OIOC.

1851 the Bombay Temple Commission advocated the compilation of a similar corpus. This idea, which had been in the air for many decades, finally found concrete expression with Cunningham. In 1875 he submitted to the Government of India the manuscript and plates of a volume that he proposed should be published under the title of *Corpus Inscriptionum Indicarum.*[83] He presented this as the first of a projected four- or five-volume series, which would include all the most important ancient Indian inscriptions, each volume being complete in itself. The series would place in the hands of enthusiasts a set of accessible and affordable volumes which would contain a complete collection of authentic copies of all the stone and copper inscriptions found thus far.

The project was approved by the government and the first volume of *Corpus Inscriptionum Indicarum*, on the inscriptions of Ashoka, edited by Cunningham, was published in 1877. The transcribing of the inscriptions in the plates was carefully done by Cunningham himself, 'in order to preclude even slightest error'. The book gave a general account of the sites, dimensions, and condition of the rocks, caves, and pillars, and a detailed account of the inscriptions, their chronology, script, and language. The text (with all the variations) of the Ashokan inscriptions was given in the Roman script, based on fresh copies and impressions taken by Cunningham and Beglar. The volume also contained the various translations of the Ashokan inscriptions made by scholars such as Prinsep, Burnouf, and Wilson. Cunningham saw his *Inscriptions of Aśoka* as the first of a series which would 'bring together in a few handy and accessible volumes all the inscriptions of India which now lie scattered about in the Journals of our different Asiatic Societies.'

Cunningham's volume on the Ashokan inscriptions came in for criticism from certain quarters. W.F. Sinclair of the Bombay Civil Service complained to the government that the text of the Girnar inscriptions had been given from the almost obsolete versions, and that no reference had been made to the excellent transcripts taken at

[83] Letter No. 112, dated Simla, 2 September 1875, from Cunningham to the Officiating Secretary to the Government of India, Home Proceedings/Public, October 1875, No. 123, Part A, OIOC.

the behest of the Government of Bombay and published in the Annual Report of the Archaeological Survey of Western India. 'The Government is wronged by the publication in its name of a work not up to the present state of knowledge on the subject.'[84] In spite of such negative comments, it cannot be denied that the publication of the first volume of *Corpus Inscriptionum Indicarum* marked an important stage in the history of epigraphic research in India, the beginning of a series considered authoritative even today.

Cunningham also recognized the need to create a special post for an epigraphist in the Archaeological Survey. The second volume (on the inscriptions of the Indo-Scythians) was on its way, and J.F. Fleet of the Bombay Civil Service had agreed to prepare the third volume of the *Corpus Inscriptionum Indicarum* on the Gupta inscriptions. Cunningham thought highly of Fleet's ability as a translator of inscriptions. He did not, however, think that Fleet could handle the enormous task of publishing the texts and translations of an ever-increasing number of inscriptions unless he was allowed to devote his attention exclusively to this work. Cunningham was keen that a special post be created for Fleet, but he was equally keen that the appointment be made by the imperial government and that Fleet be associated with the Archaeological Survey: 'I am so strongly impressed with the necessity and importance of making this appointment at once that I am quite willing to give up a portion of my own salary to assist in providing the requisite funds. Accordingly, I now beg to offer Rs 500 a month from my own pay for this purpose from such date as Mr Fleet may be appointed to the duty.'[85] The Bombay government initially refused to release Fleet from his regular duties on the grounds that it would find it difficult to replace him. Ultimately it gave in, and in January 1883 J.F. Fleet relinquished charge of his duties as assistant collector of Belgaum, taking on a three-year appointment as epigraphist to the Government of India. His duties included the editing of texts and translation of all

[84] Letter dated Royal Asiatic Society's Rooms, 22, Ablemarle Street, 30 May 1878, from W.F. Sinclair, Bombay Civil Service to the Under Secretary of State for India, Home/Public, September 1878, Part A, No. 11, OIOC.

[85] Letter No. 74, dated Simla, 18 July 1881, from Cunningham to the Secretary to the Government of India, Home Proceedings Archaeology and the Conservation of Ancient Monuments, September 1881, No. 25, Part A, OIOC.

inscriptions discovered in India, along with historical comments and indexes. Local governments and administrations were urged to assist the epigraphist by procuring and forwarding inscriptions, and passing on relevant information. Another urgent need was to ensure that no important inscription found its way out of the country without the epigraphist's knowledge. Cunningham's insistence on the importance of this appointment was ultimately vindicated. Fleet was a diligent and indefatigable scholar who went on to leave his mark in the field of Indian epigraphy.[86]

Photographic Documentation

The preparation of lists of objects of antiquarian interest and the collection of photographs was part of the ongoing project of the colonial government. Till the 1870s progress in this area was rather haphazard, and was dependent on the initiatives and interest of government officers. Cunningham recognized the importance of photographic documentation and exerted himself in this direction after taking over as director general of the Archaeological Survey. The survey reports were increasingly accompanied by photographs, many of which were taken by Beglar. Other officers were also appointed for the project of photographic documentation. One of these was Captain W.G. Murray, assistant surveyor general, who was employed for a period of six months in 1872 to take photographs of Kashmiri architecture.

Cunningham himself was involved in the task of helping the government to acquire photographs and negatives from various individuals. In September 1874 he sent to A.C. Lyall, secretary to the Government of India, a detailed list of some 1,800 photographs of Indian buildings, indicating the size of the pictures and the names of the owners of the negatives. Cunningham added that he was aware of many other photographs, but did not have the means of referring to any lists of them. 'Doubtless the Asiatic Society and the School of Art in Calcutta will be able to increase this list very considerably, as they have been placed in possession of many sets of photographs by Government which have not been supplied to me, although the necessity

[86] The third volume of *Corpus Inscriptionum Indicarum* edited by Fleet, consisting of the text and translation of the inscriptions of the Guptas and their contemporaries, was published in 1887.

of being able to refer to and consult photographic pictures of buildings is of paramount importance to the Archaeological Department, while their possession can be of comparatively little use to the Asiatic Society or to the School of Art.'[87] Clearly, apart from the Archaeological Survey, certain other institutions were also involved in the collection of photographs, and Cunningham was peeved at the fact that they had been handed many sets of photographs which were inaccessible to him.

Apart from compiling lists and details of photographs, Cunningham was also called upon, on occasion, to give his opinion about the value of various private photographic collections that the government was considering for purchase. Asked to comment on the value of Peppe's collection,[88] Cunningham indicated that the collection was rich in several respects, and listed the photographs that he thought the government should buy: 'At the same time I beg to ask for a set of the pictures for my own use as head of the Archaeological Survey, as many of them are of buildings that I have not hitherto heard of.'[89]

The importance that Cunningham attached to photographic documentation was indicated in his choice of the successor to Beglar. There were two candidates for the job of assistant in the Archaeological Survey. One was J.R. Sandfore, a tea-planter in Assam, a man who Cunningham thought was likely to be hardworking, and would turn out to be the better assistant in the long run. The other applicant was H.B.W. Garrick, a young draughtsman and photographer, with a certificate from the South Kensington School of Art. Cunningham ultimately decided on Garrick.

The Director General and the Government

As we have seen, in the years preceding the establishment of the Archaeological Survey, archaeology was an area in which the initiative of local governments and officers played a decisive role. The degree of

[87] Home Proceedings/Public, September 1874, No. 46, Part A, OIOC.

[88] Peppe was the Sub-Deputy Opium Agent of the Chota Nagpur Division.

[89] Letter No. 184, dated Umballa, 30 October 1874, from Cunningham to the Secretary to the Government of India, Home Proceedings/Public, February 1875, No. 251, Part A, OIOC.

interest and involvement of local governments in these activities varied greatly. With the setting up of the Archaeological Survey and Cunningham's appointment as director general, a more systematic and focused approach to archaeological activity in India was initiated.

In September 1875 the secretary to the Punjab government sent out a circular to a wide range of officers.[90] The circular included a provisional list of objects of antiquarian interest in each district of the Punjab and the adjoining princely states. This list was supposed to be preparatory to the compilation of a more accurate and complete one. The circular also included long extracts from Cunningham's Memorandum of Instructions and a long section giving his classification of architectural remains. The aim of these extracts was to aid officers of the Punjab government in their observation and study of architectural remains and in the preparation of the list of such remains.

Throughout his career as director general, Cunningham had a fairly smooth working relationship with the Government of India. He had been the undisputed choice for the post. His long and distinguished army record and his strong credentials as a scholar and archaeologist were recognized and respected. The government was, however, quite stringent in its demands and unstinting in its criticism when these demands were not met.

When Cunningham was appointed director general of the newly established survey, he was supposed to immediately attend to three tasks. These, as we noted earlier, were: first, a compilation of a brief summary of the nature and results of previous inquiries; second, the preparation of a general scheme of systematic archaeological inquiry for the guidance of his staff; and third, a report of every year's proceedings before the beginning of the next year's operations. The first requirement was met swiftly and published in the Introduction to Volume 1 of the *Archaeological Survey Reports.* The second, and more so the third, requirement—that of annual reports—continued to be a sore point for many years.

In December 1872 the secretary of the Royal Asiatic Society wrote to the secretary of state for India, complaining that nothing had been heard of the proceedings of General Cunningham since he had taken

[90] Circular No. 30, dated Lahore, 21 September 1875, Home Proceedings/ Public, November 1875, No. 67, Part A, OIOC.

over charge of the Archaeological Survey, and asking whether the government had any information regarding the results of his research. The secretary of state in turn sent off a despatch to the Government of India, asking for a response to these queries.[91] The Government of India responded a few weeks later, enclosing a sketch of the plan of operations for the Archaeological Survey of India that had been submitted by Cunningham and approved by the government in February 1871. It went on to state that the reports of Cunningham's pre-1871 work had just been collected and published in two volumes (these were the reports for the years 1862–5), copies of which had recently been forwarded to the India Office. Cunningham's report for 1871–2 had also been received and was in press, and copies of this would be sent to England as soon as they were ready.[92]

The matter did not end here. Several years later, in late 1876, the secretary of state for India wrote a strongly worded despatch to the viceroy about the same issues.[93] A year later, the same complaint was made, this time accompanied with a warning: 'I trust that you will forthwith take steps to obtain from General Cunningham a proper record of his proceedings. If no results are forthcoming, it becomes a question how far the continuance of the expenditure is permissible; but I should deeply regret if, owing to the continued failure to obtain these reports, I would be compelled to bring to a premature close investigations which, entrusted as they were to an officer of General Cunningham's known qualifications, ought to be productive of results of high interest.'[94] Matters had evidently reached a head, and the threat seems to have worked. Cunningham soon submitted to the

[91] Letter dated 13 December 1872, from T. Eggeling, Secretary of the Royal Asiatic Society to the Secretary of State for India in Council, Despatch No. 38, dated India Office, London, 31 December 1872, from the Secretary of State for India to the Government of India, Home/Public, May 1873, Nos. 53–4, Part A, OIOC.

[92] Letter No. 7, dated 14 February 1873, from the Government of India to the Secretary of State for India, Home/Public, May 1873, No. 57, Part A, OIOC.

[93] Despatch No. 44 (Geographical), dated India Office, London, 21 December 1876, from the Secretary of State for India to the Governor-General-in-Council, Home Proceedings/Public, February 1877, Nos. 255 and 256, Part A, OIOC.

[94] Despatch No. 42 (Geographical), dated India Office, London, 18 October 1877, from the Secretary of State for India to the Governor-General of India in Council, Home/Public, December 1877, Nos. 98 & 99, Part A, OIOC.

Government of India a detailed statement of work done each season from 1871 onwards by him and his assistants.[95] He also gave a list of the *Archaeological Survey Reports* that had been published and those that were in the process of publication. Referring to the difficulties in obtaining information regarding antiquities due to the 'combined ignorance and apathy' of the natives, he went on to give his general estimate of what had been accomplished by the Archaeological Survey and what remained to be done: 'I believe that about two-thirds of Northern India, as described above, has already been so far explored that all the *principal remains* of antiquity, which diligent search and repeated enquiries could bring to light, has been examined and reported on. I have no doubt, however, that some few have escaped our search, but I believe that whatever discoveries may hereafter be made in the districts which have been explored by the Archaeological Survey, will be mostly due to excavation.'[96]

Cunningham and His Contemporaries

Cunningham had chosen his assistants Beglar and Carlleyle on the basis of their interest in and zeal for the archaeological project. In this respect, his assessment proved accurate. Over the years, Beglar and Carlleyle (and later, Garrick) operated under Cunningham's direction and supervision, and the results of their explorations were incorporated into the *Archaeological Survey Reports.* The published version of the assistants' reports was sometimes accompanied by Cunningham's comments or disagreements on certain points of detail.

In the post-Cunningham era, Cunningham's contribution to Indian archaeology came in for a barrage of criticism from his contemporaries. Beglar and Carlleyle's work was even more strongly criticized. This criticism was, to a certain extent, valid. Neither of these two men had the wide range of scholarship or experience that Cunningham himself brought to bear on his archaeological explorations. Their reports were often replete with inaccuracies, untenable theories and

[95] Letter No. 233, dated Camp Gooneer, on the Ganges, near Mohar Railway Station, 2 February 1878, from Major-General Alexander Cunningham to the Officiating Secretary to the Government of India, Home Department, Home/Public, March 1878, No. 13 & 14, Part A, OIOC.

[96] Ibid.

long, unnecessary ramblings on matters not archaeological, often reflecting their own peculiar idiosyncratic views and prejudices. Beglar and Carllelye *were* amateurs, and their work, especially in the initial years, carries the mark of this.

Over the years that they were associated with the Archaeological Survey work, Beglar and Carlleyle learnt while on the job. Carlleyle, however, became the victim of a psychological disorder that became increasingly acute. Cunningham was no doubt aware of his assistants' shortcomings and problems, but the *Archaeological Survey Reports* and the archival material reveal his extremely supportive attitude towards his team. His disagreements with them on academic points were always couched in measured terms. A striking reflection of Cunningham's attitude towards his assistants is the request he made to the Government of India in September 1878, that the salary of his hard-working assistants be raised, and that the increase be deducted from his own salary.[97] For their part, the respect in which Cunningham's assistants held him comes out frequently in remarks they made, especially Beglar, in their reports and in their correspondence.

Cunningham's relationship with James Burgess, on the other hand, was marked by a number of tensions. At the beginning of the enterprise of establishing an Archaeological Survey of India, Cunningham had spoken to the government in glowing terms about Burgess, and had suggested that he would be the best person to succeed him as director general of the survey. Burgess became the guiding force behind the Archaeological Survey of Western India and of the Archaeological Survey of Southern India. He did eventually succeed Cunningham as the superintendent of the survey in 1885 and director general in 1886.

One of the problems between Cunningham and Burgess arose over the question of jurisdiction. Burgess regarded the Narbada river as the boundary between his and Cunningham's domain, and demanded from the government a confirmation or clarification of this issue. He was also peeved that the government had instructed district officers to forward inscriptions collected by them to Cunningham, and that it was up to Cunningham to decide which ones ultimately reached the Government of Bombay and Burgess. The reason for this arrangement

[97] Letter No. 76, dated Simla, 4 September 1878, from Cunningham to the Officiating Secretary to the Government of India, Home Proceedings/Public, March 1879, Nos. 89 & 90, Part A, OIOC.

was so that the same inscriptions should not end up getting published twice—by Cunningham in Calcutta and by Burgess in Bombay. But according to Burgess, the denial of his access to all discovered inscriptions 'is only calculated to retard, if possible, my investigation.'[98]

Cunningham apparently never let things get acrimonious or unpleasant from his end. He continued to be supportive of Burgess's applications for grants for new work and for extensions of leave. The question was not merely of the geographical boundaries of their respective operations, it was also of approach and emphasis. Cunningham's approach and interests were primarily those of a field archaeologist, while Burgess's were architectural.

When the Archaeological Survey was established in 1871, the Government of India had expressed its hope that Indians would be associated with the new department at various levels. And yet, for almost three decades after its inception, the survey remained a department in which Indians had a presence only at the lower levels, as draftsmen and clerks. During the 1880s the debate on the formal admission of 'natives' into antiquarian enterprise gained momentum. The special focus was on epigraphic research, where the facility of natives in the Indian languages was weighed against their intellectual capabilities of taking on such work.[99]

With minimal representation in the Archaeological Survey, the contribution of Indians to archaeological and antiquarian research remained dependent on individual interest, initiative, and contacts. The relationship between members of the survey and Indian scholars varied a great deal. In this respect, Cunningham's attitude was significantly different from that of many of his contemporaries. While the writings of his assistants, Beglar and Carlleyle, and those of certain other contemporary scholars such as Fergusson, clearly reveal their racist attitude towards Indians, little of this attitude is apparent in Cunningham's published work as well as his official correspondence.

Cunningham's reports contain frequent references to Indian scholars. In his early work on the Kashmir temples, he had cited the work of Ram Raz. In his report on Delhi, he referred to the writing of Sayyid

[98] Letter No. 35, dated Bombay, 8 November 1876, from James Burgess, Archaeological Surveyor and Reporter to the Government of Bombay to the Secretary to the Government of Bombay, Home/Public, March 1877, No. 64, Part A, NAI.

[99] On this debate, see Chapter 9.

Ahmed Khan, expressing disagreement with him on substantial issues. Among the Indian scholars mentioned in Cunningham's writings, it is Rajendralala Mitra who finds most frequent mention. There were clearly several disagreements between the two men on many issues, but Cunningham's expression of his disagreements was always measured and matter-of-fact. In 1872 the Government of India sent a manuscript of Mitra's *Antiquities of Orissa* to Cunningham, for an opinion on whether or not the government should subsidize its publication. Cunningham was generous in his criticism as well as praise for the work, and wholeheartedly recommended that the government support its publication.[100] Apart from Rajendralala Mitra, Cunningham relied on scholars such as Bhagwanlal Indraji and P.C. Ghosh (librarian of the Asiatic Society) for the translation of inscriptions. His habit of getting Indian scholars to help in these tasks was regarded with disapproval by some of his contemporaries.[101] Cunningham also consulted his friend Babu Deva Sastri, professor of mathematics in the Benaras College, on matters of ancient chronology. He acknowledged discoveries made at Bhita, Bhitargaon and Garhwa by another associate, Raja Siva Prasad. For the interpretation of Buddhist texts and narrative reliefs he consulted his friend Subhuti, a Buddhist priest of Sri Lanka. Cunningham was also particular about mentioning the discoveries made by his draftsman Jamna Shanker Bhatt. Such positive acknowledgement of the contributions made by 'natives' was not typical of European scholarship in nineteenth-century India, and here, as in his professional work, Cunningham appears an unusual and exemplary archaeologist, in addition to pioneering this major field of historical inquiry within the subcontinent.

[100] Letter No. 94, dated Simla, 22 August 1872, from Cunningham to H.L. Dampier, Officiating Secretary to the Government of India, Home Proceedings/ Public, October 1872, No. 6, Part A, OIOC.

[101] 'In the translation of inscriptions—like other early pioneers—he depended for guidance on native pandits, rather than on European scholars best able to help him, and but seldom consulted those whose willing aid he could readily have commanded.' From Cunningham's Obituary in *JRAS*, 1894, p. 177.

CHAPTER 5

J.D.M. Beglar: Enthusiastic Apprentice

As he prepared to take over as head of the newly created Archaeological Survey in early 1871, Cunningham faced the problem of identifying individuals who could form part of its staff. There were no ready-made archaeologists, and assistants would have to be trained before the Archaeological Survey could be brought into full operation.

The search for assistants ultimately narrowed down to two—J.D.M. Beglar and A.C.L. Carlleyle. Beglar was at the time an assistant engineer in the Public Works Department of Bengal: 'Mr Beglar is already favourably known for his zeal and success as a photographer, and his remarks on the Buddhist ruins and sculptures at Bargaon in Behar show that he has a taste for archaeology, which gives good promise for the future.'[1] As for Carlleyle, he was at the time curator of the Riddell Museum at Agra: 'He has already made himself known by his zealous activity in antiquarian research, which, properly guided and directed, promises to be of much value.'[2]

Joseph Daviditch Melik Beglar, son of David Fridomitch Melik Beglar, was an Armenian settled in Chinsurah in Hooghly zilla in Bengal.[3] He obtained his technical training in the Civil Engineering

[1] Letter dated 7 February 1871 from Cunningham to A.O. Hume, Officiating Secretary to the Government of India, Home/Public, 30 July 1870, Nos. 204–16, Part A, NAI. Cunningham says in this letter that both Beglar and Carlleyle had been strongly recommended to him, but does not specify who had made these recommendations.

[2] Ibid.

[3] R&A/Archaeology, July 1890, Nos. 5–9, Part B, NAI. It may be noted that Armenians played an important part in Asian trade in the seventeenth and eighteenth centuries. There were flourishing Armenian settlements in Bengal in the

College in Calcutta and joined the Public Works Department in 1863 as an assistant engineer. He was transferred from the imperial to the local establishment in 1867. Beglar had a particular interest in photography and historical monuments. In 1870 he photographed architectural remains in the Burhee division and submitted the results, accompanied by a description of the ruins and sculptural remains, to the Government of India. Beglar's services were lent to the Archaeological Department in 1871, and he continued to work with this department till his retirement from the Public Works Department on 31 December 1879. In 1880 Beglar was chosen by the Bengal government to supervise repairs to the temple at Bodh Gaya, a project he worked on till 1884. In 1885 the Bengal government appointed him archaeological surveyor for Bengal, a post he held till 1890. Beglar's archaeological career and work thus consisted of three parts—as Cunningham's assistant in the Archaeological Survey during the 1870s; as restorer at Bodh Gaya; and as archaeological surveyor for Bengal.

The first twenty-three volumes of Cunningham's *Archaeological Survey Reports*, as we have seen, embody the results of surveys he conducted along with his assistants. Beglar's reports are contained in Volumes 4, 7, and 8 of this series. At the beginning of each season Cunningham assigned a survey area to Beglar and Carlleyle. The director general sometimes accompanied his assistants on certain legs of their tours, but a large part of their surveys were conducted independently. As mentioned, Cunningham had drawn up a set of instructions for his assistants, a document as important for what it tells us about his ideas regarding archaeological research as for being a blueprint guiding the investigations of his assistants. Beglar and Carlleyle's reports were prefaced by Cunningham's remarks, which reveal him in his role as teacher and guide. His comments also appear scattered in footnotes, although these tended to become more and more rare in the later reports. Cunningham's ideas thus played a major role in moulding the work of his apprentices, more so with Beglar than with Carlleyle. At the same time, Beglar and Carllyle's work can be examined in its own

second half of the eighteenth century at Chinsura, Saidabad, Chandernagore, and Dacca (Sinha, 1995).

right. It is possible to identify the characteristics of their individual approach towards archaeology, their achievements and their limitations.

Beglar's Survey of Delhi 1871–2

Final arrangements to begin the Archaeological Survey were not completed till the end of February 1871, by when it was too late to go into camp. So Cunningham directed Beglar and Carlleyle to explore the cities of Delhi and Agra respectively, tasks that could be carried on through the summer without too much exposure to the sun. The results of these surveys are embodied in Volume 4 of the *Archaeological Reports.*[4] Beglar was acutely aware of his own scholarly limitations. Since he could neither read nor interpret inscriptions, he confined himself to copying them. Beglar's report on Delhi can be scrutinized for academic merit, but it can also be read as the work of an apprentice who, in the early stage of his archaeological training, got a number of things completely wrong.

Prior to Beglar's report on Delhi, there were two major studies of the monumental remains of the city—Volume 1 of the *Archaeological Survey Reports* which contained the results of Cunningham's survey, and Sayyid Ahmed Khan's *Asar-al-Sanadid.* Beglar's main focus was on the remains in the Mehrauli area—particularly Lal Kot and the Qutb complex. He made several additions to Cunningham's account of Lal Kot, describing the tank known as the Anang Tal and discovering another gateway in the southern half of the western wall of the fortifications.

Like Cunningham, Beglar drew a plan of the circuit of the walls of Lal Kot and Qila Rai Pithora.[5] But Beglar differed with Cunningham on an important point: he argued—and presented detailed evidence, quoting profusely from translations of medieval texts to support his case—that Lal Kot actually represented two different structural phases. The western part represented the original Lal Kot of Anangapala, while the eastern part represented the enlargement made by Ala-ud-din Khilji. Beglar was the first to excavate sections of the fortification

[4] Beglar (1874).

[5] Ibid.: Plate I.

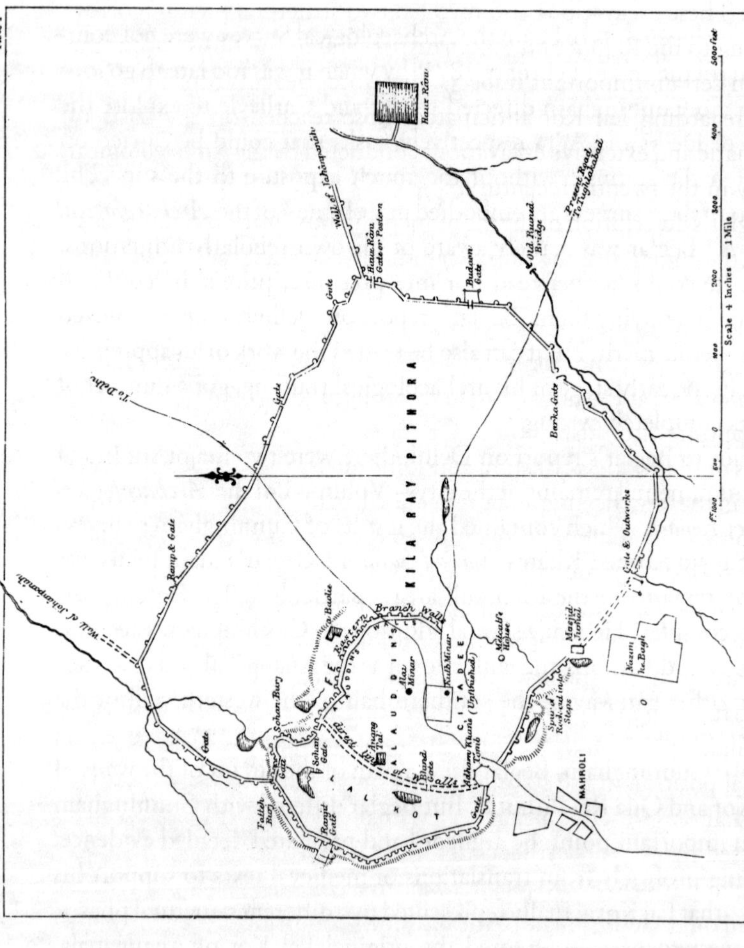

7. Beglar's map of Qila Rai Pithora and Lal Kot. Beglar (1874), Plate I.

walls of Lal Kot. He identified their different structural phases, giving drawings of the sections he had excavated. He also had the proportion of lime in mortar from different sections of the wall analysed.

Beglar's insistence on two phases in the building of Lal Kot was confirmed by excavations conducted at the site from the 1950s onwards. These excavations also revealed two structural phases (corresponding to the Rajput and Sultanate periods) in the ruins within the fort. In certain important respects, therefore, Beglar's broad conclusions regarding Lal Kot anticipated those reached on the basis of systematic and extensive excavations conducted by the Archaeological Survey in the twentieth century.[6]

Beglar's description of the monuments in the Qutb complex focused on the minar and the Jami Masjid. He sketched their plans, elevations, and sections, and drew a general plan of the Qutb complex as a whole, showing the portions ascribed to the reigns of Qutb-ud-din Aibak, Iltutmish, and Ala-ud-din Khilji. He excavated at the base of the iron pillar, at the north, east and south inner gates of the mosque, and opposite Iltutmish's tomb. He mentioned the discovery of two images of the goddess Lakshmi and some old earthen lamps that were found in the trenches dug at the inner north gate. Giving a detailed description of the minar, and the walls and colonnades of the mosque, Beglar proudly claimed to have discovered the series of geometrical progressions that governed the spacing of the bands of the minar.

The problem with Beglar's description of the monuments of the Qutb area is that he made what he later admitted was 'a grave error' on certain fundamental points. He argued long and hard in his report that the pillars in the Qutb mosque, although rearranged, were in their original position in the colonnade of a single Hindu temple. He also argued at length—this being a view that Sayyid Ahmed Khan had expressed many years earlier—that the Qutb Minar was originally a Hindu monument. With regard to the first contention, Cunningham pointed out that the pillars of the mosque's collonade belonged to not

[6] The point on which more recent excavations do not bear Beglar out was his identification of a section of the original fortifications—what he referred to as the 'direct line' of the walls extending southwards from the Sohan Gate. See Mani (1997): 45. It may be noted that this recent book reproduces Beglar's plan of Lal Kot and Qila Rai Pithora, and his plans and sections of the fort wall.

one but several temples, and that only two of the pillars were *in situ*. As for the hypothesis of the Hindu origins of the minar, Cunningham had already given a detailed critique of this hypothesis in his own report on Delhi.

Beglar had got hopelessly muddled. He revisited the Qutb together with Cunningham, who pointed out the errors in his hypothesis, and Beglar realized as much. 'At present therefore I gladly and unhesitatingly acknowledge the grave error I committed . . . I now accordingly hold that whatever in the masjid and minar I have maintained in my report to be undisturbed Hindu, is Muhammadan of the period of Kutb and Alitmish [*sic*], and that whatever I have there called Muhammadan is due to subsequent repair and alteration.'[7] Beglar's report on Delhi included a list of the principal objects of interest in Delhi, which in arrangement follows Sayyid Ahmed Khan's work, omitting those buildings which he considered of little interest. It included plans and sections of various monuments mentioned in the text and notes on the styles of architecture of the city's 'Hindu' and 'Muhammadan' buildings based on Cunningham's classification.

Towards the close of his report Beglar could not resist making a rather wild speculation which transported the Qutb masjid back from its supposedly earlier Hindu incarnation to a still older Buddhist one: 'The speculation is, I admit, very bold to consider the temple to have been originally a Buddhist structure, appropriated afterwards and added to by the Hindus, and lastly by the Muhammadans; but the coincidence is too tempting to be dismissed without some notice.'[8] The report closed, as it began, with Beglar's admission of his limitations. The report, he admited, was rather long; perhaps it would have been shorter if the material and arguments had been better arranged. The work involved enormous intricacies, and a range of knowledge and skills, of which 'I cannot pretend to lay claim to more than the veriest fractional part.'[9] And finally, a tribute to Cunningham: 'Before concluding, I wish to acknowledge the obligations I am under to General Cunningham. Although aware that my views were opposed to his, he has nevertheless, with a spirit of great liberality, not only

[7] Beglar (1874): Beglar's Note, xvi.

[8] Ibid.: 83.

[9] Ibid.: 91.

given me permission to state my views, but has assisted me with his advice and sustained me by encouragement; and in opposing his views I have not forgotten the distance between him—the foremost of the higher authorities on Indian Archaeology—and myself, a learner of the science of which he is master.'[10]

Tours in Bundelkhand and Malwa 1871–2

Beglar's work in 1871–2 was not confined to his survey of the monuments of Delhi; he also toured Bundelkhand and Malwa. The next year was devoted to a survey of the Central Provinces. The results of work in these areas are contained in Volume 7 of the *Archaeological Survey Reports.*[11] The report of the 1871–2 tour in Bundelkhand and Malwa lists forty sites; that of the 1873–4 tour in the Central Provinces lists fifty-five. Some of these places were already known, others were discovered in remote areas as he journeyed along the solitary road, 'with scarcely a cart or traveller to enliven its dreary monotony.'[12]

One of Beglar's main objectives in Bundelkhand was to photograph the Khajuraho temples, which had already been surveyed and described by Cunningham. He also photographed the richly carved temples at Pathari and Udaypur, as well as many other old temples in little-known places. Beglar's accounts of temples of different ages, many hitherto unknown and undocumented, are of value not only for the history of Indian architecture but also because they provide important archaeological data for the reconstruction of the religious history of this region. Among the important temple sites discovered and documented was Pathari, about twelve miles north of Teonda. Beglar refrained from detailed discussion of the stylistic aspects of the temples he described on the grounds that this was something he would write about later, when he had collected more material on the subject.

Beglar's report of his tour in Bundelkhand and Malwa has features of the classic Cunningham survey and corresponds broadly to the instructions he had been sent into the field with. Among other things, Cunningham had instructed his assistants to look out for village

[10] Ibid.: 90.

[11] Beglar (1878a).

[12] Ibid.: 5.

shrines consisting of assemblages of miscellaneous sculptural fragments. Beglar noted many instances where villagers had collected fragments of sculpture under one or two of the largest *vat* or pipal trees near the village. While most of the sculptural fragments were 'rude', Beglar noted that on occasion there were finely executed specimens. Glimpses into other aspects of contemporary religious life include a description of the annual fair in honour of Bateswar Nath Mahadeva at Bateswar.

One of the interesting sets of data in this and later reports is the composite picture of different sorts of historical remains located at different places. This included the changing appropriations and connotations of religious shrines. The site of a modern temple at Bateswar, seemed to have originally been a *dargah*. But the surface of the graves, with their headstones or head-pillars of brick and mortar and their niches, were being used as *chabutaras* to place Hindu images: 'There are many examples of Muhammadans appropriating to their religious use buildings dedicated to Hindu divinities, but instances of the reverse are very rare. It shows that, had the Hindus succeeded in driving out the Muhammadans from any part of India, their masjids and dargahs would probably have been used for Hindu divinities and sanctified with some Hindu legends.'[13] At Gyarispur, Beglar found evidence of the active worship of the Buddha incarnation of Vishnu.

Cunningham was particular about recording local traditions and legends and his assistants were expected to do the same. In his report on Delhi, Beglar had been rather dismissive of 'native' traditions. In his subsequent work, he was more accommodating. At Bateswar, where he found evidence of the diversion of a section of the Yamuna river from its original course, he pointed out that such a diversion was spoken of in one of the local legends of the area. His report also contains a detailed account of the story of Alha and Udal, a popular folk legend in the area between the Jamuna and Sagar.

Beglar occasionally veered into speculation on mythology and religion. He suggested the possible tribal origin of Manya Devi, a tutelary goddess of the Chandelas. He put forward the hypothesis that the phallic symbol may originally have been associated with Vishnu, and was at some later time appropriated for Shiva. He wondered if the avataras of Vishnu represented successive forms of images worshipped

[13] Ibid.: 8–9.

by the Aryans, some of them perhaps the symbols of conquered tribes.

In Bundelkand and Malwa Beglar confronted Indian erotic sculpture. He was shocked at the scenes of 'degradation and obscene immorality' carved on the walls of the Khajuraho temples. He thought it quite possible that these represented scenes from everyday life in ancient times and used this evidence as the basis for a hypothesis regarding the history of female morality (or rather immorality) in India:

> With the advent of the Muhammadans a new era opens for the history of Indian female morality. No doubt Muhammadan ideas of morality were very low, but they never indulged publicly in such scenes as the Khajuraha sculptures depict; their vices of this stamp were confined to the interiors of their houses, and were not paraded on their structures, and immortalised by the sculptor; far from corrupting previously existing female morality or decency, they improved it, however imperfectly, and lastly, the extent of the debt that female morality and decency owes to British rule and Western ideas can only be realized by a comparison of existing customs with the representations on the holy temples, not of Khajuraha alone, but of a great portion of India.[14]

Tour through the Bengal Provinces 1872–3

In 1872–3 Beglar toured the provinces of Patna, Gaya, Mongir Bhagalpur, the Santal Parganas, Manbhum, Singhbhum, Bankura, Raniganj, Bardwan, and Hughli. The results of this tour were published in Volume 8 of the *Archaeological Survey Reports.*[15] The report lists 103 sites. More than 120 photographs were taken to illustrate the ancient remains visited. Some of these were included in the report, as were plans and sections of several important structures.

Beglar followed Xuan Zang's route from Patna to Gaya and for the first time tried his hand at the identification of ancient places. He was only partially successful in this enterprise. For instance, his identification of Silao, a large village about three miles from Bargaon, as the site of the ancient Vikramashila monastery was wrong.[16] In his preface to Beglar's report, Cunningham gave a detailed rebuttal of Beglar's

[14] Ibid.: 58.

[15] Beglar (1878b).

[16] Ibid.: 75, 84. Vikramashila can be identified with Antichak in Bhagalpur district.

claims that the Eranoboas river of the Greeks was the Gandak and not the Son. Beglar had suggested that the Son Bhandar cave at Rajgir represented a cave where the Buddha had meditated and not (as Cunningham had argued) the Sattapani cave, where the first Buddhist council was held. Cunningham described Beglar's opinion on this matter as completely untenable.

While his report was still in press, Beglar revisited some portions of Magadha with Cunningham and realized that he had made a number of mistakes. For instance, he had been wrong in his hypothesis about the identification of the Eranoboas, and now saw it could indeed be identified with the Son river. The first time Beglar had visited Rajgir, he had used Fa Xian's account as his guide. This time round, Cunningham provided him with extracts from Xuan Zang's account.[17] Using this new source, Beglar re-examined the identifications he had proposed in his report and found them to be 'hopelessly wrong'. He concluded that Cunningham was right—the Son Bhandar cave did indeed represent the Sattapani cave.[18]

Beglar was on surer footing in his discussion of the ancient course of the Son river, which forms one of the most significant aspects of this report. His discussion of the issue was based on his own detailed observations (he had worked as an engineer in the Patna, Gaya, and Bihar districts for one-and-a-half years), and the opinions of other professional engineers. Tracing the ancient course of the river, Beglar argued that the Son had once joined the Ganga near Fatuha.[19] He also tried to identify various places in this area with those mentioned in the Epics and *Puranas*. Although many of his identifications remain speculative, his attempt to document the history of the changes in the course of a major river system was in itself important, as was his recognition of the relationship between river regimes and settlement history.

In spite of a very careful examination of modern Patna, Beglar failed to find any trace of the ancient city. He concluded that it must have

[17] Beglar writes that when he first visited Rajgir, the translations of Xuan Zang's account were out of print and not available.

[18] Beglar (1878b): xiv. Cunningham's identification of the Son Bhandar cave with the Sattapani cave is not generally accepted. See Chapter 4, fn. 26.

[19] Beglar (1878b): 6–9.

been swallowed by the Ganga. This hypothesis was wrong.[20] However, he gave a useful and detailed account of the history of Patna and of the remains to be found in the city.

At Rajgir, the new discoveries made by Beglar comprised two inscriptions embedded in the ring of an old well and another inscription engraved on a rock face 'in curious shell letters'. He also located an old stupa which he could not investigate because of the surrounding dense jungle. Beglar's description of the ruins of Rajgir included a description of the circuit of the outer walls and of the numerous caves in and around the place, along with the various legends associated with them.

The report contains a detailed description of temples sites such as Baijnath, Telkupi, and Bahulara, but at certain places Beglar was denied access. This happened at Kispa, about twelve miles from Barabar, and Beglar sent his servant into the temple to investigate. The latter peeped behind the sari of the image worshipped as Tara Devi, and came back with a report indicating that behind her accoutrements Tara Devi was male and Buddhist. At the stupa site of Indappe, Beglar could only make a rough survey of the area due to 'active opposition from the Raja's people'.[21] At Pandra, he had heard of an inscription embedded in one of the walls of the main temple but was not permitted to enter.

Bodh Gaya had already been dealt with by Cunningham and others. Beglar therefore confined himself to making some additional points about the nature of the vault over the sanctum of the great temple and estimating its original size.[22] He agreed with Cunningham that the present Bodh Gaya temple was not substantially different from the original one and that James Fergusson ('notwithstanding the weight of his name in all questions as to style of architecture') was wrong in assigning its external form to the fourteenth century.

According to Beglar, the task before a surveyor such as him was to

[20] Excavations made by Waddell in 1892–9, P.C. Mukharji in 1897–8, Spooner (1912 onwards), and those of most recent times have unearthed the remains of an ancient city in Patna and its subarbs.

[21] Beglar (1878b): 120

[22] Ibid.: 66–7.

describe, not to analyse or detail. The problem was that even description did imply certain assumptions about the chronology and history of architectural style, which were at the time still extremely contentious issues. In spite of his disclaimers on venturing into a general discussion of larger architectural issues, Beglar did discuss the question of the antiquity of stone architecture in India.[23] Like most European scholars of the time, he held that the beginnings of stone architecture in this region were the result of Greek influence, and that the history of artistic 'development' was for the most part a history of decline: 'The history of Indian sculpture is one of retrogression; not a single step forward have the Indians made since Asoka's time, but backwards they have only too readily moved.'[24]

There are only two references to excavation in the report for 1872–3. At Raghogarh Beglar dug at the site of what he describes as a singularly beautiful pillar and found two bases of plain granite, one perhaps *in situ.* The more significant excavation was at nearby Nongarh, a village on the western bank of the Kiyul river, six miles south-south-east of Jaynagar. Here, Cunningham had begun the excavation of a stupa and had instructed Beglar to continue the digging, which he did, continuing the shaft sunk by Cunningham. Below the floor of the lower chamber that had already been laid open, he found the remains of a shrine with a vaulted roof. The temple, perhaps Buddhist, but more probably Brahmanical, was dated by Beglar on the basis of an inscription to the first century BC or AD. The importance of this discovery was that this was one of the few examples of the use of the true arch in pre-medieval India. The bricks of the arch were laid edge to edge, and not face to face, as in modern arches.

Beglar was critical of the damage caused by the removal of inscriptions, statues and other artefacts from their original place by British officers. Captain Kittoe, for instance, had taken away an important inscription from Afsand. The inscription had got lost and since it had not been clearly copied, proved irretrievable. There was also the problem posed by unscientific excavation by various government officers. A case in point were the excavations at Nalanda, undertaken without

[23] Ibid.: 122–3.

[24] Ibid.: 123.

professional assistance by a magistrate named Broadley, who had destroyed the shrine he was supposedly excavating. Worse was the fact that the destruction was not preceded by adequate documentation.

Beglar's recognition of the importance of tracing old routes, apparent in the report on the Central Provinces, is evident in this one as well. In a section titled 'Old Lines of Road', he reconstructed old routes and demonstrated the correlation between these and ancient sites in the Magadha area, between Patna and Tamluk (ancient Tamralipti), and between Tamluk and Benaras.

The report for 1872–3 faithfully recorded local legends connected with Patna (even though Beglar thought the story of a great magician named Patan Deo was 'very silly'), Dharawat, Kauwa-dol, the Sudama cave in the Barabar hills, Mokama, Mari, Bawan Ganga, and the important pilgrimage spot of Baijnath. The 'immoral' practices of the *jogis* and the pilgrims at Nagor (and *tiraths* in general) come in for disapproving comment. This report also indicates that Beglar's disapproving comments on the immorality of Indian women were becoming somewhat habitual:

> The . . . unmeasurable distance between modern Western ideas of propriety and Indian ideas, even of the present day, is evident: the one tries to provide against the awakening of even a passing impure thought by an unguarded word or gesture, the other not only does not attempt to preserve purity of thought, but does not even guard sufficiently against purity of conduct. In short, the circumstances alluded to bear out the conclusion one would naturally draw from Hindu sculptures, that female morality during the Hindu period was of a very low standard.[25]

Beglar's report for 1872–3 contains occasional incursions into the ethnography of the tribal communities of the Bengal Provinces. But ethnography turns out to be a scarcely veiled vehicle for expressing a low opinion of tribal character. Beglar was scandalized by tribal promiscuity and claims to have discovered the prevalence among Santals of a custom (missed by Dalton) that was 'nothing less than a modification of the Babylonian mylitta.'[26] From here it was a short step to wild speculation:

[25] Ibid.: 82–3.
[26] Ibid.: 177–8.

> The aboriginal races of India are generally, I believe, admitted as Turanian, and there is good reason to believe that the Turanian races formed the substratum of the population of Babylon: the Sântals of India, and the lower classes of the people of Babylon would, therefore be branches of the same race, and the prevalence among the former, even at this day, of a custom, however modified, which we know prevailed in Babylon, may be more than an accidental coincidence: the speculation is, however, too wide for me to venture on.[27]

Tour in the Central Provinces 1873–4

Beglar's 1873–4 tour covered the eastern half of the Central Provinces and portions of Rewa, beginning at Jabalpur and ending at Bharhut.[28] The total distance marched was almost 1,100 sq. miles, exclusive of rail. The remains at Jabalpur, Tewar, Bhera Ghat, Nagpur, and Bharhut were examined by Beglar and Cunningham together. Beglar concentrated on the eastern half of the Central Provinces while Cunningham explored the western. Beglar collected many ancient and medieval inscriptions in the course of his tour. He also made a copy of the Ashokan inscription at Rupnath.

Concentrating on the places he visited on his own, Beglar described a total of fifty-five sites in his report. His fieldwork in this season was greatly aided by the information in settlement reports and the Central Provinces gazetteer, although he pointed to various errors in the latter. The clumsiness that marks Beglar's early reports is less visible in this one. We see him confidently assigning approximate dates to temples on stylistic grounds. He notes inscriptions and estimates their age on the basis of palaeography. But a detailed treatment of their content and age is left for Cunningham, 'who will do them that justice which I fear is beyond my powers'.[29]

Beglar frequently faced problems when he tried to enter and examine temples in the Central Provinces. At Ramtek, the Brahmins showed him a board on which was posted a paper signed by the commissioner, requesting visitors not to insist on entering the temples. Beglar could not get near the main temple and had to get a copy of the

[27] Ibid.: 178.
[28] Beglar (1878a).
[29] Ibid.: 118.

inscription there through his Hindu servant. Beglar was very keen to visit Bandhogarh but writes that the *tahsildar* of the Rewa raja would not allow him there, threatening to imprison him if he tried to enter. At Rajam (i.e. Rajim), he says, he was 'pounced on' by Brahmins, who tried to prevent him from examining the temples. In spite of these incidents, Beglar did succeed in visiting and describing a large number of Hindu, Buddhist, and Jaina shrines.

Apart from large temple sites such as Rajim, Arang, Sirpur, Rayapur, and Amarkantak, Beglar recorded many smaller and less spectacular remains in Central India. At Balod, for instance, he referred to an inscription on a sati stone. The characters of the inscription had been assigned by Prinsep to the second century AD. At Sorar, he found the remains of what seemed to be a quarry which may have been a source of stone for temples in and around the area.

Beglar tried to identify various places around Ramtek in terms of their associations with the *Ramayana* story. He also examined a number of local traditions. Some were of dubious value, others were more useful. For instance, Beglar interpreted a local legend at Rajim as an allegorical record of rivalry between Vaishnavism and Shaivism in the area. He documented the legends connected with Amarkantak and recounted the legend of the thirty-six forts at Chhattisgarh, using this as a launching pad for a description of the people of the area, their language, attire, and food.[30]

The most significant part of Beglar's report on the Central Provinces, however, is his recognition of the importance of ancient routes and their correspondence with modern ones. While describing the temple at Gowror, he writes:

> There can be no doubt that many places in this portion of Central India, though now thinly inhabited and consisting in great part of waste land, were once of great importance and possessed numerous inhabitants; indeed it must have been so, for one of the most important roads of ancient times passed this way; this Old Road is to this day used by pack animals, and is the basis, to a great extent, of the modern customs line and local roads; it appears to me, then, not uninteresting to trace this great line of communication.[31]

[30] Ibid.: 225–6.

[31] Ibid.: 139–40.

Beglar proceeded to delineate the old route that emerged from near Bhandak or Dewalwara to Gowror, branching into two before it eventually reached Katak. He referred to ancient remains found along such ancient routes.[32]

Tour in the South-Eastern Provinces 1874–6

Between 1874 and 1876 Beglar toured the 'the little known and unexplored places of the South-eastern Provinces lying between Chhattisgarh and Katak.'[33] He also visited various parts of Rewa, the Central Provinces, and Orissa. Sixty sites are listed in the report. Among the significant discoveries were the three major temple sites of Rewa, Turturia in the Central Provinces, and Ranipur–Jurial (Ranipur–Jharial) in Karund state in Orissa. The report also gives detailed descriptions of sites such as Khandagiri, Udayagiri, and Dhauli. Apart from drawings of ground plans and sections, this report included several photographs of temples.

The report contains detailed descriptions of Kichand, the area in and around Katak, and Udayayagiri and Khandagiri. At Udayagiri and Khandagiri, Beglar found two new caves. He did not discuss Bhubaneswar, which had already been documented by Rajendralala Mitra. At Dhauli, Beglar identified the remains of two stupas near the Ashokan rock and added that veneration of the elephant (in the form of Dhavaleswari Mata) was widespread in the area.

The hypaethral (open-air) temple of the 64 yoginis at Ranipur–Jharial was an important discovery. The report contains a detailed description of the temple and its images. Beglar was not far off the mark in assigning the temple to the eighth/ninth century. Another important temple site discovered in this season's tour was Turturia, a few miles south-west of Seorinarayan. The remarkable point about this temple was that the *pujaris* here were all women. Coupled with the numerous Buddhist remains (sculptures and the ruins of a brick stupa) scattered about the place, this led Beglar to suggest it may have been the site of an ancient Buddhist nunnery. He began excavating an old temple at this site but was forced to suspend operations and leave due to the hostility of local zamindars.

[32] Ibid.: 140–2.

[33] Beglar (1882).

Beglar highlighted the importance of the passes in the Kaimur range for north–south traffic in the area. He listed passes and roads, and noted the presence of ancient remains along them, corroborating their antiquity and the striking element of the continuity of routes over time.

> No one who has noticed the inherent conservatism of men, especially of ignorant men, will need any proofs to show that such tracks, however circuitous within certain limits, once made, are seldom abandoned even when across a level plain with freedom of choice to adopt a better line, indeed, so great is this conservatism (or shall I call it laziness?) that officers seldom care to strike out the best line if an old track is to be found in existence. In hilly and wild districts the tracks never change; accordingly, a review of the various roads will certainly help us in finding out the sites of old cities and villages of importance.[34]

The report also contains detailed descriptions of hills and caves in the survey area. Here, the *Ramayana* was Beglar's guide. He gave a detailed description of the ruins on and around Ramgarh hill and concurred with the tradition that this represented the Chitrakuta hill of the *Ramayana*. He went on to try to identify the locale of several *ashramas* of *rishis* mentioned in the epic. There is also an endorsement of its accounts of scenic beauty: 'I cannot speak too highly of the natural beauties of the hill tracts . . . The exquisite descriptions of the *Ramayana* are literally true—all except the "hermits'coats of bark" and their belongings.'[35]

Beglar faced a number of problems during his explorations in Eastern India. He did not know the languages of the area and found it difficult to procure labour for his excavations. The villagers seemed keen to guide him on to the next village in order to be rid of him. Beglar himself was an object of curiosity: the villagers crowded around his camp till after dark to observe his strange living habits and his extraordinary beasts of burden—camels, which they said they had never seen before. At Jaugada, for instance, Beglar complained of difficulties in obtaining impressions of the Ashokan inscription due to the 'passive resistance of the neighbouring villagers' who were convinced that the inscription was the key to the whereabouts of a hidden treasure. Beglar

[34] Ibid.: 11.
[35] Ibid.: 66.

dug trenches in the earthen fort walls of the Jaugada fort, down to ground level. He found nothing but earth, but did notice two distinct strata in the walls. He also excavated within the fort walls but found nothing of significance.

Here, as in Beglar's previous reports, archaeology veers into a virulent critique of the character of the people of the surveyed region. Beglar's description of the temples around Bhanpur breaks off into a diatribe against the Oriyas of the Katak and Ganjam districts, especially the tribal communities. He complains that the Oriyas are compulsive liars and that his explorations in the area were thwarted by 'the stolid bigotry of the people and the active opposition of the Brahmans'. Female morality seems to him lower here than anywhere else in India. 'Archaeological enquiries have been prosecuted by me since the establishment of the archeological [sic] survey in India, not merely without heart-burning, but with pleasure in every part of India I have been sent to, with the single exception of the province of Orissa and such adjacent places where Uriyas resided in any considerable numbers. The character of the Uriya-speaking people as a body combines the most abject servility with a vindictively vengeful disposition. . . .'[36]

Beglar energetically contradicted the stereotype of tribal character (constructed on the basis of certain ethnographic works) which highlighted the bravery, hospitality, and truthfulness of tribal people, and the chastity of their women. He attributed most of these so-called virtues, and also tribal backwardness in general, to their singular lack of imagination. There is a long section in the report in which Beglar tried to demonstrate the psychological connections between chastity and lack of imagination. As for truthfulness, how could this be an attribute of people who scarcely had an idea of God, and none of ethics? 'It is with regret that I demolish the fairy castles resting on the assumed high moral virtues of the aboriginal tribes, but justice and truth demand that I should expose the true origin of so-called virtues. The only path of progress for the aboriginal tribes is, first, a cultivation of the imaginative faculties in which they are especially deficient . . .'[37]

[36] Ibid.: 103.
[37] Ibid.: 108.

The Reorganization of the Survey and the Beglar–Burgess Conflict

Between 1880 and 1884 Beglar was assigned to supervise restoration work at the Bodh Gaya temple.[38] Two years later, when Cunningham retired, archaeological survey work was restructured. The provinces of Madras and Bombay were to continue to be under the charge of James Burgess. The rest of India was entrusted to three small, independent survey parties which were to deal with the following areas—the Punjab, Sind and Rajputana; the North-Western Provinces, Oudh, the Central India Agency, and the Central Provinces; and Bengal, Assam, and Chota Nagpur. Each of these three divisions was to be entrusted to a surveyor with a suitable establishment. Each survey party would consist of one surveyor, one assistant surveyor, one draftsman, and one writer. Burgess was to supervise the activities of the various survey parties. Apart from conducting survey work, the archaeological surveyors were supposed to play the role of professional advisers to local governments and administrations, offering advice on the preservation and repair of historical monuments. The work of repair was to be carried out by the public works departments of the various local governments and administrations under the general supervision of the surveyors. The choice of archaeological surveyors was the prerogative of local governments. The Bengal Public Works Department selected Beglar as archaeological surveyor for the Bengal division. A. Rea was to be his assistant surveyor.

The new arrangement provided the basis for a series of intensely acrimonious relationships between Burgess (who was ultimately given the designation of director general) and the surveyors; between Burgess and the local governments (who generally supported their surveyors in their conflicts with the director general); and between the surveyors and their assistants. The most acrimonious disputes were between Burgess and Beglar. Burgess complained continuously to the Bengal government and the Government of India about deficiencies in Beglar's conduct, his refusal to consult the director general, his lack of scholarship, the poor quality of his drawings, inordinate delays in

[38] For a detailed discussion of the controversial restoration work at Bodh Gaya, see Chapter 7.

the submission of his badly written reports, and the wild speculations he was wont to make in them. Work of this kind, Burgess asserted, was simply a waste of public money.

Burgess's view of the kind of persons required for fruitful archaeological work was linked to his perception of what constituted such work. He was keen to change the direction of the Archaeological Survey from field surveys to architectural studies. In Burgess' opinion, the time had come for the creation of a new kind of cadre in the Archaeological Survey, one that possessed a different range of skills. He was relentless in his attempts to oust dead wood (which surveyors like Beglar and Keith represented) and make way for the new. The problem was that local governments stood in his way. The Bengal government's response to Burgess' incessant complaints about Beglar's work and behaviour and his suggestion that survey work in Bengal be radically reorganized was curt:

> the Lieutenant-Governor regrets to find that you have taken so unfavourable a view of the work done by Mr Beglar and his assistants since the commencement of the operations of the survey under its new constitution. Mr Beglar has now been employed for many years on Archaeological work in Bengal, and has always carried out the work entrusted to him with zeal and efficiency. The Lieutenant-Governor is not therefore prepared, without further information, to endorse your opinion that any radical change is required in the organization of the Archaeological Survey party in Bengal, so far as Mr Beglar is concerned.[39]

In the midst of this situation and his ongoing feud with the director general of the survey, Beglar tried to independently put forward certain proposals to the Government of India. In Easter 1889 he took the unorthodox recourse of writing directly to the governor general, the Marquis of Lansdowne, outlining a proposal for the conservation of ancient monuments in India.

> This is one of the rare days on which the meanest subject may by the customs of my fatherland approach his sovereign with offerings of good will; and I one of the least important of the servants of your great Government

[39] Letter No. 613 dated Calcutta, 2 April 1887, from W.B. Bestic, Under-Secretary to the Government of Bengal, PWD, to the Director General of the Archaeological Survey of India, R&A Proceedings/Archaeology, May 1888, Part A, No. 2, NAI.

take advantage of it to approach your Excellency with my humble offering of good will and my respectful expressions of Loyal Service and good wishes.

I beg to be forgiven if pursuaded [sic] of the futility of my attempt to approach your Excellency on any other day through the regular official Channel owing to the Notorious want of sympathy between the present head of my Department (the Director General of the Archaeological Survey of India) and myself, I avail myself of this auspicious day of the Commemoration of mans [sic] Salvation by Divine love, when the Customs of my fatherland give me the right to approach you directly with my humble petition for the preservation of the monuments of my birthland over which it has pleased God to constitute your Excellency ruler. . . .[40]

Beglar had submitted his proposal to the previous viceroy, Dufferin, but had got no response. This time he was admonished to submit correspondence through the 'proper channels'. The 'Outline of a Scheme for the Conservation of Ancient Monuments in India'[41] suggested a Board for the Conservation of Ancient Monuments in each province, with the Public Works Department secretary as its *ex officio* director general. As for funds, the scheme involved not a paisa of expense for the imperial or provincial exchequers. Beglar proposed that the funds could come from a small but regular contribution made by district boards and municipalities. Details of the budgeting were also provided. But the Government of India was not interested.

Beglar also put forward a proposal, after his retirement, for privately taking on and financing the publication of a series of volumes on the Archaeological Survey of Bengal. The idea was to supplement the material he had collected as archaeological surveyor to produce the books. What Beglar wanted from the government was a commitment that it would buy a certain number of copies to ensure him against loss.[42] This proposal too was rejected.

Beglar's long association with the Archaeological Survey ended on a sour note. The director general had tried hard to get rid of him and

[40] Letter dated Easter eve, 1889, from Beglar, to the Marquis of Lansdowne, R&A/Archaeology, June 1889, Nos. 2/3, Part B, NAI. The details of the proposed scheme are given in R&A/Archaeology, April, 1890, Nos. 64–5, Part B, NAI.

[41] R&A/Archaeology, April 1890, Nos. 64–5, Part B, NAI.

[42] R&A/Archaeology, June 1889, Nos. 16/17, Part B, NAI.

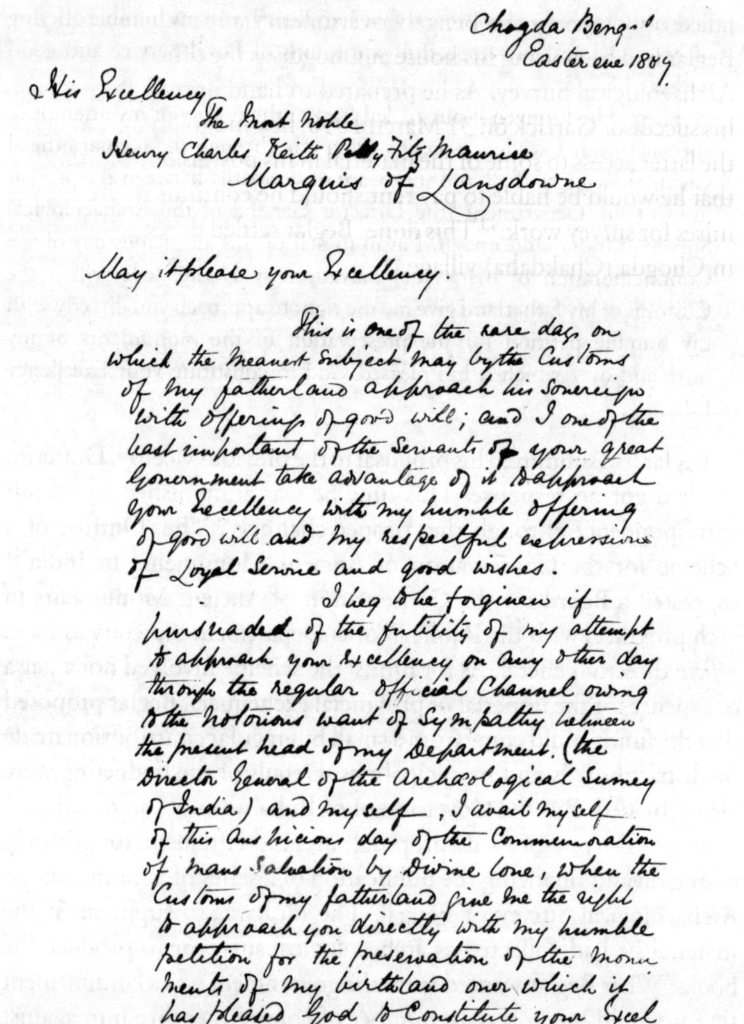

Chogda Beng.[l]
Easter eve 1889

To His Excellency
The Most Noble
Henry Charles Keith Petty Fitz Maurice
Marquis of Lansdowne

May it please your Excellency.

This is one of the rare days on which the meanest subject may by the Customs of my fatherland approach his Sovereign with offerings of good will; and I one of the least important of the Servants of your great Government take advantage of it to approach your Excellency with my humble offering of good will and my respectful expressions of Loyal Service and good wishes.

I beg to be forgiven if persuaded of the futility of my attempt to approach your Excellency on any other day through the regular Official Channel owing to the notorious want of Sympathy between the present head of my Department (the Director General of the Archaeological Survey of India) and myself, I avail myself of this auspicious day of the Commemoration of mans Salvation by Divine love, when the Customs of my fatherland give me the right to approach you directly with my humble petition for the preservation of the Monuments of my birthland over which it has pleased God to constitute your Excellency ruler.

Some time ago, (about the end of last year) I submitted to your

8. The beginning of Beglar's letter to the Marquis of Lansdowne.
Courtesy: National Archives of India

failed only because the Bengal government had solidly backed him. Beglar had been using his house at Chogda as the office of the Bengal Archaeological Survey. As he prepared to hand over all his papers to his successor Garrick on 31 March 1890, he grudgingly agreed to give the latter access to some of the material in his possession, warning him that he would be liable to pay rent should he continue to use the premises for survey work.[43] This done, Beglar settled down to retirement in Chogda (Chakdaha) village.[44]

[43] Letter dated 12 March 1890, Chogda, from Beglar to Garrick; and additional notes in file, R&A/Archaeology, January 1891, Nos. 14/34, Part B, NAI.

[44] Chakrabarti (1988: 119, n. 160) writes that he went to school in Chakdaha and remembers the ruins of Beglar's house. A black basalt Buddha image which lay in its garden was removed at some point of time to the Ashutosh Museum of Calcutta University. Chakrabarti adds that Beglar was one of the founders of the Chakdaha municipality.

CHAPTER 6

A.C.L. Carlleyle: Amateur Prehistorian

Archibald Campbell Carleyle (he spelt his name thus, with a single 'l', at first) came to India as tutor to the sons of the raja of Vizianagram. He went on to work in the Indian Museum in Calcutta, and then in the Riddell Museum in Agra as its curator. At some point of time after his arrival in India, Carleyle changed the spelling of his name to Carlleyle.[1] In 1871 he joined the Archaeological Survey as Cunningham's assistant.

In an age dominated by interest in the archaeology of the historical period, Carlleyle had his sights fixed firmly on the study of India's prehistoric remains. His zeal in exploring the mountains of Central India in search of these dated to years before his appointment with the Archaeological Survey. In 1867–8, while exploring the area near Sohagi Ghat on the north scarp of the Vindhyas, to the south of Allahabad district, he had found some small flake tools made of agate, jasper, and chert. In the same area he had discovered some faded paintings in red in a recess of a low cliff under overhanging rocks. The results of these discoveries were never published, and reference to them survives only in Carlleyle's notes.[2] During his years with the Archaeological Survey, Carlleyle explored various areas. But his obsession with prehistoric

[1] Some of these details are to be found in Cook and Martingell (1994): 1–2; and Sieveking (1960): 98–100. Sieveking suggests the possibilities that either Carleyle changed the spelling of his name in India or that 'Carlleyle' was a curious Indian misprint. The latter suggestion is not acceptable as the name is spelt 'Carlleyle' in the various publications of the Archaeological Survey of India and also in government correspondence. The British Museum collections list him as Carleyle.

[2] These notes found their way into the hands of Revd. Reginald Gatty, a collector of stone age artefacts. Gatty passed them on to Vincent Smith, who published an article based on, and citing sections from, them (Smith, 1906).

remains in the Vindhyas shines through both in his published and unpublished reports.

Report on Agra

Carlleyle's on-the-job training as archaeological assistant began with a survey of Agra. His report on Agra is contained in Volume 4 of the *Archaeological Survey Reports.*[3] Carlleyle identified the old bed of the Yamuna in the vicinity of the city and suggested that the site of the old settlement of Agra should be sought along its course. Carlleyle's detailed description of the Mughal remains of Agra was chronological. He began with the remains traditionally assigned to Akbar's time and concluded with those belonging to the time of Aurangzeb. He left the Taj Mahal for Cunningham, who would be able 'to do so much more justice than it would ever be possible for me to do.'[4] The report also contains an account of local traditions connected with the various monuments of Agra, with Carlleyle making no attempt whatsoever to conceal his contempt for such traditions.

Carlleyle was not an architectural scholar. This is reflected in the way he described monuments, sometimes using rather graphic parallels drawn from everyday life. For instance, while talking of the domes of the Moti Masjid, we are told that from a distance 'they look, for all the world, like *great white crocus bulbs* or onions turned upside down, or like great *petrified peg-tops* or *spinning tops reversed*, and resting on a thick ugly neck'.[5] Carlleyle also suggested that this type of dome must have been copied from the Buddhist stupa. There are frequent references to Italian elements in the architectural details of some of the structures.

The report described places in the environs of Agra which may have had pre-medieval affiliations. The richest returns came from two mounds—Purana Khera and Aundha Khera, near Bhateswar. At Purana Khera, for instance, Carlleyle saw a 20-30 ft soil section studded with ancient bricks and pottery, small fragments of stone and ash—evidence of habitation over centuries. Throughout this season's work Carlleyle made no attempt at excavation. Digging was confined

[3] Carlleyle (1874).
[4] Ibid.: 159.
[5] Ibid.: 150.

to prising out sculptural fragments from debris. His interpretation of the sculptural remains was sometimes confused, indicating lack of knowledge and clarity about Indian religion and iconography. He thought for instance that Buddhism and Jainism were identical, and that Jainism was a sect of Buddhism (he was not the only one to think so at the time).

The report on Agra frequently refers to works by 'natives' such as Seal Chand's *Tafrih ul Imarat* and Raja Ram's *Tamirat Agrah*, usually in order to contemptuously deride the opinions expressed therein.

> It is seldom that natives take the trouble to give anything whatever of *historical data* in their flatulently fulsome dedicated books; indeed it is a *rare* chance if they even tell one *where* a building is *situated.* But when they *do*, on extremely *rare* occasions, attempt to go into the *history* of any place, it would be just as well perhaps if they had left it alone, and never made any attempt of the kind. One may read through the *whole* of Seal Chand's and Raja Ram's books *without* being able to find out *where any* one single building they notice is situated; but as an instance to the historical *incorrectness*, and *anachronisms* of these native would-be bookmakers, I will now quote what Seal Chand says concerning the '*Havaili Aezad Bakhsh*' . . .[6]

Carlleyle's report on Agra refers to vandalism on the monuments of Agra by various agencies. The mausoleum of Ladli Begum was pulled down and replaced by an ornamental pavilion some years earlier by a Hindu *seth.* The description of Itimad-ud-daulah's tomb is accompanied by a plea to stop the robbing by local stoneworkers of stones used in the beautiful inlay work. Carlleyle also listed many instances of vandalism by employees of the government. For instance, in 1866 the Ajmer Gate was demolished in order to widen the Shahganj Road to facilitate traffic for the exhibition of the North West Provinces to be held in Agra in early 1867. Jodha Bai's mausoleum was blown up with gunpowder by the government forty years earlier, perhaps on the excuse that it had become a favourite rendezvous for thieves, and some of the material was taken off to build barracks. The front pavement and the back of the western wall of the masjid in the Moti Bagh were cut through by a Mr Mackenzie who constructed the pontoons of the

[6] Ibid.: 201.

bridge at Agra. As for the Guru-ka-Tal near Sikandra, Carlleyle says he was sorry to hear that some road officers of the Public Works Department had taken some of the stones from the walls of this tank to repair the Sikandra road. A great part of the Firoz Khan-ka-Talab had been similarly destroyed in order to build barracks.

The Rajputana Tour

In 1871–2 and 1872–3 Carlleyle made an extensive and exhaustive tour of eastern Rajasthan, remaining in camp during the main part of the winter, summer, and monsoon months. Starting from the sites in the Fatehpur Sikri range of hills to the west of Agra, he wound his way slowly in the direction of Chittor. The results of his explorations are contained in Volume 6 of the *Archaeological Survey Reports.*[7]

Carlleyle's report on Rajputana is prefaced with a comprehensive account of the Pathar, Karkota, and Aravalli ranges that straddled the area—their extent and span, the passes and rivers that traversed them, and the nature of their rock composition. As he travelled through this difficult, uncharted terrain, Carlleyle recorded details of twenty-two sites. His description of these was accompanied with disquisitions on the etymology of place names and an attempt to reconstruct their history on the basis of local legend and political history. Apart from documenting his own observations, Carlleyle frequently cited James Tod, contradicting him on various points.

One of the important achievements of Carlleyle's explorations was his identification and excavation of a large number of 'cairn' (i.e. megalithic) burials in the Agra hills and in Rajputana. The first of these was at Khera, on a hill about four miles west of Fatehpur Sikri:

> According to a custom which I pursued, whenever practicable, throughout the greater part of my tour, of ascending any likely-looking hills in the vicinity of places where I rested or halted, I ascended the bare, brown-looking, stony ridge of hills to the north-east just after sunrise. On reaching the summit of the hill, and after walking for some distance along it, I began to meet with a few heaps of stones here and there, which, from their inconsiderable dimensions and irregular depressed shape, and (if I may so term it) dilapidated condition, I did not at first take much notice

[7] Carlleyle (1878).

> of; but presently, a little further off, I found a few genuine cairns of more regular shape and larger dimensions; and it at once occurred to me that they might be ancient, and would at least be worth examining.[8]

Carlleyle excavated three of them; two seem to have had bone ash interred in them. His report gives a detailed description and drawings of the cairns.

After this there was no looking back. Carllelye found cairns at Satmas, Machari, and Deosa, all of which he described. The village of Satmas, about two miles north-east of Jagner, lay on high ground in a cleft between two hills, close to a pass that gave access across the range of hills. Here, Carlleyle encountered a fairly large megalithic burial site. He was able to distinguish between ancient and more recent cairns. On the basis of his excavations he suggested a threefold typology and a possible correlation between typology and funerary practices.[9] Machari (also known as Sanchari), some twenty-two miles south of Alwar, was a village in a plain girded by hills, just beyond the Taltora pass. Here, Carlleyle dug into 'a very curious aboriginal tomb, formed of slabs of stone and boulders', finding nothing but some bone ash, a stone ball, and a few rude flakes of stone.[10]

Deosa (or Devanasa/Daivasa) was about thirty-two miles east from Jaipur, to the south of the Jaipur–Agra road. The most striking physical feature here was an isolated, high, rocky hill, on the summit of which lay a Rajput fort. The village was situated on the rising ground to the west of the hill. On the gently sloping ground to the north of the foot of the hills Carlleyle found the remains of four stone circles. After describing the arrangement and the dimensions of these, he went on to explain the possible astronomical and numerological significance of the arrangement.[11] Dilip K. Chakrabarti has pointed out that this may perhaps be one of the earliest attempts to find an astronomical basis of the construction of megalithic cairns.[12]

[8] Ibid.: 13.

[9] The three types of cairns he identified were: the round-topped or tumulus-shaped solid cairns, the flat-topped four-sided cairns, and the cromlech cairns. Ibid.: 36.

[10] Ibid.: 88–9.

[11] Ibid.: 105.

[12] Chakrabarti (1988): 89.

The excavation of the Deosa cairns revealed human remains in some, and prehistoric stone implements in others. Carlleyle gave a clear, detailed description of these:

> I may mention a flat piece of hard black stone, shaped exactly like the fragment of a sword blade, it having a sharp edge on one side, while the opposite one was thicker and blunt. This fragment was about 3 inches in length, by, I think, rather less than 2 inches in breadth, with a thickness at the thickest edge of about a quarter of an inch. I believe it to be a fragment of a stone knife or dagger. I also found a stone ball and a bulb-shaped or conical-shaped quartz implement, very thick at one end and sharp-pointed at the other—perhaps a rude borer.[13]

In one of the large sepulchral mounds he excavated at Deosa, Carlleyle dug till he reached natural soil, identifying and detailing the discoveries in five successive strata. The third of these contained post-cremation urn burials, and in the fourth he discovered a few quartzite flakes, the remains of human bones, and the shank bone and jaw of an animal, apparently of a horse.[14] He also reported a 15 ft high standing stone (menhir) nearby.

Carlleyle noted the pervasiveness of cairns in Rajputana and in other parts of the ancient world in Greece, Persia, and the British Isles. He recorded local traditions about the origin of cairns at Jagner and Satmas and commented on the similarity of some aspects of these traditions with certain funerary customs prevalent among the Celtic people of the Scottish Highlands. He also noted the prevalence of modern megalithism among some of the Bhil tribals.

The Rajputana tour also resulted in the discovery and documentation of a number of sites of the historical period. One of the interesting sites Carlleyle visited was Rupbas, about ten miles south-west of Fatehpur Sikri.[15] Apart from being a quarry site, judging from the many sculpted and inscribed sandstone slabs, pillars, and several colossal images at the place, it was also evidently associated with stone-working in ancient times. Carlleyle's assessment of the sculptural remains tended to be rather foggy (for instance in one case he tells us that the

[13] Carlleyle (1878): 107.

[14] Ibid.: 107–8.

[15] Ibid.: 16–23.

image in question may have been one of Vishnu or of 'the Hindu divinity Buddha, or of Surya).[16]

Among the important historical sites discovered by Carlleyle was Chatsu, about thirty-five miles south-west from Deosa. Here, there were many large, ancient bricks and the remains of an old temple. At Dhand, a deserted mound on the western side of the Karkota range of hills, near the western entrance to the Ghar pass, he found two stone tools and the remains of an ancient settlement in the form of a profusion of ancient pottery and large bricks, some of which formed the object of worship in a temple at the place.

More spectacular finds were made at Nagar, a small fortified town about fifteen miles south-east of Uniyara. The huge mound adjoining the town was almost four square miles in extent. 'I may say that there is hardly a square foot which is not thickly covered with fragments of ancient bricks originally of a very large size. Such an extent of brick-covered ground I never saw before in my life.'[17] Here, as elsewhere, Carlleyle measured the bricks. Some bricks had been placed on a platform along with some carved stones and formed the object of worship among the local people. He also found the remains of many human skeletons scattered about in a manner suggestive of some sort of catastrophic event.

Carlleyle's description of the site and antiquities of Nagar is clear, detailed, and comprehensive. He made a careful survey of the site, giving the dimensions of the mound. He identified and detailed the remains of six ancient temples and five embanked reservoirs. He partially excavated a small temple and recovered some sculptural fragments. The most dramatic finds were coins that lay in profusion all over, in places as thick as shells on the sea shore. He collected a huge number—about 6,000—ancient coins, several of which bore the legend of the Malavas. Carlleyle dated the coins to between the fourth/third century BC and the late fourth/early fifth century AD. He also found numerous small articles of gold, fragments of armlets and anklets of ivory and pieces of shell ornaments. The large number of beads of precious stones in various stages of preparation suggested that this was once a bead–making centre.

[16] Ibid.: 20.

[17] Ibid.: 184–5.

Another important early site documented by Carlleyle in this season's work was Nagari, about eleven miles north of Chittor on the east bank of the Birach river. Carlleyle surveyed the site and concluded that the ancient city had consisted of two parts—a fortified citadel towards the south, and an outlier-town towards the north. At a depth of some 40 ft, he found the soil to be full of ancient bricks, pottery, and stone, evidence of long and continued habitation. In the course of his two-and-a-half days' stay at Nagari, Carlleyle collected 170 ancient coins. A large number—117—were of the punch-marked variety, one was a Malava coin, while seven bore legends that suggested the identification of Nagari with Madhyamika, the capital of the Sibi *janapada*. Carlleyle listed the symbols on the coins. According to Dilip K. Chakrabarti, Carlleyle's description of Nagari is one of the best nineteenth-century descriptions of an early historical site, and also indicates that he had a general idea of stratigraphy.[18]

The most important epigraphic discovery of this season's work was a Minor Rock Edict of Ashoka discovered at Bairat (40 km west of Alwar) on a large isolated rock at the foot of an incline known as Pandus' Hill. Cunningham had previously visited and described the remains at Bairat, but he had missed the rock edict. Now Carlleyle took impressions of the inscription and his report contains the text and translation as given by Bühler. Immediately in front of the edict-bearing rock, Carlleyle made an interesting discovery, the significance of which he was not sure how to interpret. While trying to remove two large boulders half-buried in the ground (they were obstructing his attempt to take impressions of the inscription), at a depth of about three feet below ground level, he found a row of four urns containing human bones.

Carlleyle's interest in geology is manifest in various places in the report on Rajputana. In the hills near Vijaymandar Garh he knocked some interesting mineral specimens out of the rock with a geological hammer which he carried. At Nagar he recounted the legend preserved in the *Prem Sagar* about the city having been destroyed by demon princes raining ashes down on it and went on to cite evidence of volcanic action in the area. At Baghera, about forty-seven miles south-east of Ajmer, local tradition suggested this was the place where the *varaha*

[18] Chakrabarti (1988): 88.

(boar) avatara of Vishnu manifested himself. Carlleyle suggested that the myth of Vishnu in the form of a boar raising the earth out of the waters could be reminiscent of the gradual desiccation of an area once engulfed by the sea, a process which may have begun in the area around Baghera. The connections he makes are farfetched, and the evidence he cites to prove that much of Rajputana was once ocean are not borne out by subsequent geological research. What is interesting, however, is his attempt to establish the connection between the geological features of Rajputana (as he perceived them) and its early settlement history. He puts forward the hypothesis that the remains of the earliest human settlements in the area were to be found on gravelly and alluvial soil, and that settlement on the salt plains and sandy desert parts was much more recent.[19]

While discussing the local history of places he visited in Rajputana, Carlleyle often referred to two traditional sources—the *Ukha Charitra* and the *Prem Sagar.* He made clumsy attempts to construct genealogical lists on the basis of these, mixing up mythical rishis and kings with historical ones. He recorded and translated popular sayings current at various places. At Nagar he connected a local legend about the destruction of the ancient city by jealous demon princes with the evidence at the site of tectonic activity and burning. This coincidence prompted the remark that a grain of truth always lay beneath local traditions, howsoever absurd they might initially appear.[20]

While closing his discussion of Sikandra, Carlleyle stated that as a naturalist, he felt duty bound to report on the behaviour of monkeys that lived in the rocky heights above the fort of Vijaymandar Garh and Baiana (Bayana). He recounts these, adding the droll thought that such detail might interest advanced theorists such as Darwin and Huxley.[21]

Tours in the Central Doab and Gorakhpur 1874–6

Carlleyle's survey of Rajputana was followed by several years' work in the Central Doab and Gorakhpur area. Like the previous ones, the

[19] Carlleyle (1878): 136–48.
[20] Ibid.: 169.
[21] Ibid.: 75–6.

reports of the tours of 1874–5 and 1875–6 attempt a general documentation of sites.[22] But there was now a special accent on the historical geography of early Buddhism and an attempt to identify and describe places mentioned in the accounts of the Chinese pilgrims, and on excavating important sites.

At Gohana Khera (to the east of Sasni, on the road between Hatras and Koel), Carlleyle found the remains of what he thought were a Buddhist stupa and a few sculptural fragments. Little else remained, because of the activities of railway contractors: 'Such vandalism ought surely to be checked in some way; or at least some kind of bound should be set to the vagaries of railway contractors, and certain defined limits beyond which their unprincipled acts should not be allowed to transgress or trespass.'[23] At Bhuila Dih Carlleyle vented his ire against the natives, accusing them of maliciously destroying of ancient monuments: 'This, however, is the invariable policy of the brutish, ignorant, and evil-disposed natives of this part of the country, who have, moreover, already destroyed some ancient monuments since I have been here, simply because they knew I wanted to preserve them!'[24] The two major sites Carlleyle excavated were Indor Khera and Bhuila. He estimated the dimensions of the mound of Indor Khera (ancient Indrapura) as about 80 ft in diameter, 240 ft in circumference, and about 20 ft in height. He located traces of the ancient fortifications of the city, identified the position of the ancient gateways, and the foundations and walls of ancient buildings. He was mystified by a building consisting of a maze of walls running in all sorts of directions (the walls may have represented different structural phases). The site also yielded a large number of antiquities of various kinds, including coins, copper artefacts, semi-precious stones, pottery, numerous terracotta and stone figures,[25] ornamental bricks, a large earthenware vessel with Buddhist symbols stamped on it, and a clay die. Carllelye gives a detailed description of pottery shapes. Much of the winter of 1874–5 was absorbed in the opening of three large mounds which lay to the

[22] Carlleyle (1879).

[23] Ibid.: 5.

[24] Ibid.: 180.

[25] According to Chakrabarti (1988: 90), this seems to be one of the earliest reports of early historical terracottas in Indian archaeological literature.

west and north of Indor Khera. Judging from the description and the drawings of structures, these seem to have been fairly intensive excavations.

After completing work at Indor Khera, Carlleyle spent many months excavating at Bhuila Dih in Basti district. He proposed that this site should be identified with ancient Kapilavastu, the birthplace of the Buddha. He disputed Cunningham's identification of the place with Nagar Khas; Cunningham's preface to the report indicates that he visited the site and concurred with Carlleyle's correlation. The identification of ancient Kapilavastu was connected with the identifications of a number of other places mentioned in the Chinese accounts. Carlleyle's guides to this area were translated excerpts of the accounts of Fa Xian and Xuan Zang, to which he had been introduced by Cunningham.

The documentation of sites in the report on Rajputana is often interspersed with long, rambling forays into ethnography, to which Carlleyle even threatened to devote a separate treatise. The account of Nagar Khas contains a long aside on the Aryans and the Hindus, which, apart from other things, displays the highly prejudiced presuppositions that informed Carlleyle's understanding of India's past and present. After talking about waves of Aryan colonists who invaded India at various times, he went on to compare the levels of purity of Aryan blood among different groups in India. The Parsis, because they were obliged to marry among themselves, were genuine, pure, and typical Aryans, while the Hindus, with their crude caste system ('a sure index of hybridism, mongrelism or miscegenation') were degenerate Aryans. Further,

> we British Europeans are *Aryans*, and far more pure and genuine *Aryans* than the Hindus! . . . It is the *Hindus* who have altered and deteriorated, and not we! The *Hindu* has become the *coffee dregs*, while we have remained the cream of the *Aryan race*. The Hindus are like the monkey, who pretended to treat some men with contempt because they had bare white skins without any fur! The Hindu has become a sooty, dingy-coloured earthen pot, by rubbing against black aborigines rather too freely; and he consequently pretends to despise the white porcelain bowl![26]

[26] Carlleyle (1879): 104–5.

Further Explorations in the Gorakhpur, Saran, and Ghazipur districts 1875–7

Carlleyle continued his survey of Gorakhpur district during the rest of the 1875–6 season and in 1876–7. The report of this work was published as Volume 18 of the *Archaeological Survey Reports.*[27] This was followed by further explorations in the Gorakhpur, Saran, and Ghazipur districts, the account of which is contained in Volume 22 of the series.[28] Carlleyle suggested a fresh identification of ancient Ramagrama with Rampur Deoriya (he had previously identified it with Karaon Dih), and also offered identifications of several places mentioned by Xuan Zang. In place of Cunningham's identification of ancient Pava with Paraona or Padraona, he suggested Chetiyaon Dih, a site about ten miles south-east of the ruins of Kushinagara.[29]

The most important work of survey and excavation was conducted at Kasia.[30] Cunningham had already confirmed H.H. Wilson's suggestion that this site represented ancient Kushinagara, the place of the Buddha's death. Carlleyle's explorations corroborated this identification and led to the discovery of the Nirvana temple on the Matha-Kunwar-ka-Kot. In the ruined inner shrine chamber, Carlleyle unearthed the colossal Buddha statue (the 'Nirvana Buddha') mentioned by Xuan Zang. The sandstone image, representing the dying Buddha, was lying in a broken, fragmentary state on a broken *simhasana.* Carlleyle subsequently found many missing pieces of the statue buried in soil under the throne.

Carlleyle's work at Kasia involved discovery and documentation as well as repair and restoration. He describes how he set about repairing the statue, the simhasana, and the temple.[31] The tops and outer sides of the walls were broken and unstable, and so he had many of their parts taken down and rebuilt. The walls were raised to a height of 12 ft. Carlleyle assessed that the roof of the inner chamber had been in the form of a pointed arched vault. This he proceeded to have constructed, along with several arched windows. He adds that had he

[27] Carlleyle (1883).

[28] Carlleyle (1885).

[29] Cunningham was correct and Carlleyle wrong.

[30] Carlleyle (1883): 57–101.

[31] Ibid.: 61–3.

not restored the temple and the statue at his own expense, and placed men to take care of the temple, the villagers would no doubt have totally demolished the structure.

Carlleyle made other excavations in various parts of the mound at Kasia. The stupa lying immediately to the east of the temple was cleared of its thorny jungle cover and laid bare to its foundations. The depth of the excavation was about 30 ft. The stupa turned out to be a ragged pile of brick tottering dangerously towards one side.[32] Carlleyle identified three structural phases in its construction. He excavated a row of small stupas near the east side of the base of the lower plinth of the big stupa and found several small sculptures, including one apparently of the monk Sariputta. In a deep excavation in front of the Nirvana temple, he found a small copper plate inscribed in characters of about the fifth century. At the rear of the temple he found over twenty terracotta seals with the same legend in characters of a later period. Elsewhere, he uncovered sections of various structures including walls, a pavement, and a drain.

On the basis of his survey and excavation of the site, Carlleyle suggested that the ancient city of Kushinagara had consisted of two parts—the city proper ('the secular city') and an outer monastic or religious city. He also gave an account of the old river channels at Kushinagara. Giving arguments why relics were unlikely to be found in the Nirvana stupa,[33] Carlleyle added that he hoped the arguments would deter relic hunters trying to tear it open. 'There was once a mania for digging into the bowels of every stupa that was known, and leaving them thus, in a hopelessly ruined and dilapidated condition for the rain-water to collect inside and burst the building asunder! But I hope that this mania has exhausted itself and subsided; and I fervently trust that the aims and energies of the Archaeological Survey will not any longer be directed to the injury, disfigurement or destruction of ancient historical buildings, but to their preservation, and, where practicable, to their repair!'[34]

[32] Carlleyle refers to Cunningham having on a previous occasion run a horizontal gallery though the stupa.

[33] He pointed out all the Buddha's relics were supposed to have been removed from the original stupas and relocated by Ajatashatru. Nor was this an Ashokan stupa.

[34] Carlleyle (1883): 76.

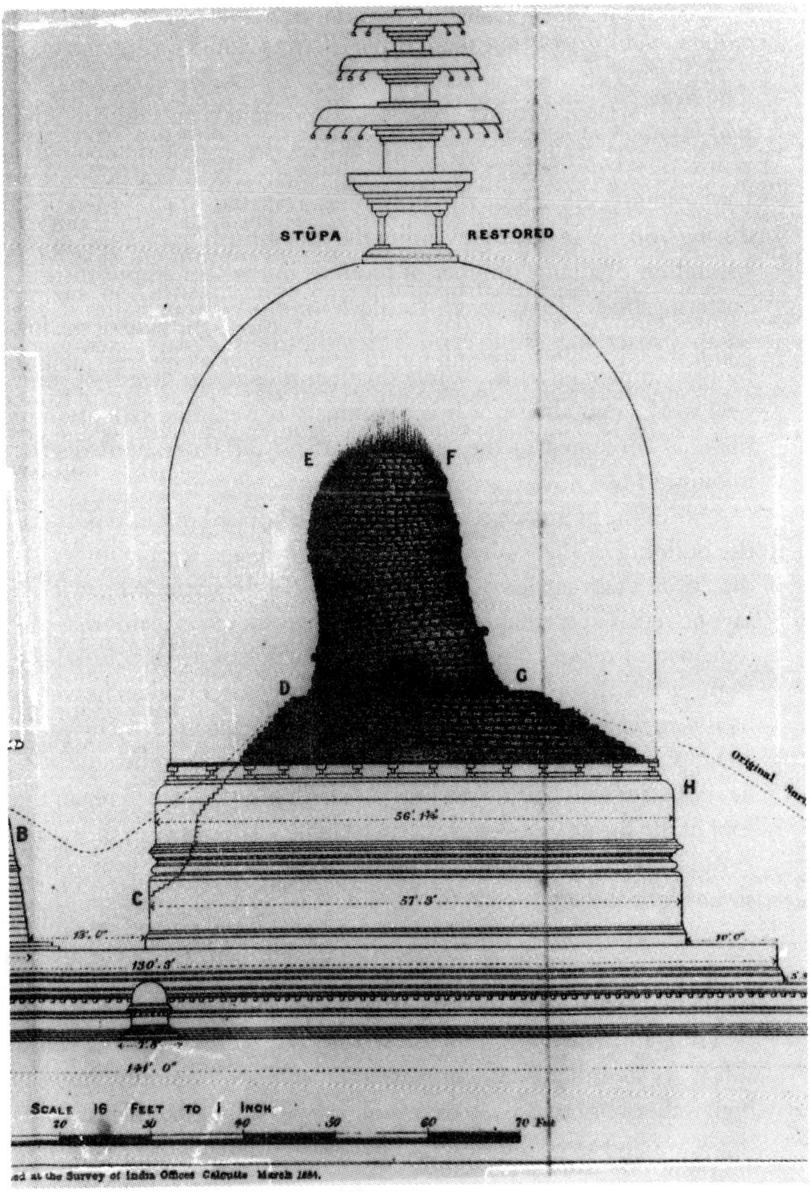

9. Carlleyle's reconstruction of the original contours of the dilapidated stupa at Kasia.
Courtesy: Archaeological Survey of India

More Tours in Gorakhpur, Saran and Ghazipur Districts, 1877–80

The *Report of Tours in Gorakhpur, Saran, and Gazipur in 1877-78-79 and 80* was Carlleyle's last published report.[35] Dilip K. Chakrabarti points out that the maps of site distribution in this area produced by Carlleyle are still about the only ones available.[36] The operations during 1887–9 included revisiting the site of Kushinagara and documentation of a large number of mounds in the Gorakhpur district. Suffering from 'Tarai fever', Carlleyle trudged through sites in the Saran district, suggesting various identifications of places mentioned by the Chinese pilgrims. While this report contains details of some new work, a good part of it is a summary or verbatim repetition of material contained in the earlier report on the Gorakhpur district (Volume 18).

One of the points on which Carlleyle elaborated in this report was the building of the vaulted roof over the Nirvana temple under his direction, a task carried out *after* the repair of the statue lying in it (he says he repaired the statue with his own hands). He explains that this sequence of repairs was necessary because, when he discovered the statue, it was in such a broken state that he was not confident he would be able to repair it. And if the statue could not be repaired, there would be no point in trying to repair the structure that gave it shelter. Once he succeeded in repairing the image, Carlleyle proceeded to repair the roof of the shrine. 'How this was to be done was a puzzle to the native masons; and one head mason and his men actually ran away out of sheer fright at the difficulty of the undertaking! But I at once saw how it was to be done and I would have undertaken to build an arched wall over a shop full of glass and crockery without removing or injuring a single fragile article. It only required a little gumption!'[37]

The statue was completely covered with successive layers of cloth, soft mats, and then a cage of mats and bamboo. Then, two six-feet-high walls of brick and clay were built at two ends of the chamber and this was covered with a casing of bamboo and mats. Over this were

[35] Carlleyle (1885).
[36] Chakrabarti (1988): 91.
[37] Carlleyle (1885): 21.

placed a close series of strong bamboo ribs on end, the top parts of which were joined to meet in the form of an arch. These were then bound together and tied to a strong ridge pole that extended from wall to wall. The framework thus constructed was covered with cowdung mixed with clay, and this formed the mould for the masons to build the arch. Once the roof was complete, the frame and the various layers were removed and the statue was uncovered, unscathed. Carlleyle made some other arrangements as well: he fixed a strong iron railing around the statue, iron bars in the windows, and an iron-bar swivel door in the temple doorway. Much of this he did using his own resources.

The new work Carlleyle reported on included his excavations during the season of 1877–8 on the mounds near Lauriya. The area had already been surveyed by Cunningham, and Carlleyle's instructions were to excavate. A 45 ft deep excavation, which yielded little of interest, caved in twice before being abandoned, luckily without casualties. At Lauriya Nandangarh Carlleyle excavated at the base of the Ashokan pillar. At a depth of a little over 10 ft, he found the foundation stone of the pillar. Just below a circular projection that encircled the pillar, at about 2 ft below ground level, there was the carving of a peacock. Carlleyle noted that the pillar was smooth down to the circular projection and rough thereafter. After filling in the excavation carefully, he replaced the dilapidated bamboo railing around the pillar with a new one. In the mounds to the west of the site Carlleyle identified (this had already been suggested by Cunningham) the *cetiyas* (stupas) of the Vrjjis. He also suggested a tentative identification of Alakappa (the Bulis of Alakappa received a share of the Buddha's relics) with one of the two sites named Lakheraj, 5 to 5½ miles away from Lauriya Nandangarh.

The most sensational discovery of this season was that of a new Ashokan pillar which Carlleyle found lying in a slanting position, partly buried in the ground, at Rampurwaparsa (i.e. Rampurva).[38] Carlleyle laid a long trench north–south on each side of the pillar and exposed the length of about 40 ft of the shaft. He took impressions of the inscription and reported the remains of ruins in the vicinity, including what may have been a stupa.

[38] Ibid.: 51–3.

The report for 1879–80 includes a description of the sites of Charaoti/Chandravati, Kahira Dih, Bairat, and Joharganj. The most important work was done at a mound called Masaon Dih near Joharganj. This site was located on the north bank of the Ganga, just over twenty-four miles south-west from Ghazipur. The mound of Masaon Dih measured about 1,500 ft by 1,000 ft and rose to a maximum height of almost 50 ft above the surrounding fields. Traces of the old bed of a river—perhaps the Ganga—could be seen about three-fourths of a mile north of Joharganj. Masaon Dih was clearly an important ancient site. Carlleyle identified it with an ancient city called Dhanawar or Dinawar. He excavated the mound to a depth of about 33 ft. 'I excavated this mound of ruins, near Joharganj, in the centre, vertically downwards, to a considerable depth, even down to about even with the level of the river; and found in it a regular historical epitome, ranging from recent times back to the stone age!'[39]

Carlleyle's account of his excavations at Masaon Dih clearly indicates his awareness of the principle of stratigraphy. At the uppermost levels of the mound he found the remains of an old house. Below this were the ruins of an old temple in which he found some sculpted stones, two of which bore short inscriptions. Other antiquities included sculptural fragments, old coins, certain metal artefacts (including two iron arrowheads), earthen vessels, clay objects, and several agate beads. At a level below that of the temple Carlleyle found a worn copper punch-marked coin. Still further down, in a layer of firm clay interspersed with layers of sand and *kankar*, he found prehistoric remains, including a polished celt. These he described carefully. Another broken stone artefact was found at the same level, as were two pieces of *geru* (red haematite used for making paint or colour). Still further down, Carlleyle found several cores and flakes of jasper and agate. He noted that not a single article of metal or pottery was found in association with the stone tools at the lowest level. Dilip K. Chakrabarti points out that the credit of discovering a neolithic-mesolithic level in the Gangetic valley belongs to Carlleyle, but the significance of his work was regrettably forgotten in the subsequent period.[40] Apart from this, what is

[39] Ibid.: 97.

[40] Chakrabarti (1988): 92.

significant is the clear description of a long stratigraphic sequence—one of few such accounts to be found in the Indian archaeological literature of the time.

The last few pages of Carlleyle's report mention the prehistoric finds he had made at various sites during his career as archaeological assistant—at Bairat, Joharganj, Indor Khera (where he found a stone hatchet or celt along with fossilized bones in an excavation), and Bhuila (where he found some stone hammers along with fossilized fragments of deer's antlers in a deep excavation). Carlleyle also referred to worked flakes he found nearly nine years earlier in various parts of Rajputana, as also stone implements he found in the neighbourhood of Banda, throughout the whole of Bundelkhand and Patar Kachar, in the Sohawal State, in the Nagod state and to the south of Mahiyar, in the hills of the Rewa plateau, and in the southern parts of Mirzapur district.

> The question now, therefore, is not—'where are stone implements to be found?' but rather—'where are they not to be found?' For, as far as my own experience goes, they appear to be findable almost everywhere in India, at least!
>
> Might it not perhaps turn out to be the same in other parts of Asia, as well as in Europe and America; or possibly in all parts of the world? Indeed, if people only had eyes to see such things! Stone implements have hitherto been looked upon as rare wonders, but they cannot, and should not, be so any longer.[41]

It is somehow fitting that Carlleyle's last published report should end on this note. He was the only member of the Archaeological Survey with an active interest in documenting the details of prehistoric remains. In the course of his explorations he had identified certain sites with a cultural sequence ranging from the prehistoric to early historic and still later. And he underlined the pervasiveness of prehistoric finds in India.

Discoveries, and a Time of Trouble

Carlleyle continued to work for the Archaeological Survey till 1885, when his position was wound up as part of the reorganization of the

[41] Carlleyle (1885): 117–18.

Archaeological Survey preparatory to Cunningham's retirement. During these years he continued his survey work, the results of which were never published but which are contained in his notes and in the reports he submitted to Cunningham (and which the latter passed on to the Government of India). A paper by him on the coins of the Mitra kings of Ahichchhatra was published in 1880.[42]

The most spectacular discoveries were made in 1880 and 1881, when Carlleyle discovered rich microlithic sites in the caves and rock shelters in Baghelkhand, to the south of Mirzapur district and in the northern part of Rewa state. Many of the sites were very inaccessible and could be reached only by arduous walks and climbs. Carlleyle spent much time living in caves and rock shelters. He obtained a total of about 4,000 implements of various kinds from his explorations in this area. As many as 1,200 crescent-shaped microliths came from two caves and two rock shelters. He noted the similarities between these and other stone tools he had found previously in the Kaimur range further south, and in Bundelkhand.

Some of the microliths were discovered as surface finds in the caves and rock shelters, but the majority were dug out in the course of excavations made in cave floors and in front of their entrances. Carlleyle also found pieces of geru in association with the tools. This was obviously the material with which the numerous rock paintings in the area were made. Carlleyle recognized the fact that although the paintings belonged to different periods, some were obviously contemporaneous with the stone tools. He describes them as illustrating 'in a very stiff and archaic manner scenes in the life of the ancient stone chippers; others represent animals or hunts of animals by men with bows and arrows, spears, and hatchets.'[43] He also found fragments of 'very rude pottery' (presumably hand-made pottery) in some of the caves, but observed that no ground or polished implements occurred.

Excavations in some of the burial mounds in the area revealed skeletal remains and grave goods in the form of fragments of handmade

[42] Carlleyle (1880). Carlleyle pointed out that he himself had found about 100 coins of the Mitra kings in deep excavations he had made at Bhuila in Basti district. He also suggested a rough chronology of the kings on the basis of the number and degree to which they were worn. His theory was that a larger number of coins indicated more recent kings.

[43] Cited in Smith (1906): 187.

pottery and small stone tools similar to those found in the caves. The evidence he discovered enabled Carlleyle to establish important correlations between habitation sites in the caves and burials, and between 'pygmy flints' and rock paintings.

Carlleyle's report for the season 1881–2 gives a summary account of the prehistoric and other remains he found in Banda district and Rewa, into which he ventured again.[44] In the hill fort of Marpha he reported a curiosity of palaeontological interest—strange animal footprints preserved in the exposed sections of the stratified limestone on the hill. But much of the report is taken up with his description of how he was separated from his camelmen and baggage, and the problems he had on account of their intransigence.[45] Carlleyle intended to publish a comprehensive account of his important prehistoric discoveries in Central India. The title and contents of a paper on the subject were announced in the *Proceedings of the Asiatic Society of Bengal* for February 1883, but the paper was never published.[46]

At the time when he was feverishly—but unnoticed—making his momentous discoveries, Carlleyle was also descending rapidly into mental illness and questions were raised about his fitness for continued service in the Archaeological Department. The raja of Nagod had complained about the activities of a certain English gentleman who had set up a makeshift hut in the Shankargarh fort in Nagod territory. When an official of the state had turned up to inquire who he was and what he was up to, he had apparently come out of his hut with a gun in his hand and refused to divulge any information whatsoever. The raja had made various further inquiries about this man and concluded he was an escaped criminal. D.M.K. Barr, the political agent of Baghelkhand, discovered he was none other than Carlleyle of the

[44] 'A summary report of operations for the season of 1881–2, Home/Archaeology, Nov. 1882, No. 5, Part A, NAI.

[45] Interestingly, the report for the previous year refers to a similar incident.

[46] According to Smith (1906: 49), the Vindhyan cave drawings had been discovered simultaneously but independently by Carlleyle and Cockburn. Cockburn published his account in *JASB*, 52 (1883), part I, pp. 56–64, and copies of the drawings in *JRAS*, 1899, p. 99. Whether the non-publication of Carlleyle's paper was due to his ill health or due to his being pre-empted by Cockburn's publication, or some other reason altogether, is not known. Cockburn suggested that Carlleyle did not publicize his discoveries because he wanted to keep them to himself and work on them further.

Archaeological Survey and sent an urgent telegram to the Foreign Department to have him removed as soon as possible. The gentleman's servants had informed Barr that their master had been strange in his manner, ordering them not to disclose his name to anyone—and, in answer to enquirers, to say he was a manager of mines named Mr Jacob. On the same day a messenger arrived bearing a letter from Mr Carlleyle, addressed to his servants, in which he accused them of gross misconduct and of abandoning him. The letter was signed 'Mr C. Gillespie.'[47] The political agent wrote to Carlleyle, requesting him to report to Sutna at once, since his presence in the Nagod and Mahiyar districts was unauthorized. Carllelyle obliged.

Now, Cunningham was ordered to explain the circumstances in which Carlleyle had been found in non-British territory. He clarified that, from the very beginning, Carllelye had only been employed for survey work in British territory, and that if he had strayed, it was on his own initiative. Cunningham also expressed his inability to send down a European (or even a native, for that matter), as he had no one to send ('my whole establishment consisting of one Draughtsman, and two Chaprassees').[48] Carlleyle was ultimately declared to be sane and fit and made his way to Allahabad, where he joined his family.

The matter caused ripples in official circles. Lepel Griffin, the agent to the governor general for Central India, wrote to the Government of India pointing out that Carlleyle had caused much alarm and embarrassment in the native states. He urged that a medical board look into the matter for it appeared that Carlleyle was totally unfit to continue in government employment. Whatever the outcome of such an inquiry might be, Lepel Griffin was adamant in his insistence that Carlleyle not be allowed into Bundelkhand or Baghelkhand ever again, and instructions to this effect had been conveyed to the political agents.[49]

[47] Letter No. 367 of 1882, dated Baghelkhand Agency, Sutna, 12 April, from the Political Agent to the Agent Governor General for Central India Indore to the First Assistant to the Agent Governor General for Central India Indore, Home/Archaeology, May 1882, No. 4, Part B, NAI.

[48] Letter dated Simla, 17 April 1882, from Cunningham to the Secretary to the Government of India, Home/Archaeology, April 1882, No. 32, Part B, NAI.

[49] Letter No. 46G-107, dated Indore Residency, 17 April 1882, from Lepel Griffin to the Secretary to the Government of India in the Foreign Dept., Home/Archaeology, May 1882, Nos. 4–5, Part B, NAI.

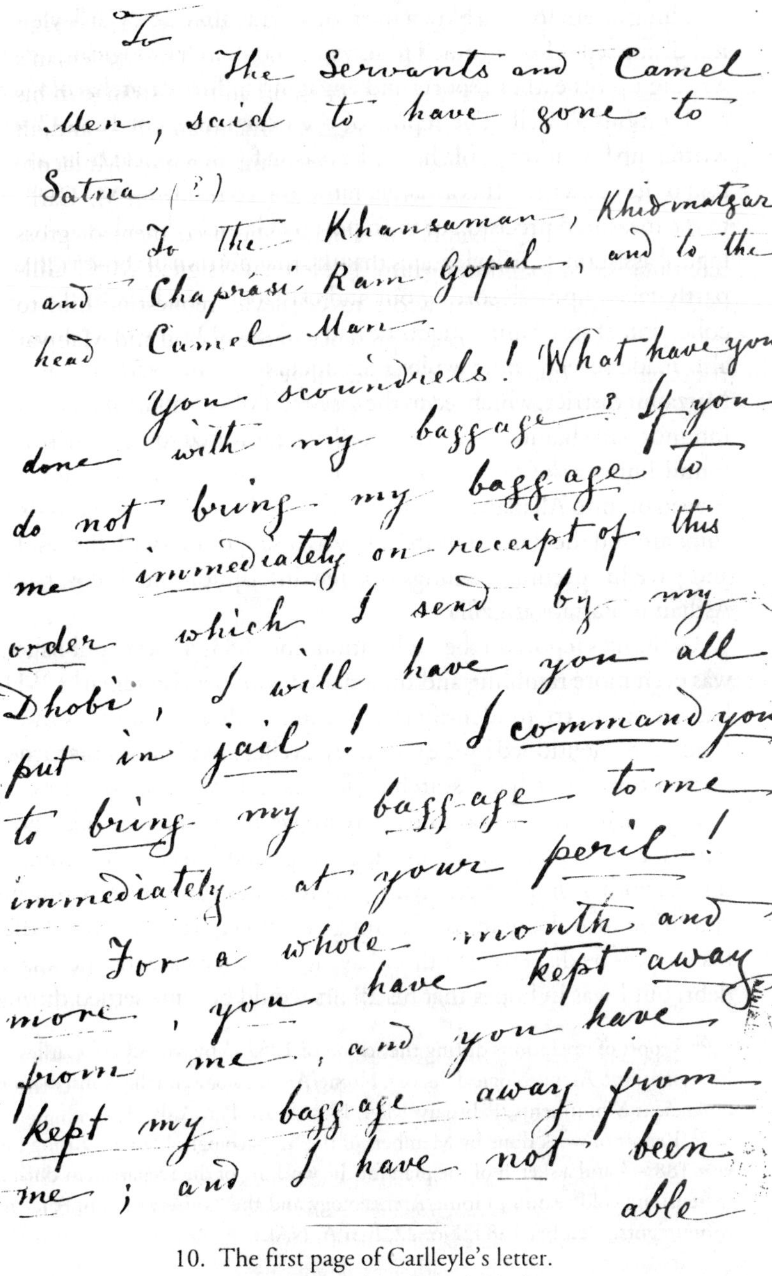

To

The Servants and Camel Men, said to have gone to Satna (?)

To The Khansaman, Khidmatgar and Chaprási Ram Gopal, and to the head Camel Man.

You scoundrels! What have you done with my baggage? If you do not bring my baggage to me immediately on receipt of this order which I send by my Dhobi, I will have you all put in jail! — I command you to bring my baggage to me immediately at your peril!

For a whole month and more, you have kept away from me, and you have kept my baggage away from me; and I have not been able

10. The first page of Carlleyle's letter.
Courtesy: National Archives of India

Things seem to have blown over for a while after this. Carlleyle was not dismissed. He continued to serve with the Archaeological Survey, writing up his earlier reports and engaging in further archaeological explorations as well. The report of the explorations of 1882–3 was written up but never published. The reason for this is clear from a perusal of its content.[50] It is a vague, rambling account, a sharp contrast to the measured precision of the report by Garrick, the other archaeological assistant. Carlleyle states that the first portion of the season was partly taken up with sorting out and classifying the large and varied collection of stone implements he had amassed. During this period he also made several short exploratory incursions into various parts of Mirzapur district, which led to the discovery of a number of sepulchral mounds and chambered cairns. Carlleyle excavated some of these and found human skeletons and stone implements. From Mirzapur he moved on into Allahabad district. He visited a number of mounds of ruins around the Rae Bareli area but was disappointed with the results, and gave his peculiar readings of a few inscriptions he discovered at Asthan in Partabgarh zilla.

Carlleyle's report on the explorations for 1883–4 (never published) was even more rambling and punctuated with peevish remarks.[51] He had set out to try to identify the location of three vihara sites in the Oudh area mentioned by the Chinese traveller Hwui Lun. This turned out to be 'very much like searching for a couple of particular straws in a *hay-field*, where you may find many straws, but perhaps not just those particular ones you *want*.'[52] During this period Carlleyle was coming under another cloud, overdrawing on his account and exacerbating his condition of indebtedness. Cunningham finally recommended that his services be dispensed with. 'I have long been aware that he was in debt, but I was in hopes that his affairs would become settled during

[50] Report of operations during the season of 1882–3 by Mr A.C.L. Carlleyle, First Assistant, Archaeological Survey, Home/Archaeology and the Conservation of Ancient Monuments, February 1884, Nos. 8–13, Part A, NAI.

[51] 'Report of work done by Members of the Archaeological Survey during the year 1883–4 and a sketch of the plan for the working of the Department during the ensuing cold season', Home/Archaeology and the Conservation of Ancient Monuments, October 1884, No. 22, Part A, NAI.

[52] Ibid.

the present year. I am afraid, however, that his affairs have become worse . . . Under these circumstances it seems to me that the further retention of Mr Carlleyle's services would most probably lead to further complications, and would thus entail more troublesome references to Government. His retirement from Government employment therefore appears to be the only real remedy.'[53] The termination of Carlleyle's services coincided neatly with the reorganization of the Archaeological Survey in the wake of Cunningham's retirement: 'It is intended to abolish Mr Carlleyle's appointment under the revised arrangements to be introduced on the 1st October next; and as he is now over 54 years of age and of eccentric habits, which have led on more than one occasion to embarrassment, and even raised doubts as to his sanity, it is not considered desirable to attempt to provide him with any other appointment.'[54]

An Estimate: A Rediscovery

Carlleyle's contribution to archaeological research in India (as was that of his fellow assistant Beglar) was dismissed as of little or no value by his contemporaries. More recent assessments have recognized the importance of his discoveries. Dilip K. Chakrabarti, for instance, highlights Carlleyle's recognition of the possible astronomical significance of the arrangement of stones in megalithic monuments, his very competent description of the site of Nagari, his documenting of ancient terracottas at Indor Khera, his detailed mapping of numerous ancient mounds in the Gorakhpur, Saran, and Ghazipur districts, and his discovery of a mesolithic-neolithic horizon in the Gangetic valley.

This resurrection of Carlleyle, however, tends towards an unwarranted extreme in a recent publication of the British Museum, which

[53] Letter No. 52, dated Simla, 20 May 1885, from Cunningham to the Secretary to the Government of India, Home Proceedings/Archaeology and the Conservation of Ancient Monuments, Nos. 3–5, Part A, OIOC. I am not sure why the same document suggests to Imam (1966: 61, n. 2) that Carlleyle's premature retirement was due to recurring financial irregularities and embezzling practices.

[54] Decision made by the Dept. of Finance and Commerce, Pensions and Gratuities, Home Proceedings/Archaeology and the Conservation of Ancient Monuments, Nos. 3–5, Part A, OIOC.

projects Carlleyle as a misunderstood genius.[55] The man's assertiveness and non-conformism, it is argued, were mistaken for insanity. The strange letter Carlleyle wrote to his servants 'reveals a charming if patronizing mixture of emphasis and humour, much in the manner of letters written to children at this time.' The signing of the note as Mr C. Gillespie was not odd at all as the use of nicknames was common at the time.[56]

Such assessments seem far-fetched. What can be said is that at a time when other archaeologists in India were preoccupied with remains of the historical period, Carlleyle was one of the few directing attention to prehistoric remains, be they in the form of stone tools, burials, or rock paintings. He was the first to discover and document the microlithic tradition in India, and to bring out the richness of the Vindhyas as sites of prehistoric tools and prehistoric art. In fact Carlleyle's discovery of the prehistoric paintings at Sohagighat in 1867–8 preceded the discovery of such paintings at Altamira in Spain, several years later, in 1879. This means effectively that Carlleyle was the first to discover and recognize the significance of prehistoric rock art anywhere—not only in India, but in the world. Unfortunately, the significance of his discoveries was not realized at the time.

Carlleyle left India for England in 1885. Among his most prized possessions were a large collection of stone artefacts (dominated by microliths) that he had collected during his years in India. He published nothing during the remaining twelve years of his life, but he did make a list of his extensive collection of stone tools. His financial problems caused him to sell his artefacts piecemeal to private collectors and various museums in Britain. Some of these eventually found their way into the British Museum, Europe, and America.

Many, many years after Carlleyle had roamed the Central Indian highlands in search of the vestiges of stone age humans, the prehistorian Bridget Allchin made an interesting rediscovery.[57] She spent several months in the winter of 1957–8 in the area in and around Mirzapur and Rewa districts. At Bhainswar (Bhainsod), forty-two miles south of Mirzapur, she discovered that the sites mentioned by

[55] Cook and Martingell (1994).
[56] Ibid.: 13.
[57] Allchin (1958).

Carlleyle in his lists were known, and even Carlleyle was remembered.[58] In one of the westerly caves at Morhana Pahar, a group of caves in the Mirzapur district, where the Vindhyas look out on to the Gangetic plains, Allchin found a painting in dark red of two horse-drawn chariots carrying riders with weapons. The painting had been carefully overlaid in white. Perhaps the chariot scene represented a raid by chariot-riding plainsmen into the hills inhabited by tribal hunters. Carlleyle's report for 1880–1 had mentioned paintings of horses and chariots. Was the careful tracing of the scene in white done by A.C. Carlleyle in order to make it easier to photograph?

[58] A letter written by Seidler to Canon Greenwell in 1888, urging the latter to send the money for the tools he had purchased at the rate of fifty for a guinea, gives an inventory which mentions Morhana Pahar several times. This seems to confirm Bridget Allchin's proposed identification of the site visited and described by Carlleyle with Morhana Pahar (Sieveking: 1960: 99).

CHAPTER 7

The Description and Care of Monuments

The description of historical monuments was an important strand in nineteenth-century Indian archaeology and was crucially linked to the ultimate emergence of a concern for conservation. But, for a very long time, measures for the delineation of monuments were not matched with effective measures for their preservation. The second half of the nineteenth century was an age of archaeological discovery and documentation in India, but it was also a time of the destruction of many ancient sites and structures. The official correspondence of the colonial state constantly blamed the indifference and vandalism of ignorant natives, but there were occasional murmurs of awareness of other agents of destruction. One of these was the colonial archaeologist whose enthusiasm for discovery was not sufficiently tempered or curbed by a concern for preservation. Other culprits were road builders and railway contractors under whose direction countless ancient structures silently crumbled into rubble and ballast for the swiftly expanding network of road and railway lines. Much of this destruction went unreported, but occasionally it was publicized and assumed the proportions of a scandal. One such scandal was created in 1885 by the revelations of a French scholar, Gustave le Bon.

Le Bon had made plans to travel to Gujarat in order to visit Chandravati, the ancient capital of the Abu branch of the Paramaras, famed for its many exquisite Brahmanical and Jaina temples. He was on the verge of leaving on his journey when someone informed him that the temples he was going to see no longer existed—they had been destroyed by an engineer in order to build a road. The Frenchman was incensed and shot off a furious letter to *Le Temps.* He condemned the

British, whose ferocious vandalism, he alleged, was causing monuments in India to disappear at an alarming rate. The barb struck home and an official inquiry initiated by James Burgess (who was by then director general of the Archaeological Survey of India) proved that the allegation was correct. Some 40,000 cubic feet of stone from the Chandravati temples had been sold to contractors of the Rajputana Railway by the Sirohi durbar (within whose jurisdiction the site fell) under the advice of the British political resident.[1]

Early Conservation Measures

In the early nineteenth century, during the East India Company's raj, a few sporadic steps were taken towards the conservation of historical monuments.[2] Through regulations issued in 1810 and 1817, the Madras and Bengal governments empowered themselves to intervene if public buildings were exposed to misuse by private individuals. A lot of the actual conservation work during these years was centred in and around Agra. During Lord Minto's tenure (1807–12), a Taj Committee was set up and Lieutenant Taylor appointed to supervise repairs, the cost of which ultimately exceeded Rs 100,000. In 1815 the Marquess of Hastings ordered the repair of the monuments at Fatehpur Sikri and Sikandra. In 1816 local agents of the government negotiated to acquire control over the grounds around Akbar's tomb, and Lieutenant Taylor was sent to live in Sikandra to supervise its preservation. In 1826, during the governor generalship of Lord Amherst, the Qutb Minar was repaired under the supervision of Major Smith of the Royal Engineers.

On the other hand, during these decades there was a practice of leasing out the gardens of historical monuments to cultivators in order to augment municipal funds.[3] During William Bentinck's tenure (1828–35), the government seriously considered a proposal to lease

[1] Home/Archaeology, November 1886, Nos. 5–8, Part A; and Home/Archaeology and the Conservation of Ancient Monuments, January 1887, Nos. 3 & 4, Part A, NAI.

[2] Many of these details are given in Cole (1882): 4–10.

[3] As late as in the 1880s, the gardens of Humayun's tomb in Delhi were being used to grow cabbages and tobacco. See Cole (1882): xxvii.

the Sikandra gardens to the executive engineer at Agra for speculative cultivation. It was at about the same time that Shah Jahan's bath in the Agra Fort, dismantled during the time of Lord Hastings in order to present it to George IV (but for some reason never actually presented), was sold at a public auction. There was also a plan to demolish the Taj for its marble, but luckily this was not executed.

Sporadic conservation initiatives resumed in the post-Bentinck era. In 1842, during the governor generalship of Lord Auckland, local agents at Agra were instructed to take charge of Itimad-ud-daulah's tomb and keep it in repair. In the next year Viscount Hardinge disbursed a small sum for the repair of the tomb. In western India Sir Bartle Frere, Resident of Satara, appointed Captain Hart of the Bombay Engineers to survey the medieval remains at Bijapur. In 1850, during Dalhousie's tenure, the lieutenant governor of the North-Western Provinces authorized an expenditure of Rs 10,493 per annum for various activities connected with Salim Chishti's tomb at Fatehpur Sikri; Rs 1,500 of this was for repairs. In 1855, at the urging of J. Gibbs (assistant commissioner in Bombay) and Sir Bartle Frere (at the time commissioner of Sind), the governor of Bombay, Lord Elphinstone, sanctioned Rs 5,000 for the repair of the Jami Masjid and the tombs at Thatta in Sind.

Apart from its political impact, the Revolt of 1857 left its scars on the social, cultural and physical landscape, particularly in Delhi.[4] During the Revolt, the rebels targeted buildings that symbolized the British presence in Delhi. The capture of the city by British troops was followed by large-scale looting and destruction. Apart from plundering private residences, British soldiers carried off everything of value in the Red Fort—from the marble slabs and fabulous inlay work to the ornaments, weapons, and clothes of the family of Bahadur Shah, the Mughal emperor.[5] For several months after the fall of Delhi there was serious debate on whether the city should be destroyed to punish the rebels and set an example. The decision to clear a space of 450 yards around the walls of the Red Fort led to the destruction of a number of historic structures, and the fort and the Jama Masjid were turned into

[4] See Gupta (1981): Chap. 1. For a more detailed account of the manner in which the Revolt of 1857 left its mark on Delhi's landscape, see Lahiri (2003).

[5] Lahiri (2003): 38.

an army camp. It took over three decades before the impact of the military occupation of historical sites was raised concertedly as an issue of concern.

During the 1860s and 1870s the Government of India became more active in promoting the illustration and conservation of historical monuments. Pressure from England had a role to play in this. The most vocal and influential spokesmen on these issues were Henry Cole, director of the South Kensington Museum, and James Fergusson, the scholar who had done much to give international exposure to Indian antiquities and architecture. In 1874 the many individuals who shared this concern for preservation included Salisbury, Ripon, Fergusson, Bartle Frere, Northcote, Meadows Taylor, Trevelyan, and Duleep Singh—all these jointly submitted to the Government of India a memorial urging the preservation of the country's historical monuments.

Initiatives were meanwhile being taken, both at the level of the imperial as well as the various provincial governments. In 1863 Sir Bartle Frere, who was now governor of Bombay, sanctioned an annual grant for the repair of the monuments of Bijapur. In 1867 the Government of India sanctioned funds for the repair of the buildings at Ahmedabad and Sirkhej. In 1871–2 the Bombay government repaired the tomb and mosque of Rani Sipri in Ahmedabad. The establishment of the Archaeological Survey of Western India in 1873 gave a new impetus to archaeological and architectural documentation in this region. In 1879 Major Mant was appointed conservator of archaeological and architectural remains in Bombay by Sir Richard Temple, and he furnished a report on the buildings in Ahmedabad. The Madras government did not lag far behind. In 1868 Lord Napier initiated the restoration of Trimal Nayaka's palace. Over the next decade repairs to historical structures were initiated at Gingi, Chandragiri, Vellore, Halebid, and Mysore. The overgrowth of vegetation among the ruins of Hampi was cleared in 1878.

An archaeological survey had been instituted in the North-Western Provinces in 1868. A few years later, in 1875, the lieutenant governor, Sir John Strachey, established a special archaeological division. The provincial government took a number of measures to continue repairs to monuments in and around Agra. Between 1871 and 1875 over

Rs 1,00,000 was spent on repairs to buildings in the Agra Fort, the Taj Mahal, and Fatehpur Sikri. In 1879 Lytton's government helped out with a generous grant of Rs 375,000 from imperial funds for the purpose.

The conservation of historical monuments was not envisaged as one of the primary functions of the archaeological surveys. This was supposed to be the responsibility of the Public Works Departments of local governments.[6] Apart from occasionally allocating funds for specific conservation work, the imperial government issued a number of instructions on the subject to local governments and administrations. Official circulars and government resolutions began to mention the importance of *in situ* preservation of archaeological remains. The 1860s and 1870s also saw some legislation on this matter. For instance, an act of 1863 gave the Government of India the authority to protect and preserve buildings remarkable for their antiquity or for their historical or architectural value. The Treasure Trove Act of 1878 authorized the government to claim any unearthed treasure whose value exceeded ten rupees. But there was a big gap between directives and legislation on the one hand, and effective implementation on the other. These measures proved woefully inadequate, and ancient Indian artefacts and remains continued to drift into the hands of private owners and dealers, and into museums, in India and abroad.

James Burgess and the Archaeological Surveys of Western and Southern India

James Burgess was a trained architect who had been forced to give up his profession because of problems with his vision. He was a close associate of the architectural historian James Fergusson, and the two collaborated with each other, labouring for many years to produce the monumental work, *Cave Temples in India*, which was ultimately published in 1880. Over the years Burgess had conducted a number of architectural surveys of Brahmanical, Buddhist, and Jaina shrines in western India, and had built up a reputation as a fine and dedicated architectural scholar.

Burgess's areas of interest lay principally in western and southern

[6] Circular No. 9, PWD, 13 February 1873.

India. In 1867, when the Bombay government sent out circulars to its officials requesting them to submit lists of architectural and other remains, Burgess was entrusted with the task of compiling these lists. He corrected, compiled, and added to the information received. It was quite clear to him, however, that much more needed to be done. In August 1870 he submitted to H. Pendock St. G. Tucker (member of the governor's council), a memorandum proposing a survey of ancient remains in the Bombay Presidency.

Burgess's memorandum contained a plan, replete with an estimate of expenses, for an archaeological-cum-architectural survey of the Bombay Presidency and adjacent areas.[7] While he urged the compilation of lists of *all* ancient remains, even those devoid of beauty or ornamentation, Burgess had a special interest in the history and styles of Indian architecture, which he enumerated in his memorandum. He suggested that a good superintendent with a small staff of native assistants could in a few years complete a survey of Indian art and ascertain the conservation measures necessary. He also suggested that the Asiatic Society and students of the schools of art be involved in the project. He emphasized the importance of a photographic documentation of India's architectural heritage and stressed the importance of tracing and collecting manuscripts, inscriptions and coins. He urged the Government of India also to take the initiative in areas that lay beyond its political frontiers, in the territories of Indian princes such as the nizam of Hyderabad. He argued that the delineation and conservation of ancient monuments in India was a duty that the British government of India must discharge.

The problem was that Tucker just sat on Burgess's memorandum, and also on other letters and documents relating to the same issue, thereby delaying the establishment of the Archaeological Survey of Western India.[8] In mid 1873 Burgess was still waiting for the government's response; in fact he had delayed his departure to England two

[7] *Memorandum on the Survey of Architectural and Archaeological Remains*; Extract from the Proceedings of the Government of India in the Home Department (Public), dated Fort William, 17 March 1871, Home/Public, 1871, No. 132, Part A, NAI.

[8] The documents that Tucker tucked away included two despatches (dated 20 January 1870 and 11 October 1871) from the Secretary of State, the second

years, and now, having retired from his job as principal of the Jamsetjee Jeejebhoy School of Art, was on the verge of leaving India. At this point the initiative was suddenly seized by J. Gibbs, member of the governor's council, who urged that the Bombay government take some action in response to Burgess's proposal.

Given this nudge, the wheels of officialdom moved swiftly. The Archaeological Survey of Western India was sanctioned in August 1873 and Burgess took charge of it on 15 January 1874 with the unpretentious designation of Archaeological Surveyor and Reporter. Gibbs had suggested that Ajanta, Ellora, and other groups of caves in Hyderabad state be included in the survey's purview. The scheme ultimately sanctioned by the Government of India, however, explicitly restricted the scope of Burgess's survey activities to the Bombay Presidency. In fact the government made it clear that it did *not* want him to venture into the Central Provinces, Berar, or the nizam's territory. This was for reasons of economy and also ostensibly to prevent any possible clash or duplication of activities with Cunningham's survey, and to avoid intruding into the princely states. Burgess found this restriction extremely annoying.[9] Equally galling were the insufficient funds and staff made available. He managed to recruit one Bombay School of Art student as an assistant, and an assistant for photography—which, for the most part he was forced to handle himself.

Burgess's Archaeological Survey of Western India was independent of the Archaeological Survey of India headed by Cunningham. The reasons for this are clearly stated by E.C. Bayley, secretary in the Home Department:

---

of which included as an attachment a memorandum by Forbes Watson on the suggestions made by James Fergusson for a comprehensive work on the rock-cut temples of western India. It was only when the Secretary of State sent another despatch, dated 6 November, asking what had been done in response to the earlier communications, that Tucker, who was on the verge of leaving India, handed over the entire correspondence to the secretariat. Gibbs' Minute, in Home/Public, August 1873, Nos. 330–3, Part A, NAI.

[9] These restrictions were lifted in November 1874 at Burgess's insistence and with Cunningham's concurrence. James Fergusson had also put in a word with the home government urging that this be done.

I have discussed this matter with General Cunningham.

I was very desirous that in this matter Mr Burgess should have worked under the direction of General Cunningham, for I can see that Mr Burgess is ignorant on many points as to which General Cunningham could teach him; and *2ndly*, I wished all Government Archaeological work to fit into the General Survey.

But General Cunningham, while admitting the force of these arguments, thinks that the arrangement will not work.

The truth is that Mr Burgess is very aggrieved at the creation of General Cunningham's appointment and would not work willingly under him.

Secondly, he is a disciple of Mr Ferguson [*sic*], who is at issue with General Cunningham on some very important points.

In fact, the present sketch of operations in Bombay has, General Cunningham says he knows, been sketched by Mr Ferguson [*sic*], and he is content to leave the work which will undoubtedly be useful, without any interference on his part, which, he knows, will be distasteful . . .[10]

So, Burgess was left free to do as he pleased in the Bombay Presidency. The terms of his appointment allowed him to spend six months of the year in India and the other six in England, to write up his material and prepare it for publication. The arrangement was convenient for Burgess, but a superintendent absent from the country for half the year was not ideal. All the same his appointment, initially made for three years, was subsequently extended.

In 1872, a year before taking over the Archaeological Survey of Western India, Burgess became the founding editor of an important new journal, *The Indian Antiquary*. The journal was intentionally given a very wide scope and aimed, among other things, at publicizing important discoveries, stimulating discussion, and facilitating communication between Eastern and Western archaeologists.[11] Burgess visualized it as supplementing the journals of the various Asiatic societies. He also hoped it would aid the Archaeological Survey of India by early publication of its progress and discoveries, and by communicating useful information to its officers.

[10] E.C. Bayley's Note of 8 August 1873, in Home/Public, August 1873, Nos. 330–3, Part A, NAI.

[11] The full title of the journal was *The Indian Antiquary: A Journal of Oriental Research in Archaeology, History, Literature, Languages, Folklore, etc.*

11. James Burgess.
Courtesy: Archaeological Survey of India

The idea of setting up an archaeological survey for South India was in the air for many years. In 1874 James Fergusson submitted to the secretary of state a memorandum endorsed by a number of signatories, urging the institution of systematic measures for the preservation of historical monuments in India. At the insistence of the secretary of state, the Government of India directed Cunningham to undertake a classification of the monuments of the northern and eastern provinces, Rajputana and the Central Provinces. Burgess was asked to do the same thing in the Bombay Presidency, and the Madras government was told to nominate an officer who would undertake a similar classification for the Madras Presidency. The problem was that although the Madras government was willing to underwrite some of the expenses, it was not willing to provide a salary for such an official. So, no appointment was made.

In the meantime, the pressure was building up from a number of international scholars. In 1875, at the instance of Sir Walter Elliot (who had spent many years as collector of Guntur district), the president of the Congress of Orientalists urged the secretary of state to establish an archaeological survey of southern India. W. Rost, librarian of the India Office, made a similar representation. The secretary of state supported the proposal, being of the opinion that the southern provinces had not got as much attention as the northern ones and that the results would fully justify the expense.[12] The crucial issue was to identify a person to whom the archaeological survey of southern India could be entrusted. The names of Dr A.C. Burnell (district and sessions judge at Tanjore) and Captain H.H. Cole (an engineer working in the Public Works Department of the North Western Provinces) were considered. Burnell could not take on the job because of additional responsibilities that had come his way with the closure of the separate court of North Tanjore.[13] Cole was willing, but the

[12] Letter No. 31 (Geographical/Archaeology), dated India Office London, 29 July 1875, from the Secretary of State for India to the Governor General in Council, and Enclosures, Home Proceedings/Public, September 1875, No. 76, Part A, OIOC.

[13] Rost's Memorandum dated London, 28 June 1875 described Burnell as the 'only one man living who possesses *all* the qualifications required of an Archaeological Surveyor of Southern India.' Cunningham disagreed. While Dr Burnell's

government decided to wait till the end of an ongoing famine before it undertook the additional expense. In November 1876 the Government of India gave qualified approval to the idea of appointing Captain Cole for the job, but pointed out that it would be better to find an officer who had some knowledge of the South Indian languages. The idea of getting Cunningham's assistant Beglar for the job at a future date was also toyed with. However, the only decision eventually made was to postpone the whole scheme.

The India Office seems to have been more keen than the Government of India to see the establishment of an archaeological survey of southern India. The secretary of state was disappointed at the delay:

> In view of the rapid decay to which, from climatic and other causes, monuments and antiquarian remains in India are especially liable, I cannot but regret that circumstances have rendered necessary the decision at which you have arrived, more especially as, from information in this Office, it would appear that the authority given in 1868 to incur expenditure on archaeological investigation in the Madras Presidency was not acted upon, and that no efforts have been made, in this important administrative division of India, to carry into effect the measures planned by the Supreme Government, for obtaining records of the principal archaeological monuments throughout the Presidency.[14]

Agreeing that it was important to identify an official properly qualified for the job, the secretary of state passed on Fergusson's recommendation of R. Chisholm of the Public Works Department in the Madras Presidency for the smaller task of investigating the rock-cut temples at Mahabalipuram.

In spite of all this flow of correspondence, the subject of an archaeological survey for South India continued dormant for a long time. Things picked up in 1879, when Robert Sewell of the Madras Civil

---

knowledge of the southern languages was an asset, he did not think him suitable for survey work. Being a senior civil servant, he would also expect too a high salary. Letter No. 117, dated Simla, 8 September 1875, from Cunningham to the Officiating Secretary to the Government of India, Home Proceedings/Public, January 1876, Nos. 184–6, Part A, OIOC.

[14] Despatch No. 22 (Geographical), dated India Office, London 10 May 1877, from the Secretary of State to the Governor General in Council, Home/Public, June 1877, No. 247, Part A, OIOC.

Service was appointed as officer on special duty (with the designation of Superintendent, Archaeological Survey) in connection with the archaeological survey of the Madras Presidency. His job was to compile lists of monuments and inscriptions that could form the basis of a more detailed survey. Sewell established contact with Cunningham and Burgess. He busied himself by circulating hundreds of appeals in various languages, urging people from different walks of life to come forward with relevant information. At the same time, he was keen that some sort of permanent machinery be set up for a systematic survey of the Madras Presidency under Burgess. In April 1881 he forwarded to the Government of Madras several letters he had received from 'gentlemen of the highest scientific reputation', including James Fergusson, A.W. Franks,[15] and Sir Walter Elliot (formerly of the Madras Civil Service). They all urged that James Burgess be entrusted with an archaeological survey of the Madras province. The Madras government finally gave in, and in November 1881 James Burgess, superintendent of the Archaeological Survey of Western India, was given additional charge of the Archaeological Survey of Southern India.

These archaeological surveys of western and southern India differed significantly in aims and methods from Cunningham's Archaeological Survey of India. The collection of material for the publication of a comprehensive work on the rock-cut temples of western India (on which Fergusson and Burgess had already been working many years) was one of the principal reasons why Burgess's appointment had been made in the first place. It was clearly understood at the outset that the Archaeological Survey of Western India was supposed actually to be an *architectural* survey.[16] The archaeological surveys of western and southern India focused on the description and illustration of architectural remains, and went on to produce a series of fine, meticulously detailed and lavishly illustrated monographs on the monuments of

[15] A.W. Franks was Keeper of the Department of British and Medieval Antiquities in the British Museum. A keen collector of antiquities, he played a very important role in building up the museum's collections.

[16] See, for instance, Telegram dated Simla, 20 August 1873, from Home Secretary to the Government of Bombay: 'Your letter dated 24th July. Proposals for employing Mr Burgess on ancient architectural remains in Bombay sanctioned.' Home/Public, August 1873, Nos. 330–3, Part A, NAI.

Belgaum and Kaladgi districts, Kathiawad and Kutch, the Bidar and Aurangabad districts of the nizam's dominions, and the Buddhist cave-temples in the Deccan.

Cunningham's long, fifteen-year innings as director general of the Archaeological Survey of India came to an end on 1 October 1885.[17] On the eve of his retirement Cunningham made a number of recommendations about the future conduct of archaeological research in India. He said that, in view of the considerable achievements already made, the establishment of the Archaeological Survey be reduced and decentralized. He also suggested that conservation be squarely placed within the purview of the Archaeological Survey. Cunningham's most intriguing and drastic recommendation concerned the post of director general of the Archaeological Survey of India: he argued that there was no longer any need for it and suggested it be abolished.

Cunningham's retirement was followed by a reorganization of archaeological survey activities. Upper India was divided into three survey circles, each under the charge of a surveyor with a subordinate establishment. The three survey circles were Punjab (with Sind and Rajputana); the North Western Provinces and Oudh, the Central India Agency and the Central Provinces; and Bengal with Assam and Chhota Nagpur. J.D.M. Beglar was appointed surveyor for Bengal, J.B. Keith for the North-Western Provinces (with Führer as his assistant), and C.J. Rodgers for the Punjab. Burgess was to continue in charge of the Archaeological Survey of Western India and of Southern India, and in addition was to loosely coordinate the activities of the provincial surveyors. Burgess was ultimately given the designation of director general on 25 March 1886. The new arrangement amounted to a significant decentralization of survey activities during the tenure of Burgess (1885–9). The surveyors of the provincial circles became increasingly independent and were answerable to the provincial governments rather than to the director general. One of the major concerns behind the new arrangements was of cutting costs, reflected in a significant drop for the budget of the Archaeological Survey Department between 1885 and 1886.[18]

[17] A fall from an elephant two years previously had injured him severely, and this was one of the factors that led him to contemplate retirement.

[18] Resolution of Government of India in the Home Department, No. 2—87–143 of 6 June 1885, on the subject of the reorganization of the Archaeological

The transition from the Cunningham era (1871–85) to the brief Burgess era (1885–9) also marked a shift in the priorities of the Archaeological Survey—from extensive field surveys to detailed architectural studies. The focus that had characterized the archaeological surveys of western and southern India was now extended to the central establishment of the survey, and was reflected in the volumes published as part of the New Imperial Series of the Archaeological Survey.

> One of the principal aims of these Surveys ought to be a pretty full illustration and history of ancient and medieval Indian Architecture, down at least to the decline of the Muhammadan styles, and even inclusive of all that is best in structural and decorative art down to the present time. For all practical purposes this has hitherto been neglected in the Survey of Northern India.[19]

Burgess had cited the urgent need to prevent ill-advised restoration work as one of the principal reasons why he had accepted the post of director general of the Archaeological Survey, in spite of a heavy load of pending academic work and the enormity of the responsibility that the job entailed. He minced no words in his criticism of the ill-conceived restoration of the Mahabodhi temple at Bodh Gaya, remarking that he hoped no other building in Bengal would be treated so ignorantly.[20] He also spoke out against the destruction of stupas and

---

Survey in Upper India; Home/Archaeology and the Conservation of Ancient Monuments, January 1886, No. 23, Part A, OIOC. The desire to reduce or even totally eliminate expenditure on archaeology continued in the 1890s, when the Secretary of State proposed that the job of archaeological investigations be entrusted to the Asiatic Society of Bengal. The Asiatic Society responded that the idea did not seem practical and that continued state support for archaeology was necessary. (Revenue and Archaeology/Archaeology and Epigraphy, July 1895, No. 2, Part A, OIOC.) In fact, some years later, a major reason for the government's decision to allow Burgess to retire prematurely in 1889 was the prospect that it presented for further pruning the department and its expenditure. All these decisions spanned the viceroyalty of Dufferin (1884–8) and Lansdowne (1888–94).

[19] Letter No. 26, dated Junagadh, 27 January 1886, from James Burgess to the Secretary to the Government of India, Home Department, Home/Archaeology, August 1886, No. 25, Part A, OIOC.

[20] Letter No. 25, dated Ahmedabad, 23 January 1886, from Burgess to the Secretary to the Government of Bengal, Public Works Department, in Home/

mounds caused by unscientific excavation, urging the government to prevent antiquarian objects—which ought to be regarded as national property—from finding their way into private residences in England and foreign museums. He also urged a rule that no officer or employee of the Archaeological Survey be allowed to collect antiquarian objects for themselves.[21]

With his expertise as an architectural scholar, Burgess was one of the best people around to deal with monument conservation. At his insistence, exploration, conservation, and epigraphy had been amalgamated and placed under the purview of the director general of the Archaeological Survey. However, there was little direct scope for him to play a major role in conservation projects because these continued in effect to be the responsibility of the local governments and their Public Works Department, to whom the surveyors tendered their advice. The director general was simply a post office. Communications addressed by surveyors to local governments about conservation matters were supposed to be sent under flying seal through Burgess, who could comment and give his advice. But the responsibility for action thereafter lay squarely with the local governments. This arrangement meant continuous friction between the director general and the local governments.

The post-Cunningham arrangements for the Archaeological Survey loaded the new director general with an unmanageable range of duties and responsibilities, and armed him with inadequate powers. Burgess had had no choice in the appointment of the provincial surveyors; the appointments had been made before he took over. The men appointed were (with the exception of one), in his opinion, unfit for their job. During his brief tenure Burgess was repeatedly entangled in conflicts with local governments, with his surveyors (particularly with Beglar, who was at the time archaeological surveyor for Bengal), and with the Government of India.[22] The new arrangements for the

Archaeology and the Conservation of Ancient Monuments, April 1886, No. 4, Part A, OIOC.

[21] Letter No. 43, dated Bijapur, 6 February 1886, from James Burgess to Secretary to the Government of India, Home Dept, Home/Archaeology, August 1886, No. 26, Part A, OIOC.

[22] At the outset, Burgess was cross about the salary he was being given. He had

Archaeological Survey of India were acknowledged as a failure by all concerned, most of all by Burgess, who remained their most vocal and bitter critic.

Burgess retired prematurely in 1889 to devote his time to writing up some of the voluminous material he had collected during his tenure in India. One of his major contributions to Indian epigraphy was made during these years. The first volume of *Corpus Inscriptionum Indicarum* had been published in 1871, and the volume edited by Fleet had appeared in 1887. At the same time, it was clear to Burgess that it would take much too long to collect inscriptions of ancient and medieval India in separate volumes arranged according to dynasty or chronological period. It was therefore necessary to produce a companion to the *Corpus Inscriptionum Indicarum* series—a journal in which the text, facsimiles, translations, and analysis of inscriptions could be swiftly published as and when the inscriptions were discovered. The result was the publication, after many delays, of the first volume of *Epigraphia Indica*, in 1892. This was edited by Burgess, with Hultzsch and Führer as assistant editors. It was a valuable parting gift from Burgess to Indian epigraphy.

H.H. Cole: Curator of Ancient Monuments

As we noticed, the increasing British interest in Indian art and architecture in the second half of the nineteenth century was to a considerable extent because of the movement for the reform of industrial design in Britain. Spearheaded by people such as Owen Jones, Richard

---

a point. 'If it is considered . . . that I have double the work and double the responsibility I have had hitherto, and quite double General Cunningham's work and area of supervision, there can hardly be any ground in reason why I should be paid less than he was. . . .' Burgess finally threatened to resign his post as head of the archaeological department and revert to his archaeological work in Bombay and Madras if his pay was not raised. This threat worked, and Burgess' pay was raised by Rs 300 per month by abolishing the post of assistant surveyor in the Punjab Archaeological Circle. (Home/Archaeology and the Conservation of Ancient Monuments, August 1886, No. 32½, Part A, OIOC). It may be added that with the premature termination of the appointment of J.F. Fleet as government epigraphist, Burgess was expected to handle, along with all his other duties, all matters relating to the deciphering and translating of inscriptions.

Redgrave, Mathew Digby Wyatt, Gottfried Semper, and Henry Cole, this aesthetic movement saw the decorative art of other cultures as helpful in resuscitating British industrial design. The 1851 London Exhibition had showcased the richness of Indian crafts and design. The 1867 Paris Exhibition, where Fergusson had displayed photographs and sculptures from the Amaravati stupa, gave unprecedented international exposure to ancient Indian sculpture and architecture.

In England, the government department that liaisoned this and related initiatives was the Department of Science and Art. A key role was played in this department by Henry Cole (1808–82),[23] a remarkable man with varied interests and talents.[24] The application of art to industrial manufactures became his chief mission. He helped revive the Society of Arts as a forum dedicated to the improvement of British manufactures through the application of fine arts and science.[25] With the backing of Prince Albert, he played a leading role in organizing the Great Exhibition of 1851. For Cole, art was a living and important part of the everyday life of ordinary people. This was the underlying philosophy and conviction behind the South Kensington Museum, founded by him in 1857.[26]

Although the main impact of the movement for industrial design was felt in Britain, it had its reverberations in India as well. In the second half of the nineteenth century the colonial government extended its control over the schools of art in Bombay, Calcutta, and Madras, and a confused art curriculum designed in Britain was introduced in these.[27] Henry Cole and his fellow reformers were interested in Indian

[23] This Henry Cole should not be confused with Lieutenant Henry Cole, who became Curator of Ancient Monuments in India. I mention this because I myself was for a long time confused and mystified by the relationship between the two Coles. I was not the only one. Mitter (1977) gives the father credit for many of the achievements of the son. The fact that Lieutenant Cole was Sir Henry Cole's son helps explain some of his radical ideas and suggests that the father had a strong influence on the son.

[24] For an account of the personality and career of Sir Henry Cole, see Alexander (1995): 143 ff.

[25] The society had been founded in 1754. It was languishing at the time when Prince Albert took over its presidentship in 1843.

[26] The museum was renamed the Victoria and Albert Museum in 1899.

[27] See Mitter (1994): 30–6.

crafts and ancient monuments.[28] In 1866 and 1867, as both secretary of the Science and Art Department as well as director of the South Kensington Museum, Cole urged the British government to procure photographs, plans, and casts illustrating Indian architecture. The home government passed on these inquiries to the Government of India, adding to them an offer of funds, and the Department of Science and Art offered to finance the project of making casts of select pieces of ancient Indian sculpture and architecture.

At about this time, Place, the French consul, had been busy corresponding with the begum of Bhopal, trying to persuade her to let him remove one of the gateways of the Great Stupa at Sanchi and carry it off to France. The begum consulted the British Resident, who immediately vetoed the idea. The begum then offered the gateway to the British Museum. The Government of India declined this generous offer. It was decided instead to prepare casts of the most interesting parts of the Sanchi stupa, starting with one of the gateways, and as a goodwill gesture to offer one set of casts to the French government.[29] The man chosen to supervise the casting project was H.H. Cole.

Cole was an engineer employed in the Public Works Department of the North-Western Provinces. In 1868 he was given charge of conducting an archaeological survey of these.[30] In 1868–9 he surveyed the temples of Kashmir, Mathura, Brindaban, and Govardhan, and the monuments at Deeg and Fatehpur Sikri.[31] Cole was, initially, not particularly enthusiastic about the casting project, believing that the results were unlikely to be satisfactory; but once appointed to the job, he got to work energetically. He and his team, consisting of three

[28] Mitter (1977: 221) points out that this interest did not extend to sculpture or painting.

[29] Notes in Home/Public, 30 July 1870, Nos. 204–16, Part A, NAI.

[30] Cole was not given any specific designation while on this job. He seems to have chosen one himself, because in some of his official correspondence, he styled himself as Superintendent, Archaeological Survey. This self-created designation did not find favour with bureaucrats in the Home Department. See E.C.Bayley's Notes in Home/Public, October 1870, No. 127, Part A, NAI.

[31] Cole's *Illustrations of Ancient Buildings in Kashmir* was published by the India Museum under the authority of the Secretary of State for India in 1869. His *Illustrations of Buildings near Muttra and Agra, Showing the Mixed Hindu-Mahomedan style of Upper India* appeared in 1873.

sappers of the Royal Engineers—Corporals Heath and Jackson and Sergeant Bullen—proceeded to London in May 1869, where they spent many months acquiring training in the casting process at the South Kensington Museum. Cole returned to India with his team in November 1870. He brought along 88 boxes containing 28 tonnes of material and equipment. The begum of Bhopal had offered to assist in the project and when Cole arrived at Sanchi on 7 January 1870, a tahsildar sent by the begum was waiting for him, along with a large quantity of scaffolding material. The European team was assisted by seven Indian modellers.

Cole chose to cast the eastern gateway because it was more secure than the others, with its carvings sharper and clearer, and decided that elastic gelatine moulds would be better and cheaper than plaster of paris. The work was laborious and had to be done fast, because it had to be completed before the temperature exceeded the optimum levels at which gelatine retained the requisite elasticity. The operations evidently aroused considerable interest among local inhabitants around Bhopal and Bhilsa. The site was visited every day by curious people who wanted to look at the casts drying in tents. The project was a success. After over a month of work the master cast—consisting of 112 pieces—was ready and dispatched to England. Replicas of the eastern gateway were displayed in the South Kensington Museum and the Edinburgh and Dublin national museums, and one set was presented to France.

Cole followed up his Sanchi work with casts of other buildings, such as the Qutb Minar and the buildings at Fatehpur Sikri (again subsidized by the Department of Science and Art). He was keen to follow up his book on the temples of Kashmir with similar volumes illustrating other aspects of Indian architecture. Unfortunately, while quite happy with the quality of his work, neither the home government nor the Government of India wanted to encourage projects that involved what was seen as unnecessary and excessive long-term financial commitment. Cole faded out from the scene for the time being, spending some time in London studying and preparing a descriptive catalogue of Indian objects in the South Kensington Museum.[32]

[32] Cole's *Catalogue of the Objects of Indian Art Exhibited in the South Kensington Museum* was published in 1874. Cole states that the opportunity he had at this

He resurfaced some ten years later, in 1880. By this time he had risen from Lieutenant to Captain and was busy investigating the condition of monuments in various cities as an officer on special duty. In 1880 Lytton's government proposed to the secretary of state, Lord Salisbury, the idea of creating a special office—that of Curator of Ancient Monuments. The proposal was finally translated into reality in 1881, during Ripon's tenure. The idea was to replace the desultory and piecemeal conservation initiatives of past decades by a longer term (but not permanent) arrangement whereby local governments could benefit from the professional advice of an experienced officer specially appointed to supervise all conservation work in British India. On 28 January 1881, the new post was created and H.H. Cole became India's first (and, as it happened, the last) curator of ancient monuments. The post was sanctioned for a period of three years. The curator was to function as the head of a separate department under the Home, Revenue and Agriculture Department.[33] Cole set up his headquarters in Simla.

The curator was supposed to advise local governments on matters pertaining to the conservation of old, but not necessarily ancient, historical monuments in their areas. He had no responsibilities for the *execution* of operations, which lay with local governments. In 1881–2, Rs 50,000 was held in reserve by the Public Works departments of local governments for grants-in-aid towards the repair of historical monuments. Cole took his duties seriously and toured the country at breakneck speed, examining and preparing drawings of historical buildings. In 1883–4 he was involved in explorations and excavations

time of examining the collections in the South Kensington Museum and the British Museum 'served to strengthen and stimulate the interest I have always taken in the general subject of Indian art and architecture.' (1882: Appendix G, p. xvii.) Mitter (1977: 256) describes Cole's *Catalogue* as 'containing the very first history of Indian art.' However, he mistakenly attributes this work to Sir Henry Cole, director of the South Kensington Museum.

[33] Actually, the home government was unhappy that a separate department had been created for Cole to preside over. It would have preferred to let him operate through the Public Works Department. Despatch No. 15 (Public Works), dated India Office, London, 9 March 1882, from the Secretary of State for India to the Governor General of India in Council, Home Proceedings/Archaeology and the Conservation of Ancient Monuments, April 1882, Part A, NAI.

at a number of sites in the Yusufzai area, which led to the unearthing of stupas, monasteries, houses, and granaries, and a large number of sculptures.[34]

One of the things Cole was required to do was compile and update lists of India's important historical monuments. He expanded the conventional listing by cataloguing British monuments in India, such as isolated tombs and battle obelisks. For the first time, there was a concerted attempt to liaise with Indian princes on conservation issues in a systematic way. Cole toured many of the princely states, offering specific suggestions and advice, scrutinizing estimates and evaluating results. He thought this the best way of ensuring the proper repair and restoration of historical monuments in these principalities. In British India, Cole emphasized the importance of taking photographs to show the condition of buildings before, during, and after conservation. He extended a general sort of supervision over officers engaged in conservation. In October 1882 Major Keith was designated Assistant to the Curator of Ancient Monuments. It was clear to Cole that bad repair work was worse than no repair work, and that the job required full-time, specialized attention. He urged local governments and administrations to create a special subdivision for conservation. The Punjab government was the only one to respond positively.[35]

Cole had some very clear and definite ideas about why the study of Indian art and architecture was so important. There is a clear congruence between his ideas and those of his father, Sir Henry Cole, the most powerful and influential ideologue for the reform of industrial design in Britain. Lieutenant Cole's family roots, in fact, go a long way in explaining both his radical ideas on art and the confidence and messianic zeal with which he propounded and tried to implement them. Like other antiquarians and archaeologists of his time, Lieutenant Cole saw the study of Indian art as a window into Indian culture and civilization. However, unlike most, he was naturally deeply inspired by the movement for the reform of industrial design. For him, ancient and medieval Indian sculpture and architecture had something from which contemporary architects and craftspersons could learn.[36]

[34] Cole (1885c).

[35] Lieutenant Abbott was appointed and given charge of a newly created archaeological subdivision via a Resolution dated 3 November 1882.

[36] Cole had made these points a few years earlier in 1867 in a letter addressed

Cole's *First Report as Curator of Ancient Monuments* contained his considered opinions on the conservation of historical monuments in India. Apart from listing the various monuments in the country that required conservation, he emphasized the government's responsibility for the *in situ* preservation of historical remains. He pointed out that although investigation had hitherto been given priority over conservation, much remained as far as the accuracy of documentation was concerned. He also pointed out that the interests of investigation and conservation could sometimes clash: 'Experience has shown that the keenest investigators have not always had the greatest respect for the maintenance of monuments. Archaeological research has for its object the elucidation of history, and to an enthusiast the temptation to carry off proof of an unravelled mystery is undoubtedly great.'[37]

For Cole, conservation involved a number of things: custody, preservation, restoration, and illustration. The first two—custody and preservation—could be left to local authorities. The third and fourth—restoration and illustration—required special staff with special qualifications and skills. Cole was not an advocate of rampant restoration. Good restoration work was both expensive and difficult, and should therefore be generally avoided. The focus should be on maintenance rather than restoration. He urged that historical buildings under the occupation of British military establishments be freed from such control. He suggested the creation of a special post of conservator of monuments. He highlighted the importance of photographic documentation as well as the preparation of drawings of the plans and elevations of important monuments. He urged that replicas of ancient

to the Secretary of the Science and Art Department (cited in Letter No. 512, dated Simla, 10 November 1881, from Cole to the Officiating Secretary to the Government of India, Home/Archaeology and the Conservation of Ancient Monuments, February 1882, No. 6, Part A, NAI). He reiterated them in an appendix to his report for 1869–70 (Home/Public, 29 October 1870, No. 127, Part A, NAI). He went over the same ground in his *Note on the Industrial Arts in India*, dated May 1879, which was reproduced as Appendix G of his *First Report*. Cole was not one to cut corners for the sake of economy. He recommended that the reproduction of illustrations of Indian art be entrusted to Morel and Company of Paris, 'the best firm in the world for architectural and art works'. Letter No. 512 dated Simla, 10 November, from Cole to the Officiating Secretary to the Government of India, op. cit.

[37] Cole (1882): 11.

remains be made and that museums be satisfied with these rather than hanker after originals.

The responsibility for calculating costs and executing conservation projects still lay with local governments and administrations. But they could now avail of the advisory services of the curator of ancient monuments. Cole's preliminary reports were circulated widely within the administration. Local governments were free to apply to the Government of India for additional grants if the estimated cost of a particular conservation work project was on the high side.

While Cole saw a great need for government intervention to preserve old monuments, he also recognized the importance of harnessing local interest. This was both with the objective of making the 'natives' active participants in the preservation of their heritage, and to ensure greater chances for the success of conservation work. The generation of such an interest would also help revive Indian crafts, which were becoming increasingly corrupted by European influence. Cole suggested that high-quality illustrations of Indian sculpture and architecture be displayed in schools of art, colleges, and museums with notes in the vernacular languages. They should be circulated and made available for sale to artisans. The rejuvenation of Indian industrial crafts would result in a revival and enrichment of indigenous crafts, which would in turn translate into higher earnings for the government.[38] Cole was speaking a language that most of his contemporaries in India neither understood nor had much patience for.[39]

Cole was one of the first persistently vocal critics of the damage done to historical monuments by the British: 'architectural monuments have suffered, and are suffering, more from the acts for which Government has been responsible than from the natural decay and ruin

[38] Cole (1882): xvii–xix.

[39] Cole seems, however, to have infected his associate Major Keith. Keith's requests for municipal funding towards setting up a *karkhana* (craft workshop) in Agra, on the lines of one that the Gwalior durbar was apparently willing to contribute towards, exasperated the bureaucracy no end. Keith seems to have got progressively distracted from his duties of archaeological survey work and obsessed with the need to revive Indian handicrafts (Revenue and Archaeology/Archaeology, August 1887, Nos. 1–2, Part B, NAI). By this time, Keith had also become a fierce critic of the transfer of Indian antiquities to European museums, robbing the natives of what was rightfully theirs. Home/Archaeology and the Conservation of Ancient Monuments, 1885, No. 11, Part A, OIOC.

produced by rain or vegetation in the jungle and deserted places.'[40] One of the issues he constantly railed against was the occupation of historical monuments by military authorities. His reports give a graphic indictment of the damage caused by the transformation of medieval monuments into British garrisons in Delhi, Agra, and Lahore. In the fort in Delhi, the Rang Mahal had been re-roofed and partitioned to function as a mess-house, one of the marble pavilions in the centre of the Haiyat Baksh garden was being used to serve out meat rations, while the other had been put to use as a gymnasium. The moulded fretwork in the centre of the wooden ceiling of the Diwan-i-Khas had been garishly repainted in black, red and gold as part of the preparations for a ball to be held in honour of the Prince of Wales. The greatest incongruities were in the Diwan-i-Am, which had been transformed into a canteen, with a liquor bar to the right of the throne and a coffee shop to its left. In the Agra Fort the Diwan-i-Am was being used as an armoury, and European-style windows had been built on the west front. In the Saman Burj, a hole made by one of Lord Lake's cannonballs in 1803, in the western marble screen, was still very noticeable. The beautiful inlay work had 'suffered much through the combined influences of time and the British soldier, the latter having extracted a great number of the stones and therefore damaged the marbles.'[41] In the Lahore fort, the Moti Masjid had been transformed into a treasury, the *hammam* nearby into a hospital, and other buildings into officers' quarters. The Diwan-i-Am and the throne-room were being used as a common barrack room and the rooms behind the throne as a dining area. The Khwabgah (bedroom) of Shah Jahan had been enclosed by ugly wadded cloth screens and given a modern timber roof; it was functioning as a garrison chapel ('from its traditions about as unsuitable a place for Christian worship as could be selected'). Cole could only thunder against the ill effects of military occupation on historical monuments; he could do nothing about it.[42]

[40] Cole (1882): 20. Another person who had raised this issue was James Fergusson.

[41] Ibid.: vii.

[42] The fact that sections of these forts continue to be occupied by the army even today (although the Indian army has now withdrawn from Delhi's Red Fort) shows just how premature—or perhaps ahead of their time—Cole's demands were. It may be noted that Cole was not against the use of historical monuments

A lasting testimony to Cole's career was the production of a series of large folio volumes illustrating Indian architecture. Titled *Preservation of National Monuments in India*, these were published by order of the governor general in council for the office of the curator of ancient monuments in India. The beautiful drawings and photographs were accompanied by minimal text. Ironically, Cole's interest in producing expensive volumes illustrating Indian architecture was one of the very things that landed him in official disfavour. It was felt he seemed to be spending more time and money illustrating rather than conserving monuments—which was supposed to be his primary duty. He also seemed to frequently be side-tracked into projects that were even further from his official brief, such as designing telegraph and railway offices in Ajmer, and suggesting a design for new shops around the enclosure of the Fatehpuri Masjid in Delhi. Cole's justification for the latter intervention was that the new shops would increase the revenues of the mosque, and these could in turn be used for its better maintenance.

The outspoken curator of ancient monuments swiftly got enmeshed in conflicts all around—with archaeologists, provincial governments, and the Government of India. Cole's conflict with archaeologists was primarily one between him and James Burgess. Both shared a keen interest in Indian architecture. However, they were at loggerheads over questions relating to who was encroaching on whose turf. Burgess complained to the Government of India about Cole's interference with the activities of the archaeological surveys of western and southern India, his unnecessary interest in conserving temples being managed by private trusts (such as those at Srirangam), and his habit of directly communicating with local governments.[43] The Government of India frequently admonished Cole for such misdemeanours.[44]

---

for *civil* purposes per se; his main concern was that the structure or appearance of the monuments should not be damaged.

[43] Letter No. 10, dated Amaravati, 20 January 1882, from James Burgess to the Officiating Secretary to the Government of India, Home Proceedings/Archaeology and the Conservation of Ancient Monuments, February 1882, No. 9, Part A, NAI.

[44] See, e.g., Letter No. 24, dated Fort William, 25 February, 1882, from A. Mackenzie, Officiating Secretary to the Government of India to the Curator of

Cole was neither moved nor intimidated by such admonishment. He continued to insist that there was a difference between survey for archaeological research and survey for conservation, and that Burgess's drawings were not good enough for the latter purpose. As for offering advice, 'It appears to be as much my duty to advise the Madras Government about the means of preserving the temples at Srirangam, endowed by the State for Native use, as it is to advise the Agent to the Governor General in Central India about the Sanchi Topes, which belong to the Begum of Bhopal, or as it is to advise the Agent to the Governor General in Rajputana about the temples at Mount Abu used by the Jains. . . .'[45] Apart from his problematic relationship with the Archaeological Surveys of Western and Southern India, Cole also ran into trouble with the governments of Madras and Bengal. Cole wanted each and every case involving the removal of objects or conservation to be submitted to him. At his own initiative, he had passed on to local governments a series of directions on the matter. Unfortunately, local governments found the tone of these directions dictatorial and took offence.[46]

In three cases Cole became involved in prolonged debate and dispute with various agencies, and was unable to have his way. These were the issues of the Amaravati sculptures, the restoration of the Mahabodhi temple at Bodh Gaya, and the restoration of Sher Shah's tomb at Sasaram. Tensions between Cole and Burgess assumed the form of a blatant and bitter conflict over the Amaravati sculptures.[47] Apart from a dispute over their jurisdiction, this also became a trial of strength over

---

Ancient Monuments in India, Home Proceedings/Archaeology and the Conservation of Ancient Monuments, February 1882, No. 18, Part A, NAI.

[45] Letter dated Madras, 27 March 1882 from Captain Cole to the Officiating Secretary to the Government of India, Home Proceedings/Archaeology and the Conservation of Ancient Monuments, April 1882, No. 22, Part A, NAI.

[46] See, e.g., Letter No. 46T. dated Darjeeling, 30 June 1883, from Col. S.T. Trevor, Officiating Secretary to the Government of Bengal, PWD to the Secretary to the Government of India, Home/Archaeology and the Conservation of Ancient Monuments, August 1883, No. 10, Part A, NAI. The tone of Cole's instructions/suggestions was described by S.C. Bayley as 'equal, if not superior, to that of His Excellency the Viceroy in Council'. Home/Archaeology and the Conservation of Ancient Monuments, December 1883, Nos. 3–6, Part A, Notes on file, NAI.

[47] For details, see Chapter 8.

the *in situ* preservation of historical remains. According to Cole, archaeologists were not the best persons to look to for advice on this question. 'The question really is how is a decision to be arrived at about what is to be kept *in situ*. . . . Archaeological officers go about searching for things to enrich museums. Neither General Cunningham nor Dr Burgess care to keep any thing *in situ*. General Cunningham, so far back as 1843, wanted to remove the Sanchi Gates to England, and has ever since been active in damaging buildings and monuments by the extraction of their most valuable parts . . .'[48] Cole argued persistently for *in situ* preservation, while Burgess argued in favour of removing the best pieces of the Amaravati sculptures to Madras. Ultimately, Burgess won.

The restoration of the temple at Bodh Gaya and Sher Shah's tomb at Sasaram had begun under Beglar's supervision before Cole took over as curator. Cole thought the restoration work in both places shoddy and tantamount to introducing modern elements into old structures.[49] He expressed this opinion in no uncertain terms to the local government. The Government of Bengal complained to the Government of India about Cole's constant interference and criticism, and Cole was directed even more strongly than before to recognize and remain within the limits of his position and role.[50]

Apart from the publication of a number of works illustrating Indian art and architecture, what was the tangible outcome of Cole's three-year term as curator of ancient monuments? Judging from the information provided by Cole himself, there seems to have been an increase in conservation activity and also a greater degree of general supervision and care invested in the process during his tenure. But, as Cole bitterly observed, he was just on the threshold of achieving results. He had been able to visit only a small proportion of the important monuments on his list, had surveyed an even smaller proportion, and not one

[48] Letter dated 10 June 1883, from H.H. Cole to Sir Stewart Bayley, Home/Public, December 1883, Nos. 3–6, Part A, NAI. Also see Cole's note on this file.

[49] See Home/Archaeology and the Conservation of Ancient Monuments, August 1883, Nos. 10–27, Part A, NAI.

[50] Letter No. 124, dated Simla, 18 August 1883, from A. Mackenzie, Secretary to the Government of India to the Curator of Ancient Monuments in India, Home/Archaeology and the Conservation of Ancient Monuments, August 1883, No. 27, Part A, NAI.

monument in India had seen conservation work completed according to his specific recommendations.[51] Even as Cole protested that he had simply offered advice and just wanted to be consulted about conservation measures, and even as he urged that central direction was crucial to these endeavours, the post of Curator of Ancient Monuments was allowed to lapse in January 1884. From all points of view, including that of Cole himself, his tenure as curator seemed a dismal failure.[52]

In retrospect, this apparent failure seems to have been the result of ideas too radical for his time, a desire to accomplish too much too soon, an impatience with bureaucratic procedure, and an inability to get along with people. And yet Cole's tenure as curator was not inconsequential. It marked the first attempt by the colonial state to coordinate conservation work all over India. For the first time, conservation activity in different parts of India was assessed, monitored, and reported on. Professional and sensitive advice regarding such work was made available to the provincial governments of British India as well as to the Indian princely states. For the first time, Indian monuments had a committed and spirited spokesperson who passionately advocated the *in situ* principle and did not hesitate to delineate the damage inflicted on these monuments as a consequence of British rule. Although Cole did not make a major impact on actual conservation projects, he did successfully highlight the enormous amount that needed to be done.

With the abolition of the post of curator of ancient monuments, responsibility for conservation devolved once again on local governments, who were to solicit the advice of Archaeological Survey officers

[51] Letter No. 262 dated 22 September 1883, from Major Cole to the Secretary to the Government of India, Home/Archaeology and the Conservation of Ancient Monuments, December 1883, No. 4, Part A, NAI.

[52] A few years later, Cole was apparently lobbying to succeed Cunningham as director general of the Archaeological Survey. Cunningham vetoed his candidature, using uncharacteristically strong language. Cunningham declared that Cole had no credentials as an archaeologist, and that he was unreasonable and tactless in dealing with people. 'No doubt he has had very good opportunities of seeing the finest remains of Indian architecture. But a man is not to be judged by the opportunities which he has had of becoming fit, but by the use which he has made of these opportunities. A man may travel from the Hamalaya [*sic*] Mountains to Cape Comorin and return no wiser than when he set out. Such I believe to be Major Cole's case.' Home/Archaeology, July 1885, Nos. 5–9, Part A, NAI.

whenever required. Within the next few years, imperial grants for conservation work were drastically reduced.[53]

In situ Preservation versus the Removal of Antiquities to Museums

Over the years, the Asiatic Society had become the repository of a large number of antiquities gifted to it by its members. This led to the establishment of the Society's museum in 1814, the first museum in India. The holdings of its museum eventually became so large that the society did not have the resources to manage or maintain them. In 1866 the society and its museum parted ways, its collection becoming for all practical purposes the property of government, under the management of the trustees of the newly designated Indian Museum in Calcutta. The archaeological objects in the Asiatic Society's museum collection were formally transferred to the Indian Museum in 1876. This was now developed as the showcase of the splendour of the British Indian empire.[54]

At the same time, provincial and local museums had sprouted all over. In the 1840s steps were taken to set up museums in Madras and Bombay. The establishment of a museum in Madras was mooted by the Madras Literary Society and subsequently approved by the Court of Directors; the Madras Government Museum (also known as the Central Museum) was founded in 1851. The Lahore Museum was established in 1864 and the Victoria and Albert Museum in Bombay

[53] This went hand in hand with the reduction of the budget of the Archaeological Survey Department. The cuts were made in 1885, when local governments were informed that no grants-in-aid from imperial revenues would be made towards the conservation of ancient monuments during the current year. This included the withdrawal of grants already made. (Home /Archaeology and the Conservation of Ancient Monuments, July 1885, No. 12 and No. 73, OIOC.) In July 1885 the Government of India informed the Bombay government that the grant of Rs 7,500 that it had sanctioned earlier in the year for conservation work in the province was being withdrawn due to financial exigencies. Letter No. 119, dated Simla, 7 July 1885, from A. Mackenzie, Secretary to the Government of India to the Government of Bombay; copy in Mysore Residency File No. 118, 1885, No. 34, NAI.

[54] See Guha-Thakurta (1997).

in 1871. Local museums mushroomed in the second half of the nineteenth century—at Lucknow and Nagpur (1863), Mathura (1875), Raipur (1876), and Srinagar (1886). This 'museum movement' picked up momentum after the celebration of the jubilee of Queeen Victoria in 1887. The museums that emerged in the ensuing years included those at Jaipur, Udaipur, Rajkot, and Vijayawada. The impetus intensified in the early twentieth century, during the viceroyalty of Curzon and the director generalship of the Archaeological Survey by John Marshall.[55]

The continuing discovery of ancient sites and artefacts and the growth of imperial, provincial and local museums raised questions about their custody, removal, and display. While these questions had been in the air for some time, a systematic debate on them was set off in the 1880s by the trustees of the Indian Museum. Not unexpectedly, there was considerable difference of opinion among scholars, officials and institutions on these matters. A Government of India Resolution of 1882, while endorsing the importance of the *in situ* principle, supported the central museum (i.e. the Indian Museum in Calcutta) as the prime claimant to antiquities that had to be removed from their original place. After a round of soliciting opinions and reactions, the Resolution of 1883, in trying to accommodate the interests of provincial and local museums, left the decision as to the place of deposit of antiquities in the hands of local governments and administrations.

Cunningham's views on these issues are fairly clear. Through most of his career, he was not a particularly ardent supporter of the *in situ* principle. As far as the most appropriate place for the deposit of antiquities was concerned, he thought the most important ones should be housed in the Indian Museum in Calcutta, where they would be both safe and accessible. He argued that there was a great disadvantage in having too many museums, as objects of interest tended to get dismembered and scattered all over the country. Even in the Agra, Delhi, and Lahore museums, most of the descriptions of the items on display were written on loose slips of paper or cards which tended to get interchanged. A competent curator could set things right, but the funds for this were lacking:

[55] Sivaramamurti and Roy (1953).

This being the case, I think it very undesirable that any valuable articles should be kept in local museums where they are generally unappreciated, and are constantly exposed to the risk of theft, partly from the keeper's ignorance of their value and partly from the want of means to maintaining an efficient safeguard over them.

On the question of local museums, I hold a very strong opinion that they are worse than useless; in fact that they are positively mischievous, unless an intelligent, zealous and permanent Curator can be secured who will take the trouble to keep an accurate list of all the articles in the museum, and see that the numbers or names are not changed every time that the articles are dusted. During the present year, I have visited the local museums at Agra, Delhi, and Lahore. Not one of them has the objects numbered, or any list of its collection.[56]

Under the circumstances, it was better for small museums to surrender their most valuable artefacts to the larger one. To satisfy the aspirations of local museums, Cunningham suggested that electrotypes or plaster casts substitute the originals at the cost of the central museum.

Cunningham had no qualms about sending Indian antiquities out of the country. For instance, he thought that the sculptures discovered in the Yusufzai district should be safely housed in London, while good casts could be made for the Calcutta and Lahore museums.[57] While he was all for sending these (and other choice) sculptures to London, specifically to the proposed India Office Museum, he was quite vehement in his views regarding the British Museum which, he felt, did not give sufficient importance to Indian antiquities: 'I must enter a strong protest against any Indian sculptures being sent to the *British Museum*, even temporarily, as they would no doubt share the same fate as their predecessors, and be concealed in the vaults of the Museum, where some years ago I discovered a number of Indian sculptures as well as seven Indian inscriptions.'[58] Ultimately, however, though Cunningham

[56] Letter No. 106, dated Simla, 11 August 1871, from Cunningham to E.C. Bayley, Secretary to the Government of India, Home/Public, September 16, 1871, No. 94, Part A, OIOC.

[57] Letter No. 89, dated Simla, 12 August 1875, from Cunningham to the Officiating Secretary to the Government of India, Home Proceedings/ Public, September 1875, No. 197, Part A, OIOC.

[58] Ibid. Ironically, many of the most valuable antiquities from Cunningham's personal collection eventually found their way into the British Museum.

remained a strong supporter of the claims of large museums such as the Indian Museum, there was a problem. The trustees of the Indian Museum were worried that their archaeological collection was not growing in the way it had with the Asiatic Society. It appeared to them that the establishment and subsequent activities of the Archaeological Survey and the mushrooming of small museums must be responsible for this situation. Further, the reports produced by the survey rarely specified where the objects identified or discovered by its officers had been deposited: they pointed out that a very small proportion of the discovered artefacts were finding their way to the Indian Museum. Where, they asked, were the rest going?[59] In his response to this complaint Cunningham detailed the dispersal of objects discovered by his officers—some had been left in their original place, others sent to various local museums, or to provincial museums such as the Lahore Museum, and to the Indian Museum in Calcutta. His list was a long one but it did not account for all the innumerable artefacts that been discovered over the decade or so since the survey had been in existence.

The Government of India supported the primacy of the claims of the Indian Museum, yet it also recognized the legitimacy of the claims of provincial and local museums. Thus, the debate on the place of deposit of antiquities initiated by the very pertinent inquiries made by the trustees of the Indian Museum was ultimately inconclusive. And, regardless of official pronouncements and degree of compliance with government directives, the Indian Museum remained one of many rival claimants to Indian antiquities, many of which ended up in private hands or in museums in India and abroad.

Cunningham and Conservation

Despite the fact that conservation did not fall within the explicit purview of the Archaeological Survey of India and that southern and much of western India lay outside its jurisdiction, by virtue of Cunningham's stature and official position as director general he was often called upon to give his opinion or advice regarding conservation

[59] Letter No. 49, dated 23 August 1882, from Major J. Waterhouse, Officiating Honorary Secretary to the Trustees, Indian Museum to the Secretary to the Government of India, Home Proceedings/Archaeology and the Conservation of Ancient Monuments, 1882, Part A, No. 3, NAI.

matters. In 1874 the Government of India asked him to make some general suggestions on the matter of the preservation of ancient monuments. Cunningham strongly urged that all ancient buildings not actually in use as places of worship be placed under the sole charge of the chief civil authority of the district in which they were situated, and that this officer be held responsible for their preservation. He pointed out that, in old stone buildings, the main causes of ruin were the fracture of beams and the splitting of pillars under pressure. In such instances (and he cited the case of the Jaina temple in the Gwalior fort, where he had effected such repairs in 1844) upright stones or square masonry pillars should be set up in place of missing or broken pillars, and some sort of support provided where beams were broken. As for brick buildings, the main reason for their decay was the gradual disintegration of bricks near the bottom of the wall 'from the action of the saltpetre, and the pernicious neglect of the Natives, whether Hindu or Muhammadan.' The remedy for this was the replacement of the lower portions of the outer faces of the walls with sound bricks set in mud plaster.[60]

In some more specific recommendations, Cunningham displayed surprisingly little regard for aesthetic damage; in others, he was not particularly bothered about removing major archaeological remains from their location on the grounds of the requirements of safety and accessibility. Fortunately, in several cases his suggestions were considered inappropriate and not implemented.

In 1872 Cunningham was asked by the government to give his opinion regarding repairs to buildings in the Agra Fort.[61] His suggestion was that the roof and ceiling of the Diwan-i-Khas, which was suffering damage due to damp, should be replaced by a corrugated tin roof.

[60] Letter No. 208, dated Bharhut, 10 December 1874, from Cunningham to the Officiating Secretary to the Government of India, Home Proceedings/Public, February 1875, No. 51, Part A, OIOC.

[61] Letter No. 131, dated Simla, 24 September, 1872, from Cunningham to H.L. Dampier, Officiating Secretary to the Government of India. Also, Letter No. 4121, dated Simla, 19 October 1972, from H. Wellesley, Officiating Under Secretary to the Government of India to C.A. Elliot, Secretary to the Government of the North West Provinces, Home Proceedings/Public, October 1872, Nos. 361 and 362, Part A, OIOC.

This, he suggested would be the lightest and cheapest material. As for the Jahangir Mahal, he suggested partial restoration of the structure: complete restoration would be too expensive. The front entrance and the two interior halls could be restored. Other parts of the building not utterly in ruins could be repaired to prevent their collapse. The suggestion about redoing the roof of the Diwan-i-Khas with corrugated tin sheets, so utterly out of tune with the rest of the structure, made even government bureaucrats wince.

In 1874 the Government of India was seriously considering a proposal to peel the Ajanta frescoes off the cave walls. The idea had come from G.W. Terry, superintendent of the Sir Jamsetjee Jeejebhoy School of Art in Bombay, who suggested that the frescoes could be removed from the cave walls by a special peeling-off method. They could thereafter be removed from Ajanta—where they could neither be properly seen nor appreciated—to the safe custody of the nizam of Hyderabad, or the Bombay or Imperial museums, or, even better, the India Museum in London, 'where all the antiquarian and artistic world could see them.'[62] Of course, the procedure was not free of risk.

The Government of India referred the matter to Cunningham, who expressed himself wholeheartedly in support of Terry's proposal:

> In reply to your letter . . . regarding the proposal made by Mr G.W. Terry, of the Bombay School of Art for the removal of the frescoes in the Ajunta Caves, I have the honour to state that, in my opinion, their removal as proposed appears to offer by far the best chance for the preservation of these ancient paintings. The method proposed by Mr Terry is similar to that which has been successfully employed in splitting sheets of paper, and I see no reason to doubt that it would generally be successful.
>
> In their present position, the Ajunta frescoes are accessible only to a few, and to those few are only dimly visible. It seems to me, therefore, an object of very great importance that they should be removed to some place of more easy access and where they will be better cared for. At present many of them must be liable to injury from the percolation of moisture through fissures in the rock. This source of danger will be entirely got rid of by their removal.

[62] Letter No. 247, dated Bombay, 5 December 1873, from G.W. Terry to F.S. Chapman, Chief Secretary to the Government of Bombay, Home Proceedings/ Public, May 1874, Nos. 344–6, Part A, OIOC.

> By beginning with the smaller frescoes the workmen would gradually gain experience, which would enable them to decide whether the removal of the larger frescoes would be attended with any risk. If the risk be not great I would strongly advocate their removal as proposed by Mr Terry, as I look upon their ruin or destruction as quite certain, if they remain in their present position . . .[63]

Luckily, Cunningham's advice was not ultimately accepted. The procedure in question was risky and could have led to the damage and even destruction of the priceless Ajanta frescoes.

Proposals for rebuilding Aurangzeb's Adhai-din-ka-Jhompra in Ajmer were referred by the government to Cunningham in 1877 and 1878.[64] In response to the question of whether mortar should be used when rebuilding the structure, his answer was no, it would not look good. Cunningham also spoke against the proposal to build new arches of white marble, immediately under the old ones, for their support. He suggested that the old arches be simply rebuilt, like the great arch of the Qutb Masjid in Delhi. Cunningham said Beglar had visited Ajmer to photograph the monument and had reported that, as in the case with some of the Qutb inscriptions, mistakes had been made in restoring the broken inscriptions at the Ajmer masjid too. In 1878 the political agent of Rajputana sent Cunningham two alternative plans and estimates for renovating the masjid. One involved demolishing the gateway to the mosque. Cunningham strongly rejected this proposal, pointing out that the gateway was integral to the masjid; it should be restored, not removed.

The Restoration of the Bodh Gaya Temple

The great Buddhist temple at Bodh Gaya, the place of the Buddha's enlightenment, had attracted the attention of scholars since the late eighteenth century. One of the earliest Western notices of the place

[63] Letter No. 169, dated Simla, October 1874, from Cunningham to A.C. Lyall, Secretary to the Government of India, Home Proceedings/Public, November 1874, No. 40, Part A, OIOC.

[64] Letter No. 132, dated Simla, 2 October 1877, from Cunningham to the Officiating Secretary to the Government of India; Letter No. 208, dated Calcutta, 8 January 1878, from Cunningham to the Officiating Secretary to the Government of India, Home/Public, April 1878, Nos. 28–31, Part A, OIOC.

was Charles Wilkins' translation of a temple inscription.[65] Copies of the inscriptions at Bodh Gaya appeared from time to time in the pages of the *Journal of the Asiatic Society of Bengal.* The place was visited by Francis Buchanan in 1809, and its sculptures described many years later by Markham Kittoe.

Cunningham visited Bodh Gaya in 1861 and recommended immediate excavation of the area around the temple. The job was assigned to Major Mead, but no report of the proceedings or discoveries was ever published by him. Luckily, Mead described his activities at the site in a letter to Cunningham.[66] A trench dug in front of the brick archway attributed to Amarasimha had revealed a large quantity of masonry and many carved model stupas.[67] Mead enlarged the trench to a width of about 20 ft to trace the walls. These turned out to be the lower sections of four small single-cell shrines. In one of the shrines he found a colossal Buddha with an inscribed pedestal, with its head broken off. There was also a bronze bell and part of a bronze ornament. A trench dug along the southern face of the temple exposed the southern basement of the temple, made of plaster. Here, Mead discovered the corroded remains of two or three small bronze trumpets. About 28 ft from the south-west corner of the temple, this trench revealed a broken pillar and a Buddhist railing. Mead took the internal western trench along the line of this railing and found the latter to be *in situ* but broken in the upper levels, except for two carved pillars that were intact. He found traces of the same railing on the northern and southern sides of the temple.

The arches of the Bodh Gaya temple soon became a matter of discussion and dispute among scholars. Ranged on one side were Rajendralala Mitra and Cunningham, who argued that the arches in the

[65] Wilkins (1788).

[66] Letter No. 2077, dated 3 November 1863; extracts quoted in Cunningham (1873a): 87–8 and Mitra (1878): 62–3.

[67] Mead reported that hundreds of such stupas were found in the course of the excavations. A propos of which Cunningham remarked that not one of these 'hundreds' were now visible at the site. 'I suppose they have been carried off to Gaya, and are now doing duty as lingams, or symbols of Mhâdeva [*sic*]. No conversion is required, as the people accept one of these votive stupas of the Buddhists as a ready-made lingam.' Mead, cited in Cunningham (1873a): 87.

temple represented an early, pre-seventh-century phase in its construction and that this was proof that the ancient Hindus knew the use of the arch.[68] The most vociferous representative of the other side was James Fergusson, who argued that the Bodh Gaya arches were much later accretions, and that the absence of the arch was one of the chief defects of Hindu architecture.

In January 1877 three Burmese gentlemen arrived in Bodh Gaya. They had been sent by the king of Burma to repair the Mahabodhi temple. Obtaining permission from the *mahant* of the temple, they zealously got to work. It was not till months later, in mid 1877, that the attention of the government was directed towards the goings-on at Bodh Gaya. The Bengal government asked Rajendralala Mitra if he could visit the site and report on what was going on.

Mitra proceeded to Bodh Gaya and spent some three weeks there in September-October 1877. During this time he collected a large amount of information on the site and the temple, had a number of sketches made and photographs taken. This material ultimately found its way into his book on Bodh Gaya, published in the following year under the orders of the Government of Bengal. As to what the 'Burmese gentlemen' had been up to, Mitra's report was grim:

> The Burmese gentlemen are doubtless very pious and enthusiastic in the cause of their religion, but they are working on no systematic or traditional plan. They are ignorant of the true history of their faith and perfectly innocent of all knowledge of architecture and the requirements of archaeology and history and the mischief they have done by their misdirected zeal has been serious. The demolitions and excavations already completed by them have swept away most of the old land-marks, and

[68] According to Mitra (1878: 110), the arches and the temple were of roughly the same period; the arches had been inserted some time after the completion of the temple. It was difficult to say when exactly this was done, but the arches were definitely in place long before Xuan Zang visited Bodh Gaya in the seventh century. *Mahâbodhi*, published in 1892, contains Cunningham's last statement on this contentious point. Here (pp. 85–6), although he reiterates his view that the voussoir arch was known (although sparingly used) by the ancient Indians, he gives evidence to suggest that the arches and vaults of the Mahabodhi temple were not part of the original construction but were added later to give support to the older walls. He does not indicate when he thought these additions might have been made.

nothing of ancient times can now be traced on the area they have worked on.[69]

The damage was extensive. The Burmese gentlemen had cleared away a large area around the shrine, built an enclosing wall, rebuilt the retaining walls of the temple's terrace, and re-plastered the interior. The Ashokan rail and pavement had been demolished and the outer courtyard and its antiquities had been swept away. Of the large number of votive stupas, images, and other objects that had been uncovered, some had been built into the new enclosing wall while others lay scattered about. The inner ornamentation of the spire had been plastered over. What made it worse was that there was no documentation indicating what the temple had looked like before all this was done. The Government of Bengal politely requested the Burmese to pack up and leave and took on the task of repairing the Bodh Gaya temple itself.

This task was assigned to C.A. Mills, district engineer, who was to work in consultation with the collector of Gaya and Rajendralala Mitra. Mill's cost estimate for the work, including the restoration of the stucco sculptures plus redoing the whole outer casing of the temple, was Rs 20,000–25,000. There was uncertainty whether such a large expense should be borne by the Bengal or the Imperial government. The Bengal government also contemplated asking the king of Burma to contribute something to the repairs.[70]

The matter was referred to the director general of the Archaeological Survey. Cunningham approved the reconstruction of the outer casing of the temple with bricks laid with mortar, but advised against repair of the statues as this would bring the cost down by about Rs 5000.[71] He also recommended that the cost of repairs be borne entirely by the Government of India. The king of Burma could be asked to contribute towards the new buildings—including residences for Buddhist priests—that might be constructed at the place. He also urged that the new buildings be quite detached from the objects of

[69] Letter dated Bakipur, 31 October 1877, from Rajendralala Mitra to the Secretary to the Government of Bengal, Home/Public, March 1878, Nos. 229 and 230, Part A, OIOC.

[70] Home/Public, November 1878, No. 228, Part A, NAI.

[71] Ibid.

worship to prevent disputes between Hindus and Buddhists.[72] The Government of India accepted Cunningham's suggestions, except that it passed responsibility for defraying the costs of repair to the Bengal government. This is the background to what went on to become a highly contentious issue.

Cunningham visited Bodh Gaya again in 1879 in order to assess the condition of the temple.[73] Telltale signs of the haphazard activities of the three Burmese were everywhere. A number of votive stupas (including those lately restored by Beglar) had been thrown down in the course of clearing. Luckily the Burmese had not dug deep enough to expose or affect the earlier structural phases of the temple. Cunningham reported to the Bengal government that the temple was in a ruinous condition and required urgent repair to prevent its total destruction.

In 1880 Sir Ashley Eden, lieutenant governor of Bengal, appointed Beglar to supervise the repair of the Bodh Gaya temple. Beglar began work in 1880 and his activities at the site uncovered the complex early history of the temple. The accumulated debris turned the interior of the temple every year into a small tank by encouraging the accumulation of rain water. This clearance, and the re-laying of the interior pavement (which had become very uneven) revealed various alterations and additions to the temple over the centuries. Among the dramatic discoveries were the vestiges of an older Ashokan temple, fragments of railings, and the old vajrasana throne. Below the vajrasana was discovered a ball of stiff clay which, on being broken, revealed a collection of relics. Several structures were uncovered inside and outside the courtyard, including the enclosure of a large monastery to the north of the temple. Votive stupas and sculptures of different ages and styles were found in profusion.[74]

At an early stage of these operations a small stone model of the

[72] These disputes began in the last decade of the nineteenth century, but the potential of future conflict was evidently recognized by Cunningham in 1879.

[73] The following details are given in Cunningham (1892a).

[74] Cunningham's *Mahâbodhi* gave a detailed account of the results of Beglar's operations. It gave a comprehensive account of the site—the different phases in the history of the temple, the other structures, the sculptures and the inscriptions. It also included detailed references to the descriptions and notices of the Mahabodhi temple in the accounts of the Chinese pilgrims, especially Xuan Zang. The book included a large number of photographs and several plan drawings.

12. The Bodh Gaya temple before restoration.
Courtesy: British Library

Mahabodhi temple was discovered among the ruins. This gave a good idea of what the structure had looked like in medieval times. Due to the discovery of this model, repair soon assumed the form of restoration and this restoration brought Beglar into the eye of a storm. The curator of ancient monuments, H.H. Cole, was initially positive in his assessment of the restoration work, but subsequently, as his relationship with the Bengal government soured, he became extremely critical. Much more vitriolic was James Fergusson, who described the restoration work as unnecessary, expensive, and hideous.[75] These strong reactions were reflections of other differences—the conflicts between various individuals, and serious disagreements over the issue of repair and restoration.

The fourth chapter of Fergusson's *Archaeology in India with Especial Reference to the Works of Babu Rajendralala Mitra* contains strong condemnation of the repair of the Bodh Gaya temple and questions the need for repair as well as the credentials of the restorers: 'A building which has stood, at all events, for 500 years, without showing any symptoms of cracks, or shakes, that would in the least endanger its stability, might well have waited a year or two, till some architect, or some other qualified person, could be procured from England, or elsewhere, to make careful drawings of the building and of its details before undertaking its restoration.'[76] Fergusson alleged that the temple had been practically rebuilt and almost all its ancient features obliterated.

Beglar had sought Fergusson's advice regarding the restoration work he proposed to commence at Bodh Gaya. According to Fergusson, his reply had been something like this: 'For heaven's sake, don't! Fill up all the cranks [*sic*] with cement, cover the roof with either asphalte or cement to prevent infiltration. If buttresses or arches are necessary to maintain the fabric, build them with modern bricks, and in modern forms, so that they may not possibly be mistaken for ancient work. In short, do anything that may be necessary to maintain the fabric; but restore nothing, and, above all, destroy no feature, however insignificant it may appear; you cannot know of what value it may be

[75] Fergusson (1884): 78–9.
[76] Ibid.

eventually.'[77] To Fergusson's annoyance, Beglar chose to do the exact opposite. The southern basement of the temple, which on Major Mead's authority was 'singularly perfect and handsome', and made of plaster, had been rebuilt in brick according to Beglar's own design. The western face, which Cunningham had described as being in very bad shape, would according to Fergusson have stood for at least a hundred years if it had been left alone. Beglar's proposal for roofing over the porch on the east face was utterly unlike what the original must have been. The temple of Tara Devi, which required no repairs whatsoever, was now 'as hideous as a modern restorer could require.'[78]

Fergusson went on to observe that the Rs 80, 000 or so that had been spent on this restoration was a colossal waste. The sum would have sufficed to effect necessary repairs to the building. Even now, if Cunningham had enough photographs to record the different stages of the renovation, and would employ a competent architect to take measurements and make drawings of what remained, some of the damage might be compensated. If Cunningham succeeded in publishing a competent monograph on the temple, 'it would go far to atone for his destruction of the building . . .'[79] But although a certain amount of prosaic information concerning the history of Buddhism and Central Indian architecture might still be extracted from the structure, the poetry and beauty of the temple had been destroyed forever.

In assessing the debate over the restoration of the Bodh Gaya temple, the two crucial questions concern the state of the temple prior to commencement of the restoration work, and whether what was done amounted to renovation rather than restoration. Cunningham and Fergusson gave two very different answers to the first question. But Cunningham had seen the temple recently, while Fergusson's pronouncements on its condition were based on what he had seen decades previously, when he was in the indigo business between 1835 and 1842, and based on photographs he had taken at that time. Rajendralala Mitra had commented on the poor condition of the structure when he saw it in 1871. Photographs taken in the 1880s indicate that the temple was indeed in a very dilapidated state.

[77] Ibid.: 78.
[78] Ibid.
[79] Ibid.: 79, n.

13. The Bodh Gaya temple today.
Courtesy: Archaeological Survey of India

As for the quality of the restoration work, apart from Fergusson's opinion there are the assessments of Burgess and H.H. Cole. Burgess was very critical of Beglar's work at Bodh Gaya—'I can only express the hope that no other building in Bengal will be treated so ignorantly.'[80] He was not quite the impartial commentator in this particular context, but the sharpness of his reaction was also no doubt due to the fact that, as an architectural scholar, his sensitivity to the issue was greater than that of archaeologists.

Cole's testimony on this issue is contradictory. He visited Bodh Gaya in March 1882. Restoration work had started before the establishment of his office, so he had not seen the original state of the temple and could only go by the illustrations in Fergusson's *History of Indian and Eastern Architecture* and Mitra's book on Bodh Gaya.

> Looking, however, to the character of the masonry, which I examined in company with Mr Beglar, and which is merely a case of mud and brick, and considering that the original was nothing but plaster, I do not see how the security of the building could have been provided for in any other way than that carried out under Mr Beglar. The careful renewal of the exterior plaster envelope on the old architectural lines seems to be the only manner of successfully conserving such a building; and although the cost has been considerable, the great historical value and exceptional importance of this relic of Buddhism, in my opinion, fully justify a large outlay.[81]

Cole added that too much seemed to have been done in the votive structures surrounding the temple, but he hesitated to criticize this considering his meagre knowledge of the prior condition of these monuments.

About a year later, however, Cole was singing a completely different tune: 'The ancient temple at Buddha Gaya, which has been restored at great cost, now presents the appearance of a modern structure—a result which is certainly to be regretted, and possibly to have been

[80] Letter No. 25, dated Ahmedabad, 23 January 1886, from Burgess to the Secretary to the Government of Bengal, PWD, Home/Archaeology and the Conservation of Ancient Monuments, April 1886, No. 4, Part A, OIOC.

[81] Letter No. 276, dated 23 June 1882, from Cole to the Secretary to the Government of Bengal, Home/Archaeology and the Conservation of Ancient Monuments, August 1883, No. 12, Part A, NAI.

avoided.'[82] Part of the reasons for this *volte face* may be that he had got deeply embroiled in a conflict with the Bengal government. At the same time, as one who had consistently recommended careful and tasteful repair, the restoration of the Bodh Gaya temple must have hurt Cole's sensibilities.[83]

Cunningham was firm in his defence of Beglar's work. He stated that in the six centuries or so subsequent to the Muslim conquest, the Bodh Gaya temple had lain deserted and become more and more dilapidated. Most of the stucco facing had disappeared and many of the bricks had caved in, especially on the west face. Nevertheless, enough remained of the mouldings and niches on the other faces to enable the restorer to faithfully reproduce the original. The front pavilion of the temple, Cunningham continued, had been almost a complete ruin, and he had advised that the ruined walls should be plastered with cement in order to prevent further decay. This was begun, but shortly thereafter a small stone model of the temple discovered in the ruins provided evidence of the design of the shrine as it existed in medieval times. It was on the basis of this model and the extant parts of the façade that Beglar designed the front pavilion and the four corner pavilions: 'This additional work has been much criticized, and I have been roundly abused for it in company with Mr Beglar, although I had nothing whatever to say to it. At the same time, I must confess that, since I have seen it, I think his design of the front Pavilion is a very successful completion of the entrance in the style and spirit of the original work as shown in the model. It is of course a *Restoration*, which as it was based on the double authority of existing remains and an ancient model I consider as legitimate and justifiable.'[84]

The argument over the Bodh Gaya restoration work had yet

[82] Letter No. 47, dated Simla 26th April 1883, from Cole to the Secretary to the Government of Bengal, PWD, Home/Archaeology and the Conservation of Ancient Monuments, August 1883, No. 11, Part A, NAI.

[83] Strangely, Cole did not hold Beglar personally responsible for the want of taste displayed in the restoration work at Bodh Gaya and Sher Shah's tomb, as he thought that in the former case, he was simply following instructions and in the latter case the work was taken out of his hands altogether. In fact, he urged the Bengal Government to retain Beglar's services and place his work on a basis of permanency. Ibid.

[84] Cunningham (1892a): ix.

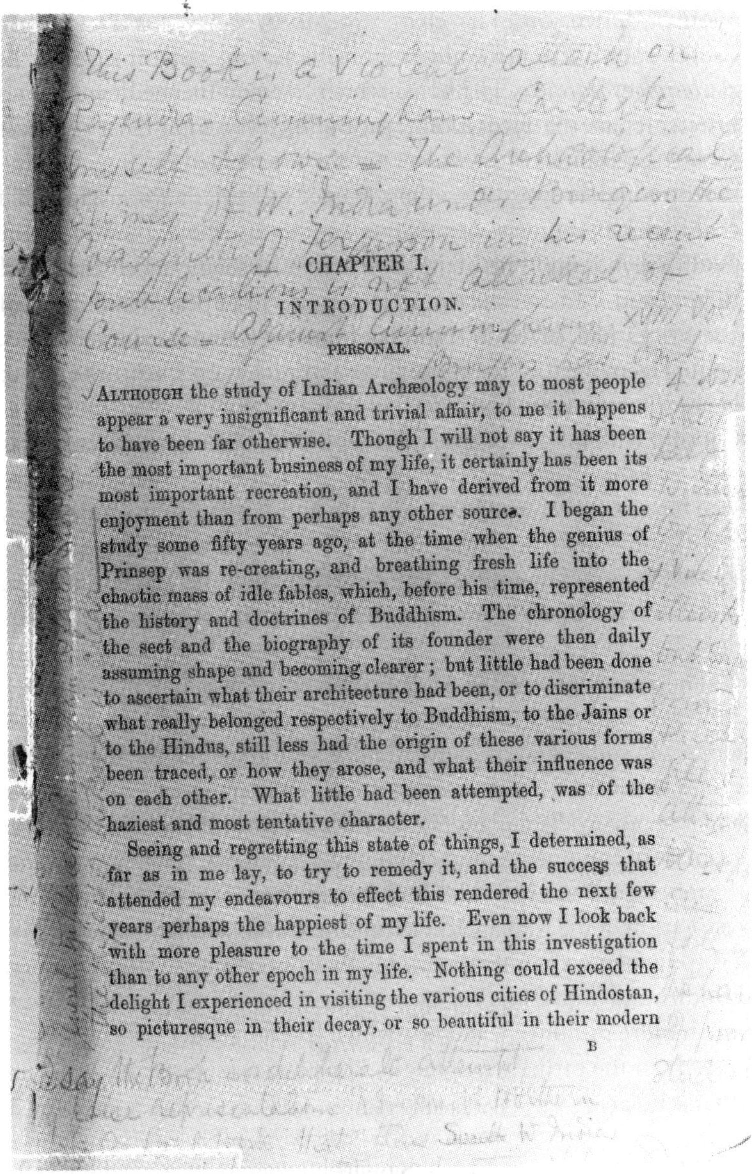

CHAPTER I.

INTRODUCTION.

PERSONAL.

Although the study of Indian Archæology may to most people appear a very insignificant and trivial affair, to me it happens to have been far otherwise. Though I will not say it has been the most important business of my life, it certainly has been its most important recreation, and I have derived from it more enjoyment than from perhaps any other source. I began the study some fifty years ago, at the time when the genius of Prinsep was re-creating, and breathing fresh life into the chaotic mass of idle fables, which, before his time, represented the history and doctrines of Buddhism. The chronology of the sect and the biography of its founder were then daily assuming shape and becoming clearer; but little had been done to ascertain what their architecture had been, or to discriminate what really belonged respectively to Buddhism, to the Jains or to the Hindus, still less had the origin of these various forms been traced, or how they arose, and what their influence was on each other. What little had been attempted, was of the haziest and most tentative character.

Seeing and regretting this state of things, I determined, as far as in me lay, to try to remedy it, and the success that attended my endeavours to effect this rendered the next few years perhaps the happiest of my life. Even now I look back with more pleasure to the time I spent in this investigation than to any other epoch in my life. Nothing could exceed the delight I experienced in visiting the various cities of Hindostan, so picturesque in their decay, or so beautiful in their modern

B

14. Beglar's notes in his copy of Fergusson's *Archaeology in India.*
Courtesy: Archaeological Survey of India

another dimension. The charges made by Fergusson are fiercely contested by Beglar in the notes within his personal copy of Fergusson's *Archaeology in India.* The book, which as noted (in the Preface), was pre-eminently a virulent attack against Rajendralala Mitra, was clearly seen by Beglar as having a wider target. The pencilled writing spanning the top of the first page states that the book was a violent attack not only on Mitra but also on Cunningham and his assistants The comments pencilled on the bottom of the same page state that Fergusson had tried to attempt, by false representation, to discredit the Archaeological Survey of India, so that Burgess and his surveys would appear in better light. The writing across the left-hand margin suggests that the object of the book was quite clear to those who knew of Burgess' close relationship with Fergusson and his disappointment at not succeeding as director general of the Archaeological Survey, instead of Cunningham. The bitter conflict between Fergusson and Burgess on the one hand, and Cunningham and his team on the other, is borne out by other sources as well. The conflict may have had a personal dimension, but, as indicated earlier, it also involved fundamental differences of approach and methodology.

The restoration of the Mahabodhi temple was one of the major conservation works initiated and completed during Cunningham's tenure. In spite of Cunningham and Beglar's best efforts, the restoration was executed at a time when the expertise required for such work was scarcely available, and so it is not surprising that architectural scholars found much fault with the final result. In the last decade of the nineteenth century, this bitter disagreement over the quality of the restoration of the Mahabodhi temple made way for the beginnings of a dispute of a very different kind. The newer dispute—that between Hindus and Buddhists for custody over the shrine—proved to be much more prolonged, and one which had far greater social implications than the earlier wranglings among archaeologists and architectural scholars.[85]

Sanchi

The Buddhist site of Sanchi lay within the territory of Bhopal state. When discovered by General Taylor in 1818, the monuments of

[85] For the history of the early stages of this dispute, see Lahiri (1999): 33–43.

Sanchi were apparently in fairly good shape.[86] In 1834 they were described by Captain Edward Fell. At that time, three of the four gateways of Stupa No. 1 were still standing, and the southern one was lying at the place where it had fallen. The dome of the stupa was intact and a part of the balustrade on its summit was still *in situ*. Stupa Nos. 2 and 3 were also intact. There is no record of the state of preservation of the eight small stupas, apart from the other buildings, near Stupa No. 2.

In 1822 T.H. Maddock, the political agent at Bhopal, and Captain Johnson, assistant political agent, visited the site and dug a shaft from top to bottom on one side of Stupa No. 1 in search of relics. This breach damaged the body of the stupa and led to the collapse of the western gateway and parts of the enclosing balustrade. The Maddock–Johnson duo were also probably responsible for the partial destruction of Stupa Nos. 2 and 3, which till their visit, had been in perfect condition. Many years later, Cunningham and Maisey made their contribution to the process of destruction.[87]

Captain F.C. Maisey had first heard of the Buddhist ruins at Sanchi in 1849 from Captain J.D. Cunningham, political agent at Bhopal (Alexander Cunningham's brother).[88] At the time Maisey was on

[86] Many of these details are given in Marshall and Foucher (1940): 7 ff.

[87] The most scathing criticism came from Lepel Griffin, agent to the governor general for Central India: 'A thousand years of time and weather have not done so much injury to the invaluable Topes at Sanchi as was caused by the action of Major-General Cunningham, the Director General of Archaeology, who years ago mined deep into the Topes in the vain search for coins or inscriptions, and never filled in his excavations, reducing a quarter of this ancient and unique monument to complete ruin. This damage is being slowly and partially repaired, but the building is irremediably injured.' (Letter No. 51G.-119, dated Indore, 21 April 1882 from Lepel Griffin to the Secretary to the Government of India, Foreign Department, Home/Archaeology and the Conservation of Ancient Monuments, October 1882, Part A, NAI. Many years later, John Marshall (Marshall and Foucher, 1940: 8) expressed a similar view: 'in 1851, Major (afterwards Gen. Sir) Alexander Cunningham and Capt. F.C. Maisey together contributed to the general spoliation of the site by hasty excavations in several of the monuments, and, though they succeeded in recovering a most valuable series of relic-caskets from the Second and Third Stupas, their discoveries hardly compensated for the damage entailed in their operations.'

[88] These details are given in Maisey (1892): Introduction. J.D. Cunningham (1847) went on to publish an accurate plan and section of Stupa No. I and an account of the gateway sculptures.

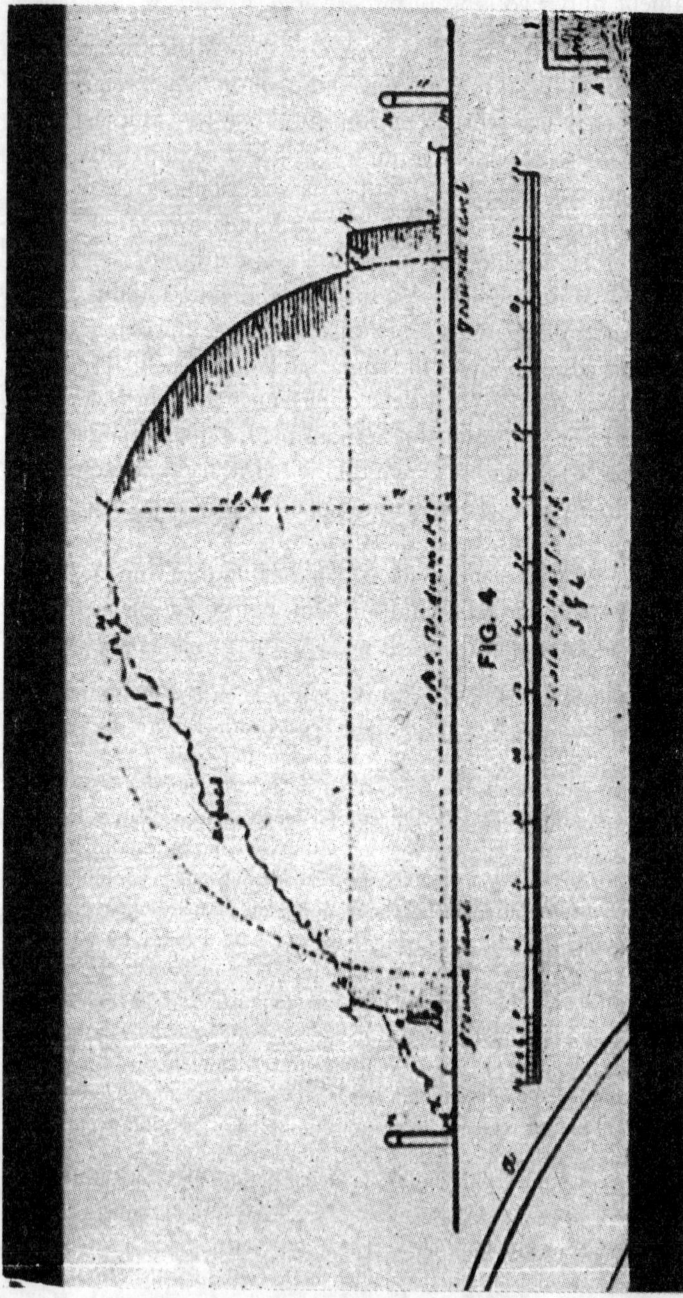

15. The damage caused to Stupa No. 1 due to the excavations of Maddock and Johnson. Maisey (1892).

government duty, working on archaeological work in the Upper Betwa districts of Central India. At J.D. Cunningham's suggestion he was directed to drop all other work and proceed to Sanchi in order to prepare an illustrated report on its structures, sculptures and inscriptions. Maisey spent the winter of 1849–50 working on this project. In October 1850, on his way to resume work at Sanchi, he spent a few days with Alexander Cunningham in Gwalior. Cunningham was at the time executive engineer of Gwalior state. Cunningham was keen to explore the site but, being busy with official duties, persuaded Maisey to defer operations till he joined him.

Cunningham arrived at Sanchi in January 1851, and he and Maisey proceeded to systematically open the many stupas in the area in order to find relic caskets. Cunningham reports that the method they adopted—of digging a single vertical shaft right down the exact centre of the stupa—was aimed at minimizing damage to the structure. That the operation was brisk is suggested in the following remark by Cunningham, referring to the first of the stupa openings: 'I arrived at Sanchi on the 23rd of January 1851, and the same morning, after only a few hours' work, we found the relics of Sariputa and Mogalana, the two chief disciples of Buddha, in the ruins of No. 3 Stupa.'[89] The opening of numerous other stupas at Sanchi, Sonari, Satdhara, Andher, and Bhojpur is described in Cunningham's *The Bhilsa Topes*. While the relic boxes and caskets discovered were carried away by Cunningham and Maisey, nowhere does he mention filling up all the shafts that they had dug in so many stupas.[90] Clearly, this was not a priority.

Maisey submitted a preliminary report on Sanchi to the Government of India in October 1851.[91] He never managed to prepare the supplementary report he intended to submit as he did not receive translations of the inscriptions he had sent to the Asiatic Society. His submission of the drawings he had made of the structures and sculptures of Sanchi was delayed because of an accident: the baggage in which they were packed fell into a river. Moreover, in March 1852

[89] Cunningham's Introductory Note to Maisey (1892).

[90] According to Lahiri (2004), the inscribed stone box containing Mahamogalana's relics was left at the site and was rediscovered there by John Marshall more than sixty years later.

[91] Mss. Eur. D., 572, OIOC.

Maisey was sent off on duty to Burma and soon after his return, in May 1854, his special archaeological appointment was terminated. Maisey's book on the subject was likewise delayed by many years and appeared in 1892. He argued in this book that the Sanchi stupa was pre-Buddhist and belonged originally to a cult worshipping the sun, fire, and the elements.[92]

Cunningham, on the other hand, swiftly brought out his volume on the Bhilsa 'Topes', in 1854. This included, as we have seen, a detailed account of the remains at Sanchi, Sonari, Satdhara, Andheri, and Bhojpur, framed within a broader account of the history and doctrines of Buddhism. Cunningham suggested that the two fallen southern and eastern gateways of the Sanchi stupa be removed to the British Museum to ensure their preservation and appreciation.[93]

Several years later in 1868, Place, the French consul, sought the begum's permission to remove one of the gateways of the Great Stupa at Sanchi to France, but the British Resident used his influence on Shahjahan Begum to induce her to reject the idea. The begum then offered the gateway to the British Museum.[94] The matter went up to the viceroy's council, which was unanimous in the view that the architectural remains of Sanchi should remain at Sanchi itself, and that to remove them to a European museum would be an act of vandalism. The begum's generous offer was politely but firmly refused. As for the French, it was decided to present them with a cast of the eastern gateway in lieu of the original.[95]

[92] Cunningham vigorously refuted Maisey's points in his Introduction to Maisey (1892). He remarked here that Maisey's argument that Buddhism was born not in the sixth century BC but around the beginning of the Christian era, may have been motivated by the pious desire to prove that Christianity was older than Buddhism.

[93] Cunningham (1854b): xi.

[94] According to Lahiri (2004), this was the second time that such an offer was made. Many years earlier, in 1853, H.M. Durand, the political resident, had persuaded Sikandar Begum to make such an offer. The gateway was not carted off to England at that time because of the cost and difficulties involved in the task. When arrangements were finally made for the transfer, the Revolt of 1857 broke out and the whole thing fell through.

[95] Foreign Dept.—A (General), June 1868, Nos. 59–61; and Home/Public, 30th July 1870, Nos. 204–16, Part A, NAI.

The architecture and sculpture of Sanchi and Amaravati formed the subject of James Fergusson's *Tree and Serpent Worship*, published in 1868. The book included copies of many of Maisey's drawings and photographs of Sanchi, taken by Lieutenant Waterhouse, with a general introduction and detailed description of plates by Fergusson.[96] The author here described the three main stupas at Sanchi and discussed the sculptures, quoting frequently from Maisey's report. He identified two major 'races' in the Sanchi sculptures—the *dhoti*-clad Hindus (these, he explained, were Aryans who had degenerated due to miscegenation), and the kilt-wearing, cloaked Dasyus (the aboriginal people), who sported beards and strange hair-do's. He identified Buddhist and historical themes in the sculptures, and saw the Mauryan emperor Ashoka as the hero of all or almost all the bas-reliefs in the latter category. The most striking aspect of the Sanchi sculptures, in Fergusson's opinion, was the testimony they bore to an ancient tree cult, for he identified the tree as the most frequent object of worship. The Sanchi sculptures were superior to those of ancient Egypt, but inferior to those of ancient Greece. Fergusson had no doubt that this school of Indian art owed its origin to the influence of the Bactrian Greeks.[97]

Over all the decades after its discovery, nobody thought of repairing or preserving the Sanchi structures. This seems to have been partly the result of information given by officers deputed to assess the situation, who reported that the monuments were so damaged that no repairs were possible.[98] The first measures in the direction of conservation of the site were taken under the direction of Cole when he became curator of ancient monuments. By this time the site had been further damaged by the inhabitants in the vicinity and the encroaching jungle. Restoration work at Sanchi was begun in 1881 under the supervision of Austin Mears, superintendent of public works at Sehore. Expenses for the restoration work were shared by the imperial government (a sum

[96] Maisey (1892: vii, fn. 2) later complained that several of his sketches had been incorrectly reproduced, with the result that they had led to erroneous conclusions.

[97] For a more detailed discussion of Fergusson's ideas on Indian architecture, history, and ethnography as reflected in *Tree and Serpent Worship*, see Chapter 8.

[98] Lahiri (2004).

16. The re-erected gateway of Stupa No. 3. The heap of rubble behind it is what remained of the stupa.
Courtesy: Archaeological Survey of India

17. Stupa No.1 in 1920. Courtesy: Archaeological Survey of India

of Rs. 2000 was initially sanctioned for the purpose) and Shah Jahan Begum of Bhopal. The begum was more than willing to contribute towards the preservation of this important historical monument lying within her dominion.

Mears was instructed to clear the area of jungle, to collect all the carved stones and railing pieces and place them together, to clear a way the debris from the breach in Stupa No. 1 and begin the work of repair.[99] The dome of the stupa, which had suffered extensive damage over the years, was repaired. The shaft (5 ft in diameter and about 40 ft deep) sunk though the centre of the dome by Cunningham and Maisey some thirty years earlier was filled. The roots of trees that had damaged the railings and the stupa itself could not be removed easily, and had to be bored into and destroyed with sulphuric acid. The ground was carefully sloped to prevent waterlogging. The northern gateway was partially cleaned. The stone pavement was exposed, sections of the railing re-erected, and several Buddha images restored to their original places. The northern gateway, which had developed a crack due to an earthquake, was repaired. The fallen southern and eastern gateways, as well as the gateway in front of Stupa No. 3, were re-erected. Mears was pleased with his handiwork: 'For the dome having been put in thorough repair, there will be nothing to prevent its standing another 2000 years as it had hitherto done till wrecked by blundering Archaeologists.'[100]

The restoration work required judgement, and the restorers sometimes erred. When Major J.B. Keith (assistant to the curator of ancient monuments for Central India) stepped in to assist Mears in the conservation work at Sanchi 1882, he had to undo some of the work done previously. Mears had, by mistake apparently, used railing slabs to reconstruct a stairway. Keith in turn faced the top and bottom lintels of the southern gateway of Stupa 1 incorrectly and made the same mistake in one of the gateways of Stupa No. 3.[101] Apart from such mistakes, much remained undone. The task of rescuing the numerous

[99] Letter dated Sehore, 20 January, 1882, from Austin Mears to Sir Lepel Griffin, Agent to the Governor General for Central India, Home/Archaeology, March 1882, No. 1, Part B, NAI.

[100] Ibid.

[101] Lahiri (2004).

other crumbling structures at the site—shrines, monasteries, stupas—from vegetation and debris, and of protecting the hundreds of sculptures and inscriptions lying about at the site, was left to be done some three decades later by John Marshall.[102]

The Bharhut Stupa

The remains of the Buddhist stupa at Bharhut in Nagod state were discovered by Alexander Cunningham in November 1873. On the maps, the place was called Bharaod, which Cunningham suggested might well be the Bardaotis of Ptolemy. The evidence at Bharhut indicated that this was the site of an ancient city. The ruins of a large brick stupa stood in the midst of the jungle overgrowth. Cunningham estimated that it must have been 68ft in diameter, surrounded by an 88 ft diameter and 9 ft high stone railing:

> The whole of the Stupa has been carried away to build the houses of the present village, but more than half of the stone railing still remains, although it has been prostrated by the weight of the rubbish thrown against it when the Stupa was excavated. When I first saw the place only 3 of the Railing Pillars near the Eastern Gateway were visible above ground, but a shallow excavation soon brought to light some pillars of the south gate,—from which I obtained the measurement of one quadrant of the circle. I was thus able to determine the diameter of the enclosure, the whole of which was afterwards completely excavated,—partly by myself, and partly by my assistant Mr J.D. Beglar—In many places, the accumulation of rubbish rose to 8 feet in height.[103]

According to Cunningham, Bharhut village consisted of over 200 houses built entirely from the bricks removed from the stupa. The removal of bricks had gone on till quite recently, and Cunningham was informed that a small box discovered in the middle of the brick

[102] In 1912, the whole site was once again almost totally covered with jungle and debris. Except for Stupa No. 1, little else was visible. John Marshall's operations at Sanchi extended from 1912 to 1919. Marshall ordered the clearing of the site and repair of the structures. A small site museum was set up for the protection of the movable antiquities. Marshall and Foucher, 1940: 8–9.

[103] Extract from General Cunningham's Brief Report of Proceedings for 1873/74, in Baghelkhand Agency File no. 2 [A], 1874, NAI.

mound had been given over to the raja of Nagod. Cunningham's inquiries about this relic casket—for that is what it must have been—'were met by persistent ignorance, both as to its contents and as to whether it was still in the possession of the Râjâ.'[104]

The *jagirdar* of the place did, however, inform Cunningham that the site of the stupa had been covered completely by dense jungle till as recently as sixty years ago, when the land first came into his family's possession. According to the jagirdar, at that time the railing was in perfect condition, a claim Cunningham doubted, judging from the evidence of many railing stones embedded in the residence of the *thakur* of Batanmara, which was over two hundred years old. Clearly, the thakur had had many pieces of the stone railing removed from the site. Pieces too heavy to be moved easily were split lengthwise and some of these still lay about the place. Cunningham and Beglar surmised that the removal of the Bharhut stones may have come to a sudden end when the land on which the stupa lay was granted to the ancestor of the present jagirdar. Being a poor Brahmin, he was no doubt disinclined to let the thakur of Batanmara carry off stones from his land without adequate recompense. But, not having the resources to split and move heavy stones, he confined himself to removing bricks from the mound to use in building his house.

Cunningham's first halt at Bharhut was brief as he was, at the time, on his way to Nagpur. He was at Bharhut long enough to ascertain that portions of two gateways, along with a quarter of the circular railing between them were still *in situ*, although nearly all the stones were thrown down and buried under debris. In February 1874 Cunningham came back to Bharhut and stayed ten days.[105] During this period he uncovered the *in situ* south-east quadrant of the buried railing. He excavated the whole space inside the railing, which revealed the sole remaining fragment of the stupa, 6 ft in height and about 10 ft in length at the bottom. While all this activity was going on, hundreds of curious people from the vicinity visited the site. They were intrigued by the sculptures, by the inscriptions, and by this Englishman who could actually read them.

[104] These details are given in Cunningham (1879b).

[105] Ibid.: v ff.

18. The Bharhut mound after clearance, with sculptures lying about in the foreground.
Courtesy: Archaeological Survey of India

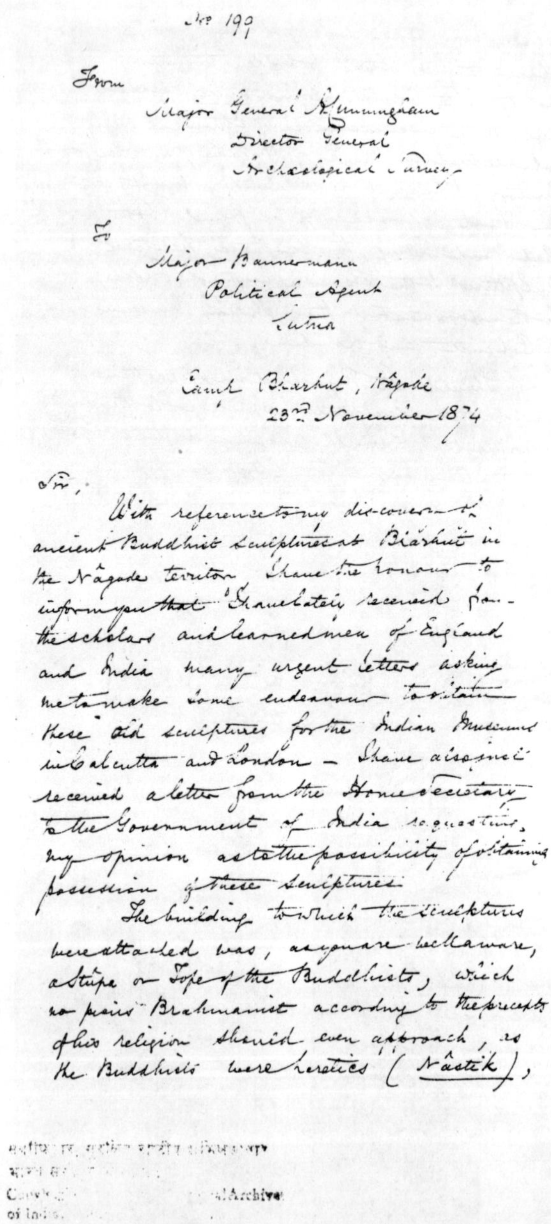

No 199

From

Major General A Cunningham
Director General
Archaeological Survey

To

Major Bannerman
Political Agent
Sutna

Camp Bharhut, Nâgode
23rd November 1874

Sir,

With reference to my discovery of ancient Buddhist sculptures at Bharhut in the Nâgode territory I have the honour to inform you that I have lately received from the scholars and learned men of England and India many urgent letters asking me to make some endeavour to obtain these old sculptures for the Indian Museums in Calcutta and London — I have also since received a letter from the Home Secretary to the Government of India requesting my opinion as to the possibility of obtaining possession of these sculptures.

The building to which the sculptures were attached was, as you are well aware, a Stupa or Tope of the Buddhists, which no pious Brahmanist according to the precepts of his religion should even approach, as the Buddhists were heretics (Nâstik),

19. The first page of Cunningham's letter to Bannerman.
Courtesy: National Archives of India

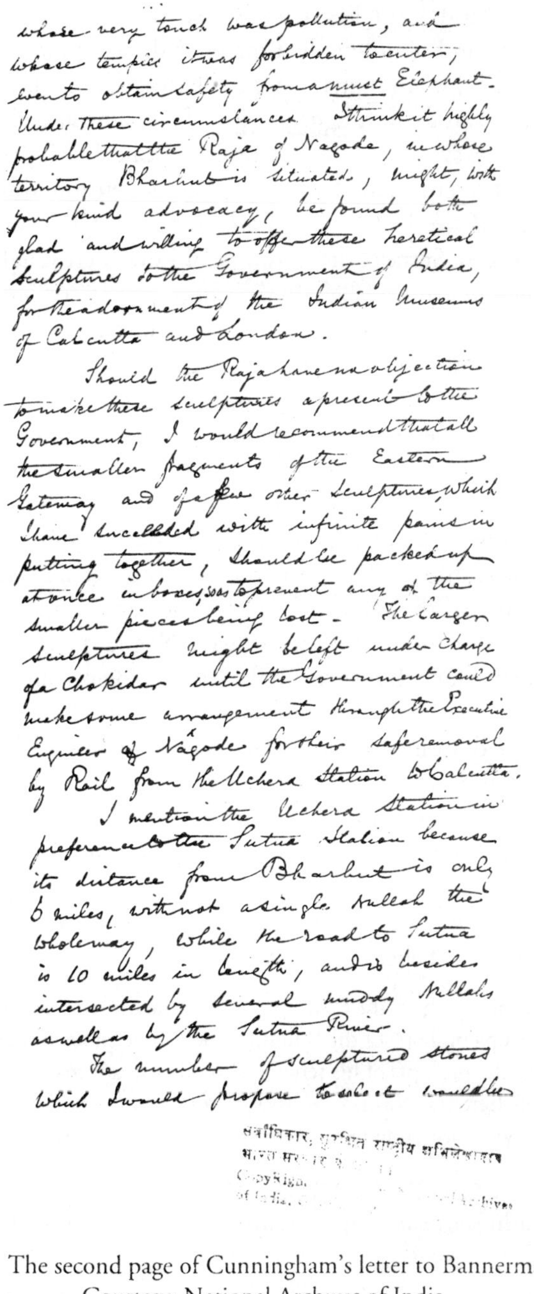
whose very touch was pollution, and whose temples it was forbidden to enter, even to obtain safety from a must Elephant. Under these circumstances I think it highly probable that the Raja of Nagode, in whose territory Bharhut is situated, might, with your kind advocacy, be found both glad and willing to offer these heretical sculptures to the Government of India, for the adornment of the Indian Museums of Calcutta and London.

Should the Raja have no objection to make these sculptures a present to the Government, I would recommend that all the smaller fragments of the Eastern Gateway and of a few other sculptures, which I have succeeded with infinite pains in putting together, should be packed up at once in boxes, so as to prevent any of the smaller pieces being lost. The larger sculptures might be left under charge of a Chokidar until the Government could make some arrangement through the Executive Engineer of Nágode for their safe removal by Rail from the Uchera Station to Calcutta.

I mention the Uchera Station in preference to the Sutna Station because its distance from Bharhut is only 6 miles, without a single nullah the whole way, while the road to Sutna is 10 miles in length, and is besides intersected by several muddy Nullahs as well as by the Sutna River.

The number of sculptured stones which I would propose to select would be

20. The second page of Cunningham's letter to Bannerman. Courtesy: National Archives of India

In March-April 1874 Beglar excavated the entire railing of the Bharhut stupa and photographed many of the sculptures. Then, in November 1874, Cunningham and Beglar together returned to the site. Their aim was to thoroughly explore the mound and photograph all the sculptures systematically on a uniform scale. During these excavations the smaller pieces of the eastern gateway were found and restored by Cunningham. By the end of December the whole railing area had been exposed. Some of the missing sculptures were sought for and found in neighbouring villages. In the summer of 1876 Cunningham and Beglar visited Bharhut yet again, and thoroughly explored the neighbourhood, discovering still more sculptural fragments belonging to the stupa.

Cunningham's report on the discoveries at Bharhut found its way into London newspapers and led to wide publicity for the finds. Cunningham received many letters from scholars in India and England, urging him to secure the sculptures for the museums in Calcutta and London. The home secretary to the Government of India had also written to him on the subject.[106] The matter was a little tricky for Bharhut lay within the territory of the raja of Nagod. The Baghelkhand area was one in which the officers of the Archaeological Survey did not have a free run. Permission had to be sought from local rulers, and *parwanas* obtained for movement through their territory. It was the job of the political agent, Major Bannerman, to interface between the native princes and the officers of the survey. It was he who had to prise the spectacular Bharhut sculptures out of the hands of the raja of Nagod.

Cunningham did not think that this would be a very difficult task. His reason for this belief is interesting.

> The building to which the Sculptures were attached was, as you are well aware, a Stupa or Tope of the Buddhists, which no pious Brahmanist according to the precepts of his religion should even approach, as the Buddhists were heretics (Nastik), whose very touch was pollution, and whose temples it was forbidden to enter, even to obtain safety from a *must* Ele-

[106] Letter dated Camp Bharhut, Nagode, 23 November 1874, from Cunningham to Major Bannerman, Political Agent, Sutna, Baghelkhand Agency File No. 2[A], 1874.

> phant. Under these circumstances I think it highly probable that the Raja of Nagode, in whose territory Bharhut is situated, might, with your kind advocacy, be found both glad and willing to offer these heretical sculptures to the Government of India, for the adornment of the Indian Museums of Calcutta and London.[107]

Major Bannerman swiftly got in touch with the Nagod durbar, pointing out that the raja had custody over the Bharhut sculptures. The raja then graciously gifted them to the British Government of India.[108] The thakur of Batanmara, who was in possession of a few Bharhut stones (a gateway piece formed part of a wall of his mansion), was persuaded to present them to Cunningham.

Cunningham wanted to have the Bharhut sculptures photographed as they stood at the site and then to quickly move them via rail (the station of Uchera was some miles away from Bharhut) to Calcutta. Although he thought the Bharhut material should be housed in the Indian Museum, he did initially express a hope that the eastern gateway, which he had restored from numerous fragments, be sent to London along with a portion of the railing on each side of it.[109] While this issue was being deliberated upon, the government also received certain suggestions regarding the matter from Rajendralala Mitra, who appears to have had more or less the same opinion about what should be done about the Bharhut sculptures, and seems to have been in favour of removing them to Calcutta.[110] In January 1875 the Home Department sanctioned the removal of the Bharhut sculptures to the Indian Museum in Calcutta.[111]

[107] Ibid.

[108] Letter No. 706, dated Sutna, 28 November 1874, from Major P.W. Bannerman, Political Agent Baghelkhand to Major General Alexander Cunningham, Home/Public, January 1875, Part A, Nos. 153–5, NAI.

[109] Letter No. 209, dated Camp Bharhut, near Sutna, dated 10 December 1874, from Cunningham to A.P. Howell, Officiating Secretary to the Government of India, Home/Public, January 1875, No. 153 Part A, NAI.

[110] This was a letter dated 18 October 1874. I could not trace Rajendralala Mitra's letter, but this is the impression given in the notes on the file cited in the previous fn.

[111] Guha-Thakurta (1997: 39–40) highlights the significance of the fact that the Bharhut sculptures were sent to the Indian Museum in Calcutta rather than

During the years after the discovery of the Bharhut stupa, Cunningham was corresponding with the noted Pali scholar Childers and the Buddhist priest Subhuti of Ceylon. Childers was very critical of the idea of removing the Bharhut sculptures from their original site to Calcutta. This, to him, carried the distinct aroma of vandalism ('fancy carting away Stonehenge!').[112] What Childers really seemed to be complaining about was that the sculptures were being sent to Calcutta rather than London.

Cunningham defended himself staunchly against the charge levied against him.

> I am willing to accept the aroma, since I have saved all the more important sculptures. Of those that were left behind every stone that was removable has since been 'carted away' by the people for building purposes. So inveterate is this practice in India that Babu Rajendra Lâl, when he first heard of the Bharhut discoveries, boldly addressed the Government of India, suggesting that the sculptures should be removed to a place of safety to prevent the people from carrying them off . . . In his letter already quoted Professor Childers expressed a 'hope that the sculptures may find their way to the India Office [in London] instead of being consigned to the peaceful oblivion of an Indian Museum.' In this hope, I should most cordially agree were I not afraid that they might be consigned to the still more oblivious vaults of the British Museum, where some ten years ago I discovered no less than seven Indian inscriptions in the full enjoyment of undisturbed repose, unseen, uncared for, and unknown. At present there is no Indian Museum in London, while there is one in Calcutta, where the sculptures are now deposited.'[113]

---

the British Museum in London. The Bharhut sculptures were a valuable addition to the archaeological collection of the Indian Museum. A special archaeological gallery was opened in the museum in April 1878 to display them. Guha-Thakurta also observes that the transfer of the Bharhut remains to Calcutta and some of the Amaravati remains to the Madras Museum signalled the arrival of archaeology in Indian museums, and that their arrangement and display in these museums marked the museumization of entire sites.

[112] Childers, cited in Cunningham (1879b): vii.

[113] Ibid. The India Museum in London was finally wound up in 1879, when its antiquities were divided between the South Kensington Museum and the British Museum.

Postscript

James Burgess and H.H. Cole were the two officers in British India who, at the time, probably had more expertise and experience in the sphere of Indian architecture than anyone else. Their ideas and opinions played a role both in the artistic delineation of historical monuments as well as in matters relating to their conservation. However, given the ever-present financial constraints, the institutional inadequacies, and the tensions and conflicts (ideational, personal, and departmental), and the lack of effective, centralized direction in conservation matters, neither Burgess nor Cole made an immediate or major difference to the way in which conservation work tended to muddle along during these years. Of the two, Cole was irrevocably committed to the *in situ* principle, while Burgess's opinion varied with the specific context.

The Bodh Gaya temple became a controversial case involving an acrimonious debate over the issue of restoration *versus* repair. The ruinous state of the Bharhut stupa was a deciding factor in the decision to acquire the sculptures from the raja of Nagod and remove them from the site. The fact that the India Museum in London was on the decline and that the Indian Museum in Calcutta was being prepared as an imperial museum signifying the greatness of the British Indian empire, seems to have been crucial in keeping the Bharhut remains in India. Sanchi, which was in much better condition when discovered, eventually became a case of successful *in situ* preservation. However, it may be noted that the principle of *in situ* preservation was applied to *structural* remains at the site, not to objects from which the sacrality of the structures ultimately derived. The reliquary material that Cunningham and Maisey had prised out of numerous stupas of Central India—relic caskets, boxes, and the relics themselves—was divided up between themselves and ultimately found its way to the British Museum and the Victoria and Albert Museum.[114]

Given the multitude and diversity of officials and agencies involved in conservation projects, it is not surprising that such projects were

114 The twentieth-century history of the relics is another complex story and involved some of the material being eventually sent back to India, while some was dispatched to Sri Lanka. On this, see Willis (2000).

undertaken in a haphazard, *ad hoc* manner, and were uneven in their quality of planning, execution, and results. Official reactions to, and the outcome of, all these archaeological situations varied, sometimes drastically: no clear, uniform policy was applied consistently towards the conservation of ancient monuments. This lack of a policy *vis-à-vis* ancient antiquities, sites, and monuments, and the fumbling attempts to formulate one, emerge most clearly from the story of the Amaravati stupa, which forms the subject of the next chapter.

CHAPTER 8

The Dismembering of the Amaravati Stupa

Situated on the banks of the Krishna river, on the outskirts of the great city of Dharanikota, Amaravati (in modern Guntur district, Andhra Pradesh) was one of the major Buddhist centres of ancient India. The architecture and sculpture of the Amaravati stupa shared certain stylistic features with those of Sanchi and Bharhut in Central India, but it also had its own peculiarities. Unlike the solid brick core of the latter, the stupas of the Andhra country were generally built with a number of brick walls radiating from a central point (like a spoked wheel), the interstices packed with mud. Five tall free-standing pillars (*ayaka-stambhas*) stood majestically at the four cardinal points along the circumambulatory path around the stupa. But the most distinctive aspect of the Amaravati stupa was that, unlike the plain exterior of the stupas of Sanchi and Bharhut, its dome was faced with a large number of beautifully sculpted limestone slabs, once probably painted over in red.

The history of the Amaravati complex spans some seventeen centuries, from its inception in the third century BC to its demise in the fourteenth century AD. Once abandoned, nature took its course, and the great stupa—known as the *mahachaitya*—gradually came to be enveloped in layers of dust and debris which eventually obscured it completely from sight. Then, towards the end of the eighteenth century, Amaravati was discovered by a local zamindar. The result of several decades of exploration and excavation that subsequently ensued at Amaravati was the steady dismembering of the mahachaitya. Ironically, the steady disappearance of the magnificent structure was accompanied by attempts by scholars to reconstruct its lost design.

This chapter is a new, revised version of Singh (2001).

The Discovery of Amaravati and the First Documentation

Colonel Colin Mackenzie of the Mysore Survey had heard, in the course of his travels, of some interesting finds unearthed in the town of Amareswaram in the Krishna valley. In February 1797 he had the opportunity to investigate them. Having set up camp at Ibrampattan, Mackenzie despatched his interpreter Cavelli Venkata Boria along with some Brahmins and two *sipahis* to Amareswaram 'with directions to make some previous inquiries into the history of the place: and to conciliate the inhabitants; particularly the *Bráhmens,* who are apt to be alarmed on these occasions.'[1] Mackenzie himself left Ibrampattan the next morning by moonlight and reached Amareswaram at daybreak.

The town was a new one. The ancient remains were situated on a mound nearby called 'Dipal-dina' (the hill of lamps). About a year earlier, in the course of removing a large stone from the place to a temple being built by the local raja, workmen had hit on the brickwork. This had induced them to dig the trench in search of more building material. Their shovels had turned up several white stones, many of which broke in the process of exhumation.

Mackenzie was the first to document the remains at Amaravati.[2] His account indicates the condition of the site at the end of the eighteenth century. The central part of the mound was still untouched, but around it was a circular trench about 10 ft wide and 12 ft deep. A few carved white stone slabs lay in and around the trench. Mackenzie conjectured that the whole mound may once have been faced with similar carved stone slabs. He identified the stone as a white marble, locally known as 'pal-rayi' or milk-stone.[3]

He described eight sculpted slabs which he saw at or near the site. Two were inscribed, but he could not read the undeciphered Brahmi letters. Mackenzie was puzzled. Local tradition connected the sculptures with the Jaina religion, but he could find no conclusive proof of

[1] Mackenzie (1807): 273.

[2] Ibid.

[3] Although the stone in question was limestone, over the next few decades, the stones were routinely referred to as the 'Amaravati marbles', perhaps an echo of the celebrated 'Elgin marbles'.

this. That he did not suspect a Buddhist connection is not surprising given the very limited understanding of Buddhism among Western scholars at the time.

Mackenzie's 1797 visit to Amaravati had been very brief, as was his account of what he saw there. In March 1816 he came back to Amaravati.[4] As the recently appointed surveyor general of India, he now had greater resources at his command. He remained at Amaravati till August and left his draftsmen working there till the end of 1817.[5] Mackenzie left no detailed written account of his operations at Amaravati; his understanding of the site had, however, increased substantially, judging from a paper written by him and published posthumously.[6] Local tradition held Dipal-dina to be the place where an ancient king named 'Mookunty-maharaze' had held his durbar. Mackenzie had come to realize that the ancient remains at the contiguous sites of Amaravati, Dipal-dina, and Dharanikota were of great historical importance. We can get some sort of idea of his operations at Amaravati from this account and from a comparison of two site plans that are included in the Mackenzie manuscript collection (see Figures 1 and 2).[7]

Amaravati was famous for its Shaiva temple of Amareshvara, built in the ninth century by the Eastern Chalukya king, Bhima. Towards the close of the eighteenth century, Raja Vassareddy Venkatadry Naid, zamindar of Chintapalli, visited the shrine and decided to move his residence to this place (his headquarters Lachmipuram had been occupied by English troops). The raja invited brahmins, banias, and others to come and settle in the new town, offering them financial assistance for building their homes. In the course of executing this plan

[4] He may actually have visited Amaravati several times between 1797 and 1816. Fergusson (1868): 149, n.

[5] Sewell (1880): 13. According to Mildred Archer, however, Mackenzie's draftsmen continued to work at the site till August 1819, and the fair-copying continued till 1820. Archer (1969): 530.

[6] Mackenzie (1823).

[7] The first of these was published in Sewell (1880): Plate I. Its title reads: 'Sketch of Deepauldinna at Amrawutty in its present state, March 1816.' The second plan was published in Fergusson (1868): Plate XLII. The original title of the second plan read: 'Plan Descriptive of the Present State of the Mound of Depaldenna at Amravutty shewing what has been cleared out and what still remains to be removed. Laid down from actual Measurements. June 1817.'

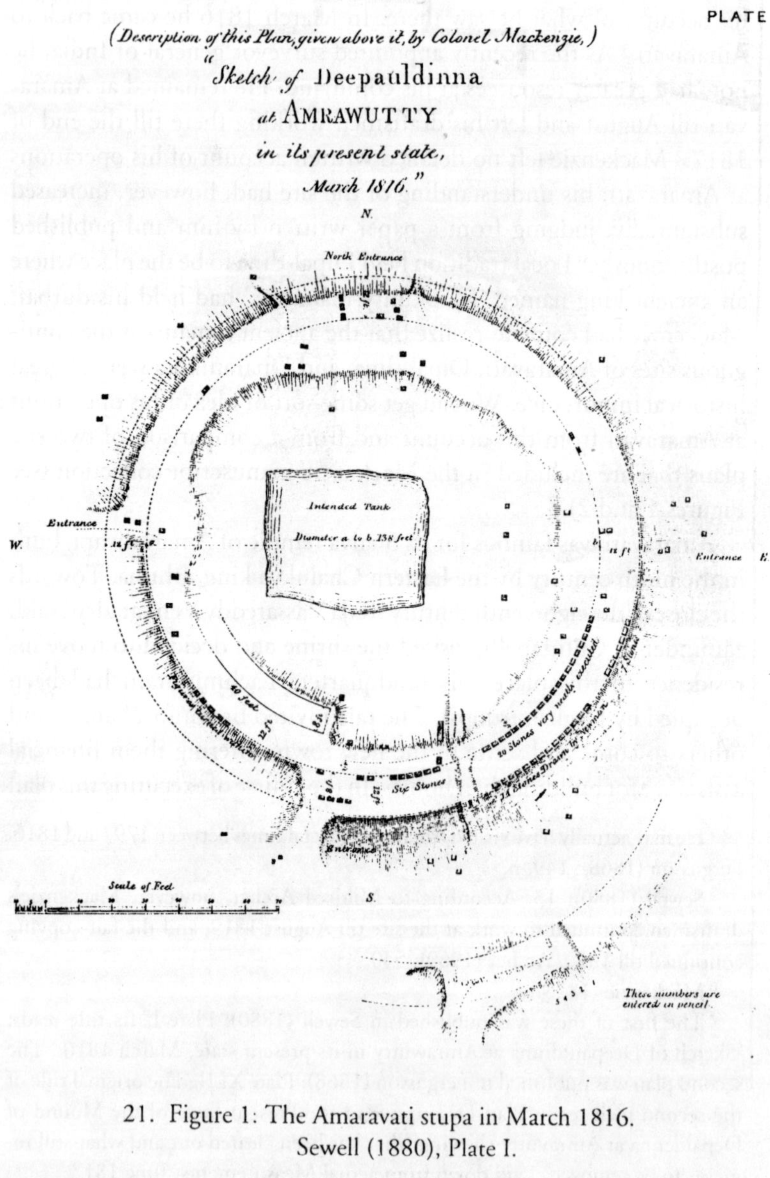

21. Figure 1: The Amaravati stupa in March 1816.
Sewell (1880), Plate I.

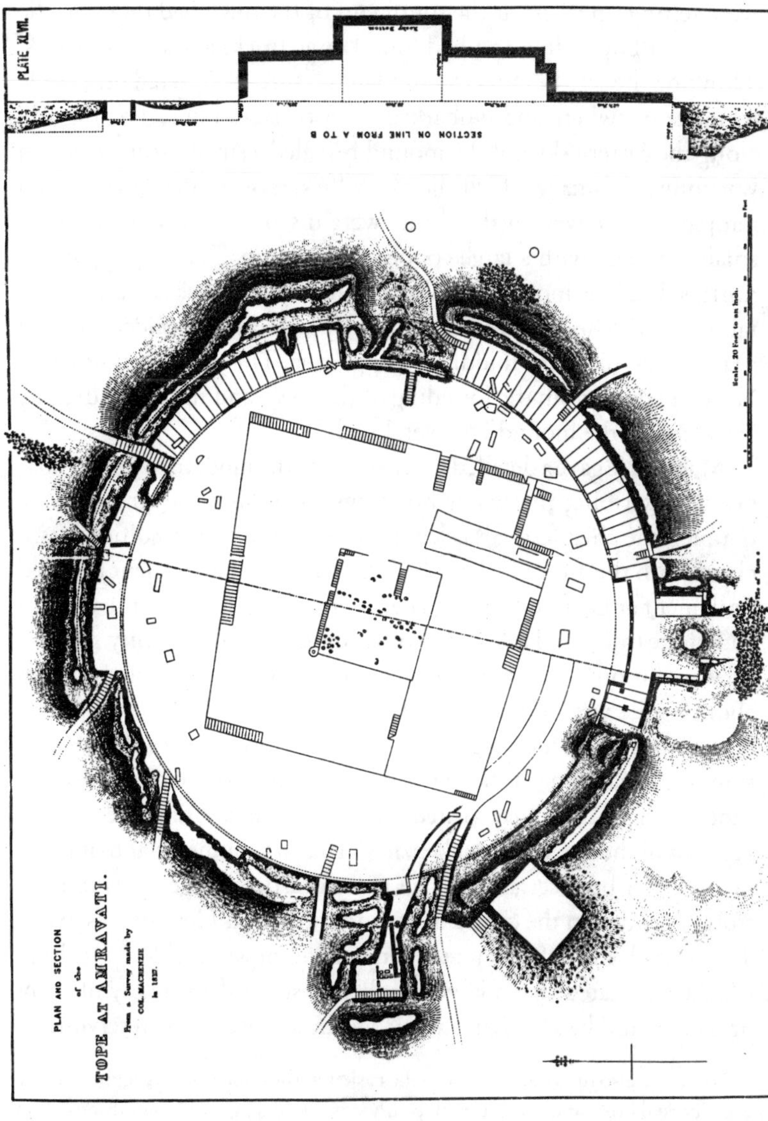

22. Figure 2: The site in 1817. Fergusson (1868), Plate XLII.

he hit on the idea of digging in the mounds around the place for bricks which could be used for his own residence.

While all this was going on, the raja heard that some people who were setting up house at the south end of the town had dug into the mound of Dipal-dina and had found large bricks and carved stones. Thinking these to be clues to a hidden treasure, he ordered the people to move elsewhere and embarked on a treasure hunt. The digging along the eastern skirt of the mound revealed a small shrine in which was found an image which the raja whisked off to the Amareshvara temple. To the west of the shrine were discovered two pillars and a small structure with a large copper votive lamp. The digging on the north side of the mound revealed a four-pillared brick structure containing a cross-legged headless image.[8] The raja next decided to build a large reservoir in the middle of Dipal-dina. This event seems to have been separated from the founding of the town and the initial digging activities on the mound by several years.

Mackenzie gave a detailed description of the modern town of Amaravati, describing the major buildings (including the Amareshvara temple), the chief festivals celebrated there, and local traditions associated with the area. He described the remains of an ancient fortified settlement at Dharanikota, situated some 500 yards from the western end of the town, and referred to other mounds in the vicinity. He also drew attention to some seventeen or eighteen megalithic stone circles about a mile west of Dharanikota.

The most important aspect of Mackenzie's account was the description of 'Depauldina' as he saw it in 1816 and 1817, close to two decades after he had first visited the place. Juxtaposing the written account of the site with Mackenzie's plans, its condition at that point of time can be ascertained. The most drastic change was the large trough opened in the centre of the mound for building the reservoir. This was about 108 ft square, and for the most part 24 ¼ ft deep. Mackenzie stated that a large number of stone slabs, many of them broken, could be seen lying about on the surface of the reservoir.

[8] The raja also discovered a stone relic casket in the course of his digging. Inside was a crystal box containing a small pearl, some gold leaf, and 'other things of no value'. These he kept in his *tosha khana* till, in 1863, they were secured by Walter Elliot and deposited in the Madras Museum. Fergusson (1868): 164, n; Boswell (1872): 149–55.

He identified an inner and outer ring of stones, 13 ft apart. The inner and outer circuit of stones together were fully exposed only in the south-east quadrant. The whole of the inner ring lay exposed in the other quadrants as well. Some of the stones of this ring in the south-west quadrant and a much smaller number in the north-east quadrant were still in place; the rest had disappeared. Mackenzie states that they had been used in repairing the temples of the town, and that several had been used to make a flight of steps to the Shivaganga tank (another tank in the town).[9] A large part of the outer ring seems to have been still largely covered with debris and Mackenzie described some sections that seem to have been *in situ*, referring to stones joining each other through projecting rims fitting into grooves. Mackenzie described the inner ring of slabs (which actually lined the stupa) as 'cemented to each other with strong mortar, and supported by a wall of masonry rising to a moderate height in the rear . . .'[10] The stone pavement between the stupa and the railing could be identified. It had been exposed mainly in the north-eastern and south-eastern quadrant. Mackenzie stated quite clearly: 'A great part of the mound remains uncleared; of the exterior row only the south-east quarter, and the entrance in that direction have been opened. . . .'[11]

He commented on the very fine and unusual nature of the carving on the stones, observing that they seemed to have originally been painted red and varnished; over time the colour had faded to a copperish red. He also referred to the discovery of coins and inscriptions at Dipal-dina. But as far as the purpose of the main structure on the mound was concerned, he remained mystified. He hazarded a guess that it belonged to 'a different sect from the Hindoos of the present day.'[12]

[9] In present times there is a belief that the lingam enshrined in the Amareshvara temple is a portion of a pillar from the mahachaitya. The unusual height of the pillar (over 20 ft) makes this possible, as do the many instances of pillar fragments of different kinds being transformed into shivalingas. The absence of any reference to or comment on this issue in the eighteenth and nineteenth century writings on Amaravati may have either been because such a belief was not current at the time or that the British officers did not have access to the interior of the temple.

[10] Mackenzie (1823): 438.

[11] Ibid.: 469.

[12] Ibid. In a footnote on the same page, Mackenzie suggested that the structure at Dipal-dina may have been connected with Druid religion.

The Mackenzie Collection in the British Library includes a bound volume containing eighty-two drawings—eighty-six sheets in all, including duplicates and loose sheets.[13] The title inscribed on the volume is: *India Antiqua Illustrata or An Essay to Illustrate the Ancient History, Inscriptions, and Religion of India—by Drawings of Remarkable Sculptures Inscriptions, Buildings, Coins & other existing Remains of Antiquity.* Its contents comprise a map of the site of Amaravati, two plans of the mound (one with a section drawing), a sketch of the stone circles in the neighbourhood, and a large number of drawings of sculptures and inscriptions. These drawings were made by the artists and draftsmen who were part of Mackenzie's team: T. Anderson, C. Barnett, M. Burke, J. Gould, H. Hamilton, J. Mustie, J. Newman, W. Sydenham, Najibullah, Pyari Lal, and Sheikh Abdullah. The drawings are inscribed with dates, and occasionally with comments, but the position or location of the sculptures they depict are not clear.

The Amaravati drawings, like the rest of the enormous amount of material Mackenzie collected in the course of his extensive travels, were, as we noted earlier, never published by him.[14] Some of the drawings later found their way into works by James Fergusson (1868), Robert Sewell (1880), and James Burgess (1887). In 1881 W.A. Franks privately published a *List of Drawings from the Amaravati Tope, Southern India, made for Colonel C. Mackenzie.*

Mackenzie removed a number of sculpted stones from Amaravati. A fragmentary note written by him, dated 7 April 1817 and pasted onto the volume of drawings, states that eleven stones of Dipal-dina, including an inscription (i.e. an inscribed stone) were given over to the charge of Major Cotgrave at Masulipatam. According to James Burgess, seven sculpted slabs were sent by Mackenzie to the museum of the Asiatic Society of Bengal, four were transmitted to the India Office via Madras, and at least sixteen others reached London (probably after

[13] Shelf mark reference: WD 1061, OIOC.

[14] James Fergusson refers to three copies of the Mackenzie drawings—one was sent to the Asiatic Society in Calcutta, the second deposited in Madras, and the third despatched to the Court of Directors. On the other hand, Douglas Barrett asserts that apart from the original, there was only one copy, the one preserved in the Library of the Asiatic Society of Bengal. This was borrowed by Walter Elliot in 1846 and submitted to the Governor of Madras in 1854, and was not heard of thereafter.

Mackenzie's death). Burgess states it is likely that most of the stones cleared by Mackenzie's assistants in order to make drawings were left exposed at Amaravati itself, where they must have been taken off or burnt into lime by local inhabitants. When Burgess visited the site in 1881, he was able to identify only one.[15]

The stones sent by Mackenzie to Masulipatam remained there for many decades. In 1830 Francis W. Robertson, collector of Masulipatam, brought down some more sculpted slabs from the site. He went on to arrange thirty-three slabs in the square of a new market-place named after himself. Details on which part of the Amaravati stupa complex these were removed from are not known. In 1835 the unusual stones of 'Robertson's Mound' caught the attention of Sir Frederick Adam, governor of Madras, who ordered them sent to Madras to be placed in the more appropriate environs of the museum of the Literary Society.[16] This removal eventually took place in 1856, twenty years after the order was given. During this period, some of the most beautiful pieces ended up adorning the garden of a Mr Alexander, Master Attendant. The government succeeded in retrieving these only in 1880, when they were sent by Burgess to Madras.

The 'Elliot Marbles'

Many years elapsed between Mackenzie's second visit to Amaravati and the next series of investigations at the site. In 1845 Sir Walter

[15] Burgess (1887): 17. According to Jennifer Howes (2002: 59), a total of 132 known stones can be connected with Mackenzie's activities at Amaravati between 1798 and 1817. All the seven stones illustrated in Mackenzie's 1809 article are missing. Of the 103 stones illustrated in the drawings of the Mackenzie Collection, 29 depict stones now in museum collections in India and Britain, and the other 74 are missing.

[16] Howes (2002: 58 and Plate 5) points out that there is a loose sketch and plan of the proposed 'Robertson's Mound' in the Mackenzie Drawings Collection. It shows a square, three-tiered monument made out of sculpted stones from Amaravati. A note on the drawing states that 88 large sculpted stones and about 38–40 smaller stones would be needed to complete the monument, and that the best part of the mound of Dipal-dina would have to be opened to acquire these stones. According to Howes, this drawing and note indicates that Mackenzie was in communication with Robertson over his plan to construct this structure. The stones from Robertson's Mound were eventually sent to the British Museum. Howes (2002): 63.

Elliot, commissioner of Guntur, visited Amaravati and indulged in some haphazard excavation. The site had not been disturbed significantly over the previous few decades and Elliot found the mound in much the same condition as Mackenzie had left it in 1816.

Elliot's operations at Amaravati began with his discovery of the western gateway of the mahachaitya. The sculpted stones he found included two lions that had flanked the entrance, the shaft of a monolithic column and a miniature stupa that had probably surmounted it, portions of other pillars that had formed the entrance, and five slabs on the dome of the stupa opposite the entrance.[17] Two sketches of sections of the western gateway pencilled by Elliot corroborate the fact that a large proportion of the stones that were uncovered under his supervision in this sector were *in situ*.[18]

On the basis of the sculptures he unearthed, Elliot was able to form 'a tolerable idea of the plan and purpose of the edifice'.[19] He was of the opinion that the structure which occupied the site of the mound was probably one of the largest and most magnificent Buddhist stupas ever built. On the other hand Fergusson (to whom Elliot had communicated his notes and sketches) thought the Amaravati stupa must have been fairly small, one of many structures on the Dipal-dina mound.

Elliot's excavations at Amaravati added next to nothing to the documentation of the site. What they did lead to was one of the largest hauls of sculpture from the place. Elliot sent a large number of pieces to Madras, where they lay for many years in the open in front of the College of Fort St George. In 1853, after the court of directors made inquiries about them, they were placed at the front entrance of the Central Museum.

In 1856 Edward Balfour, who had recently taken over as superintendent of the Madras Museum, asked Rev. William Taylor to compile and publish a description of the 'Elliot Marbles'. Taylor did the

[17] Elliot's notes and papers were lost in passage to England, and we only have bits of information about his activities at Amaravatī in his correspondence. The most detailed of these accounts is contained in a letter written many years later by him, dated 18 February 1871, to the Under Secretary of State for India, Home Proceedings/ Public, August 19, 1871, No. 76, Part A, Enclosure No. 2, OIOC.

[18] These are reproduced in Knox (1992): 17, Figure 5 and p. 227, Figure A).

[19] The Buddhist affiliations of the site had been established many years earlier in 1837, when G.T. Marshall read the inscriptions.

job but his account of the sculptures and inscriptions was of little value, 'for having no idea of what was put into his hands, and discarding the Pali alphabet, which had been recovered by scholars of note, he evolved one of his own, and gave transcriptions that are simply nonsensical, while his account of the sculptures is utterly useless except as a list of the stones and their dimensions.'[20]

Taylor listed 79 pieces of sculpture, of which two were already missing. He added to these 37 pieces which had arrived from Masulipatam in April/May 1856. Seven additional pieces had also surfaced by the time the whole collection was photographed in Madras by the government photographer, Captain Tripe, in 1858 or 1859.[21] Elliot managed to procure 44 more pieces; these included those wrested with some difficulty from Mr Alexander. By 1859, 121 pieces of the 'Elliot Marbles', as the lot had come to be known, were sent to London.[22] Other pieces were sent to the Central Museum, Madras, some to the Bezwada Museum, and a few remained in the possession of Captain Maiden, master attendant in Masulipatam.

The 121 'Elliot Marbles' arrived in London in 1860 and remained at Beale's Wharf in Southwark for a year. This was the aftermath of the 1857 Mutiny, and with the rule of the East India Company giving way to that of the crown, there was no place for the sculptures to go. In 1861 they were finally moved to the stables of Fife House, where the India Museum had been housed. A few of the best pieces were placed along the outer wall of Fife House, while the rest continued to languish

[20] Burgess (1887): 18.

[21] Tripe's photographs were published without any text in an album titled *Photographs of the Elliot Marbles and Other Subjects in the Central Museum, Madras.*

[22] According to Sewell (1880: 20), the sculptures sent by Mackenzie, Robertson, and Elliot were by this time hopelessly mixed up. Howes (2002: 62–3) points out that it is possible to distinguish between the stones from Robertson's Mound and the 'Elliot Marbles' by cross referencing the Tripe album and Taylor's catalogue. Out of the 121 'Elliot Marbles' sent from Madras to the British Museum in 1859, at least 50, if not more, had been discovered by Mackenzie in 1816–17. Twelve had been found at the site in 1845, and 38 were those that had formed part of Robertson's Mound. As for the 'Mackenzie stones' that remained in India, Howes points out that one can be found in the National Museum in New Delhi, at least one in the Indian Museum in Calcutta, and at least three in the Chennai Government Museum.

in the stables. Here they lay till, in January 1867, Fergusson found them.

James Fergusson and the 'Elliot Marbles'

In the fall of 1866 Henry Cole, whom we saw earlier as a leading figure in connection with the reform of Western industrial design, suggested to Fergusson that he put together a display of Indian art and architecture for the Paris Exhibition, scheduled to he held in 1867.[23] Fergusson agreed, and decided to prepare a collection of photographs for the event. He thought the effect of his display would be enhanced if supplemented with plaster casts of Indian sculpture and architectural fragments. His search for models for casting led him to the India Museum at Fife House, where he decided on four sculptures from Amaravati. Here, he received the startling information that a large collection of sculpted stones from the same site were stored in the coach-house. Investigating this, Fergusson found the stones.

The discovery made Fergusson alter his plans. He abandoned the idea of making casts and decided instead to send four or five specimens of the Amaravati sculptures to the Paris Exhibition. More important, he decided to have all the pieces of sculpture photographed to the same scale, in order to effect a photographic restoration of the monument. Forbes Watson, director of the India Museum, supported the plan, and provided the services of Griggs, the museum photographer. The Amaravati sculptures were brought into the open and photographed on a scale of 1/10th their actual size. Using as his guide the frequent depiction of the stupa in the sculptures themselves, Fergusson put together his photographs like pieces in a jigsaw puzzle, and at the end of the exercise he was confident he knew the position of at least nine-tenths of the 160 fragments in the India Museum collection.

The Amaravati photographs and some of the best pieces of sculpture were exhibited in Paris. Subsequently, in June 1867, Fergusson exhibited them and read a paper on the subject (later published) to the Royal Asiatic Society.[24] He went on to apply to Sir Stafford Northcote, secretary of state for India, for financial assistance to enable him to publish the most important photographs with an explanatory text.

[23] These details are given in Fergusson (1868): iii ff.
[24] Fergusson (1867): 132–66.

Having obtained this, he got to work on the project. Around this time he stumbled on the beautiful sketches of Sanchi by Lieutenant-Colonel Maisey and received a set of photographs of the same site from Lieutenant Waterhouse. Fergusson decided to enlarge the scope of his work to include Sanchi as well as Amaravati. The result was *Tree and Serpent Worship* (1868).

Tree and Serpent Worship contained the first detailed photographic and textual account of the Amaravati stupa. Sanchi had already been dealt with by Cunningham in *Bhilsa Topes* (1854). However, Fergusson's work included reproductions of Maisey's drawings and Waterhouse's photographs of Sanchi and also some of Mackenzie's material on Amaravati, making these available for the fist time to a wider audience. The series of maps, drawings and photographs were accompanied by an explanatory text. Fergusson placed the Amaravati remains a few centuries later than the Sanchi stupa. According to him, the history of the Amaravati stupa stretched from *c.* AD 200 to *c.* AD 500. He assigned the stupa itself to the third century and the 'outer rail' to the fourth century (on the basis of architectural style and inscriptions). The 'inner rail' he held to be more modern. *Tree and Serpent Worship* included an appendix by Cunningham, giving the text and translation of twenty Amaravati inscriptions.

Fergusson thought that several structures had once stood on the Dipal-dina mound. He estimated that the stupa could not have been more that 30 to 35 ft in diameter, and must have risen to a height of about 50 ft. The rest of the area, he suggested, had been occupied by other structures made of wood, including a nine-storeyed pagoda (based on accounts in Ceylonese tradition to a place called Diamond Sands, which Fergusson identified with Amaravati), a *vihara*, a *chaitya* hall, a *dharmashala*, and other buildings. The relief sculptures found at the site repeatedly showed stupas with highly ornamented domes and railings, and five tall pillars situated at the cardinal points. This suggested to Fergusson that the stupa at Amaravati must have been very different from those of north-western and Central India and was therefore a very important addition to knowledge of ancient Buddhist stupas.

Fergusson's interpretation of the Sanchi and Amaravati sculptures is indicated in the title he chose to give to his volume. That these were

Buddhist monuments was undeniable. He was able to identify several Buddhist scenes and motifs, although the Jataka scenes eluded him.[25] What struck him as the most significant aspect of the relief sculptures was the strong substratum of tree and serpent worship they revealed. Most of Fergusson's long introduction to his book is an exercise in comparative mythology, emphasizing the ubiquitous presence of tree and serpent worship in almost all parts of the world. His interpretation of the Amaravati sculptures was strongly influenced by this presupposition and preoccupation.

Another point Fergusson emphasized was a strong Bactrian influence. This led to a more general pronouncement on the origins of art and architecture in India: 'We can now assert with confidence that all the permanent forms of art arose in India after its inhabitants were brought into contact with western civilization, by the establishment of the Grecian kingdom of Bactria.'[26] Fergusson's understanding of Indian art and architecture was closely linked to his understanding of Indian history, ethnography, and religion. He was one of many scholars of the time floundering in these waters. He identified two original races of India—the Aryan and the Dravidian (whom he saw as a Turanian race, 'Turanian', after the fashion of the time, being used as a catch-all phrase for non-Aryan groups). To these he was prepared to add a third race—the aboriginal inhabitants of North India. The Aryans, with their belief in the soul's immortality, produced literature but did not deign to build mundane edifices of brick and stone. This was left for the more down-to-earth but intellectually inferior Turanians. The intermixture of Aryan and Turanian blood had important repercussions for the history of Indian architecture. 'The result of this distinction, in so far as the present subject is concerned, is this: so long as the Aryans retained their purity of blood and supremacy of power, no permanent buildings were erected in India . . .'[27] Fergusson also identified various racial groups depicted in the sculptures of Sanchi

[25] This was no doubt because no published text or translation of the Jataka text was available at the time.

[26] Fergusson (1868): 221.

[27] Fergusson (1868): 78. It is interesting to note that in medieval India the term 'Turani' was used to refer to Central Asians, in contrast with 'Iranis' or 'Persians'.

and Amaravati. According to him, the principal race represented in the latter were the Nagas.

Boswell's Report

In June 1869 the Board of Revenue of the Madras government requested J.A.C. Boswell, officiating collector of Kistna district, to prepare a report on ancient remains worthy of note and preservation in his district. Boswell's report, submitted the following year, detailed a series of archaeological remains, arranged by him in some sort of chronological order.[28] Large extracts of it were subsequently published in 1871 in *The Indian Antiquary*. Boswell's account referred to the Buddhist remains in and around Amaravati. He had observed some ten or twelve sculpted stones lying on the surface of the Dipal-dina mound and noted that a few of the best ones had been buried as protection against injury. He urged that further research be conducted at the site.

Boswell's report led to the first serious discussion in official circles on the steps that needed to be taken to excavate and preserve the Amaravati remains. The report was sent by the Madras government to the secretary of state for India in the India Office. The secretary of state consulted James Fergusson, Walter Elliot, and W. Rost (librarian of the Royal Asiatic Society) on the Amaravati issue and passed on their opinions to the Madras government. 'I will only add', he wrote, 'that I shall be ready to sanction any well-considered plan for preserving these valuable archaeological remains, and making fresh excavations, and that Major-General Cunningham, who has lately been appointed Archaeologist to the Government of India, should be consulted as to the best method of proceeding in the matter.'[29]

Rost emphasized the desirability of obtaining accurate copies of the ancient inscriptions. Elliot suggested that supervision of further excavations be entrusted to a skilled officer of the Public Works Depart-

[28] Letter No. 1301, dated 31 March 1870, from Boswell to the Acting Secretary to the Board of Revenue, Home Proceedings/Public, 27 May 1871, No. 1, Part A, OIOC.

[29] Letter No. 9, dated India Office, London, 12 April 1871, from the Secretary of State for India to the Government of Fort St George, Home Proceedings/Public, 27 May 1871, No. 1, Part A, OIOC.

ment, and that Cunningham be consulted on the matter. He also protested that he had taken good care of the Amaravati sculptures that he had removed to Madras, and it was only after their arrival in London that the stones had suffered neglect.[30] Fergusson asserted that there was no one in England (he was obviously excluding himself as he was not in a position to take up the job) who had the knowledge or zeal to supervise excavations at Amaravati. In India, there was only one man he could confidently recommend—James Burgess, who was on the verge of being appointed archaeological surveyor to the Bombay Presidency and would therefore not be available for work at Amaravati.[31]

Boswell's report, along with the suggestions penned by Fergusson, Elliot, and Rost, were sent to Cunningham, now director general of the recently established Archaeological Survey of India. Till the very end of the whole affair, Cunningham had little role to play in the Amaravati controversy. On the occasions when he was asked to express an opinion or give advice or direction, his responses were invariably delayed and generally began with an apology and explanation of the delay. Part of the delay was no doubt due to the fact that his establishment was very small and the task of archaeological exploration and documentation enormous. Given the constraints of his situation, Cunningham's operations and interests were directed towards north and Central India. In response to the specific query directed to him at this point of time by the government, Cunningham suggested that Boswell was the best person to supervise further excavations at Dipaldina. But Boswell was seriously ill and had proceeded to England on a year's medical leave. Under the circumstances, he thought it advisable to postpone operations until Boswell's return.[32] Boswell did not survive his illness and never came back to India.

[30] Letter dated Wolfebe, Hawick N.B., 18 February 1871, from Sir Walter Elliot to the Under Secretary of State for India, Home Proceedings/Public, 27 May 1871, No. 1, Enclosure No. 2, Part A, OIOC. There is a note in the margin of this document signed by Forbes Watson refuting Elliot's charge that the sculptures had suffered damage in the India Museum and Fergusson's charge that many of them had been dumped in a pile of rubbish in the coach house.

[31] Letter No. 20, Longham Place, dated 8 February 1871, from Fergusson to the Under Secretary of State for India; Home Proceedings/Public, 19 August 1871, No. 76, Enclosure No. 1, Part A, OIOC.

[32] Letter No. 101, dated Simla, 9 August 1871, from Alexander Cunningham

Sewell Offers His Services

The Amaravati excavations remained on hold for five years till the matter was reopened by Robert Sewell, acting head assistant collector of Kistna district. In March 1875 Sewell formally applied to the collector of his district to investigate the Amaravati remains.[33] He took great pains to emphasize that he would exercise the utmost care and caution in the operations. Since it was doubtful whether any of the sculpted rails of Amaravati remained in their original place, he would devote himself to clearing the debris in the area. If he found any *in situ* stones, he would leave them in their place and report at once. If he found any loose stones, he would note their exact position and store them, till such time as the government wanted to remove them to a museum. If the government thought it too 'dangerous' to entrust a non-expert such as him with this work, Sewell said he would be content to confine himself to certain other explorations in the area.[34]

Sewell's request for a grant of Rs 1000 was approved by the Madras government. At the same time, the matter was referred to the Government of India. While the Madras government expressed its willingness to take up Sewell's offer, Sewell himself had confessed he was no expert. It was therefore thought desirable to try to secure the services of Lieutenant Cole of the Royal Engineers, a man who was considered to have the expertise required for the job and who was on the verge of leaving England for India. Cunningham's advice was sought on the matter.

Cunningham responded several months later, explaining that he had not replied immediately as he wanted to examine Colonel Mackenzie's manuscript volumes in the library of the Asiatic Society, particularly the map and plan of the site. Unfortunately, he had been unable to do so, and not being able to locate the notes he had made in London after examining the Mackenzie manuscripts in the India Office, he

---

to E.C. Bayley, Secretary to the Government of India, Home Proceedings/Public, 27 May 1871, No. 1, Part A, OIOC.

[33] Letter No. 96, dated Mangalagherry, 19 March 1875, from Sewell to the Collector of the Kistna district, Home Proceedings/ Public, May 1876, No. 61, Part A, OIOC.

[34] Ibid.

was constrained to rely on his memory in making his recommendations:

> As well as I can remember, the whole of the Stûpa itself has been removed, even including its foundations, so as to form a circular tank surrounded by a high mound. This mound I believe to have been formed due to the rubbish and earth thrown out from the excavated Stûpa, and beneath it lie the remains of the double railing which once surrounded the monument. It is therefore very much to be desired that the whole of this circular ring of the mound should be explored; and I would recommend that the work should be begun from the interior of the circle, the whole of the excavated earth and rubbish being thrown into the circular tank.
>
> In making these explorations it is especially desirable that all standing stones, or stone-work *in situ*, should be left undisturbed until the exact position of each piece and a general plan of the whole have been made by some competent surveyor. As Mr Sewell himself seems to be fully alive to the importance of leaving such stones in their original places, the work of exploration might safely be entrusted to him; and I would most strongly recommend that the sum of one thousand Rupees, which he has asked for this purpose, should be granted to him.[35]

He also urged that a meticulous search be made for carved stones in the town of Amaravati and its neighbourhood, that impressions be taken of all inscriptions, and that if possible they be photographed as well. Cunningham concluded on a note that emphasized the importance of collecting and analysing inscriptional rather than sculptural evidence from Amaravati, alluding to his continuing disagreement with James Fergusson over the general issue involved.

> In conclusion, I beg to express my opinion that inscriptions should be most diligently sought for as it is to them that we must look for the *history* of the Stupa. We already possess more than a sufficient number of sculptures to show the style of art which prevailed when the Stupa was erected. From the sculptures Mr Fergusson has inferred that it must have been built in the 4th century AD. From the inscriptions, on the contrary, I infer that it was erected towards the end of the 1st century AD. As the forms of the alphabetic characters afford a much surer criterion than the style

[35] Letter No. 295, dated Agra, 6 March 1876, from Major General Alexander Cunningham to the Officiating Secretary to the Government of India, Home Proceedings/Public, May 1876, No. 62, Part A, OIOC.

of the sculptures for determining the date of any building, I trust that the importance of securing every fragment of inscription may be kept in mind.[36]

Sewell's Operations

In June 1876 the Madras government gave Robert Sewell the green signal to proceed with explorations at Amaravati. Sewell was, however, so preoccupied with routine administrative duties that he did not find the time to visit Amaravati till May 1877, when he spent a week at the site. In a letter written some three years later, Sewell stated that the site 'had not been disturbed to any purpose since Sir Walter Elliot's explorations in 1840 . . .'[37] He was talking about a period of thirty-seven years.

At the time of Sewell's visit, a hollow cup-like basin was all that remained of the Chintapalli raja's reservoir.[38] This was surrounded by a mound of earth and stones, sloping more steeply on the inner than on the outer side (see Figure 3). On the mound, which varied from 150 to 200 feet across, were smaller undulating mounds, intersected by the courses of water channels. A few 'somewhat damaged and discoloured marbles' were lying about, and 'a fine but terribly mutilated slab', originally unearthed for display for the district collector, lay fully exposed on top of the mound on the west. Sewell made 'a slight excavation' in the south of the mound and found two small stones embedded near the surface. He then had all the exposed stones covered with earth and left.

Sewell came back to Amaravati at the end of 1877. He took measurements, drew a plan of the site, and fixed the cardinal points as accurately as possible. In the south-east quadrant he uncovered seven unsculpted stones. Towards the south of the circle he exposed two stones he had excavated when he was there last. His main excavations were concentrated in the north-west quadrant, where he found a portion of a platform (see Figure 4).

[36] Ibid.

[37] Letter from Sewell to the Under Secretary of State for India, dated Isle of Wight, 5 April 1880; Home Proceedings/Surveys, July 1880, No. 25, Part B, NAI.

[38] Sewell (1880): 31.

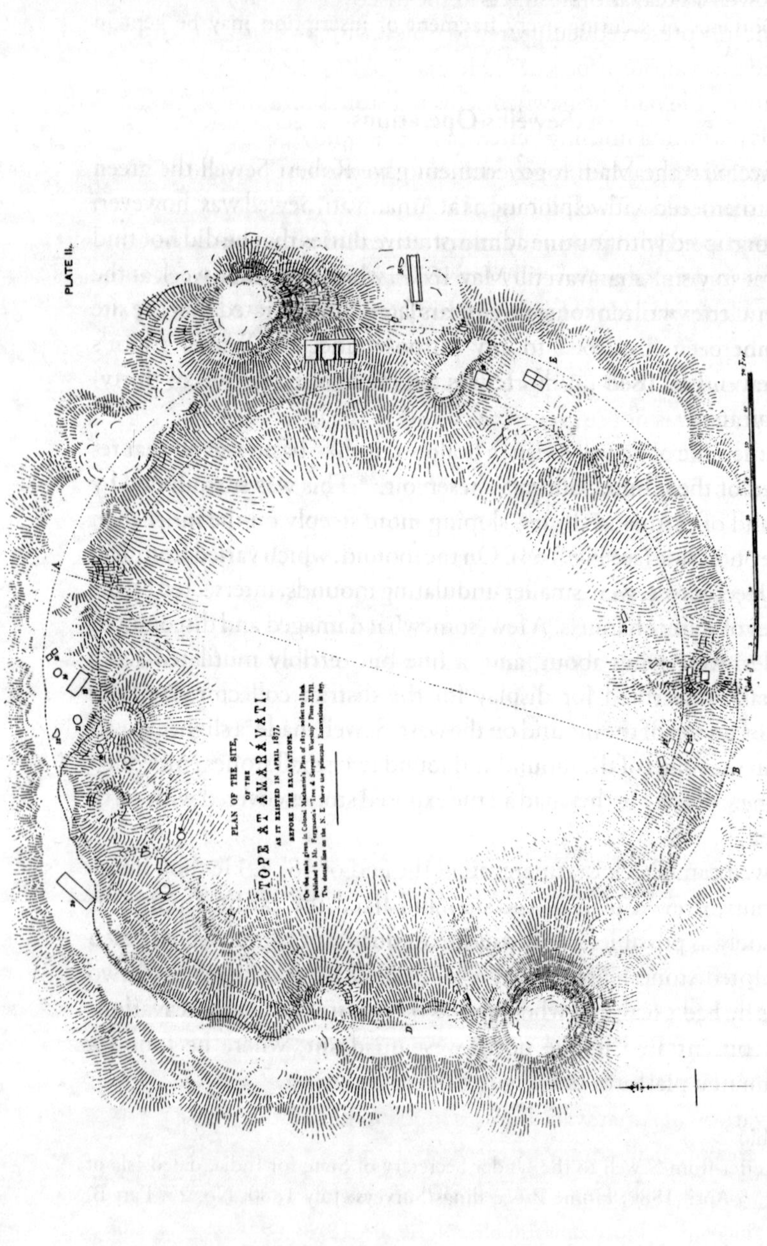

23. Figure 3. The site in 1877. Sewell (1880), Plate II

Sewell's excavation resulted in the discovery of about 90 'new and splendidly preserved sculptured marbles, with promise of plenty more as the excavations proceed.'[39] He managed to clear only 100 ft of the platform. He had the newly discovered stones photographed, but his funds permitted nothing better than the employment of 'an unskilled Native photographer' for the job, and he was not particularly happy with the results. Sewell thought the Amaravati sculptures ought to be photographed professionally and prepared for publication by a school of arts student or engraver. An even better solution, he suggested, was to send the whole lot of stones to England, to join those already shipped there.

Sewell had used up more than half his sanctioned grant and the remainder was not sufficient to complete the work. More funds were urgently required. It was equally important, Sewell emphasized, to put someone exclusively on the job: 'The best proof that this is so will, perhaps, be found in the fact that, though extensively interested in the subject, I could not find leisure from my ordinary official duties *for a whole year*, to commence the excavations at Amravati, only 17 miles from my headquarters.'[40] Sewell suggested that Burnell was the best man in the presidency to handle the work of translating the inscriptions, but since he was a senior official on judge's pay, the government would no doubt be reluctant to release him from his regular official duties. So, Sewell went on to humbly offer his own services for conducting an archaeological survey of the area. Appealing to the bureaucratic concern for economy, he urged that this would cost the least. Justifying the sanction of additional funds for the project, he pointed out that in 1868 the Madras government had been authorized to spend Rs 13,000 per annum on the archaeology of the presidency, not a penny of which had been spent to date. This fact, he asserted, had recently been brought to the notice of the viceroy by the home government. Rs 13, 000 was precisely the amount he now sought government sanction for. The project Sewell outlined included further excavations at Amaravati, but was much larger in its scope—it was for an archaeological survey of the Kistna and Godavari valleys, on the

[39] Letter dated Charing Cross, 18 August 1877, from Robert Sewell to Col. Yule, Home Proceedings/Public, November 1877, No. 88, Part A, OIOC.

[40] Ibid.

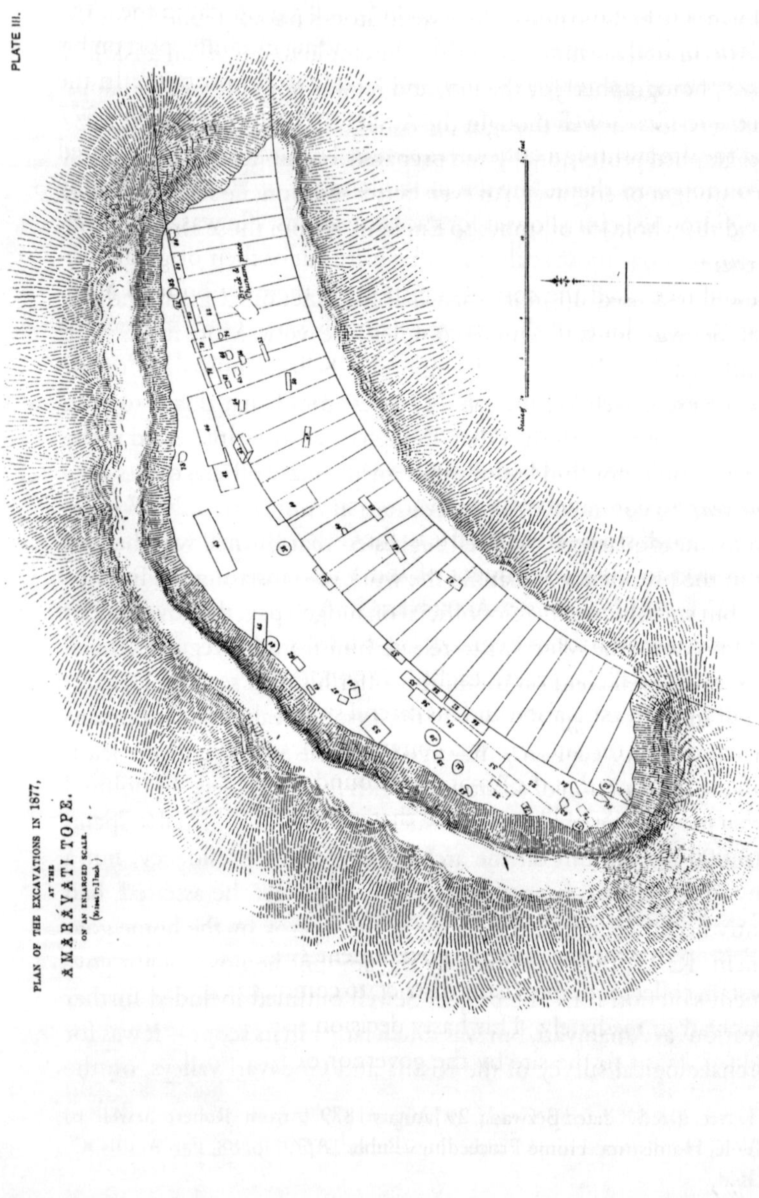

24. Figure 4: Sewell's excavations in the north-west quadrant. Sewell (1880), Plate III.

basis of which he could compile a history of the area in the ancient period. Sewell wanted to be released from his regular duties so that he could devote himself to this work on a full-time basis.

The Madras government passed on Sewell's proposal to the Government of India. Sewell refrained from sending in a full report on his excavations at Amaravati, waiting for a reply to his proposal. In the meantime, the sculptures he had unearthed at Amaravati in May 1877 lay at the site awaiting a decision as to their fate. Sewell had appointed a peon to guard them, but the monthly salary of Rs 5 was steadily eating into the grant allowed for the excavations. He was, moreover, anxious to move those sculptures that were out of their original position and estimated the cost of transporting them by punt to Madras as Rs 150. Some of these were eventually sent to the Vijayawada museum. As for the stones that were *in situ*, he suggested the simple expedient of loosely covering them with a foot or so of earth till more permanent arrangements were made.[41]

The Madras government ultimately sanctioned the retention of the peon stationed at Amaravati, as also the sum required for the removal of the sculpted stones from the site to the Central Museum at Madras. It appealed to the Government of India for an additional grant of Rs 1000 for explorations at Amaravati. In April 1879 Sewell packed his bags and went back to England. He had received no response to his proposal. He had, however, reached an important conclusion on the basis of his own excavation and his careful study of Mackenzie's plans and account of the site. He was convinced that Fergusson had been wrong in thinking that the Amaravati mound was the site of a number of structures. To Sewell, it was clear that it was the site of a single, huge stupa.

Horsfall Steps In

In February 1880 the Madras government suddenly directed J.G. Horsfall, collector of the Kistna district, to complete the excavation of Amaravati immediately. This hasty decision seems to have been the result of a visit to the site by the governor of Madras, the Duke of

[41] Letter No. 52, dated Bezwada, 29 January 1879, from Sewell to the Collector of the Kistna district, Home Proceedings/Public, April 1879, No. 107, Part A, OIOC.

Buckingham. The long prevarication over the issue was brought to a sudden end by giving a free hand to a man who had no qualifications for the job. The result was a hastily conducted, sloppy excavation, which resulted in the removal of still more sculptures, adding little of value as far as the documentation of the site was concerned.

Horsfall began excavation work at Amaravati on 16 February 1880 and continued to personally supervise it up to 3 March.[42] It was not until 1st March, when all the work was nearly done, that a draftsman arrived to assist him. Horsfall proudly reported that, unable to get the work taken up on contract, he directly hired the labour for the job at highly economical rates. On 3 March Horsfall had to leave Amaravati for Bapatla *taluk*. He placed the draftsman in charge of 'the trifling work that remained to be done'. When he came back to the site on 24 March, Sergeant Coney had already photographed much of the stupa.[43] Horsfall was thus not present for the most part when the work of drawing and photography was being conducted.

As for the results of the excavation, Horsfall himself admitted he was disappointed. He had hoped to discover stones of the outer and inner circles in their entirety. Instead, he found broken sculptures, 'wretched brick hovels', and evidence of vandalism and destruction everywhere, for which he blamed religious iconoclasts. Horsfall did not give many precise details regarding his operations at Amaravati. He did refer to the discovery of a brick basement running around the inner side of the circle, about 1 ft below the level of the pavement. He also mentioned having encountered very large quantities of bricks, suggesting that there were once many brick buildings immediately next to the stupa. He ascertained the position of the southern gateway. He also uncovered pottery, coins, inscriptions, and an unspecified number of sculpted stones. The sculptures, according to him, were similar to those already described by Fergusson and gave plenty of evidence of tree and serpent worship. Horsfall himself was quite confused about the significance of the motifs on the sculptures.

[42] Horsfall gave an account of his activities at the site in letter No. 794 to the Chief Secretary to the Government of Madras, dated Masulipatam, 16 April 1880, Home Proceedings/Archaeology, October 1881, No. 17, Part A, NAI.

[43] Coney's photographs included a panoramic view of the site, consisting of twelve joined pictures, which brings out the pathetic condition of the site as a result of Horsfall's excavations. Cited in Howes (2002): 56, and p. 55, Plate 3.

The fallout of Horsfall's operations included the discovery of a relic casket a little to the east of the southern gateway. This contained what seemed to be human relics, a tooth, and some fragments of bones. Although stones continued to be dug up, for unspecified reasons Horsfall considered it inadvisable to go on excavating. He ordered the draftsman to cease work and wound up the operations. Some of the excavated material, including four sculpted stone heads, were sent to Masulipatam, from where they were to move on to Madras.

The Madras government sent Horsfall's brief report for comments to Sewell, who had finally been recalled to India in January 1881 as officer on special duty in connection with the archaeological survey of the Madras Presidency. Sewell found Horsfall's details and copies of inscriptions of little value, for they were neither sufficiently accurate nor clear. Although the site plan seemed to have been carefully made, it would be difficult to work from it as sections were missing and there were no descriptions showing the levels at which the stones had been found. The fact that new numbers had been given to all the stones made the task of correlating the two plans (Horsfall's and Sewell's) difficult. The photographs taken by Sergeant Coney were good, but not good enough. Sewell expressed regret that the 'wretched hovels' mentioned by Horsfall were not preserved or at least drawn. And what were they—Buddhist shrines? Votive stupas? How old were they? Horsfall's report suggested no answers to these important questions. Sewell recommended further excavation at Amaravati, but a scientific one, which Horsfall's excavation certainly had not been.[44]

Horsfall's clumsy doings at Amaravati had set off a series of alarm bells in England as well, and with good reason. The India Office wrote to the governor of Madras on the matter, sending a copy of the letter to the viceroy.[45] Secretary of State Hartington pointed out that the instructions given to Horsfall should have included the making of

[44] Letter No. 639, dated Greenwood, Ootacamund, 20 August 1881, from R. Sewell, Madras Civil Service, Officer on Special Duty, to the Chief Secretary to the Government of Madras, Home Proceedings/ Surveys, Oct. 1881, No. 17, Part A, NAI.

[45] Despatch (Statistics and Commerce) No. 38, from Hartington, India Office to the Governor-in-Council, Fort St. George, dated 30 September 1880, Proceedings of the Home, Revenue and Agriculture Department, Surveys/Archaeology, 1880, No. 56, Part B, NAI.

accurate plans and sections showing the location and relative height of every stone uncovered in the course of the work. He also expressed his apprehensions about the care and expertise that had been invested in the operations, and questioned the collector's qualifications as an archaeologist.

> I am therefore under some anxiety to hear further from Your Excellency as to the steps taken for the proper excavation and conservation of the Amravati Tope. If these operations are not already completed, it should be borne in mind that the work of the examination and survey of an ancient monument of such unique value should be entrusted only to some competent archaeologist and scholar with such engineering assistance as you can most conveniently place at his disposal. When an accurate record has been furnished of the results of the excavations you have ordered, it will then be necessary to determine what further steps should be taken for the preservation of these sculptures which have excited a keen interest in Europe.[46]

A copy of the secretary of state's despatch was sent for comments to Alexander Cunningham, who remained silent almost two years, in the course of which several reminders were issued to him. By the time he got around to replying, the Archaeological Survey of Southern India had came into being under the charge of James Burgess, and Amaravati fell within his jurisdiction.

Burgess *versus* Cole

James Burgess' appointment as superintendent of the Archaeological Survey of Southern India in 1881 roughly coincided with that of H.H. Cole, who had taken charge as curator of ancient monuments in January of the same year. As we have seen, Burgess and Cole both had definite ideas about their role in the documentation and preservation of Indian antiquities and monuments, making Amaravati a trial of strength between them, while causing a full-blown discussion and acrimonious debate over the broader issue of conservation policy.

At the time that Burgess and Cole took up their respective appointments, a batch of Amaravati sculptures was lying exposed at the site since Horsfall's excavation. Burgess visited the site and was there from

[46] Ibid.

December 1881 to January 1882. He reported that the stone slabs had been pounded to pieces in the most regardless way during the 'rough and ready' excavations in February 1880.[47] The site had the appearance of a large, roughly circular pit, about 75 yards in diameter, with extensions at the cardinal points (see Figure 5). Burgess counted 255 slabs (these included those uncovered and then buried for safety by Sewell) laid around the circle, 44 stored by Sewell in a shed, and 29 in the Bezwada Library (a total of 328). He discovered about 90 more in the course of his own excavations.

Burgess's detailed account of the Amaravati stupa identified several structural phases belonging to different periods.[48] His description and interpretation of the sculptures was integrated with the inscriptional evidence and accompanied by the text, translation, and photo-lithographs of a large number of inscriptions. Burgess estimated the diameter of the Amaravati stupa as about 138 ft at the base, narrowing to over 90 ft near the summit, and placed its height at between 80 and 100 ft. He thought that this huge stupa had been faced with sculpted slabs and surrounded by a double rail, carved on both sides.

Many of the exposed stones Burgess found were not *in situ* and he thought that the best of the lot (he identified over 170) should be immediately removed to Madras where they could be placed in the Central Museum. This had to be done at once as the water levels in the Krishna were fast receding, and it would soon be impossible to move them downriver. Burgess asked for immediate despatch of the necessary equipment and an experienced officer to Amaravati.

In January 1882 a large number of selected Amaravati stones lay packed at the site, ready for shipment down the river. The heavier stones were wrapped in straw ropes and some of the smaller ones were given the additional protection of wooden cases. However, the arrival of a telegram from the Madras government froze all operations. The curator of ancient monuments had been in communication both with the Madras government and the viceroy regarding the Amaravati sculptures. The Government of India had intervened and decreed that

[47] Letter No. 15, dated Amaravati, 30 December 1881, from Burgess to the Chief Secretary, Government of Madras, Home Proceedings/Archaeology and the Conservation of Ancient Monuments, July 1882, No. 2, Part A, NAI.

[48] Burgess (1887).

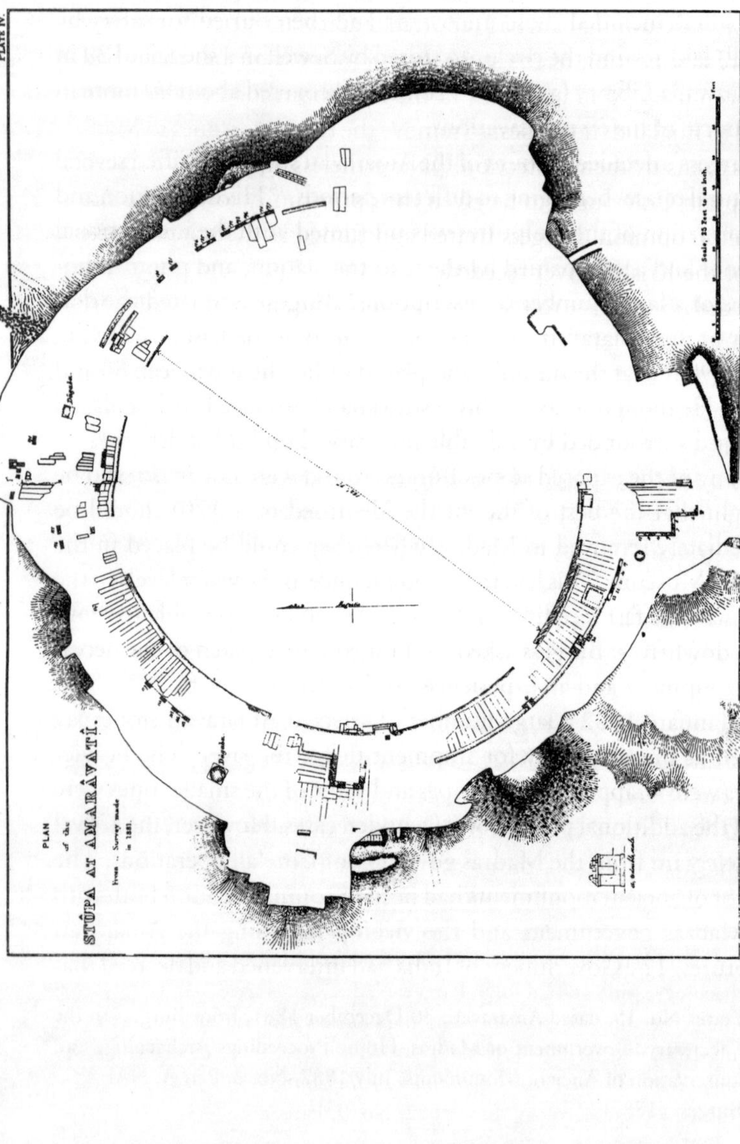

25. Figure 5: The site in 1881. Burgess (1887), Plate IV.

Captain Cole should be allowed to visit the site and give his opinion on the matter before further action was taken.[49]

Opinions had been sought from Sewell and Cunningham. Sewell had reported that some of the Amaravati stones were so out of place that there was no harm in removing them, while others could be preserved *in situ*. Cunningham had reported that it was utterly impossible to restore any portion of the stupa *in situ* as most of the stones had either been used up in buildings in the neighbourhood or had been shipped to England. It was best to remove the remaining ones to Madras, so as to ensure their protection.[50] Nevertheless, the viceroy decreed that Captain Cole ought to be given the opportunity to visit the site and give *his* opinion. Burgess fretted and fumed as the waters in the canals of the Krishna river receded.

Cole did not manage to visit Amaravati till the end of the year as he had to prepare for his examinations for promotion. In the meantime, he did prepare and submit to the government a memorandum on the condition of the Amaravati stupa. Referring to Burgess's visit to the site he stated: 'I now learn . . . . that Dr Burgess was engaged at Amravati *over a month* this last cold season, and packed up everything that he thought worth packing, and has in fact *ransacked the place* of all valuable stones.'[51] Cole's memorandum put forward a strong case for *in situ* preservation: 'How far it may be possible *now* to restore any of the sculptures to their original positions is a question to which I cannot reply until all the facts are investigated; but I have no hesitation in counselling the preservation of the marbles (now at the Madras Museum and those lying packed) in a suitable manner on the site *at Amravati*. Even should it prove impossible to replace them as they stood, I recommended the erection of a small building where these carvings would be properly displayed and absolutely safe, and the railing-in of the site of the great Buddhist Tope, securing, as far as

[49] Letter No. 9, dated 16 June 1882 from A. Mackenzie, Secretary to the Government of India to the Secretary to the Government of Madras, Home Proceedings/Archaeology, June 1882, No. 9, Part A, NAI.

[50] Home Proceedings/Archaeology and the Conservation of Ancient Monuments, July 1882, No. 1, Part A, NAI.

[51] *Memorandum on the Present Condition of the Amravati Tope in Madras*, Home Proceedings/Archaeology, June 1882, No. 9, Part A, NAI.

possible, all the existing masonry of the building.'[52] Cole expressed the opinion that valuable ancient antiquities should on no account be removed from India to England. He spoke of the Sanchi stupa having escaped two great dangers—one when in 1853, General Cunningham had advised the removal of the fallen gateways to the British Museum, the second in 1868, when the eastern gateway was nearly carried away to the Paris Exhibition (at the last minute it was decided to display a cast). If beautiful and valuable remains were to be ruthlessly torn from their ancient sites, the outlying districts of the country would be rapidly robbed of all their interesting records. According to Cole, a policy of preserving ancient monuments *for India* was a sounder one than carting them away to European museums. Cole suggested that the needs of the British Museum in London and the Central Museum in Madras (which already housed several valuable marbles from Amaravati) could be met by displaying plaster casts, and that there was no need to send any more stones to these places: '. . . it seems to me *a suicidal and indefensible policy to allow the country to be looted of original works of ancient art when there exist the means of making facsimiles scarcely distinguishable from the original!*'[53]

One of the arguments made by Burgess for the removal of the Amaravati sculptures from the site was the inaccessibility of the place. Cole pointed out that India was being rapidly opened up by communication networks of different kinds. Travellers and scholars from many countries were visiting its ancient cities and temples. Cole also contested Burgess's argument that there was no point in leaving the sculpted pieces where they were because the ignorant natives were unaware of their significance. He cited an 1881 order of the governor general in council[54] which expressed satisfaction at the 'cordial interest' displayed by 'natives of various classes', in Sewell's operations at Amaravati. Besides, since the Amaravati case was a matter concerning the conservation of an ancient monument, and not of archaeological research, it came within the jurisdiction of the curator of ancient monuments and not of the Archaeological Survey.

Throughout the whole controversy, Burgess maintained that the

[52] Ibid.

[53] Ibid. Italics in original.

[54] No. 985 of 20 January 1881. Cited in ibid.

stones that remained at Amaravati were too scattered to permit the restoration of even a small part of the stupa.

> Amaravati has not been an 'Architectural Monument' for centuries. No two complete stones are together *in situ*, nor can three be found entire that were originally in juxtaposition . . .
>
> If Captain Cole only condescended to ask me what was the character and extent of the remains at Amaravati, I would have most readily given him every information. The Amaravati Stupa has been so utterly destroyed, and the remaining fragments are so few relatively to its original extent, that the ablest living archaeologists differ in their views of its original form; and as the villagers destroy and carry off the slabs to burn into lime, any attempt at conservation on the spot would be futile. No one, who had informed himself as to the amount and condition of the materials, and recognised the difficulty of the problem, would suggest such an attempt.[55]

Burgess alleged that Cole's stand on the matter was motivated by something other than a commitment to the principle of *in situ* preservation. His real aim, he asserted, was to wrest South Indian architecture out of Burgess's hands and to prepare an illustrated work on the subject at government expense. If Cole were allowed to have his way, this 'would cut my department off from all connection with architecture—the branch which of all others I am best fitted to deal with.'[56]

Cole's Recommendations

Cole visited Amaravati in November 1882 and submitted his report in December of that year.[57] He had inspected the 175 fine stones packed and stored in a fenced enclosure about half a mile north of Amaravati by Burgess. They seemed to be in good condition. They had been taken out of their cases and straw cocoon; the flood waters had cleaned them and had not harmed them in any perceptible way.

[55] Letter dated Edinburgh, 27 July 1882, from Burgess to the Secretary to the Government of India, Home Proceedings/ Archaeology and the Conservation of Ancient Monuments, September 1882, No. 12, Part A, NAI.

[56] Letter dated Edinburgh, 2 August 1882, from Burgess to the Secretary to the Government of India, Home Proceedings/Archaeology and the Conservation of Ancient Monuments, September 1882, No. 11, Part A, NAI.

[57] *Memorandum on the Present Condition of Amaravati.*

Cole gave the following list of the sculpted stones that still lay at Amaravati:

Sculptures of Dr Burgess's selection on the river-bank	175
Sculptures at Tope—	
In a shed to the North, in boxes	8
In a shed to the North, loose	43
In situ	195
	256
Total	421

According to Cole, a large number of stones were obviously in their original place, and it was possible on the basis of these to trace the position of the railing and of the structure that must have stood in the centre of the mound. The stones listed as deposited in the shed to the north of the mound were those placed there by Sewell in 1877. In the western part of the circumference of the structure, a part of the stone terrace, although much damaged, was still in its original place. The southern entrance could be traced. Elsewhere, portions of the railing were in position. Various smaller fragments and masonry slabs in position indicated the demarcation of the railing and the plinth of the stupa itself.

Cole's report exonerated the Hindu natives of Amaravati of responsibility for the shattered condition of some of the masonry and the sculptures. It was true, he wrote, that many years ago the grandfather of the present zamindar had removed bricks and stones from the mound for his buildings, but he would have been concerned with simple removal of the material, not with smashing and destroying sculpture. Cole insisted that any damage suffered by the sculptures must represent the handiwork of the iconoclast Aurangzeb, when he conquered the area and established himself in the forts of Kondapilli and Kondavid nearby. But there was not much of this sort of thing either: 'The place is now easily accessible to any idle boy who wishes to pass away his time in hammering off carved surfaces, but it is really surprising to me how little evidence there is of damage of this kind.'[58]

Cole recommended that the masonry terrace-rails and fragments still standing in their original position should be rendered secure. The

[58] Ibid.

existing portions of the terrace should be re-laid on concrete and in cement. The rails should be supported in their places by a solid foundation of concrete and by using iron bars to prop the uprights and hold them in position. All the fragmentary sculptures should be collected and placed under a permanent shed in the centre of the circular enclosure. The embankment of earth formed around the stupa by the demolition of the mound in past years should be gently sloped off so as to prevent the falling in of earth, which had happened during the last rainy season. A 7 ft high masonry wall should be built around the ruins and the entrance gate placed under lock and key. A small house for a custodian should be built near this gate.

Cole vetoed in strong terms the idea of moving the 175 stones selected by Burgess to the Madras Museum, saying that there was no indoor room there for them and that an open-air display would expose them to the destructive atmospheric conditions of the town. The Madras Museum (or any other museum that was interested) could display plaster casts. The Amaravati stones should be left at Amaravati.

Cole was advocating *in situ* conservation, not restoration. Considering the fact that it was not possible to identify the exact original position of the removed stones, any attempt at restoration was neither possible nor desirable. What he did suggest was that, since it was certainly possible to identify the part of the stupa complex to which the stones belonged, they could be placed on the ground in these positions, where they might be easily examined and appreciated. Cole also advocated that all the best sculptural pieces be photographed by a professional photographer. He estimated the cost of preparing casts and photographs to be about Rs 5000. A special officer should be appointed to implement all these recommendations.

Cole's recommendations were sent to Burgess for comment, and the slanging match between the two continued. Burgess opposed Cole's recommendation of re-laying the slabs of the old terrace on concrete and cement as it would alter what remained of the original structure.[59] He even opposed Cole's suggestion that a stone wall be built around the site on the grounds that this would only amount to a

[59] Letter No. 24, dated Gujarat, 9 March 1883, from Burgess to the Chief Secretary to the Government of Madras, Home Proceedings/Archaeology, July 1883, No. 9, Part A, NAI.

temptation to Telugu boys, natives of a hilly country, to jump over it and damage the sculptures. On the other hand he found the suggestion of building a shed to protect the stones remaining at the site and appointing a custodian acceptable. If the Madras Museum lacked space to house the stones, some of them could be displayed in the School of Art. Provided funds were available, there was no harm in having casts of some of the pieces made under the supervision of the superintendent of the Madras School of Art; it would be cheaper to have the casts made at Madras rather than at Amaravati.

According to Burgess, the fact that Cole himself admitted that the restoration of any part of the Amaravati stupa was impracticable amounted to an admission that there was no structure worth the name left to conserve. This clearly indicated that the remains at Amaravati fell within the domain of archaeology and not within conservation. He argued that the disposal of the Amaravati marbles fell squarely within the jurisdiction of the Archaeological Survey of Southern India. If General Cunningham had been permitted to do as he pleased at Bharhut, why should he, Burgess, be subject to undue interference at the hands of the meddlesome curator of ancient monuments? Burgess argued that he did not stand alone in his point of view on the matter of the Amaravati sculptures. His opinion was shared by all those who had been connected with the site over the years—the collector, Horsfall; the sub-collector, Mackenzie; the engineer, Grant; and the former first assistant collector, Sewell. If the government required further advice, it could consult Cunningham.

Meanwhile, Sewell continued to urge the Madras government to do *something* about the Amaravati sculptures. He pointed out that apart from the stones that lay exposed at the site after Horsfall's excavations, those that he himself had excavated in 1877 had been lying exposed for the last six years. The stones that Burgess had packed and removed to the river bank had lain there waiting for Cole's inspection, and in that period had been exposed to great danger due to the flooding of the river. While this had not caused any appreciable damage, their continued exposure to sun, wind and rain could not but harm them: 'As each year passes by and nothing is done to save them, the process of destruction is steadily going on, and if this treatment is continued, all the rare beauty of the lately-excavated marbles will be lost by their becoming weather-worn like *all* the rest previously excavated. I would, therefore, earnestly entreat Government to take some immediate steps to save them.'[60]

Cunningham's Verdict

The Madras government took up Burgess's suggestion that the director general of the Archaeological Survey of India be asked for his opinion on the matter. This time, Cunningham obliged with a fairly swift response, requiring only one reminder:

> There is so little now remaining on the side of the Amaravati Stupa that I do not think it is worth while to attempt any kind of restoration. I am a strong advocate for the conservation of all ancient buildings that actually exist, and also for the restoration of such as can be restored. When I suggested in 1853 that the gateways of the Sânchi Stupa might, with advantage, be removed to the British Museum, my sole object was their preservation, as I was but too well aware of the danger to which they were exposed if left much longer neglected. But since Major Cole obtained his present appointment, I have been a staunch advocate for the complete restoration of the Sânchi Stupa.[61]

Cunningham's solution to the impasse fell more or less in line with Burgess's views on the matter. Since so many of the sculpted stones had already been removed from Amaravati, he suggested that the best course of action would be to remove the selected stones to the Madras Museum. There they would be safe as well as accessible and could be displayed to give a fair idea of their original arrangement. As for the rest of the stones lying scattered at the site, they could, as suggested by Cole, be placed under a shed in the centre of the circle of the ruins, under the care of a chowkidar. The best specimens of sculpture should be photographed, and, if casts were to be made, Burgess was correct in stating that it would be cheaper to have this work done in Madras rather than at Amaravati.

[60] Letter No. 2, dated Chingleput, 29 April 1883, from Sewell, Acting Sub-Collector, Chingleput to the Chief Secretary to the Government of Madras, Home Proceedings/Archaeology, July 1883, No. 9, Part A, NAI.

[61] Letter No. 24, dated Simla, 30 May 1883, from Major-General Cunningham to the Chief Secretary to the Government of Madras, Home Proceedings/Archaeology, July 1883, No. 9, Part A, NAI.

Presented with Cunningham's verdict on the matter, the Madras government decided to accept Burgess's plan of action. Orders were issued to that effect. Cole was not, however, a man to give up easily. He still had one more card (not an ace, but a card nevertheless) up his sleeve. He wrote to the viceroy directly, referring to the recent Government of India Resolution of 8 June 1883 concerning the preservation of archaeological remains.[62] He argued that this resolution could not have been before the Madras government when the orders on the Amaravati case had been passed. The resolution and the orders must have crossed each other on their respective ways. Cole pointed out that the resolution, which laid down principles to guide local governments, endorsed the principle of *in situ* preservation. It clearly stated that only isolated remains, the original site of which was unknown, were to be removed to museums. Cole stated that he had met the governor of Madras some months previously, on 2 December 1882, and that the latter had supported his proposals. After going over Burgess's and Cunningham's letters on the matter, Cole said that he saw in them no argument whatsoever to induce him to alter his recommendation of *in situ* preservation of the Amaravati sculptures. In fact General Cunningham's suggestion of setting up slabs and pillars to give an idea of their original arrangement could be done at Amaravati, rather than in the Madras Museum. Cole attacked the archaeologists: 'I submit that the province of the Archaeological Surveys is to write ancient History and not to go about the country pilfering tons of sculptures from well-known monuments.'[63]

The Removal of the Amaravati Sculptures to the Madras Museum

Cole's last shot proved in vain. His had all along been a lone voice. The Government of India declined to reopen an issue that had dragged on inconclusively and in which the majority opinion was clearly ranged against Cole. Burgess's recommendations were implemented and the stones awaiting removal near the bank of the Krishna for some twenty months were sent to the Madras Museum in 1883. Yet Burgess did not

[62] Letter No. 138, dated Simla, 2 July 1883, from Cole to the Government of India, Home Proceedings/Archaeology, July 1883, No. 11, Part A, NAI.

[63] Ibid.

have the last laugh. He had his way as far as the removal of choice sculptures from Amaravati to Madras was concerned, but he was far from happy with what happened to them once they reached Madras.

The sculptures lay in the museum for two years. During this time there was talk of the possible construction of a special covered area between the wings at the back of the Central Museum for their display. In March 1886 Burgess was appointed director general of the Archaeological Survey. He had all along maintained that he should supervise the unpacking and arrangement of the Amaravati marbles on their arrival in Madras. This did not happen. The job of arranging the stones that reached the Madras Museum was entrusted to the acting surgeon general of the Government of Madras, a man named Bidie. Bidie arranged the Amaravati stones in the Madras Museum as he thought fit, and had many of them embedded in cement for display.

Burgess was furious and minced no words in expressing his displeasure. He shot off a letter to the Madras government stating that he had heard from those who had visited the museum and seen the display that it left much to be desired.[64] His own visit there had confirmed his worst fears—the Madras government had caused irreparable damage to one of the most valuable collections of sculpture in India.

Burgess listed the 'barbarisms' that had been perpetrated in the hotch-potch arrangement of priceless sculptures, in flagrant violation of their original architectural placing or their differences in style and age. He further alleged that certain sculptures still lay about, uncared for, in the museum: 'Few museums have received so important a collection of sculptures; none has shewed itself so unworthy by such wanton and ignorant abuses of such a trust.'[65] The Madras government directed Bidie to respond to these charges. Bidie defended himself by asserting that before commencing he had consulted all the literature available on the sculptures, examined the stones carefully, and solicited the advice of Colonel Morant, an architect, 'whose respect for these valuable antiquities was just as great as my own.' He complained of the many difficulties he had faced in arranging such a heterogeneous collection. He also reported that many 'scientific visitors' from various

[64] Letter No. 240, dated Hospet, 16 April 1886, from James Burgess to the Chief Secretary of the Government of Madras, Home/Archaeology and the Conservation of Ancient Monuments, July 1886, No. 10, Part A, NAI.

[65] Ibid.

parts of the world had visited the museum and expressed their approval of his display.[66]

The Madras government was satisfied with Bidie's response. At the same time, it expressed regret at the 'extraordinary attack' on the Madras Museum by the director general of the Archaeological Survey, and on the incorporation of items of gossip in his official communication. It referred to the infrequent visits paid by Burgess to the Madras Presidency and observed that his interest in the province was chiefly manifest in fault-finding.[67] Burgess was also officially ticked off by the Government of India. He was informed that the governor general in council—

> has perused your letter in question with much regret. His Excellency in Council cannot refrain from expressing his opinion that the remarks made in your letter . . . are altogether wanting in the moderation and judgement which should characterize official documents; while they are equally open to objection as failing to show that respect which the Government of Madras has a right to expect in communications made to it more particularly when such communications relate to the proceedings of officers serving under its order.
>
> The Government of India earnestly trusts that such proceedings will not recur, and that in your future correspondence you will be careful to avoid giving any ground of offence to Local Governments, on whose cooperation the success of the Archaeological Survey must largely depend.[68]

Epilogue

The history of Amaravati in the eighteenth and nineteenth centuries is instructive from several points of view. The writings on the site and

[66] Letter No. 0–80, dated Ootacamund, 19 May 1886, from G. Bidie to the Chief Secretary to the Government of Madras, Home Proceedings/Archaeology and the Conservation of Ancient Monuments, July 1886, No. 10, Part A, NAI.

[67] Order passed by the Governor-in Council, Madras, Home Proceedings/Archaeology and the Conservation of Ancient Monuments, July 1886, No. 10, Part A, NAI.

[68] Letter No. 224, dated Simla, 20 July 1886, from A.P. MacDonnell, Officiating Secretary to the Government of India to the Director General of the Archaeological Survey of India, Home Proceedings/Archaeology and the Conservation of Ancient Monuments, July 1886, No. 11, Part A, NAI.

the stupa illustrate the gradually expanding Western understanding of Buddhism, its history, and its sacred edifices. The story of the excavations at Amaravati also forms an important part of the history of Indian archaeology. It reveals the gradual transition from sloppy, amateur operations, often poorly documented and causing greater harm than good, towards more systematic excavations in the later decades. It also graphically reveals how a spectacular and important ancient site was destroyed by repeated archaeological excavation. The history of the dispersal of the Amaravati sculptures illustrates the turbulent life-history of ancient remains in modern times and the slowly emerging concern for the conservation of historical monuments in colonial India in the later part of the nineteenth century.

Subsequent to the events detailed in this chapter, several excavations were carried out at Amaravati. Alexander Rea excavated the site in 1888–9, 1905–6 and 1908–9. In 1890, eleven stone slabs were sent by the collector of Kistna to Madras, and in 1891 Rea sent down 180. Some of the sculptures unearthed in the 1905–6 and 1908–9 excavations also found there way to the Madras Museum. These included a number of metal images.[69] Further excavations were carried out in independent India by the Archaeological Survey of India under the superintendence of R. Subrahmanyam and K. Krishna Murthy in 1958–9. In 1973–4, I.K. Sharma conducted excavations at a site close to the mahachaitya. In 1974–5, A. Ghosh's excavations established a clearer chronological framework for the cultural sequence of the site.

Some of the sculptural pieces unearthed in the course of the later excavations were assembled and displayed in a museum at the site of Amaravati. But a large number of the most beautiful stones had been slowly but steadily removed from the site during the course of the nineteenth century. Over that period every subsequent plea for the removal of stones sought justification in prior removals. Assessments of the condition of the site, and opinions on whether it was possible to conserve the sculptures there, varied considerably. Only once in the nineteenth century did the Amaravati stones have a strong spokesman urging their *in situ* preservation. But eloquent and determined as he might have been, Cole's arguments came too late; moreover, he had all

[69] Sivaramamurti (1977): 2.

the other authorities on the subject ranged against him—this in spite of all the strongly worded resolutions favouring *in situ* preservation passed and circulated by the Government of India.

The eventual distribution of major collections of the Amaravati sculptures in the British Museum in London and the Government Museum in Chennai reflects two distinct phases in the history of conservation policy in colonial India. During the early phase of colonial rule, right up to the 1860s, apart from the antiquities carried off by officers of the East India Company in their private capacity, a large number were routinely officially despatched to England, especially to the India Museum in London. The despatch of the 'Elliot Marbles' to England in 1859 was in line with this trend. But the tide was about to change towards a policy that preferred to keep Indian antiquities in India, to be displayed in Indian museums. This change was a result of a number of factors. For one thing, the need to evolve a policy on the issue of the disposal of objects of archaeological interest was for the first time seriously deliberated within the government from the 1860s onwards. Other important factors were the decline and eventual winding up of the India Museum in London in 1879, and the increase in the number and importance of museums in India. As a result, the colonial state became increasingly reluctant to despatch valuable Indian antiquities to England, or anywhere else for that matter. The decision to send the second major lot of Amaravati sculptures to the Madras Museum in 1883 reflects this change. Just as the despatch of the Bharhut sculptures marked the coming of age of an imperial museum of the British empire in India—i.e. the Indian Museum in Calcutta—the display of a major collection of Amaravati sculptures in the Madras Museum marked the coming of age of the provincial museum.

Today, those interested in a glimpse of the former magnificence of the Amaravati stupa can venture into the portals of the Government Museum in Chennai, the British Museum in London, and the small site museum at Amaravati itself.[70] They can leaf through catalogues

[70] A few sculptures and inscriptions of Amaravati are also lodged in the Musèe Guimet in Paris, the Boston Museum, the National Museum in Delhi, and the Indian Museum in Calcutta. The British Museum has digitalized the Mackenzie Amaravati album to help bring to light unidentified stones from the Mackenzie Collection (see http://www.bl.uk/collections/amaravati/mackamaravati. html).

and publications on the subject produced by these museums. However, the result of a century-and-three-quarters' exploration and excavation at Amaravati is that, today, the site of what James Fergusson described as the most elaborate and magnificent pieces of architecture found in any part of the world, is marked by a nondescript mound ringed by a few forlorn stones.

The World Corpus of Amaravati Sculptures Project of the Society for South Asian Studies aims at digitalizing the Amaravati collections throughout the world.

CHAPTER 9

The 'Ignorant Natives' and Archaeological Research

The colonial state in India saw itself engaged in a civilizing mission. The white man's burden included a retrieval of the lost history of a conquered land, the natives of which had little interest in their own past. Cast in the role of 'ignorant natives', Indians were generally considered as possessing neither the wisdom to promote historical inquiry nor the critical faculties required for engaging in it. This was the usual characterization of political and social elites, intellectuals, and ordinary Indians.

As the process of cataloguing and documenting India's historical remains got under way, and local governments started receiving circulars instructing officials to make lists and collect photographs of monuments and archaeological remains, one of the problems that presented itself was that many of these monuments and remains lay outside British territory. At its height, the British empire in India covered approximately three-fifths of the subcontinent, indigenous elites ruled over the rest. The princely states of nineteenth-century India varied greatly in size, population, and resources—from the numerous small principalities sprinkled through Central and West India to the larger and more politically important ones such as Hyderabad, Mysore, Gwalior, Baroda, and Kashmir. Although the princes ultimately emerged as 'the most obvious and ostentatious bulwark' of British control in India, the relationship between the British and the traditional rulers of India always remained problematic.[1]

Several major historical sites naturally lay in the princely states. These included Sanchi in Bhopal state, Bharhut in Nagod, Ajanta in

[1] Jeffrey (1978): 1.

the nizam's domain, and Mandu in the principality of Dhar. The challenges posed by such a situation were recognized and highlighted early in the day by James Fergusson, using language evocative of a military campaign:

> Apart from these operations in our own territory, it is even more important that photographic incursions should be made into the Nizam's territory. All our inquiries and all our speculations as to the ethnography and antiquities of India are stopped short by our utter ignorance of the great central plateau, where, if anywhere, the wrecks of the past may be expected to be found. What I would suggest, to remedy this, would be, that a party from Bombay should penetrate *via* Kallien and Kulbarga, and a party from Bengal *via* Wyaghur and Chanda.[2]

On occasion, British officers concerned with conservation work observed Indians were more willing to make financial contributions towards structures that were part of contemporary religious life than for derelict ruins. Cole, when he became curator of ancient monuments, fresh from a visit to various monuments in the Madras Presidency in 1882, observed that natives of all religious denominations could be counted on to voluntarily contribute large sums of money for repairs to religious buildings.[3] But there were certain aspects of current native worship which, according to the official British view, ran counter to the project of preserving ancient monuments. Thus, at Karle, Cole found that the Buddhist stupa inside the shrine had been painted and converted into a Shivalinga. The wall and sculptures had been whitewashed and the lighting of cooking fires was damaging the cave. All this was clearly intolerable and had to be stopped.[4]

In the long run, archaeological research and the conservation of historical monuments was not the monopoly of the British Government of India and European scholars. Some of the princely states took initiatives in this regard, and some were willing to cooperate or collaborate with the British. Because of the complex relationship between the princes and the colonial state, this collaboration was not always

[2] 'Memorandum by Mr Fergusson regarding the Architectural Objects in India, of which it is desirable Photographs should be obtained', Home/Public, 30 July 1870, No. 206, Part A, NAI.

[3] Home/Archaeology, July 1882, No. 2, Part A, NAI.

[4] Ibid.

smooth nor was it always positively acknowledged by the latter. Similarly, the role of indigenous scholars in the nineteenth-century discovery of India's past is something that needs exploration and acknowledgement.

Ancient Remains in the Princely States

An important role in interfacing between the British government and the princely states on various issues was played by residents and political agents, drawn from the Indian Political Service. The main job of the political agent was to 'advise' the rulers of his agency. The degree and nature of the interaction between political agents, Residents, and princely durbars varied, depending on the size of the agency and the degree of subordination of the native state. So, for instance, the level of British interference in the internal affairs of large states such as Hyderabad, Gwalior, and Baroda was less than in smaller states, as for instance many of the small states in the Mahi Kantha Agency of Gujarat, where the British exercised 'residuary jurisdiction' on the grounds that the rulers were incapable of discharging these duties properly. The political agent also functioned more or less as a district officer in states whose administration had been taken over completely on the grounds of gross mismanagement, or where the rulers were minors.[5] The development of railway and telegraph networks eventually transformed the political agents from powerful 'men on the spot' who wielded considerable initiative and influence to mere post offices between the Government of India and the Indian princes. But in the middle of the nineteenth century, this process was just beginning.

While some political agents were indifferent to the conservation of historical remains, others were passionately concerned. One of the best examples of the latter was Lepel Henry Griffin,[6] Resident at Indore

[5] Copland (1978): 283–4.

[6] Griffin had joined the Indian Civil Service in 1860, and went on to a distinguished career as an administrator and diplomat. In 1871, as under secretary to the Government of the Punjab, he sent out letters to all commissioners asking them to take steps to prevent unauthorized excavations, and to prevent the appropriation of coins and antiquities by private individuals. Deputy commissioners should furnish a list of all localities known or likely to contain ancient

and agent to the governor general for Central India between 1881 and 1888. The best proof of his keen interest in the historical remains of this area is the book brought out under his direction in 1886. *Famous Monuments of Central India* was illustrated with 91 autotypes of original photographs taken by the pioneering and major Indian photographer Lala Deen Dayal. The illustrations included 27 plates of Sanchi, 20 plates of Gwalior monuments, 21 plates of Khajuraho, and 21 miscellaneous plates. The book was an official publication, and profits from its sale were earmarked for the preservation of the architectural monuments described in the book. Lepel Griffin's concern for India's monuments was also reflected in his relentless, outspoken critique of the destruction caused by the vandalism of railway contractors and archaeologists.

A few political agents and residents who interfaced between the British colonial government and the princely states gave a positive report, such as this: 'It is gratifying to be able to state that the Native Chiefs respond, in general, with good will, to the invitation of the political officers to consider the subject of protection to be afforded to the architectural remains scattered through their territories. The young Chief of Dhar is stated to be quite disposed to aid in preserving the ruins at Mandoo, some of the principal of which are well deserving of the expenditure that would be required with this object.'[7] The vast majority of political agents, however, described the attitude of the Indian princes towards the preservation of historical remains as one of dull indifference. Lepel Griffin attributed the financial contributions some of them had made towards conservation projects as the result of hollow sycophancy, an attempt to ingratiate themselves with the British. This in turn was part of Griffin's larger perception of the calibre of the indigenous princes and the civilizing mission that the British had in India.

---

remains. Commissioners should ensure that all discoveries of antiquities should be immediately reported to the district officer, who should inform the curator of the Lahore Central Museum, who should in turn ask for instructions of the government. Circular No. 12–92, dated Lahore, 23 February 1871, Home/Public, 29 April 1871, Nos. 3–4, Part A, OIOC.

[7] Extract from Political Administration Report of the Central India Agency, for 1867–8, Home/Public, January 1869, No. 139, Part A, NAI.

> But seriously to compare the British administration with those which preceded it, or with the majority of those which exist side by side with it today in India, is an insult to the intelligence. There have been, it is true, Muhammadan and Hindu Princes who have ruled with strength and justice, and whose names are still held in honour. But these have been very few. Native rule in India, in former days, signified oppression of the most terrible kind, insecurity of life and property, luxury and debauchery in the Prince, misery and want in the people . . .[8]

So it is not surprising that British administrators routinely expressed scepticism about the support that the native princes could be expected to offer towards conservation. What is interesting are the arguments that they put forward to support this assessment. Griffin's explanation of why the Indian princes could not be expected to be really interested in the major historical monuments within their respective states was exactly the argument that Cunningham had put forward many years earlier, when he argued that the Hindu raja of Nagod would be quite glad to get the 'heretical' Buddhist sculptures of Bharhut off his hands:

> Sanchi, the most important, is a Buddhist monument, its supremely important carvings being much concerned with the ceremonial of that creed. It is situated in a Muhammadan State, the predominant influence in which is at present fanatical and iconoclastic. I do not doubt that I can persuade Her Highness the Begum to subscribe Rs. 5,000 towards the restoration of the Tope; but I am still more certain that the Nawab consort and his party would see the building destroyed with the greatest pleasure . . .
>
> . . . Similarly with the . . . monument of Mandu. It cannot be expected that a Hindu Maharaja should specially interest himself in the preservation of a deserted city only associated with the memory of the Muhammadans who crushed and superceded his dynasty . . . I trust, however, that the Government of India will not contract their liberality in the preservation of ancient monuments in these States within the narrow limits of the interest, and sympathy of the Native Princes, which is really non-existent.[9]

[8] Griffin (1873): ix. Griffin wrote two other books on the kingdoms of the Punjab (Griffin, 1909, 1911).

[9] Letter No. 122 G.-277, dated 15 August 1882, from Sir Lepel Griffin to the

In the same breath, however, Lepel Griffin indicated the contributions that had been made by the princes for conservation work. Maharaja Sindia had contributed Rs 5000 to the restoration of Jaina buildings in the Gwalior fortress, 'and both Dhar and Bhopal are ready to do what is reasonable, with reference to the interesting remains in their respective states . . .' The begum of Bhopal had personally promised Lepel Griffin Rs 5,000 towards the preservation of the Sanchi stupa, and the maharaja of Dhar ('always ready to meet the wishes of the Imperial Government') could be expected to contribute half that amount towards repairs at Mandu.[10]

The next year Lepel Griffin reported that the begum of Bhopal had already contributed much money and labour towards the repairs to the Sanchi stupa, and that she proposed to build a bungalow close to the monument for the use of travellers and visitors, a venture that would cost several thousands of rupees.[11] At Mandu, restoration and conservation work was being carried out by the raja of Dhar at his own expense, on the lines suggested by the curator of ancient monuments, and this support was likely to continue. In spite of all this evidence to the contrary, Lepel Griffin continued his refrain that the native princes had no desire to contribute towards the conservation of monuments located within their respective states, that any contributions they made could not be called voluntary, and that there was no point trying to elicit or to record these contributions on a regular basis.

The work of repair and conservation at Sanchi and Mandu was conducted under the supervision of British officers. The work at Sanchi was initially superintended by Austin Mears and later by Major Keith, who operated under the direct control of Cole. Keith also supervised the repair of buildings in the Gwalior fortress. The repairs to Mandu were likewise effected under the personal supervision of Colonel Biddulph, with the professional assistance of a Public Works Department officer. The funding was shared by the imperial government and

---

Secretary to the Government of India, Foreign Department, Home Proceedings/ Archaeology and the Conservation of Ancient Monuments, No. 8, Part A, NAI.

[10] Ibid.

[11] Letter No. 19, G. 41, dated Indore Residency, 10 March 1883, from Sir Lepel Griffin to C. Grant, Secretary to the Government of India, Foreign Department, Baghelkhand Political Agency Files (English), File No. 15, 1882, NAI.

the native states concerned. The Dhar grant for repairs towards repairs at Mandu was Rs 2,000 and the British government's contribution was Rs 1200.[12]

The Begum of Bhopal and her *History*

One of the nineteenth-century Indian rulers who belied the colonial stereotype of ignorant natives was the begum of Bhopal, Shahjahan Begum (r. 1868–1901), second in a line of four women rulers of this state. The begum was a learned woman, deeply interested in the history of her state. She was the author of a book on the history of Bhopal. Her *Táj-ul Ikbál Tárikh Bhopal* (The Crown of Prosperity, the History of Bhopal; hereafter referred to as *History*) was translated from Urdu into English by C. Barstow, political agent of Bhopal between 1874 and 1875.

The text of the English translation of the Begum's *History* is sandwiched between the comments of the translator at one end and those of her husband, Nawab Wala Jah Amir ul Mulk Syud Muhammad Sadik Hasan Khan Bahadur, at the other end. Both display their particular bias, one political, the other personal. Barstow notes that the only other works thus far that had touched on the history of Bhopal were Sir J. Malcolm's *Central India* and Colonel Malleson's *Essay.* In his opinion, the value of the begum's work did not lie in its historical insights but in something quite different: 'It is to be hoped that the present work may not prove devoid of interest to the English readers as affording an insight into the genuine expression of Oriental feelings and modes of thought.'[13] The Afterword to the book, on the other hand, bestows fulsome praise on the author, 'who, though she is a woman, can teach lessons of wisdom to great statesmen both in politics and finance.'[14] Muhammad Sadik Hasan Khan extols the veracity of

[12] Report submitted by P.M. Thompson, who was appointed by Cole to supervise repairs at Mandu. The Dhar durbar also contributed Rs 150 for the repair of the Lat Masjid. Home Proceedings/Archaeology and the Conservation of Ancient Monuments, February 1885, No. 11, Part A, OIOC.

[13] Shahjahan Begum (1876): Translator's Preface, iii.

[14] Shahjahan Begum (1876): 231. Muhammad Sadik Hasan Khan is at pains to point out that his effusive praise of the author and the book is objective. 'I have

the begum's account of Bhopal's history and describes it as a textbook on the science of politics, a work of great value for princes and ordinary folk alike, young and old.

The project of writing the *History* was begun by Shahjahan Begum's mother Sikandar Begum (r. 1843–68). In 1852 Major Durand, the political agent at Bhopal, had suggested to her that she write a history of the state and its rulers 'after the example set by the Emperor Babar, who wrote the annals of his reign.' Such a book, Durand impressed upon the begum, would spread her fame from Hindustan to England.[15] Sikandar Begum liked the idea and began collecting material for it from the state archives. She worked on the book for seventeen years, till her death. Her daughter decided to continue and complete the work her mother had begun.

Shahjahan Begum's *History* is a detailed and lively account of the history of Bhopal from the time of the foundation of the Bhopal principality by Dost Muhammad Khan in 1736 to the author's own time. The author was aware of other works on her area—those of Sir John Malcolm and Major William Hough. In the Preface to her *History*, Shahjahan Begum makes certain observations on the nature and utility of history: 'History is a science which engages the attention and study of rulers in every age, and claims votaries from every religion and sect, especially among the English, who are at great pains to collect and analyse facts and acquaint themselves with the customs and history of every country and society, regarding this knowledge as a key to understanding the revolutions of the world and the progress or decline of mankind. It is to historians too we should look to discern the signs of peace and war.'[16]

The book is divided into three parts. The first deals with rulers of Bhopal from the time of Dost Muhammad Khan up to the time of the death of the author's father, Jahangir Muhammad Khan. The second deals with the reign of the author's mother, Sikandar Begum. The third part deals with the early years of the reign of Shahjahan Begum

---

no interested motives in thus writing and speaking of her; am I not her husband? I am no courtier seeking for a reward. God has been pleased to give me enough and to spare.'

[15] Shahjahan Begum (1876): v.

[16] Ibid.: iii–iv.

herself. Battles, intrigues, treaties and ceremonies are described in detail. There is dramatic dialogue and long, sonorous speeches. There are quotations from official correspondence and references to financial accounts and expenses. Among the many things that emerge from the begum's *History* is the utter abjectness of Bhopal's rulers *vis-à-vis* the British in matters ranging from policy to marriage and travel, all of which required the viceroy's prior sanction.

Shahjahan Begum's account of the early years of her own reign indicates a keenness to advertise her administrative reforms and progressive measures—in the areas of education, revenue, and welfare. Towards its end her book takes on the appearance of a sort of Gazetteer—giving the extent of the state of Bhopal, a list of *parganas* and principal towns and forts, an account of the produce of the soil and its fruits, and a description of the city of Bhopal. There is also an account of 'some of the most deserving officers of the state and of the most learned of its servants'. The begum's detailed accounts of her journeys to Lucknow, Agra, Fatehpur Sikri, and Delhi display her interest in historical monuments.

Looking for reference to Sanchi, one of the most important ancient historical sites in Bhopal state, the reader is initially disappointed by the very brief reference in the third chapter of the third part of the *History*: 'We visited Sanchi Khanakhera, and inspected the stone sculptures and statues of Budha [*sic*], and the ancient gateway . . .'[17] Further reading rewards us with a long account of the site of Sanchi, with which Chapter VI closes: 'The most wonderful ancient buildings in the State of Bhopal are at Sanchi Kanakhera, a small village under the brow of a hill some 20 miles north-east of Bhopal . . .'[18] The begum goes on to describe the ruins of Sanchi. She refers to similar ruins at Sunari, Sandir, Satdhara, Bhojpur, and Andher nearby. The discoveries made at Sanchi by Cunningham are summarized, as are some of his views on the antiquity and style of the sculptures: 'The above ruins appear to be objects of great interest to European gentlemen. Major Alexander Cunningham, brother of the late Captain J.D. Cunningham, formerly Political Agent of Bhopal, stayed several weeks in this neighbourhood and examined these ruins most carefully.

[17] Ibid.: 145.

[18] Ibid.: 219.

He took drawings of the place, deciphered the inscriptions, and bored shafts down these domes. The results of his investigations were described by him in an English work.'[19] The begum had gathered from Cunningham's research that the domes at Sanchi were called 'topes'-by the English and that they were associated with the Buddhist religion.

When Fergusson's *Tree and Serpent Worship* was published in 1868, the begum expressed a desire to obtain a copy. The viceroy duly presented her with one. Shahjahan Begum went on to express her interest in the ruins of Sanchi in more material terms as well, in providing assistance for Cole's casting project and money towards the preservation of the important ancient Buddhist site. This support was continued by her successor Sultan Jahan Begum (1901–26), to whom John Marshall's volumes on Sanchi are dedicated. The sustained interest, concern, and material support extended by the Bhopal durbar towards the historical remains at Sanchi go a long way in contradicting the constant British refrain that a Muslim ruler could not possibly have any interest in a Buddhist monument.[20]

Other Princely States

Clearly, not all native princes were indifferent towards the preservation of the cultural heritage of their dominions. The nizam of Hyderabad was quite willing to cooperate with Cole and follow up his suggestions. Considerable amounts of money from the state exchequer were spent on conservation work during the ministry of Salar Jung I. In 1882 the nizam's government took steps to provide doors for some of the Ajanta caves in order to protect the Ajanta frescoes.[21] Subsequently, it communicated with the curator of ancient monuments regarding its plans for the repair of old monuments at Kalburgah.[22]

[19] Ibid.: 220.

[20] For a detailed account of the long-term role played by the Bhopal durbar in preserving the Sanchi remains and retrieving the Sanchi relics, see Lahiri (2004).

[21] Home/Archaeology and the Conservation of Ancient Monuments, July 1882, Nos. 6–12, Part A, NAI.

[22] These plans included, much to Cole's irritation, the whitewashing and painting of the structures, dome and all.

Several years later (in 1894–5), the services of H. Cousens of the Archaeological Survey were lent to the nizam's government. Cousens toured the state, surveyed its monuments, and prepared a classified list of these for conservation purposes.

At the same time, not all native princes were as interested in a close relationship with the British on preservation matters. In 1884 Colonel J.C. Berkeley, officer on special duty in Kashmir, gave the maharaja's prime minister a list of the ancient buildings and ruins of Kashmir. 'Would the Durbar be willing to arrange for their conservation as they stand? The cost would be trifling, and the object of view is one that commends itself to all.'[23] The response was cool: 'With reference to your letter . . . I shall thank you to inform the Government of India that His Highness the Maharaja himself takes great interest in the preservation of all ancient buildings within his territories, and is fully alive to the importance of conserving the specimens of ancient architectural art. I may also state here that the Governor of Kashmir has been instructed to take particular care in conserving such buildings.'[24]

The maharana of Mewar reacted similarly. At Cole's behest his attention of was drawn to the need for repairs to structures at Chittor and Nagda. The maharana informed the Resident in the course of a discussion on the matter that he was himself deeply interested in their renovation and repair, but he was opposed to the supervision of such work by British officers.[25] The written response of the Mewar durbar was polite but firm:

> the Fortress of Chittor represents the Crown of Meywar and the Rajputs, and its repair did of old engage attention. In fact repairs have been in execution during the past three years, while in the last Sambat work has been

[23] Letter No. 225, dated 30 June 1884, from Col. J.C. Berkeley, Officer on Special Duty in Kashmir to Dewan Anant Ram, P.M. to His Highness the Maharaja of Jummoo and Kashmir, Home Proceedings/Archaeology and the Conservation of Ancient Monuments, February 1885, No. 8, Part A, OIOC.

[24] Letter dated 8 July 1884, from Dewan Anant Ram to J.C. Berkeley, Home Proceedings/Archaeology and the Conservation of Ancient Monuments, February 1885, No. 8, Part A, OIOC.

[25] Letter No. 1360, dated 15 December 1882, from Col. C.K.M. Walker, the British Resident in Meywar to the Secretary to the Agent to the Governor General in the Public Works Department, Rajputana, Home/Archaeology and the Conservation of Ancient Monuments, June, 1883, No. 77, Part A, NAI.

> started on an extensive scale. The style of repair advocated by Captain Cole is deserving of approval, and regard will be paid to his recommendations. There is every determination to extend the scope of repairs.
>
> . . . With regard to what you write about the appointment of a British officer to draw up estimates and exercise supervision, there does not appear to be any necessity for this, and therefore the proposal should not be carried out . . . The work of repairs at Nagda will also be effected from here.[26]

Although it refused British assistance in the matter of repairs, the Mewar durbar was willing to allow agents of the colonial government to survey major monuments in the state. Cole was given permission to arrange for a complete survey of the monuments in the Chittor fort and at Udaipur, the only proviso being that the maharana should be informed of the name of the person who was going to do the job. The Jeypore and Sirohi durbars likewise gave permission to the curator of ancient monuments to survey the Amber Palace and the Jain temple at Mt Abu.[27]

While most of the officials who interacted with the native durbars over these issues were aware of the need for delicacy, this variety of virtue was not, as we have seen, part of Cole's style as curator of ancient monuments between 1881 and 1883. While he sympathized with the princes' desire to maintain control over the preservation of monuments in their dominion, he insisted that with this sort of arrangement it would not be possible to achieve uniformity in approach or results.[28] He referred to the harm that could befall monuments due either to neglect—through vegetation, damp, dirt, bees, bats, etc.; or to damage—through the improper use of paint, plaster, whitewash, etc. He pointed out that a glaring example of the latter sort of damage was the whitewashing of the Amber Palace in 1881 to prepare it for

[26] 'Translation of a Khatta from the Mahkama Khass, Oodeypore, to the Resident in Meywar, dated the 11 December 1882.' Enclosure to ibid.

[27] Letter No. 1375G., dated Mt. Abu, 7 May 1883, from Major E.R.C. Bradford, Agent to the Governor General in Rajputana to the Secretary to the Government of India, Foreign Department, Home/Archaeology and the Conservation of Ancient Monuments, June 1883, No. 71, Part A, NAI.

[28] Letter No. 588G, dated 6 March 1883, from H.H. Cole to Capt. E.A. Fraser, First Assistant Agent to the Governor General in Rajputana, Home/Archaeology and the Conservation of ancient Monuments, June 1883, No. 78, Part A, NAI.

Lord Ripon's visit: this was the worst sort of vandalism possible. In short, native princes could not be left to their own devices when it came to the care of historical monuments in their territories. Cole's presupposition was always that art's needs were supreme—neither his colleagues nor the princes who owned these artefacts and monuments, in his view understood this as well as he did.

Cole's strident approach to this matter was fraught with problematic potential. For of course this was not merely a matter of how best to conserve ancient monuments, but an issue that impinged on the sensitive relationship between the colonial state and the princes, something that worried officials on the spot. This is what Major E.R.C. Bradford, agent to the governor general in Rajputana, had to say on the matter:

> it must be remembered that we have not to consider this matter only from our own point of view of what is appropriate and in good taste, and that we cannot arbitrarily force the possessors of these priceless treasures to do with them that which is against their inclination or their traditions. It therefore appears to me that the subject cannot be approached too cautiously. Much has been conceded by the Maharana of Oodeypore with some reluctance as the correspondence shows; by Jeypore and by Sirohi, and it is my belief that no Native State will oppose, or be indifferent to suggestions which do not trench on their prerogatives and preconceived ideas. As I have already stated, most of the Chiefs of Rajputana prefer to make their own arrangements for the preservation and repair of their ancient buildings and the feelings that prompt this expression of their wishes are thoroughly intelligible, as it cannot be supposed that the fate of structures, with which, as is frequently the case, the annals of their ancestry and their religion are intermingled, can be a matter of no concern to them . . .[29]

Faced with the political factors involved, the Government of India decided it was best to influence the princes without imposing any 'distasteful pressure' on them: 'in the opinion of the Government of

[29] Letter No. 1375G., dated Mt. Abu, 7 May 1883, from Major E.R.C. Bradford, Agent to the Governor General in Rajputana to the Secretary to the Government of India, Foreign Department, Home/Archaeology and the Conservation of Ancient Monuments, June 1883, No. 71, Part A, NAI.

India, the Chiefs cannot be expected to abandon their control over buildings, rendered precious to them by family associations in favour of a controlling department working under the paramount power. The objects of the Government of India, however, will be fully attained if the Durbars can be induced to make a real effort to carry out Major Cole's plans by means of their own agency. . . .'[30] It is noteworthy that almost all the ruling houses of Rajputana expressed willingness to take appropriate measures to repair and preserve a large number of historical monuments within their jurisdiction.[31] These monuments not only included temples, forts, and palaces to which the princes could be expected to have a sentimental attachment, but also several medieval monuments such as mosques, *dargahs*, and tombs. Thus, the monuments in and near Dholepore included the sixteenth-century dargah and tomb of Sayyid Raj Bokhari, a mosque and tomb of Mussamut Zarina, the tomb of Surafabdal, the tomb of Sadik Muhammad Khan (one of Akbar's generals), and the ruins of a hunting lodge built by Shah Jahan. The maharaja of Dholepore was willing to undertake steps to repair these and any other monuments deemed worthy of similar attention in his state, and reported that as a matter of fact yearly sums were now devoted to this end. The fact that the ruler of this state was in principle agreeable to undertake such measures belied, in some measure, the frequently expressed British view that the interest Indian princes took in the conservation of historical monuments was necessarily limited by communal or sectarian prejudice.

During the post-Cole years, the Government of India dutifully sent out to the princely states copies of its resolution of 26 November 1883, which emphasized the necessity of compiling lists of historical monuments on a uniform plan. Attached to this were lists of monuments compiled by Major Cole. The princes were asked what precisely they

[30] Letter No. 1578 I., dated Simla, 12 June 1883, from C. Grant, Secretary to the Government of India, Foreign Department, to the Agent to the Governor General in Rajputana, Home/Archaeology and the Conservation of ancient Monuments, June, 1883, No. 78, Part A, NAI.

[31] 'List of Ancient Monuments and Buildings in the States under the Rajputana Agency Worthy of Preservation and Restoration.' Home/Archaeology and the Conservation of ancient Monuments, June 1883, No. 73, Part A, NAI.

proposed to do with regard to the repair and conservation of monuments in their domain. The replies frequently stated that the princes were well aware of the importance of conservation and did not need the British to remind them about it.[32]

In subsequent years there was an increase in cooperation between the Government of India and the princely states in survey matters. In 1889 Baroda state collaborated with the Government of Bombay for an archaeological survey of Sidhpore, Suhilwada, and Madhera. The cost of the survey was equally shared by the British and Baroda governments, while the latter agreed to shoulder the expense of the subsequent publications. The Seventh International Oriental Congress held at Vienna suggested to the nizam of Hyderabad that he organize a linguistic survey of the state. The committee set up by the nizam's government to examine the issue decided to carry out an archaeological and linguistic survey simultaneously. In 1892 the nizam's government applied to the British government for the loan of the services of Cousens of the Bombay Archaeological Survey, in connection with this project.

In spite of such instances of cooperation and in spite of the political subordination of the Indian princes to the Government of India, the fact of the matter remained that, whether they liked it or not, the officers of the Archaeological Survey had restricted access to archaeological and monumental remains in a large part of the subcontinent. On occasion they chafed: in 1886 Burgess proposed to the Government of India that he be allowed to conduct a survey of the Chalukyan temples in Mysore state, or that the purview of the Archaeological Survey be officially extended to include Mysore. The foreign department did not think it politic to even suggest the latter course of action to the Mysore durbar.[33] The crux of the matter was that although the native princes were generally willing to collaborate with the colonial government on specific tasks of survey and conservation, certain limits of propriety and decorum could not be transgressed even within this unequal relationship.

[32] See, for instance, Mysore Residency File No. 118, 1885, No. 27, NAI.

[33] Home/Archaeology and the Conservation of Ancient Monuments, October 1886, Nos. 14–16. Part A, OIOC.

The Contribution of Indian Scholars

The relationship between traditional and Western scholarship in the Orientalist enterprise has been touched upon earlier. Many Western scholars were heavily dependent on pandits and maulavis for the reading and translation of original texts and inscriptions, a dependence rarely acknowledged in part because traditional scholars were seen as lacking the intellectual apparatus necessary for a rational and critical appraisal of India's past.[34]

While many traditional scholars who participated in the Orientalist enterprise remain shadowy, anonymous figures, some can be clearly identified. Along with European names such as E. Roer, F.E. Hall, E.B. Cowell, H. Kern, H. Jacobi, A. Sprenger, W. Nassau Lees, and Alfred von Kremer, the monographs published in the *Bibliotheca Indica* series by the Asiatic Society of Bengal reveal the names of a large number of traditional scholars who were involved in the enterprise of editing and translating Sanskrit and Persian texts.[35] The men who worked on editing Vedic texts in the 1850s, 1860s and 1870s included Pandits Ramayana Tarkaratna, Hara Chandra Vidyabhushana, Visvanatha Sastri, Ananda Chandra Vedantavagisa, Rama Narayana Vidyaratna, and Satyavrata Samasrami. Pandits Rama Narayana Vidyaratna, Ananda Chandra Vedantavagisa and Chandra Kanta Tarkalankara worked on the *Shrauta Sutras and Grihya Sutras.* Pandit Visvanatha Sastri edited the *Chanda-Sutra* of Pingala, the leading work on Vedic prosody, and Satyavrata Samasrami brought out an edition of Yaska's etymological lexicon, the *Nirukta.* In 1875 Pandit Rama Narayana published a translation of the Ayodhya-mahatmya section of the *Skanda* and *Padma Puranas* in the *Journal of the Asiatic Society.*

The work on Vedic (and to a lesser extent Pauranic) literature was accompanied by the publication of texts belonging to the various Indian philosophical schools and other branches of ancient learning. In 1853 Pandit Rama Narayana Vidyaratna edited the *Brahma Sutras* along with the commentary of Shankaracharya and the gloss of Govindananda. This was also the year in which Ishwarchandra

[34] The divide between traditional scholars and academia is something that emerged in the colonial period but has lived on into the present.

[35] See *Centenary Review of the Asiatic Society*, pp. 137 ff.

Vidyasagar published his edition of the *Sarvadarshana-sangraha*. A few years later (in 1860) came the publication of the *Kanada Sutras* of the Vaisheshikha school edited by Jaya Narayana Tarkapanchanana. An edition of the *Jaimini Sutras* with the commentary of Shavarasvamin was prepared by Mahesa Chandra Nyayaratna (1863) and Jaya Narayana Tarkapanchanana's edition of the *Shankara Digvijaya* was published in the following year. In 1871, Bharata Chandra Siromani began working on the important legal digest, Hemadri's *Chaturvarga Chintamani*; the work was continued by Yogesvara Bhattacharya and Kamakhyanatha Tarkaratna. Pandit Bapudeva Sastri contributed towards bringing out an English translation of the astronomical texts *Surya Siddhanta* and *Siddhanta Shiromani.*

Similarly, several maulavis contributed towards the publication of a number of Persian and Arabic texts in the second half of the nineteenth century. Agha Muhammad Shusteri and Agha Ahmad Ali worked for several years on the Persian *Sikandarnamah.* In 1853 Muhammad Wajih and Gholam Qadir began work on editing the Arabic *Kashuz-Zunun* (Dictionary of the Technical Terms used in the Sciences of the Muhammadans). These two, along with Abdul Haqa, began working on an edition of the *Isaliah fi-tamyiz-is-Sihabah* (Bibliographical Dictionary of Persons who knew Muhammad); the project was completed by Maulavi Abdul Hai. In 1856, the Court of Directors of the East India Company complained that too much attention and money was being spent on the publication of Arabic works which had little or no connection with India. The Asiatic Society decided to institute a separate Persian series of monographs, with a special focus on historical chronicles illustrating the history of India. The first work selected for this new scheme was Zia-ud-din Barani's *Tarikh-i-Firuz-Shahi*, and Maulavi Sayyid Ahmad Khan began work on it in 1860. In 1865, Abdul Haqq and Ahmad Ali brought out an edition of the *Iqbalnamah-i-Jahangiri* by Mutamad Khan. In 1866 Khadim Husain and Abdul Hai began working on an edition of Muhammad Qasim's *Alamgir-namah* (a court chronicle of the time of Aurangzeb) and Kabiruddin Ahmad and Abdur Rahim on editing Abdul Hamid Lahauri's *Badshah-namah* (a chronicle of the time of Shah Jahan). In 1868 Kabiruddin Ahmad and Ghulam Qadir commenced work on the *Muntakhab-i-Lubab of Khafi Khan*, an important chronicle of the time of Aurangzeb. In 1870 Agha Ahman Ali started working on an edition of the *Maasir-i-Alamgiri* by Muhammad Saqi Mustaid Khan. Maulavi Agha Ahmad Ali's edition of the *Akbarnamah* of Abul Fazl was carried forward after his death by Abdur Rahim.

These lists are by no means exhaustive, but they show that traditional scholars often played a major role in preparing reliable editions of a wide range of Sanskrit and Persian texts. The appearance of such editions in print was an important prerequisite for European scholars who either could not handle or had no access to the Indian manuscript tradition. This was also a prerequisite for the translation of texts into the European languages, a major aspect of the Orientalist enterprise during this period.[36] Such publication of a vast array of primary sources opened a rich storehouse of material for textual study and historical reconstruction to scholars all over the world.

Colonial rule also saw the emergence of another sort of Indian scholar, one with expertise in the language of the traditional sources but also a facility with the English language and an interpretive approach broadly in consonance with those evolving in the West. Such scholars combined familiarity with and understanding of tradition with the critical distance required for tradition to be critically analysed. In the nineteenth century the list of such scholars was small, and the range of their scholarship often varied considerably in scope and range. It includes men such as Ram Raz, Bhau Daji, Bhagwanlal Indraji, R.G. Bhandarkar, and Rajendralala Mitra. The section that follows is not an exhaustive account of these scholars and their work, but of three who may be seen as exemplary, each with very different profiles, and each of whom made very different sorts of scholarly contributions. Ram Raz, the first Indian architectural scholar; P.C. Mukharji, one of the handful of early Indian field archaeologists; and Rajendralala Mitra, whose scholarship crossed the boundaries of several disciplines are the three who represent this new and evolving blend of East and West.

[36] One of the most ambitious ventures of this kind, The Sacred Books of the East series, was launched by Max Müller in 1879.

Ram Raz: The First Modern Indian Architectural Scholar

Ram Raz was born in Tanjore in about 1790. Although he proudly traced his lineage to the last of the kings of the great Vijayanagara empire, his family was poor. We have no details of his schooling, except that he seems to have acquired some knowledge of English somewhere along the way as he grew up. Raz was a self-taught and self-made man.

Early in his career, Raz worked as a clerk to the adjudant in one of the native regiments of the infantry in the Carnatic. Later, he rose to the position of *vakil* to the Second Battalion of the Sixteenth Regiment of the Madras Native Infantry. During these years, he polished his linguistic abilities in English and several South Indian languages. This made him a skilled interpreter. In 1815, while working as a clerk in the office of the military auditor general, he decided to translate into English a code of regulations drawn up by the order of Tipu Sultan for the guidance of his revenue officers.

The translation—so accurate and competent that it was doubted whether it could possibly be the unassisted work of a Hindu—brought Ram Raz to the attention of Richard Clarke, an official in the Madras government and also senior member of the College of Fort St George. Clarke got him a job as head of the college office. From here, Ram Raz went on to become head English master to the native classes in the college.[37] It was at this time that he came to the notice of a Captain Harkins. While living in Madras, Ram Raz pursued on his own the study of Sanskrit, mathematics, geography and astronomy, and also conducted classes in these subjects. He became a corresponding member of the Royal Asiatic Society. Harkins recommended him to the first commissioner in Mysore, and Ram Raz rose to ultimately become a judge and magistrate at Bangalore.

For many years, Ram Raz collected ancient architectural treatises and laboured to decipher their mysteries. The result was *The Essay on the Architecture of the Hindus*, posthumously published in London in 1834. The book included forty-eight fine drawings. For Captain Harkins, who wrote the preface, Ram Raz's work was remarkable not only

[37] The college employed a number of headmasters of languages, who taught Indians to become teachers.

for its contents but because of the fact that such a work had been written by a Hindu: 'The introduction to the European public of an "Essay on *Hindú* Architecture," and by a *Hindú,* would seem to mark an epoch not only in the history of the science but also in that of the Hindús themselves.'[38] From the point of view of Indian architecture, Ram Raz's *Essay* is a short but pathbreaking work. He was the first scholar to study the principles of Indian architecture as reflected in ancient Indian architectural treatises. The technical vocabulary of these treatises was not only unknown to the European world, its memory had faded among both Sanskrit pandits as well as practitioners of the craft. Ram Raz's *Essay* combined a study of the principles of architecture as laid down in the *Shilpa Shastras* with the evidence of extant South Indian temples, and a comparison with architectural features and styles found elsewhere in the world—in Greece, Rome, and Egypt. His aim was to elucidate the theory and practice of Indian architecture and make comparisons with other architectural traditions.

The sources Ram Raz used for his work included a number of texts, the manuscripts of which he assiduously acquired and collected. Many of the manuscripts were mutilated and fragmentary. The most comprehensive and complete source he used was the early medieval *Manasara.* Ram Raz was certain about the area in which his major sources had been composed—the fact that existing temples in South India corresponded to the principles they enunciated made it clear that they were of southern provenance. He was less sure about the age of the texts. Although convinced that the antiquity assigned to them by tradition was 'altogether extravagant', he could reach no definite conclusions about their actual dates. Ram Raz's knowledge of Sanskrit and the South Indian vernacular languages enabled him to interrogate both Brahmin pandits as well as artisans.

The main body of his essay deals with specific issues, such as the system of measurement used in architecture and sculpture, the qualities of an architect, the quality of the ground on which buildings should be built, rules for ploughing the ground before beginning construction, the method of ascertaining the cardinal points by means of a gnomon, and the construction of pedestals, bases, and pillars. The

[38] Raz (1834): iii.

discussion of types of pillars is particularly detailed and is illustrated by a number of sketches. The different types of *vimanas* (the sanctum and its superstructure) are also discussed and illustrated in detail.

The ancient architectural treatises laid down the minutiae of numerous religious rites to be performed before the beginning of construction of structures and on until their completion. There were also numerous rules and aphorisms that served to predict the future destiny of the builder. These sorts of things, Ram Raz asserted, were of interest only insofar as they illustrated the customs of the ancient Hindus (many of which were still in vogue), but were not his concern in the *Essay*.[39] He similarly ignored details given in the *Manasara* of certain mystical figures traced on the ground plan of villages in order to identify the appropriate location of various structures and for the performance of various propitiatory rites. He thought these would be of little interest to the European reader (which was clearly an important part of the audience he addressed), and therefore left them out.[40]

The author of the *Essay* does not merely summarize and quote from texts, he also comments on them. For instance, in one place he states that the most interesting aspect of the architectural treatises was their toleration of the worship of the Jainas and Buddhists, and the fact that they contained a discussion of the images and shrines of these religions. Another interesting aspect he noted was their reference to images of the Shaiva saints. Ram Raz was well aware of the implications of these facts for the question of the age of the texts.

He was aware too of the writings of Orientalist scholars, and at several places referred to them, sometimes expressing disagreement. For instance, he contested William Jones's view that the *Shilpa Shastras* dealt with sixty-four different arts and manufactures. The principal subject of these works, asserted Ram Raz, was sacred architecture and sculpture.[41] Elsewhere in the *Essay*, he disagreed with the dates assigned by H.H. Wilson to the ancient South Indian dynasties.

> The few facts, it is true, that have been recorded of these dynasties, or preserved by tradition, are unfortunately inadequate to the formation of a connected sketch of their history, or to trace their chronology with precision; but the various accounts which are obtainable of these ancient

[39] Ibid.: 12.
[40] Ibid.: 41, n.
[41] Ibid.: 1–2.

monarchies though they usually commence with the earliest ages, and are blended with marvellous and extravagant fictions, would still afford ample proofs of the establishment of these principalities at an earlier period than what has been hitherto assigned them by western antiquarians.[42]

As mentioned, Ram Raz's was a comparative exercise: he compared Grecian pillars with Indian ones; in the course of this comparison, he pointed out that the massiveness of Indian entablature was in striking contrast to the lightness of Grecian pillars, 'but the richness of the former may be said to be unrivalled.'[43] Then again, while discussing the proportions of Grecian and Indian columns, he suggested that the principle which governed the proportion of diminution of the columns from base to summit 'is supposed to have been discovered with great scientific skill and adduced as one of the proofs of the highly refined taste of the Greeks; but we observe, that precepts derived from the same principle have been taught and practised in India from time immemorial.'[44]

The major differences of opinion between Ram Raz and Western scholars concerned certain important issues in the history of Indian architecture—the question of the origins and originality or otherwise of Indian architecture, and its aesthetic aspects. Although Ram Raz failed to suggest any specific chronology of the architectural samples he was comparing, he was unwilling to accept the assumption of Western scholars that Indian architecture was indebted to Western inspiration. His stand on this issue was typical of his cautious, methodical approach:

Some of the Western authors have traced a certain resemblance in the leading features of the buildings in Egypt and India, and have thence concluded that there has very early been a communication of architectural knowledge between the two countries. But it is not altogether improbable that this resemblance may be merely owing to accident; inasmuch as in architecture as well as in every other art indispensably necessary to the comfort of mankind, two or more nations may possess something in common, without having any intercourse with each other, for the wants felt by man being the same, it is not surprising that the remedies resorted to for supplying them should be also similar or nearly so. If, on the other

[42] Ibid.: 11.
[43] Ibid.: 40.
[44] Ibid.: 39.

hand, however, both these countries had actually any communication in early ages, it is hard to determine which of them may have been indebted to the other. The western writers on antiquities have not placed this matter beyond a doubt. And for my own part, I will not venture to form an opinion as to this alleged affinity in the architecture of Egypt and India. I humbly presume, therefore, that until the Silpa Sástra of the Hindús is correctly illustrated and laid before the public, the question as to whether the art owes its origin to the one or the other of the two countries must remain problematic.[45]

Ram Raz's refusal to assume or accept a Western origin for Indian architecture was combined with his highlighting of the aesthetic beauty of Indian temple architecture.[46] His *Essay* marks him out as a pioneer in the history of the study of Indian architecture. Also, it will become clearer in the subsequent section that the study of Indian architecture was never a disinterested or purely academic exercise: it had a political dimension and was connected to the broader colonial context. Within this broader context, Ram Raz may be described as India's first architectural nationalist.

The Debate on 'Native' Involvement in the Archaeological Survey

When the Archaeological Survey was created in 1871 the viceroy, Lord Mayo, expressed the desire that 'so far as possible, intelligent Natives may be employed in and trained to the work of photographing, measuring, and surveying buildings, directing excavations, and the like; while as regards deciphering inscriptions, it seems probable that Natives may be found better qualified to do this work than many Europeans, whose services could be at present secured for such employment in the Department.'[47] This was part of the general perspective the viceroy had on training and involving Indians to some extent in various spheres of public administration.

[45] Letter from Ram Raz to Richard Clarke, dated Madras, 13 January 1828; cited in Raz (1834): xiii.

[46] Ram Raz's *Essay* had a certain impact among those interested in such matters in the West. For instance, it was the basis of Owen Jones's understanding of Indian architectural ornamentation. Mitter (1977): 233.

[47] Government of India Resolution, No. 649–50, dated 2 February 1871, Home/Public, 18 February 1871, No. 28, Part A, OIOC.

As nationalist aspirations acquired a greater level of coherence in the 1880s (the Indian National Congress was founded in 1885), the colonial state increasingly veered towards the pragmatic need to introduce a greater level of Indian representation at the political and administrative levels. The viceroyalties of Ripon (1880–4) and Dufferin (1884–8) corresponded with the Liberal ascendancy in British electoral politics, and saw certain limited initiatives in the spheres of local self-government, including an increase in Indian representation in legislative councils. Ripon in fact got himself into trouble and earned the grave displeasure of the European community in India when he was seen as having gone too far in this direction by promoting the Ilbert Bill. Against this background, it is not surprising that the 1880s saw pressures on the Archaeological Department to increase Indian participation in the archaeological enterprise.

When J.F. Fleet was appointed government epigraphist in 1883 he was urged by the government to employ and train native scholars. Fleet's response was that he fully agreed with the desirability of training Indian scholars in epigraphy and had been constantly on the lookout for such men but had not met with any success. There was a major problem: 'Researches of this kind require not only a large amount of special reading before hand but also a thorough knowledge of English, as well as of Sanskrit and other Oriental languages, and, further, a habit of criticism which is of very rare existence among Native students, and which, where it does exist, can only be fully developed and turned to practical account by long and continuous exercise.'[48] Fleet also referred to the institutional constraints of the situation—epigraphy was nowhere formally taught and he could not devote all his time to training raw students. The few natives he knew who could take on epigraphic work were all elderly and already enjoying salaries far higher than those that could be offered to them as epigraphic assistants in the Archaeological Survey.

Fleet proposed that professors in Sanskrit colleges should train selected students in epigraphical and archaeological research. The

[48] Letter No. 7, dated Camp Bombay, 7 March 1884, from J.F. Fleet to the Secretary to the Government of India, Home Department, Home/Archaeology and the Conservation of Ancient Monuments, November 1884, No. 14, Part A, NAI.

Government of India circulated Fleet's observations and suggestions to a number of scholars. Not all of them were convinced by Fleet's explanation of his inability to find Indian assistants and his low estimate of the abilities of natives for this sort of work. P. Peterson, professor of Oriental languages in Elphinstone College, Bombay, pointed out that the combination of accuracy, critical judgement, knowledge of Sanskrit and other Oriental languages, and English were not found together *anywhere*, so would be as infrequent among natives as Englishmen. Proficiency in English should be the least important qualification. R.G. Bhandarkar of Deccan College, similarly, could not understand why Fleet had been unable to find Indian scholars who fitted the bill, while E. Forchhamer, archaeologist in British Burma, was confident that native scholars could be trained in epigraphical studies. Ultimately, the Government of India decided to adopt a different approach from the one suggested by Fleet. The governments of Madras, Bombay, Bengal, and Punjab were instructed to take steps to introduce palaeography as an optional subject for higher degrees, and were asked to introduce prizes to stimulate and encourage epigraphic studies among native students.[49]

In 1886 the secretary of state for India sent a despatch to the Government of India, urging the training and employment of Indians in archaeological and epigraphical work. By this time Cunningham had retired and Burgess had taken over as head of the Archaeological Survey. The responses of European epigraphists and archaeologists remained the same as before—while they agreed with the idea in principle, they found it impossible to implement. Burgess said he often gave a share of the work of translating inscriptions to scholars such as R.G. Bhandarkar and Pandit Bhagwanlal Indraji. He had also routinely associated native students of the schools of art as draftsmen to prepare illustrations of monuments. But while native draftsmen could be taught to do a good job at very economical rates, it was difficult to find any who could be appointed archaeological assistants. This was because highly educated Indians (who alone could do the job) would expect high salaries.[50]

[49] *Proceedings of the Sub-Committee, Public Service Commission*: 31–4.

[50] Letter No. 639, dated Madras, 28 December 1886, from J. Burgess to the Officiating Secretary to the Government of India, Home/Archaeology and the Conservation of Ancient Monuments, January 1887, No. 13, Part A, NAI.

When a special sub-committee was set up in 1887 to enquire into various aspects of the future conduct of archaeological survey work, the participation of Indians in archaeological and epigraphic work came up again for discussion.[51] A. Rea pointed out that a major problem was that survey and conservation work required architectural training, and there were no architectural schools in India. Further, according to him, natives generally displayed great apathy in all branches of archaeology; it was only once this apathy was overcome that they could qualify for higher positions in the Archaeological Survey department.[52] The Archaeological Department of Bengal was the only one which had a well-paid post for a native draftsman, specifically for a 'Hindu gentleman of high caste'. The reason why this was an important qualification was that it provided access to temples where active worship was still going on, many of which were out of bounds for the European officers of the Archaeological Department.[53] Hultzsch reported that he had had a native assistant, V. Venkayya, since May 1886. While this young man had the potential of making a good assistant, he wasn't sure he would make a good epigraphist. Hultzsch strongly opposed the idea of leaving epigraphical work entirely to natives.[54]

The sub-committee also sought the opinion of Indian scholars such as Rajendralalala Mitra, R.G. Bhandarkar, and Pandit Natesa Sastri on the issue. Sastri was the most outspoken. He reported that he had worked in the inscriptions branch of the Archaeological Survey under Sewell and then Burgess. Although he had copied and translated inscription after inscription, not one had ever been published. Burgess had too much on his hands and was a poor supervisor, being out of the country half the year. The publications of the Archaeological Survey of Southern India were too exorbitantly priced for ordinary people to buy. Hultzsch knew Sanskrit and Pali, but did not have any real expertise in the Dravidian languages. Work on South Indian inscriptions could only be done properly by Indians who alone knew the languages well and had access to temple interiors: 'For real, useful,

[51] The sub-committee was presided over by Sir Charles A. Turner; several sittings were held at Poona, Madras, and Calcutta.

[52] *Proceedings of the Sub-Committee*: 42–3.

[53] Ibid.: 44.

[54] Ibid.: 50.

practical work an Epigraphist should, I think, be sought for on the banks of the Kaveri or Krishna rather than the Danube. Further, even if the European has all the Dravidian scholarship of a Kamban, he can do no independent work with the ancient inscriptions of South India. As a European he cannot enter the inner parts of a temple in which worship is performed, and where alone the most valuable of ancient inscriptions are to be found.'[55] Sastri observed that the way things were going, with the current staff of one epigraphist (Hultzsch) plus one assistant, it would take a hundred years to complete the task of collecting, deciphering, and translating all the South Indian inscriptions. He suggested that two native epigraphists be added to the establishment, each with at least four well-paid assistants.

P.C. Mukharji: Archaeologist

In spite of directives emanating from various quarters, during the first few decades of the Archaeological Department Indians were employed as draftsmen, clerks, and peons, but could not hope to rise to a higher position. Hardly any had the opportunity to carry out independent work. One of the first to do so was Babu Poorno Chunder Mukharji. P.C. Mukharji's is not a particularly well-known name in the history of nineteenth-century archaeology. In 1885 while deciding on new arrangements for the conduct of archaeological survey work in India, the Government of the North-Western Provinces and Oudh recommended the appointment of Mukharji as assistant surveyor in the Archaeological Survey Department. Mukharji, 'a self-made, self-taught man', had displayed a keen interest and aptitude in archaeology.[56] He sketched well. He had already produced an illustrated report on the conservation of ancient monuments in the North-Western Provinces and Oudh. Mukharji was ultimately retained as a master draftsman, with his salary increased from Rs 110 to Rs 200 a month. Subsequently, he became personal assistant to T. Bloch in the Bengal Circle and continued to hold this appointment till his death in 1903.

[55] Ibid.: 46.

[56] Home Proceedings/Archaeology and the Conservation of Ancient Monuments, October 1885, No. 24, Part A, OIOC.

One of Mukharji's first assignments—of which detailed information is available—was conducted independent of the Archaeological Survey. In 1887–8 the Public Works Department of the North-Western Provinces and Oudh employed him to survey ancient buildings and other antiquities in the Lalitpur subdivision of Jhansi district. The report on the results of the survey was published in two volumes in 1899.[57] Mukharji gave a concise history of the area from prehistoric times to the nineteenth century. He discussed the architectural styles of different periods, and described the sculptural remains and the twelfth-century paintings he had discovered on the ceiling of a Vishnu temple at Madanpur. The report included a useful gazetteer of archaeological sites in the district. It was accompanied by a number of maps, plans, and drawings made by Mukharji of the antiquities and temples at Deogarh, Dhojri-duttia, Chandpur, Dudhahi, Madanpur, Lalitpur, Chanderi, Budhni, and Banpur.

The survey of the remains in Lalitpur district was followed up by excavations at Patna in 1896–7.[58] Mukharji's work at the site added to the evidence documented by earlier explorers such as by Cunningham and Beglar, and subsequently by L.A. Waddell, who carried out excavations at Patna from 1892 to 1899, and with whom Mukharji was in communication. Mukharji excavated at several places—at Kumrahar, Chaman Talao, the Laskari Bibi mound, a mound about a mile south of Bankipore railway station, Buland Bagh, and Jamuna Dhih. His account of his activities at the site is accompanied by several sketches, some quite rough and made from memory. On the Laskari Bibi mound, he found the remains of a mud stupa, later strengthened with brick. At the other sites he found structural remains and traced various walls, floors, and drains. A vertical cutting to the north-west of the Chaman Talao revealed various structural phases of a building. On the south bank of the Kallu Pokhra he excavated the remains of a large structure that seemed to be a vihara or a palace. Near this he discovered a large, polished, semi-circular piece of a pillar (he described it as an Ashokan pillar made of granite). He conducted fairly extensive excavations at Jamuna Dhih and exposed what he interpreted as a village of the Mauryan period (on Waddell's map it had been marked as a

[57] Mukharji (1899).

[58] Mukharji (1902–3).

26. Mukharji's sketch of a temple at Chandpur. Courtesy: Archaeological Survey of India.

fort). To the south of Kumrahar village he unearthed what he thought might be remains of the wooden pallisade of ancient Pataliputra. He also obtained coins, beads, terracottas, etc. The important discoveries of the February 1897 excavations included an oval Buddhist temple at Nauratanpur, the remains of several ghats of uncertain age leading to the old bed of the Son, several large portions of a pillar, and the remains of a multi-roomed structure (probably a vihara).

Mukharji's third major assignment took him to the Nepal *tarai.* In 1899 the Government of the North-Western Provinces and Oudh sent him to explore that area with instructions to ascertain the location of ancient Kapilavastu, to plot the outline of the city on a map, and to determine the position of the stupas of Krakuchchhanda and Konagamana. Mukharji went on to prepare a *Report on a Tour of Exploration of the Antiquities in the Tarai, Nepal; The Region of Kapilavastu; During February and March, 1899.*[59] The area had already been surveyed by A. Führer, archaeological surveyor of the North-Western Provinces and Oudh, and the summary of his sensational 'discoveries' was contained in his *Monograph on Buddha Sakyamuni's Birth-Place in the Nepalese Tarai.*[60]

The location of ancient Kapilavastu had been (and still is) a vexed issue.[61] A good deal of the problem arose due to the difficulty of reconciling the accounts of Fa Xian and Xuan Zang. Early attempts at identification had placed the site of the ancient city in modern Uttar Pradesh. In 1858 Lassen had identified the site with a place on the banks of the Rohini river. Cunningham preferred to identify Kapilavastu with Nagar Khas (in present southern Basti district, UP), while

[59] Mukharji (1901).

[60] Führer (1897). Führer and Hultzsch were German nationals who were employed in the Archaeological Department because of their scholarly reputation. Dr Führer had been persuaded to leave Germany for India by Sir Alfred Lyall, lieutenant governor of the North-Western Provinces and Oudh in 1885 in order to become curator of the Lucknow Museum for three years. He went on to become assistant archaeological surveyor and then archaeological surveyor of that province. Dr Hultzsch was a professor of Sanskrit and lecturer in Tamil in Vienna University. He was invited to become government epigraphist in 1886 at the suggestion of Sir M.E. Grant Duff, governor of Madras.

[61] For a summary of the different identifications, see Srivastava (1996): 13–23. Also see Debala Mitra (1972): 5–8.

Carlleyle suggested an identification with Bhuila Dih (in the same district).

In 1896, Führer was deputed to advise the Nepal government in archaeological exploration. He had discovered the Nigali Sagar inscription of Ashoka in the previous year. Now, he also claimed to have identified Kapilavastu and the birthplace of the Konagamana and Krakuchchhanda Buddhas. He described in detail the stupa he had discovered at Nigali Sagar and asserted it was clear that the corporeal relics of Konagamana were interred therein, meaning that this was one of the oldest surviving Buddhist monuments in India. Führer pointed to the importance of the discovery of the inscription on the pillar at Rummindei, which had till then lain partly buried under the ground—it was now possible to fix 'with absolute certainty' the site of Kapilavastu and the various sanctuaries in its neighbourhood. He identified the site of Kapilavastu with the extensive ruins lying in a dense *sal* forest about eighteen miles north-west of the Lumbini pillar and about six miles north-west of Nigali Sagar.[62]

In 1897 Führer was busy at work at Sagarwa in the tarai region, where he presided over an exercise in looting and destruction in the name of archaeological excavation. Structures (including, apparently several square stupas) were destroyed in the search for relics, with no attempt towards description or documentation. At the end of it all Führer triumphantly announced that he had found the relic stupas of the Sakyas massacred, according to Buddhist tradition, by the Kosalan king Vidudabha. Vincent Smith, who had a keen interest in the history of India and was at the time commissioner of Fyzabad, paid a surprise visit to the site and put an end to the series of fraudulent claims Führer had been making. Führer had claimed to have found inscriptions of the Sakyas in certain small stupas at Sagarwa. As pointed out by Smith, in his preparatory note to Mukharji's *Report*, the inscriptions were 'impudent forgeries', and Führer had even gone to the extent of furnishing as proof fake relics of the Buddha, and a forged inscription of Upagupta, the preceptor of Ashoka. Führer's *Monograph on Buddha Sakyamuni's Birth-Place* ('every word of it is false') was hastily withdrawn from circulation by the Government of India. This must

[62] Führer (1897): 44.

count as one of the most audacious frauds perpetrated in the history of nineteenth-century Indian archaeology.

When Mukharji set off for the tarai in 1899, no map of the area existed and to survey the erstwhile Sakyan kingdom was not easy. Roads were non-existent, paths circuitous, and travelling in the area involved trudging through slushy fields and crossing streams rarely bridged. Reserved forests in the area were full of wild animals. Mukharji was almost attacked by a tiger one day near the ruins of Tilaurakot, 'so that exploration of the ruins were not altogether without risks or difficulties.'[63] He was also poorly equipped. His survey, drawing, and photographic equipment was old and in unsatisfactory condition. He was assigned only one draftsman, who joined him late. Mukharji was not the lone explorer in the area. Major Waddell had also got permission from the Government of India to join in the investigation. It is clear from Mukharji's restrained account that it was not easy to get along with Waddell, and that he had been frequently at the receiving end of that gentleman's peremptory orders.

In the two months that he was able to devote to his work, Mukharji managed to make good progress and discovered further evidence of Führer's fraud. The stupa of Konagamana, which Führer had described in detail, did not exist. Führer had also described the Ashokan pillar at Nigali Sagar as *in situ*, and had given a description of its foundations. Mukharji and Waddell excavated the pillar, found it broken, and minus a foundation. In spite of Führer having concocted much of his evidence, Mukharji reached similar conclusions on certain important points. Thus, he agreed that Kapilavastu should be located in the Nepal tarai area (specifically with the site of Tilaura-kot), and not in the Basti or Gorakhpur districts. He made trial excavations at Tilaura-kot, Chitradei, and Rummindei (where his major achievement was the excavation of a temple), and traced the Gotihwa stupa through a superficial excavation. The Nepal government pitched in, providing an establishment for the excavations consisting of a captain, and a group of twelve Pahari diggers and men from the plains—to be recruited when required. Mukharji reported on various other sites such as Piprahwa and Sagarwa. He produced a useful map of the tarai area.

[63] Mukharji (1901): 1.

In spite of certain inaccuracies, particularly with respect to chronology, Mukharji's *Report* was one of the important early descriptive accounts of the archaeological remains in the tarai region.

He also wrote a tract entitled *The Indian Chronology, Buddhistic Period*,[64] in which he put forward a number of interrelated hypotheses. He argued determinedly but unconvincingly that the Sandrocottus of the Greeks was not Chandragupta Maurya but Ashoka, and that consequent to this important conclusion major changes needed to be made to the chronology of the Buddha and the Magadhan dynasties. He put forward the hypothesis that there were two Ashokas, one belonging to the Nanda dynasty, the other to the Mauryan. He further argued that the pillar edicts belonged to the Mauryan emperor Ashoka, and the rock edicts to his grandson Samprati (who was the contemporary of the five Hellenistic kings mentioned in the rock edicts). Clearly, although Mukharji seems to have been a diligent and methodical archaeological investigator, his ideas about history and chronology were far less sound.[65]

Rajendralala Mitra

Rajendralala Mitra (1822–91) was one of the most erudite and versatile scholars of nineteenth-century India. He belonged to a learned family of Soora, a suburb of Calcutta. His father, Janamejaya, was a well-known Bengali writer. As a child, Rajendralala was sent to live with his widowed aunt in Calcutta. This is where he went to school, first at the private school of Kshema Chandra Bose and then at the Hindu Free School of Govindachandra Bysack.

Mitra's subsequent history was one of studies broken off by chance incidents. He joined the Calcutta Medical College but left after four years, before getting his degree, in 1841. The incident that precipitated this was Mitra's refusal to reveal the names of certain fellow-students who were supposed to have indulged in some sort of misdemeanour. Dwarkanath Tagore was keen to finance his higher

[64] Mukharji (1903).

[65] John Marshall (1905: 7) described Mukharji in the following manner: 'Though without the advantage of a scientific training, Babu P.C. Mukerji [*sic*] showed himself ungrudgingly devoted to his work and possessed of a variety of useful knowledge which was not infrequently turned to good account.'

27. Rajendralala Mitra.
Courtesy: National Library, Calcutta

studies in England, but Mitra's family thought it improper to accept the generous offer. After this Mitra turned to the study of law. This time round a cancelled examination (due to a report that certain papers had been leaked) led to his abandoning law as well.[66]

During these formative years Mitra acquired a number of important linguistic skills. Apart from Bengali and English (which he already knew), he learnt Persian, Sanskrit, Urdu, Greek, Latin, French, and German. His 'Dr' was the result of an honorary degree, Doctor of Law, conferred on him by Calcutta University. Along with many other Bengali intellectuals of his time, Mitra was actively involved in the nationalist currents sweeping through the province. He was an active member of the British Indian Association (founded in 1851), serving as a member of its executive committee from 1855 onwards. In 1877 he was elected vice-president of the association, and in 1881 he became its president (a post he held till his death). He was also associated with the Indian National Congress after its inception in 1885. Mitra seems to have initially espoused the cause of Hindu nationalism, and then gradually converted to Indian nationalism. He was a strong advocate of a number of reforms, particularly that of the legislative councils. Mitra's nationalism, typical of his age, was by no means revolutionary. He wanted the reform of British rule, not its elimination: 'No Hindu in Bengal would for a moment wish to see our present Government changed. On the whole India never had a Government so good in the course of her history.'[67]

Mitra was the editor of two Bengali journals—*Vividhartha Sangraha* (the first illustrated magazine in Bengali) and *Rahasya-Sandarbha*, which carried articles on a variety of topics. For seven years he was also editor of the *Hindoo Patriot*. He was, further, for a short period one of the editors of the *Tattvabodhini Patrika*. He was associated with the activities of a number of organizations and institutions—the Asiatic Society, Calcutta University, the School Book Society, Vernacular Literature Society, Central Text-Book Committee, Bethune Society, Wards Institution, Society for the Promotion of Industrial Art, Association of Friends for the Promotion of Social Improvement, the

[66] Sisir Kumar Mitra (1973): 2–3.

[67] Excerpt from speech given by Rajendralala Mitra at a meeting of the British Indian Association on 2 July 1870. In Mitter, ed. (1892). 35.

Photographic Society, the Calcutta Municipality, and the Philharmonic Academy of Bengal.[68]

One of the closest institutional links that Mitra had was with the Asiatic Society of Bengal. He joined the society as librarian and assistant secretary in 1846, continuing in this post for ten years. The Asiatic Society was an ideal place for one interested in what, at the time, went by the overlapping names of Indology, antiquarian studies, and archaeology. Mitra's duties as librarian placed him at the helm of the fine collection of manuscripts, books and antiquities that the society was building up. It meant being closely in touch with the manifold research projects of the enthusiastic members of the society. And it provided the atmosphere, exposure, and stimulus for his own research.

In 1856 Mitra left librarianship to take on directorship of the Wards Institution, an institution set up by the government to promote the education of the sons of zamindars and landlords. He occupied this position for twenty-five years, till the institution was wound up in 1880. During all these years Mitra continued to be closely associated with the Asiatic Society, and to research and write. At various points of time he served as secretary (1857, 1865) and vice-president (1861–5, 1870–84, 1886–91) to the society. In 1885, he was elected president of the Asiatic Society, the first Indian to rise to this position. Mitra produced a large number of works under the auspices of the Asiatic Society.[69] Over the years he contributed almost 120 articles to the society's journal. He edited fourteen Sanskrit texts in the *Bibliotheca Indica* series and contributed significantly to the reputation and renown achieved by the series. He published two volumes of catalogues of the society's manuscripts (apart from other catalogues of manuscripts).

Rajendralala Mitra was a remarkably versatile scholar, writing both in Bengali and English. He wrote on an amazing variety of issues—history, epigraphy, architecture, social issues, political issues, education, language and literature, cartography, applied sciences, physical sciences, etc. His interest in the technical sciences is apparent from his Bengali work *Silpik Darshan*, published in 1860, consisting of a collection of his articles on subjects as varied and practical as the making

[68] B.N. Mukherjee (1978): 49–50.

[69] Saraswati (1978): 39–42.

of soap to the techniques of dying cloth. He was the author of a book on the life of Shivaji (1860) and a history of Mewar (1861), both in Bengali. Mitra was also an amateur photographer. A difference of opinion led to his being turned out of the European-dominated Photographic Society, although he was later reinstated.

Mitra made a major contribution towards disseminating geographical knowledge in the vernacular languages.[70] In 1854 he published *Prakrita Bhugol*, a book in Bengali on physical geography for school students. Under the auspices of the Calcutta School Book Society and the Vernacular Literature Society, he prepared a series of maps and topographic charts for students in Bengali. In 1853–5 he brought out an *Atlas of the North-West Frontier Provinces* in the Hindi and Persian scripts. This project was undertaken at the request of the governor of the North-West Frontier Provinces. During these years he also brought out maps of India and Asia in Hindi, Oriya, Bengali, and Persian. His *Atlas of the Bengal Presidency* (in Bengali) was published in 1871. As the first president of the Saraswat Samaj (established in Calcutta in 1882), he worked towards the formulation of a technical geographical vocabulary in Bengali.

Mitra was one of the few men of his time (and probably of our own as well) who, although rooted in tradition, was able to dispassionately analyse aspects of that tradition and take a controversial stand on sensitive issues. The work that most readily comes to mind in this connection is his essay, *Beef in Ancient India*. Here, in a matter-of-fact way, he marshalled references from Sanskrit texts in order to prove that the modern Hindu's repugnance to beef was not shared by the most ancient texts of the Brahmanical tradition.[71] This was a radical stand even by the standards of the twenty-first century.

One of the significant aspects of Rajendralala Mitra's personality was his ability to negotiate the tightrope between tradition and modernity and reconcile what might seem on the surface to be contradictions. He was a vociferous proponent of the English language and modern Western education (at least for those whose circumstances permitted exposure to it):

[70] Banerjee (1978): 24 ff.
[71] Mitra (1881): 354–88.

> If patriotism means an insensate love of everything that is ours, whether good or bad, away with such patriotism. If it is to teach us to rest satisfied with our lares and penates, our language, and our civilisation, as they now stand, the less we have of it the better. Such patriotism requires us to hug our chains, and remain intellectual bondsmen for ever. True patriotism, however, is not a blind adherence to ancient customs, but an intelligent love for the welfare and advancement of our race, and if you really wish to serve your country, you should not hesitate a moment to spurn everything that stands in the way of progress, and import from foreign land [*sic*] whatever is calculated to raise her in the scale of nations. Our history, our traditions, our ancient glory, are preserved in a language which has long since ceased to be current, and it is impossible to revive it. It can now only serve as a monument of the past, and not the instrument of future amelioration. Our vernaculars are mere media of speech and all but totally devoid of such scientific and literary lore as can raise a nation and satisfy our intellectual wants. Our only resource, therefore, is to borrow what we want from those who will help us, and who can assist us better in this respect that the noble race which now sways the destiny of this country?[72]

And yet this was the same man who spent much of his life trying to elucidate India's ancient history and culture. One of Mitra's important contributions to scholarship was his preparation of a number of descriptive catalogues of research source material. Some of this work was done for the Asiatic Society—cataloguing its collections of manuscripts, books and antiquities. From the 1870s, at the behest of the Government of Bengal, Mitra was actively involved in tracing, collecting, and cataloguing ancient manuscripts within and outside Bengal.[73] The results included the nine volumes of *Notices of Sanskrit Manuscripts,* published between 1870 and 1888. His catalogue of Hodgson's collection of Buddhist manuscripts was published under the title *Sanskrit Buddhist Literature in Nepal* (1882). Mitra was keenly aware of dangers to the manuscript tradition:

> A new influence is now at work for the destruction of MSS. The halo of sanctity which formerly surrounded Sanskrit literature is fast fading away; the ancient Hindu religion is gradually losing its hold on men's minds;

[72] Excerpt from speech given by Rajendralala Mitra to the British Indian Association on 2 July 1870. Cited in Mitter, ed. (1892): 29–30.

[73] A list of these is given in Mitra (1978): 70–1.

> Sanskrit is no longer a paying study; European literature is rapidly replacing it everywhere; the venerable old pandits—the repositories of traditional and book knowledge of ages,—whose erudition was the profoundest, to whom no modern scholar, European or Asiatic, can for a moment be compared, and who have hitherto preserved with such unflinching zeal the oldest literary monuments of the Aryan race, are rapidly dying out, and their places are not being supplied by the rising generation. For hundreds who formerly studied Sanskrit we have not scores, and, there being little demand, very few MSS. are being prepared to take the place of those which are crumbling down by age. Many works of great literary value and age have already disappeared, and others are in eminent [*sic*] risk, and unless timely saved, will in half a century more be irreparably lost.[74]

For Mitra, concern with the future was connected with concern for the past. The two might demand different strategies and approaches, but both were important.

One of the most important scholarly contributions made by Rajendralala Mitra was his role in editing a number of ancient texts. This was a particularly important task, for only after such primary source material was published could further inquiries follow. His erudition enabled him to take on an amazing variety of texts in Sanskrit, Pali and Prakrit. Some of these formed part of the Asiatic Society's *Bibliotheca Indica* series. The texts he edited and published included Kamandaka's *Nitisara* (1849 onwards), the *Taittiriya Brahmana* of the *Yajur Veda* with Sayana's commentary, the *Taittiriya Aranyaka* (1871), the *Gopatha Brahmana* of the *Atharva Veda* (1872), the *Aitareya Brahmana* of the *Rig Veda* (1875), the Pratishakhyas of the Black *Yajur Veda* (1871), the *Brihad-devata* of Shaunaka, the *Yoga-sutras* (1880), the *Agni* and *Vayu Puranas* (1870, 1886), the *Lalitavistara* (1853), the *Ashtasahasrika Prajnaparamita* (1888).

In spite of these achievements—and in this he was unlike most other Indian scholars of the time—Mitra's vision of the subcontinent's past was not informed exclusively by texts. Mitra also left his mark in the fields of epigraphy and numismatics. He edited and commented on a number of inscriptions in the *Journal of the Asiatic Society of Bengal.* These formed an important basis for the construction of the

[74] Mitra (1875).

political history of ancient India and the attempt to solve the vexing problem of dynastic chronologies.

Mitra was a man with distinct ideas about archaeological research, and he made efforts to translate these ideas into reality. Over the years he remained on good terms with the Government of Bengal and was entrusted with various projects. In 1868 he submitted a proposal for an archaeological survey of Orissa to the lieutenant governor. He explained that he had selected Orissa because, next to Bihar, it had the most extensive and interesting ancient remains. He listed its principal places of antiquarian interest, many of which had hitherto attracted little or no attention:

> It is desirable therefore that measures should be taken for a systematic investigation of all the ancient buildings, temples and tumuli in the province, with a view to place on record full descriptions, together with all that may be rescued from oblivion of their early history. As a general rule the description of each place should include a survey of its principal ancient buildings, and a ground plan of every building or ruin of note, with measurements of its height and extent, and photographs of its front and side views, together with drawings and sections of all sculptural and architectural details of value, and accurate facsimiles of inscriptions. A brief account of the traditions current among the people regarding all objects of note should also be included.[75]

Mitra supported his proposal by pointing out that the cost of such a survey would be minimal. He himself would do the work without remuneration, during the Dussehra and winter holidays, taking leave from his job with the Board of Revenue. His estimate of the cost of the project was about Rs 1350. He would take the photographs himself, so the expense of photography would be limited to materials. He also offered to make a selection of architectural details and sculptures for the team from the Society of Arts that was proceeding to Orissa to make casts of interesting architectural features. The lieutenant governor, Sir William Grey, recommended Mitra's proposal and the Government of India sanctioned it. Mitra accompanied the group of moulders, draftsmen and photographers who made their way to

[75] Rajendralala Mitra's letter dated Manicktollah, 16 April 1868, Home/Public, August 1868, Nos. 83–5, Part A, NAI.

Bhubaneswar in 1868–9. Students of the Calcutta School of Art also participated in the project.

The cost of publication of Mitra's report on the results of his investigations ultimately exceeded the initial estimates; nevertheless the two volumes of *The Antiquities of Orissa* (including a number of drawings and photographic illustrations) were eventually published in 1875 and 1880 respectively, at government expense. Cunningham had strongly endorsed financial assistance towards publication of this important work.[76] The information contained in the volumes was extremely comprehensive. Mitra explained his goals in the preface to the first volume:

> In prosecuting my researches I had a two-fold object in view; in the first place to carry out the directions of the late Lord Canning, as laid down in his memorable resolution on the antiquities of India, that is to say, to secure 'an accurate description,—illustrated by plans, measurements, drawings, or photographs, and by copies of inscriptions—of such remains as most deserve notice, with the history of them so far as it may be traceable, and a record of the traditions that are retained regarding them;' and in the second place to notice permanently such points in them as were calculated to throw any special light on the social history of the ages to which they referred.[77]

The two volumes of *The Antiquities of Orissa* covered a wide range of subjects, from general issues such as the origins and history of Indian architecture, the principles of Orissan temple architecture, sculpture and architectural ornamentation, the history of religions (all in Volume I), to a detailed account (in Volume II) of the historical remains at Khandagiri, the temples of Bhubaneswar, Puri, Konarak, Satyabadi, and other places in Orissa. Singling out the writings of James Fergusson on the issue, Mitra gave a spirited rebuttal to the hypothesis that the origins of stone sculpture and architecture in India were indebted to foreign influence. These theories, he argued, were based on false premises such as the claim that the Aryans were not a race of builders. The lack of extant pre-Mauryan remains of stone sculpture and architecture did not itself constitute conclusive proof on this issue. A variety of factors (including 'Moslim fanaticism') could have been

[76] Home/Public, May 1875, No. 132, Part A, NAI.

[77] Mitra (1875): i.

responsible for the absence of such remains. The roots of stone architecture in India lay in an older indigenous tradition of making wooden structures. Its style and features were distinctively Indian, and very dissimilar to those of other parts of the world. Looked at in its entirety, ancient Indian architecture was 'perfectly self-evolved, self-contained, and independent of all extraneous admixture. It has its peculiar rules, its proportions, its particular features,—all bearing impress of a style that has grown from within,—a style which expresses in itself what the people, for whom, and by whom, it was designed, thought, and felt, and meant, and not what was supplied to them by aliens in creed, colour and race.'[78]

In 1877 the Bengal government deputed Mitra to investigate the activities of the three Burmese at Bodh Gaya—as we have seen earlier. It was as a result of Mitra's report that the Bengal government took up the repair of the Mahabodhi temple. Another result was the publication of Mitra's book *Buddha Gaya, the Hermitage of Sákya Muni*, published under the orders of the Government of Bengal in 1878. Different aspects of the historical remains at Bodh Gaya had been noticed and written about by earlier scholars such as Charles Wilkins, Francis Buchanan, and Alexander Cunningham. But Mitra's was the first comprehensive account of the site. *Buddha Gaya* gave a detailed description of Bodh Gaya, its location, mounds, and structures. It provided a history of the Mahabodhi temple and its *mahants*, and of its passing from the hands of Buddhists into those of Hindus. Acknowledging the legendary character of the narrative of events connecting the Buddha with this place in texts such as the *Lalitavistara*, Mitra argued that the character and personality of the historical Buddha were discernible under its hagiographical cocoon. He tried to identify the various places in Bodh Gaya mentioned in the accounts of the Chinese pilgrims. Mitra's account of the archaeological remains at Bodh Gaya included a history of previous excavations and activities at the site—those conducted by Major Mead over a decade previously and the more recent damage done by the 'Burmese gentlemen'. The rest of the book was devoted to a detailed account of the architectural features of the Bodh Gaya temple and the sculptures and inscriptions discovered at the site.

[78] Ibid.: 22.

As indicated earlier, there were at this time major differences of opinion among scholars regarding the age and the arches of the Mahabodhi temple. Mitra described the arches—all seventeen of them—in *Buddha Gaya*. He argued (against Fergusson) that the large number of arches and their position indicated that they were integral to the original temple and not later additions. According to him, the Mahabodhi temple was built between the first century BC and the first century AD. Agreeing with Cunningham on this issue, Mitra concluded that this was the very temple seen and described by the Chinese pilgrims, and that the arch was known to ancient Indians. Once again, he vigorously refuted the hypothesis that foreign influence had a major role to play in the beginnings of Indian stone sculpture or architecture.[79]

Mitra was the only Indian scholar of his time who had the stature to raise various issues related to architecture, archaeology, and conservation with the colonial state, and whose views were considered seriously. In 1874 he submitted to the Government of India a memorandum on the preservation of ancient Indian monuments.[80] He drew the attention of government to the large number of ruined monuments in India whose parts were redeployed, particularly in new construction activity. Examples of this sort of thing included, for instance, a valuable inscribed marble slab being converted into a pestle for grinding foodstuffs, another inscribed slab from Bodh Gaya which had been cut to serve as a fulcrum for a door hinge, and an Ashokan pillar converted into a road-roller. Besides, it was well known that sculpted stones often found their way into *nullahs* to build *bunds* across them or to protect the foundations of bridges; many others were pounded to pieces for road construction. Mitra urged that such sculptures and inscriptions be rescued and deposited in a public museum, preferably the Indian Museum in Calcutta.[81]

It was towards the end of his life that Mitra became the focus of Fergusson's virulent attack. Apart from the fact that it makes racy

[79] Mitra (1878): 106–13, 164–80, 242.

[80] Letter No. 30, dated Calcutta, 18 October 1874, from Babu Rajendralala Mitra to A.C. Lyall, Secretary to the Government of India, Home/Public, November 1874, No. 18, Part A, OIOC.

[81] Ibid.

reading, Fergusson's *Archaeology in India with Especial Reference to the Works of Babu Rajendralala Mitra* (1884) is important for revealing the links between architectural studies and politics during this period. The slipping away of the façade of disinterested academic discourse was on account of the bitter atmosphere of the Ilbert Bill controversy (1883–4). The version of the bill eventually passed was a much diluted version of the original (which would have allowed Europeans to be tried by Indians in the lower courts), but the months between the proposal and the enactment saw very intense racial antagonisms on both sides, particularly in Bengal.

In *Archaeology in India* Fergusson tried to kill several birds with one stone. On the one hand he tried to demolish Mitra's scholarly reputation by heaping ridicule on his architectural writings. On the other he held Mitra up as an example to demonstrate how ill-conceived the Ilbert Bill was in allowing Indians to sit in judgement over Europeans.[82] There was a third angle too—the settling of scores. Fergusson claimed he was the victim of a long-term conspiracy, that Mitra's *The Antiquities of Orissa* and *Buddha Gaya* had become 'practically gigantic pamphlets written for the purpose of exposing my iniquities and ignorance.'[83] What galled him most was that the Government of Bengal had promoted these defamatory tracts.

Among the central points of disagreement between Mitra and Fergusson was their assessment of the degree of foreign influence on Indian art and architecture, and the extent to which such influence could explain the beginnings of stone sculpture and architecture in India. Fergusson had consistently emphasized the importance of such influences, while Mitra had consistently minimized them. In *Archaeology in India* Fergusson significantly shifted his stance. He protested

[82] Fergusson (1884): vi. As already discussed in a previous chapter, although Fergusson's book had a special focus on Rajendralala Mitra, it included a virulent attack against Cunningham, Beglar, Carlleyle, and F.S. Growse. An officer keenly interested in archaeological investigations, Growse had served as collector of Farukhabad and went on to author a book titled *Mathura: A District Memoir* (1883). Fergusson spoke up against ill-conceived restoration work such as had been conducted at Bodh Gaya by Beglar and at Brindaban by Growse. On the tussle over scholarly domains reflected in the Fergusson–Mitra conflict, see Guha-Thakurta (1998): 41–3.

[83] Fergusson (1884): Preface, iv.

that, contrary to what Mitra continually suggested, he had never harped on foreign elements in Indian architecture; in fact he had always recognized its originality. He further suggested that it was the menace of white ants rather than the exposure to Greek influence that caused the shift from wood to stone as the preferred building material in India. Another contentious issue was whether style or inscriptional evidence formed the more reliable gauge of the age of historical monuments. Fergusson had always favoured the former, Mitra (like Cunningham) the latter. Discussing the Katak caves, the temples of Bhubaneswar, and Bodh Gaya, Fergusson tried to point out how Mitra had committed innumerable blunders in descriptions of these.

It is difficult to separate the personal, the political, and the academic in Fergusson's *Archaeology in India.* The fact that it shows vividly the complex interweaving of all these aspects is perhaps of greatest import.

Other Contributions

Ram Raz, P.C. Mukharji and Rajendralala Mitra were a few of the Indians of this period who made contributions to the study of ancient archaeological and literary sources. There were several others: Sir Sayyid Ahmed Khan's *Asar-al-Sanadid* (1846) attempted for the first time to give a comprehensive, descriptive account of the monuments of Delhi.[84] Prominent scholars of later years include Bhau Daji, Bhagwanlal Indraji, and R.G. Bhandarkar. Bhau Daji (1822–74) was a physician and surgeon who established a reputation as a scholar of ancient texts, inscriptions, and coins.[85] R.G. Bhandarkar (1837–1925),

[84] The voluminous Urdu work was divided into four parts. The first dealt with miscellaneous monuments of Delhi, the second with the Red Fort and its buildings, the third with the city of Shahjahanabad, and the fourth with the cultural life of Delhi. The text was accompanied by 130 free-hand sketches by Mirza Shah Rukh Beg, printed by woodcuts, and copies of a number of inscriptions. The work became accessible to the European audience with the publication of a French translation by Garcin de Tassay in the *Journal Asiatique.* Sayyid Ahmed Khan began working on an English translation, but he never completed it. Instead, a second revised and abridged edition of the work appeared in 1854. More recently, an English version of Khan's book (not a literal translation) has been published by R. Nath (1979). Sayyid Ahmed Khan was a member of the Delhi Archaeological Society.

[85] See Keer (1963): 1–19.

professor of Sanskrit at Deccan College, Poona, and subsequently vice chancellor of the University of Bombay, made a mark as an exceptional scholar of ancient texts, inscriptions and history. Bhagwanlal Indraji (1839–88) started out as a young scholar under Bhau Daji's wing, and soon made his mark both as epigraphist and archaeologist. His account of his 1882 explorations at Sopara and the Padana hill was an important contribution to the archaeological literature of the time.[86]

If we move beyond the strict spheres of antiquarian and archaeological studies, a few other contributions also merit attention. While the photographing of historical monuments was dominated by Europeans, the Indian name that stands out is that of Lala Deen Dayal, who set up a major photographic business in Indore and whose photographs of historical monuments appeared in a number of important publications. Deen Dayal's talent was recognized and used by a number of influential contemporaries. In 1882 he accompanied Sir Lepel Griffin on his tour of Central India, one of the products of which was a set of beautiful photographs of the Sanchi monuments. The most important patron of Deen Dayal was the nizam of Hyderabad. In 1884 the nizam appointed him state photographer. Over 250 of Deen Dayal's photographic views were bought by the Archaeological Survey of India. Deen Dayal also prepared volumes of photographs comprising views of the monuments of Delhi and Agra. His photographs appeared in Griffin's *Famous Monuments of Central India* and in H.H. Cole's *Preservation of National Monuments in India.*

An important but relatively unexplored area is works in the vernacular languages. In nineteenth-century India, there was a thriving Urdu *tarikh* literature which had as its theme the histories of events, cities and regions.[87] The reports of the Archaeological Survey frequently refer to vernacular works, often cited by officers of the survey solely in order to refute their contents.[88] Very few of these texts have been translated into English. Among those that have are the works of Syad Muhammad Latif, extra judicial assistant commissioner in Gurdaspur in the late nineteenth century. Latif wrote a detailed account

[86] Indraji (1882): 273–328.

[87] I was made aware of this genre of texts by Nonica Datta.

[88] An example are Carlleyle's frequent references to Seal Chand and Raja Ram's works on the monuments of Agra.

of the cities of Lahore and Agra, as well as a history of the Punjab.[89] Such histories and descriptions of monuments reflect the intersection between colonial context and indigenous discourse on the past; both individually and collectively, they merit closer attention and scrutiny than they have received.

[89] Latif (1891, 1892, 1896). The first two books contain detailed descriptions of historical monuments. The accuracy of the historical account of the third one is dubious in its earlier parts and in the later part strongly tempered by an intense, loyalist stance towards British rule in India. It is interesting that Latif should focus on Agra and Lahore, which, apart from their profusion of historical monuments, were important provincial political centres in British India. On the marginal position of archaeology in most nineteenth-century nationalist writings within the history of Bengal, see Chakrabarti (2003): 265–8.

CHAPTER 10

Archaeology, Sites, and Monuments in Nineteenth-century India

Like all branches of knowledge, archaeology was grounded, and continues to be grounded, in its specific historical contexts. Bruce Trigger has identified three distinctive types of archaeologies, each produced by and corresponding to different social-political contexts—nationalist, colonialist, and imperialist.[1] He describes colonialist archaeology as that which developed in countries where large-scale displacement of native populations by Europeans took place or where Europeans exercised political and economic dominance for a considerable period of time. In these parts of the world, archaeology was practised by colonizers who had no historical ties with the communities whose pasts they were studying. The reconstruction of the pasts of colonized people emphasized their primitiveness and lack of innovation or change, and served to justify their displacement or subjugation by European colonizers. This archaeology was closely linked to an ethnology which shared similar features.

While highlighting the fact that archaeology is rooted in its specific historical contexts, Trigger points out that the archaeological interpretation of the past is shaped by a number of other factors as well.[2] These include the ideas that archaeologists—individually and collectively—have about the past, the techniques they have at their disposal, and the steadily increasing body of physical evidence of the past. Although ideology forms a powerful factor in governing and moulding archaeological research, it intersects with a number of other important variables.

[1] Trigger (1984).
[2] Trigger (1995).

Trigger cites the examples of the United States, Canada, Australia, New Zealand, and sub-Saharan Africa as instances of colonialist archaeology and does not specifically discuss India. This omission is crucial, for although the features of colonial archaeology delineated by Trigger do by and large hold true, colonial archaeology did not assume exactly the same form in all colonized lands, nor did its features remain constant over time. Sub-Saharan Africa was cast in the mould of a land petrified in a state of primitiveness and stagnation, fit only for the study of anthropologists or pre-historians. India, with its evidence of an ancient classical literature and civilization, required far more complex negotiations. Further, the British attitude towards India's past, her texts and traditions changed with the waxing and waning of the British Indian empire.

One of the differences between early European antiquarian and archaeological investigations of their own past and European investigations of the past of the Eastern lands they encountered lay in the different degree of 'unknownness' involved. Europe's discovery of the European past was a discovery of the unknown past of a known land, often fuelled by nationalist fervour. In India, early antiquarians and archaeologists grappled with a double unknown—the unknown past of an unknown land. Another difference between the two sorts of investigation was the colonial filter through which the British, in particular, perceived and processed the Indian past, and the imperative to know in order to subdue, control, and rule.

Archaeology in nineteenth-century India was thus embedded in a colonial context and part of a larger Orientalist universe. At the same time, whether we look at the approaches and ideas of individuals, or at institutional developments, or at state policies, we are confronted with a complex picture, diverse strands, and contradictory impulses. Disinterested scholarship jostles with scholarship linked directly or indirectly to larger political agendas. Racist presuppositions and prejudice exist simultaneously with more measured approaches. Major breakthroughs in the decipherment of scripts, the discovery and documentation of sites, and construction of historical chronologies vie for attention with negative, judgmental statements about India's people and her past. Spokesmen for the removal of ancient Indian antiquities to the British Museum meet their match in those who argue for the preservation of Indian antiquities in India. Policymakers seeking to whittle down funds for archaeological research and the conservation of monuments are frequently replaced by those eager to increase financial support for such activities.

While some civil and military officials responded half-heartedly or with indifference towards such issues, others displayed a long-term commitment to this cause. Nor was archaeological research in colonial India entirely the monopoly of a colonizing elite decoding India's past in splendid isolation. However contemptuous it might have been of the ability of 'natives' to reconstruct and understand their own past, British scholarship in India did have to engage in a variety of ways with indigenous scholarship, and indigenous scholarship did have a role to play in these investigations.

In a more global context, on the other hand, the relationship between archaeology in India and in Europe, during the nineteenth century, seems to have been largely one of mutual indifference. The interests and inquiries of European archaeologists were for the most part directed towards Europe or West Asia. The same applies to interest at the more popular level. Although the discovery of the Bharhut stupa made it to the pages of the *Times*, generally speaking discoveries in West Asia excited more interest and publicity in Europe than those made in India. British archaeologists in India could not have been unaware of archaeological discoveries and techniques being employed in Europe and West Asia. Yet Cunningham's writings contain hardly any reference to these. There is only one place (in *The Bhilsa Topes*) where he refers to Layard's discoveries in Mesopotamia: 'In illustration of the ancient history of India, the bas-reliefs and inscriptions of the Bhilsa Topes are almost equal in importance to the more splendid discoveries made by the enterprising and energetic Layard in the mounds of the Euphrates.'[3] Imam asserts that Cunningham's stay in England over 1866–70 must have exposed him to the ideas of geologists such as Lyell and prehistorians such as Lubbock. Their ideas do not, however, seem to have influenced him in any remarkable way. As far as long-term intellectual interaction with European scholars is concerned, Cunningham is known only to have been in regular correspondence with the numismatist E.J. Rapson of the British Museum.

[3] Cunningham (1854b): viii.

In fact, it was Rapson who read and corrected the proofs of Cunningham's last book, *Coins of Mediaeval India.*

The cocooning of Indian archaeology from Western influences was connected with the fact that India was colonized and that archaeology became the concern and preserve of a department of the Government of India. This department did not generally recruit scholars or specialists from Europe.[4] It relied on civil and military officers of the colonial state for whom archaeology was often an ancillary, part-time or post-retirement activity. This group of officers does not seem to have had much in common, nor any significant degree of contact, with European archaeologists.[5] There is one notable exception to the relative insulation of Indian archaeology from European scholarship. This is the case of Robert Bruce Foote, one of the pioneers of palaeolithic research in India, who was in regular contact with J.D. Evans and other European scholars. Greater contact between Indian and European archaeologists had to await the twentieth century with the increasing professionalization of archaeology both in Europe and in India, and its recognition as a separate academic discipline requiring specialized training.[6]

Nineteenth-century archaeology in India had a voracious range of interests and concerns, which included anything and everything to do with India's past, sometimes spilling out into the present. Although archaeology here did gradually carve out its separate niche, till the late nineteenth century it did not fully succeed in shaking off its connections with other branches of Orientalist inquiry. This is not surprising, given the close connection among the men who worked in these fields, and the fact that sharply demarcated disciplinary boundaries had not

[4] Hultzsch and Führer, both German nationals, are exceptions to the rule.

[5] Mitter (1977: 142) suggests that Indian archaeology inherited an empirical, pragmatic approach from British archaeology. That Indian archaeology in the second half of the nineteenth century had these characteristics may not be a matter of dispute. But whether this was an inheritance from the tradition of British archaeology or from the mind and method of the colonial administration, is another matter.

[6] Although archaeology made its way in the nineteenth century into the undergraduate curricula of universities in Britain as part of classical and Near Eastern studies and Egyptology, it emerged as an independent discipline in the post-World War I period.

yet emerged. Early archaeologists shared with some surveyors an orientation towards field survey, a journal-like style of reporting, and a wide scope of inquiry. Like the adventurers, they had an inveterate interest in opening Buddhist stupas, with scant concern for the resulting damage. The links with textual scholars is evident in nineteenth-century archaeology's heavy dependence on textual sources. While archaeology gradually added a new and important dimension to the discourse on India's past, it was, after all, a part of a larger discourse. The frequent forays of archaeologists into racial ethnography, and the prejudices they reveal, reflect the larger frameworks within which Europeans of the time understood the cultures they encountered.

Assessing the Cunningham Era of Indian Archaeology

The cast of characters in the history of nineteenth-century Indian archaeology includes experienced field archaeologists such as Alexander Cunningham, zealous apprentices such as J.D.M. Beglar and A.C.L. Carlleyle, and bumbling amateurs such as Walter Elliot and J.G. Horsfall. There were James Fergusson and James Burgess, with their interest in delineating India's architectural heritage, and H.H. Cole, who combined this interest with a passion for conservation. And in spite of institutional constraints, there was a slowly growing number of Indians such as Rajendralala Mitra, P.C. Mukharji and Bhagwanlal Indraji who contributed to archaeological inquiry during these decades. Among all these individuals, the figure of Cunningham stands out most prominently.

The achievements of Cunningham and the Archaeological Survey he presided over for fourteen years fell short of the standards and expectations of many of his contemporaries. In 1887 as part of the deliberations regarding the future of the Archaeological Department, a sub-committee of the Public Service Commission held a number of hearings in various cities, receiving oral and written testimonies from a number of European and Indian scholars. These testimonies assessed the work of the Archaeological Survey and suggested how archaeological research in India should henceforth be conducted. All of them were critical of the achievements of the survey under Cunningham's leadership.

Burgess's references to Cunningham were brief and terse, but their general tenor was clear. Although Cunningham had collected important historical and geographical information, 'he had done little to illustrate architecture and art.'[7] F.S. Growse (one-time collector of Farukhabad, an official interested and involved in archaeological investigations) emphasized that all the most distinguished successes in Indian archaeology had been won by amateurs—men like William Jones, Prinsep, Wilson, Muir, and Hodgson, who in their public capacity were salaried servants of government, but as Orientalists were independent and unpaid. According to Growse, Cunningham too had made his mark when archaeology was only the recreation of his leisure hours, but he had achieved nothing worthy of his reputation during his long period of office as director general. The only two volumes of his reports that did Cunningham any credit were the first two, compiled before his appointment as director general, while the rest were so utterly deficient in method as to be useless. As for the reports of his assistants, they were best described as 'a tissue of trivial narrative and the crudest theories.'[8] Growse suggested that the interests of Indian archaeology would be better served if the Archaeological Department were abolished and replaced by government funding of private initiative. The assessment of the achievements of Cunningham and his team by J.L. Kipling, curator of the Central Museum, Lahore, was just as bleak.[9]

This low opinion of the achievements of the Archaeological Department during Cunningham's stewardship was shared by Rajendralala Mitra.[10] Mitra conceded that it was not an easy job to find officers who had the necessary qualifications—an extensive knowledge of Indian history, historical criticism, the Indian classics, surveying, architecture, fine art, drawing, numismatics, photography, and epigraphy. It was therefore not surprising that in several instances men totally unfit had been appointed for survey work. Although he admitted this

[7] *Proceedings of the Sub-Committee, Public Service Commission. Scientific Departments,* Part III: 27–56.

[8] *Sub-Committee Report,* Section IV (Written Evidence), No. I.

[9] *Sub-Committee Report,* Section IV, No. III. Interestingly, assessments of the pioneering British anthropologist Verrier Elwin by his peers and immediate successors was, in the same vein, generally disparaging.

[10] *Sub-Committee Report,* Section IV, No. II.

was with some reluctance, Mitra went on to quote from Fergusson's *Archaeology in India* on the incompetence of Cunningham, Carlleyle, and Beglar. This was amazingly dispassionate of Mitra, considering that the book, while a virulent diatribe against many, was principally against Mitra himself.

Several years later, Vincent Smith was appointed to produce an index to Cunningham's *Archaeological Survey Reports.* In his preface to the index volume (published as Volume 24 of the series), Smith could not resist making a number of criticisms.[11] The reports, he said, contained a mass of information, but presented in such an undigested form that much of it was inaccessible. Other defects were lack of specification of the territorial division in which sites lay, and the arbitrary spelling of proper names. Smith also made scathing remarks about the 'crude and unscientific speculations' of General Cunningham's assistants.

The most balanced among contemporary assessments was by the epigraphist Bühler.[12] According to him, the great progress had been made in the cataloguing and description of archaeological and epigraphic remains, even if only a beginning had been made in the preparation and publication of exact reproductions of monuments accompanied with detailed descriptions, and even less achieved in the excavation of important ruins. The publications of the Archaeological Survey contained an enormous mass of information regarding the location of many thousands of architectural monuments, sculptures, and inscriptions scattered over nearly the whole of India, and gave the archaeologist a very good general idea of the chief fields for future labour. Over the previous few decades, a large number of stupas had no doubt been opened, rifled of their deposits, and searched for inscriptions. Surface diggings and small clearings and excavations had also been made at many sites. But truly scientific excavations which laid bare entire monuments or sites had been attempted only in very few places, no doubt due to the high costs involved.

More recent assessments of Cunningham's achievements have tended to be kinder than those of his contemporaries, although the verdict remains mixed. Sourindranath Roy criticizes Cunningham's

[11] Smith (1887): v.
[12] Bühler (1895).

obsession with discovering art treasures and ignoring the ordinary artefact, his superficial excavations that led to the destruction of a large number of stupas, his indifference towards prehistory, and his missing the significance of Harappa. But Roy also points out that Cunningham's failings were not his alone; he shared them with most of his contemporaries in India, while there is no doubt of his status as a pioneer in Indian archaeology. He was the first to emphasize the importance of fieldwork and the meticulous and accurate description of sites. He evolved a standard and uniform style of reporting on sites and describing monuments. Arguing against the frequent complaint that Cunningham's was a text-aided archaeology, heavily dependent on the accounts of the Chinese pilgrims, Roy asserts that Cunningham shared with Prinsep the honour of 'liberating archaeology from its literary affiliations'.[13]

F.R. Allchin also identifies various negative aspects of Cunningham's work.[14] In his estimate Cunningham's primary interest was in inscriptional or numismatic evidence, his treatment of sculptural and architectural monuments being secondary. His interest in historical geography was confined to the identification of place names.[15] His excavation methods are not beyond reproach—at Sanchi he completed the process of destruction begun by Johnson in 1822. He left no detailed excavation reports and he seems in practice to have been oblivious to objects other than sculptures and relic caskets. 'Thus his work still lacked, in practice, those aspects which archaeology today has shown itself peculiarly suited to study.'[16] On the other hand, there was Cunningham's grand view of the scope of archaeology as expressed in his instructions to his assistants. At the end of the day, Allchin feels that one of the most impressive aspects of Indian archaeology during this phase was the close contact that scholars like Cunningham had with its soil of India, with its monuments and living culture.[17]

Abu Imam asserts that it is wrong to speak of a 'Cunningham period' in Indian archaeology: it reflects the undue importance given to North India, for Cunningham never concerned himself with South

[13] Roy (1953): 17–18.

[14] Allchin (1961).

[15] I do not think either of these two charges is justified.

[16] Allchin (1961): 247.

[17] Ibid.: 249.

India.[18] Imam also refers to the 'unbelievable unawareness' in India of developments in archaeological method and technique taking place in other parts of the world. He points to Cunningham's lack of interest in prehistory, the lack of clear understanding (or at least application) of stratigraphy, and of the significance of the typology of ordinary artefacts. Cunningham's excavations were 'scrappy, unconnected and unplanned'. The fact of limited resources does not explain why, after finding the great cities of ancient India, it never occurred to him to go in for large-scale horizontal excavations. His reports were delayed, casually written, poorly illustrated, and marred by the puerile discussions of his assistants. According to Imam, there was a gap between what Cunningham actually attempted and the goals he had expounded in his memorandum to Canning and his instructions to his assistants.[19]

This said, Imam is quick to give the other side of the story.[20] If Cunningham was innocent of developments in archaeological ideas and methods in the wider world, the same can be said for his contemporaries (including his critics) in India. So what if he was a bit obsessed with the Chinese pilgrims? Their accounts formed a handy guide for the identification of many an ancient site. It is true that Cunningham dabbled in many things–the decipherment of scripts, numismatics, epigraphy, etc.—but excelled in none; yet his contribution to Indian archaeology remains important and impressive, the chiefest being the identification and listing of a huge number of sites in northern India, many hitherto unknown.

Dilip K. Chakrabarti's assessment dwells less on failings and more on Cunningham's contributions.[21] Chakrabarti asserts that it is pointless to criticize Cunningham for not doing what he was not interested in doing in the first place. By the middle of the nineteenth century the general pattern of Indian antiquities was more or less understood, but there was little awareness of sites in all their specificity. Cunningham's surveys laid out the topographic details of a vast number of sites over a huge area. He did for Indian archaeology what the Great Trigonometrical Survey did for the Indian landmass—map things on a grand

[18] Imam (1966): 239.

[19] Ibid.: 191, 203.

[20] Ibid.: 207 ff.

[21] Chakrabarti (1988): 115–16.

scale: 'In fact, the question of scale is important to understand Cunningham's work. His Reports are basically site survey reports which occasionally come down to the level of tour diaries. It is the scale of this reporting which sets it apart from anything else in Indian archaeology for all times to come. When one adds to this element of scale the level of Cunningham's scholarship—his ability to handle a singularly wide variety of coins, architectural remains, images, etc.—one gets his true measure.'[22] Chakrabarti adds that Cunningham did not neglect excavation. In fact he conducted a large number of these and had evolved a successful method of stupa-opening. His method of excavating structural remains by tracing walls was the standard method followed in Indian archaeology till the 1940s. His 'Multan well' indicates that he understood the principle of stratigraphy in a general way.[23] Chakrabarti also highlights the forgotten contributions made by Cunningham's much-maligned assistant, Carlleyle, in the field of prehistory.

Cunningham's instructions to his assistants can either be considered a hopelessly rambling and eclectic view of the scope of archaeology or viewed as a truly remarkable statement, putting forth a vision of archaeology that touched on artefacts and institutions that were part of the everyday experiences of ordinary people. It was a vision that included much and excluded little, and its wide scope can be connected to the fact that Cunningham was never an armchair scholar. His archaeological inquiries involved extensive travel and intensive contact with the people and places of India. Imam's criticism that Cunningham did not take his instructions to his assistants seriously enough, that there was a gap between his theory and practice, is incorrect. Whether it was in the noting of cromlechs and cairns (in which Cunningham admittedly seems to have had little interest) or sati pillars, or aspects of contemporary life and ethnographic details, all these are there in Cunningham's reports.

Perhaps because he was interested in so many things, Cunningham spread himself thin, laying himself open to criticism by specialists. But, at the time when he took over the Archaeological Survey, a wide-ranging approach was necessary. The importance Cunningham attached to field archaeology made possible the basic archaeological

[22] Ibid.: 116.

[23] Although Cunningham was evidently aware of the principle of stratigraphy, it was not part of his regular method of investigation or reporting.

mapping of North India. Equally, it was he who made space for the simultaneous growth of numismatics, epigraphy, and architectural study.

Cunningham's concern with identifying the places mentioned by the two Chinese pilgrims remained an obsession, but it was an obsession that yielded a number of major breakthroughs and correlations in the historical geography of ancient India. Such correlations were, moreover, never restricted to the matching of accounts and descriptions in texts; they were tested in the field. Furthermore, because attentiveness to the relationship between settlements and landscape was an important part of his method of investigation and reporting, Cunningham's approach to historical geography involved contextualizing historical sites in relation to their physical landscape and ancient routes. It is true he neglected the prehistoric past and was often unable to understand the significance of sites which could not be anchored to literature. At the same time, his approach to the study of India's past—one which integrated data from a variety of sources, literary and archaeological—is very far from being without merit.

The fact is, Cunningham's explorations, although 'text-aided', were never completely circumscribed or restricted by textual references. The routine of regular, extensive field surveys, and the results of these surveys led to an accumulation of important data on the reconstruction of the history of settlements and localities, many of which were *not* mentioned in ancient literature. His manner of site description also offered a highly contextualized picture of historical monuments, one which is often missed in more recent writings. Cunningham's style of describing sites spanned centuries, bridging the gulf between the ancient, medieval and modern. His knowledge of ancient texts and the emphasis he routinely placed on documenting local tradition (even though he was sceptical of its historical veracity) enabled him to constantly move between the great and little traditions of India.

Imam and Chakrabarti critically assert that Cunningham's basic style of investigation and reporting remained more or less constant through his long career. There are indeed many strands of continuity in his voluminous writings. Perhaps this was because, when Cunningham set out on his archaeological surveys in 1861, his background and vast antiquarian and archaeological experience had provided him with some more or less definite ideas about his methods and goals. At the same time, if we carefully consider the whole corpus of Cunningham's writings from the 1830s to the 1880s, there are a few discernible changes in his approach after 1871. There are increasing notices of ordinary artefacts and pottery (although even then he did not assign as much importance to them as he could have). There is also an increasing focus on inscriptions. And though he is best remembered primarily as a field archaeologist, the reports and other writings indicate an increasing interest in and attempts to take further his analysis of architectural style. In fact, while the twenty-three volumes of *Archaeological Survey Reports* contain some of the most important results of Cunningham's long archaeological career, equally important are his studies of individual monuments such as *The Stûpa of Bharhut* and *Mahâbodhi.* The *Archaeological Survey Reports* also display an increasing focus on medieval monuments, inscriptions, and history.

Cunningham's most important contribution to Indian archaeology lies in his having relentlessly scoured the north Indian countryside for decades on end, meticulously collecting and recording what he saw and discovered. His twenty-three volumes remain a record that most archaeologists would find hard to match, quite apart from his numerous other papers and books. Apart from the extensive ground they cover, the detailed, vivid, and comprehensive description of sites in Cunningham's reports remains a starting point for the history of many sites in North India, even when more recent explorations and excavations have produced more important results.[24] This is because they contain a meticulous account of sites as they existed in the second half of the nineteenth century, before they were altered or destroyed in subsequent years.

As far as the long-term implications of developments in the Cunningham phase are concerned, the creation of the Archaeological Survey meant that archaeology in India remained, and remains even today, a largely state-sponsored enterprise. Secondly, many important breakthroughs in prehistoric research were made in the second half of the nineteenth century, but, leaving aside Carlleyle's unnoticed discoveries, few were the result of the activities of the Archaeological Survey. In this arena, officers of the Geological Survey of India played

[24] This is indicated by the fact that the Archaeological Survey of India has recently reprinted the entire set.

the lead role. Historical archaeology continued to be the prime focus of the Archaeological Survey in the post-Cunningham era, and it was only very gradually that prehistory received its fair share of attention.

In the history of Indian archaeology, methodical archaeological excavation and conservation are generally associated with the 'Marshall phase'. During the viceroyalty of Curzon (1899–1905) and the director generalship of John Marshall (1902–44), the Archaeological Survey of India was thoroughly overhauled. The conservation of historical monuments became top priority and conservation work came to be conducted on more careful and sound principles than before. These principles are embodied in a pamphlet titled *Conservation of Ancient Monuments: General Principles for the Guidance of Those Entrusted with the Custody of, and Execution of Repairs to, Ancient Monuments*, prepared by the director general and published in 1907, and circulated within British India and the various princely states. The Marshall years also saw the infusion of a greater degree of order and stability into archaeological investigations. Large-scale excavations based on careful attention to stratigraphic sequence were introduced for the first time in India. Greater space was created for Indians in the Archaeological Survey. It was also during the Marshall era that the most dazzling discovery of the century—the Indus civilization—was made. In comparison with all this, the achievements of the Cunningham era appear haphazard and confused. And yet it must still be emphasized that they formed the foundation on which the more systematic archaeological investigations of the twentieth century were based. Ultimately, therefore, a critical appreciation of the founding phase of Indian archaeology seems the most cogent reason for the present book.

The Modern History of Ancient Sites and Monuments

The nineteenth-century archaeological mapping of India and the documentation and illustration of monuments was accompanied by the destruction of such monuments, particularly at the hands of railway contractors, but also to a certain extent by archaeologists themselves. At the same time, during the last decades of the nineteenth century there was a growing awareness of such destruction and a concern that it should somehow be stopped. The story of Amaravati reveals a complex interplay between discovery, documentation, and destruction. The chorus of discordant voices in the story reveals the lack of coherent policy in relation to the preservation of historical monuments in this period.

The factors affecting the ultimate fate of historical sites emerge more clearly when the fate of Amaravati is compared with that of Sanchi and Bharhut. Ultimately, the fact that Sanchi was not denuded of its spectacular historical remains—in the way in which Bharhut and Amaravati were—was the result of a combination of factors. First, the timing of the discovery: Amaravati was the first of three sites to be discovered (1796), this being a time when concern with systematic archaeological research and *in situ* preservation were nowhere in the picture. The site was slowly but surely destroyed by repeated excavation and the removal of material over more than a century. Sanchi was discovered in 1818 and Bharhut in 1873, and were in this respect somewhat better poised for sympathetic treatment.

The timing of discovery, however, was not everything. Another important factor was the condition of the site at the time of discovery—even if there could be drastic differences in assessments of this aspect. Amaravati was damaged by repeated excavation and removal of material, but even in 1882 Cole was confident that *in situ* preservation could be attempted there. The problem was that nobody agreed with Cole. Contrary to early reports, Sanchi was eventually recognized as being in fairly good shape, and therefore ultimately accepted as a good candidate for *in situ* preservation, but in the 1850s it narrowly escaped losing one of its gateways. Cunningham's report of the battered state of Bharhut ruled out similar preservation there.[25]

The ultimate decisions in the 1880s to keep the Sanchi remains at Sanchi, to prevent the dispersal of its sculptural and architectural elements over museums in India or abroad, and the devising of a plan for

[25] When Sanchi was discovered by General Taylor in 1818, three out of the four gateways were still standing, and the southern one was lying at the spot where it had fallen. The dome of the *stupa* was intact as was part of the balustrade on the *harmika.* Stupas No. 2 and 3 seem to have been in good shape too. At Bharhut, the whole of the Stupa had disappeared, but over half of the stone railing was still there.

the conservation of the site were, finally, also the result of initiatives by individuals such as Cole and Lepel Griffin, both ardent proponents of the principle of *in situ* preservation and fierce critics of the 'vandalism of the archaeologists'. Cole had proved ineffectual in Amaravati but had an important say in what happened at Sanchi.

In the first half of the nineteenth century, in the absence of a conservation policy, a great deal depended on the individual interest and initiative of officers on the spot. The India Museum in London was an obvious destination for countless prized Indian antiquities. The dispatch of the 'Elliot Marbles' in 1859 to England belongs to this phase. The tide began to turn in the 1860s; by the 1870s, it had turned. The issue of what to do with antiquities had become an issue of debate within the Government of India. The winding up of the India Museum in London was paralleled by the growth of museums in India, such as those at Calcutta, Madras, and Bombay, and these now became the preferred homes. The despatch of the Bharhut sculptures to the Indian Museum in Calcutta in the early 1870s reflects a significant policy change. When the second major lot of Amaravati sculptures lay packed on the banks of the Krishna in 1881–2, the quarrel was over whether to send them to Madras or to leave them at Amaravati. Nobody talked of sending the sculptures to the British Museum.

More broadly, the policies of the colonial state *vis-à-vis* the conservation of historical monuments gradually emerged and evolved as a result of its having to grapple with specific cases and issues, and because of various pressures from Britain and within India. Particularly noteworthy are the frequent missives from the home government to the Government of India, urging the latter to take steps towards the delineation of Indian architecture, an interest that was at least in part spurred by the British movement for the reform of industrial design.

The setting up of the Archaeological Survey and the surveys of western and southern India, and the attitude of specific officers presiding over these organizations, naturally played an important part in the formulation of a policy *vis-à-vis* ancient sites and monuments. Although Cunningham did recommend sending one of the Sanchi and Bharhut gateways off to England, his attitude seems to have changed over time. Whether this was simply because of the winding up of the India Museum and his antipathy towards sending material to the British

Museum, or because of a more far-sighted approach, is impossible to know. The setting up of a government department devoted to the investigation of ancient sites and antiquities in 1871, and the establishment of similar set-ups for western and southern India, did in the long run lead to a greater volume of serious debate on these issues. Cunningham was frequently consulted by the Government of India on conservation issues, and Burgess had an important say in matters relating to the place of deposit of antiquities found in areas such as Amaravati. Carlleyle made frequent attempts to repair monuments using his own resources, and Beglar had a clear role in the repair of monuments such as the Mahabodhi temple.

The most vociferous among those who directed the attention of the colonial state to the need to protect and preserve India's historical monuments and antiquities in their original place was clearly Cole. His tenure as curator of ancient monuments (1881–3) was brief and his tangible successes few, but the strong and reasoned manner in which he argued his case brought the conservation issue centrestage for the first time. By the end of the nineteenth century, some of the ambivalences and uncertainties of earlier decades had been ironed out, and the idea that India's archaeological heritage must remain in India, for Indians, had many influential advocates and takers within the colonial regime. The issue of the extent to which the *in situ* principle should be applied, and the priority that should be given to different kinds of museums, however, remained unresolved to the end.

Just as Indians had a role to play in the nineteenth-century reconstruction of India's past, Indian political elites made their contribution towards the conservation of historical monuments. It is not surprising that, with a few exceptions (such as Cole), the British, with their perception of India's past and her monuments divided into the categories 'Hindu' and 'Mohammedan', did not think it conceivable that Indian princes could transcend sectarianism when it came to historical monuments in their realms. The fact that they often did is indicated by the contributions made by the maharaja of Dhar towards conservation work at the medieval site of Mandu, the steps taken by the nizam of Hyderabad to protect the Buddhist frescoes at Ajanta, the money given by Sindia for the restoration of Jaina temples in the

Gwalior fortress, and most eloquently by the long-standing concern of the Bhopal durbar for Sanchi.

While it is important to focus on the development of official policy in relation to sites and monuments in India, there was always a gap between legislation and enactment, between official pronouncement and actual practice. The amassing of private collections and the trade in antiquities may have slowed after 1857, but it was not possible to put an end to it.[26] Many of the custodians of India's archaeological heritage themselves saw nothing wrong in collecting, removing and exporting large and extremely valuable personal collections of antiquities. This is testified most ironically by the large number of items on display in (and the even larger number of items in the vaults of) the British Museum that ultimately came from Cunningham's private collection. All that can be said in Cunningham's defence is that at least some of this material must have been collected by him before his appointment as director general, and that he was, after all, never one of those who argued passionately against the propriety of such acquisitions by officers of the Archaeological Survey. Like many in his time, he believed in the efficacy of the private collection by the knowledgeable collector as one among many modes of conservation and preservation.

The history of Indian archaeology provides, finally, a basis for questioning the frequent assertion that Orientalist discourse perceived and invented the Orient though its texts. It is true that textual traditions were an important part of the nineteenth-century understanding of India's past. However, throughout this period there was a parallel track of inquiry, one admittedly influenced—often even governed—by textual research, but which frequently broke away from it. Because of its methods and the results of its investigations, archaeology could not be completely circumscribed by textual boundaries; it *had* frequently to confront and reveal non-textual pasts. What is equally significant is that, after 1871, although occasional support was given to the publication of ancient texts, it was the archaeological track of inquiry that was given firm organizational basis and sustained financial

[26] This continues to be a thriving trade even in our own time.

support by the colonial state. This support was no doubt inadequate in the task of investigating, documenting and protecting India's vast archaeological heritage, and there were even times when it seemed to be on the verge of being entirely withdrawn. In spite of such constraints, ancient India was ultimately discovered as much through its artefacts, coins, inscriptions, monuments, and sites, as through its texts.

Bibliography

Archival Sources

Files of the Home, Revenue and Agriculture, and Foreign Departments of the Government of India in the National Archives of India and the Oriental and India Office Collection of the British Library.

Proceedings of the Sub-Committee, Public Service Commission. Scientific Departments. Simla, 1887. Part III, pp. 27–56: Archaeological Survey.

Files of the Baghelkhand and Central India Agency, and Mysore and Hyderabad Residency in the National Archives of India.

Published Sources

Alexander, Edward P. 1995, *Museum Masters: Their Museums and Their Influence.* Walnut Creek, etc..

Allchin, Bridget. 1958, 'Morhana Pahar: A Rediscovery.' *Man* 8: 153–5.

Allchin, F.R. 1961, 'Ideas of History in Indian Archaeological Writing: A Preliminary Study.' In *Historians of India, Pakistan and Ceylon*, pp. 241–59. Edited by C.H. Philips. London.

Allen, Charles. 2002, *The Buddha and the Sahibs: The Men Who Discovered India's Lost Religion.* London.

Almond, Philip C. 1988, *The British Discovery of Buddhism.* Cambridge.

Archer, Mildred. 1969, *British Drawings in the India Office Library.* 2 vols. London.

Asher, Catherine B. and Metcalf, Thomas R., eds. 1994, *Perceptions of South Asia's Visual Past.* New Delhi, etc.

Ashton, S.R. 1985, *British Policy Towards the Indian States.* New Delhi.

Asiatic Society Bicentenary Souvenir. 1884. Calcutta.

Baber, Zaheer. 1998, *The Science of Empire: Scientific Knowledge, Civilization, and Colonial Rule in India.* Delhi.

Babington, J. 1832, 'Description of the Pandoo Coolies in Malabar.' *Transactions of the Literary Society of Bombay* 3: 324–30.

Banerjee, Bireswar. 1978, 'Contribution of Rajendralal Mitra to Geography and Technical Sciences.' In *Rajendralala Mitra (150th Anniversary Lectures)*, pp. 24–33. Asiatic Society, Calcutta.

Barrett, Douglas. 1954, *Sculptures from Amaravati in the British Museum.* London.

Bayly, C.A. 1989. *Imperial Meridien: The British Empire and the World 1780–1830.* New York.

Bayley, E.C. 1852, 'Notes on Some Sculptures found in the District of Peshawar.' *JASB* 21: 606–31.

Beglar, J.D.M. 1874, 'Delhi.' In Beglar, J.D.M. and Carlleyle, A.C.L. *Report for the Year 1871–72. Delhi. Agra. ASR,* 4. Calcutta.

———. 1878a, *Report of a Tour in Bundelkhand & Malwa, 1871–2; And in the Central Provinces, 1873–74. ASR,* 7. Calcutta.

———. 1878b, *Report of a Tour Through the Bengal Provinces of Patna, Gaya, Mongir and Bhagalpur; the Santal Parganas, Manbhum, Singhbhum, and Birbhum; Bankura, Ranigunj, Bardwan, and Hughli; in 1872–73. ASR,* 8. Calcutta.

———. 1882, *Report of Tours in the South-Eastern Provinces in 1874–75 and 1875–76. ASR,* 13. Calcutta.

Bellasis, A.F. 1857a, 'Further Observations on the Ruined City of Brahminabad in Sind.' *JBBRAS* 5: 467–77.

———. 1857b, 'An Account of the Ancient and Ruined City of Brahminabad in Sind.' *JBBRAS* 5: 413–25.

Black, Charles E.D. 1891, *A Memoir on the Indian Surveys 1875–1890.* London.

Blackburn, Stuart. 2003, *Print, Folklore, and Nationalism in Colonial South India.* Delhi.

Bose, Sugata and Jalal, Ayesha. 1998, *Modern South Asia: History, Culture, Political Economy.* Delhi.

Boswell, J.A.C. 1872, 'On the Ancient Remains in the Krishna District.' *Indian Antiquary* 1: 149–55.

Bühler, G. 1895, 'Some Notes on Past and Future Archaeological Explorations in India.' *JRAS,* NS, 27: 649–60.

Burgess, J.A.S. 1874, *Report of the First Season's Operations in the Belgaon and Kaladgi Districts.* London.

———. 1875a, *Memorandum of the Antiquities at Dabhoi, Ahmedabad, Than, Junagadh, Girnar and Dhank.* Bombay.

———. 1875b, *Memorandum of the Remains at Gumli, Gop and in Kutch.* Bombay.

———. 1875c, *Provincial Lists of Architectural and Other Archaeological Remains in Western India.* Bombay.

———. 1876, *Report on the Antiquities of Kathiawad and Kachh.* London.

———. 1877, *Notes on the Antiquities of the Talukas of Parner, Sangamner, Ankole and Kopargaum.* Bombay.

———. 1878, *Report on the Antiquities in the Bidar and Aurangabad Districts.* London.

———. 1879, *Notes on the Bauddha Rock Temples of Ajanta.* Bombay.

———. 1882, *Notes on the Amaravati Stupa.* Madras.

———. 1883a, *Report on the Buddhist Cave Temples and Their Inscriptions.* London.

———. 1883b, *Report on the Elura Cave Temples and the Brahmanical and Jaina Caves in Western India.* London.

———. 1885, *List of the Antiquarian Remains in the Bombay Presidency.* Bombay.

———. 1887, *The Buddhist Stupas at Amaravati and Jaggayapeta.* London. 1996 reprint edn, New Delhi.

———. 1896, *On the Muhammadan Architecture of Bharoch, Cambay, Dholka, Champaner and Mahmudnagar in Gujarat.* London.

———. 1905, 'Sketch of Archaeological Research in India During Half-a-century.' *Journal of the Bombay Branch of the Royal Asiatic Society Centenary Memorial Volume*: 131–48.

Burnes, Sir Alexander. 1834, *A Voyage on the Indus: Being the Third Volume of Travels in Bokhara.* London. 1973 reprint edn, Karachi, etc.

Cannon, G. 1964. *Oriental Jones: A Biography of Sir William Jones (1746–1794).* New York.

Carlleyle, A.C.L. 1874, 'Agra.' In Beglar, J.D.M. and Carlleyle, A.C.L. *Report for the Year 1871–72. Delhi. Agra.* ASR 4. Calcutta.

———. 1878, *Report of a Tour in Eastern Rajputana in 1871–72 and 1872–73. ASR,* 6. Calcutta.

———. 1879, *A Report of Tours in the Central Doab and Gorakhpur in 1874 and 1875–76. ASR,* 12. Calcutta.

———. 1880, 'Coins of the Sunga or Mitra Dynasty found near Ramnagar or Ahicchatra, the Ancient Capital of North Panchala in Rohilkhand.' *JASB* 49: 21–8.

———. 1883, *Report of a Tour in the Gorakhpur District in 1875–76 & 1876–7. ASR,* 18. Calcutta.

———. 1885, *Reports of Tours in Gorakhpur, Saran and Ghazipur in 1877 78–79 and 80. ASR,* 22. Calcutta.

Cautley, P.T. 1834a, 'Discovery of an Ancient Town near Behut in the Doab.' *JASB* 3: 43–4.

———. 1834b, 'Further Account of the Remains of an Ancient Town at Behat.' *JASB* 3, 1834: 221–7.

Centenary Review of the Asiatic Society 1784–1884. 1885, Calcutta. 1986 reprint edn, Calcutta.

Chakrabarti, Dilip K. 1976, 'Rajagriha: An Early Historic site in East India.' *World Archaeology* 7, 3: 261–8.

———. 1988, *A History of Indian Archaeology from the Beginning to 1947.* New Delhi.

———. 2003, *Archaeology in the Third World: A History of Indian Archaeology Since 1947.* New Delhi.

Chakrabarti, Pratik. 2004, *Western Science in Modern India: Metropolitan Methods, Colonial Practices.* New Delhi.

Chhabra, B. Ch., Sircar, D.C., and Desai, Z.A. 1953, 'Epigraphical Research.' *Ancient India* 9: 207–32.

Clarke, J.J. 1997, *Oriental Enlightenment: The Encounter Between Asian and Western Thought.* London and New York.

Cohn, Bernard S. 1997, 'The Transformation of Objects into Artefacts, Antiquities, and Art in Nineteenth-Century India.' In *Colonialism and its Forms of Knowledge: The British in India,* Chapter 4. Edited by Cohn, Bernard S., Delhi.

Cole, H.H. 1869. *Illustrations of Ancient Buildings in Kashmir.*

———. 1873. *Illustrations of Buildings near Muttra and Agra, Showing the Mixed Hindu-Mahomedan style of Upper India.*

———. 1882, *Preservation of National Monuments: First Report of the Curator of Ancient Monuments in India for the year 1881–82.* Simla.

———. 1883, *Second Report of the Curator of Ancient Monuments in India for the year 1882–83.* Calcutta.

———. 1884a, *Preservation of National Monuments India. Buildings in the Punjab.* place of publication of the folio volumes of series not indicated.

———. 1884b, *Preservation of National Monuments India. Dehli.*

———. 1884c, *Preservation of National Monuments India. Golden Temple at Amritsar, Punjab.*

———. 1884d, *Preservation of National Monuments India. Graeco-Buddhist Sculptures from Yusufzai.*

———. 1884e, *Preservation of National Monuments India. Great Temple to Siva and His Consort at Madura.*

———. 1884f, *Preservation of National Monuments India. Meywar.*

———. 1884g, *Preservation of National Monuments India. Temples at Trichinopoly.*

———. 1884h, *Preservation of National Monuments India. Tomb of Jahangir at Shahdara near Lahore.*

———. 1885a, *Preservation of National Monuments India. Great Buddhist Tope at Sanchi.*

———. 1885b, *Preservation of National Monuments India. Agra and Gwalior.*

———. 1885c, *Report on Explorations during the Winters of 1883 and 1884.* Calcutta.

Congreave, H. 1844–45, 'Some Observations on a Remarkable Cromlech near Pullicondah in the Carnatic.' *Madras Journal of Literature and Science* 13: 47–51.

Cook, Jill, and Martingell, Hazel E. 1994, *The Carleyle Collection of Stone Age Artefacts from Central India.* British Museum, Occasional Paper 95. London.

Copland, Ian. 1978, 'The Other Guardians: Ideology and Performance in the Indian Political Service.' In *People, Princess and Paramount Power*, edited by Jeffrey, R., Delhi: 275–305.

Court, Claude-Auguste. 1834, 'Further Information on the Topes of Manikyala, Being a Translation of an Extract from a Manuscript Memoir by C.A. Court.' *JASB* 3: 558–9.

———. 1836a, 'Conjectures on the March of Alexander.' *JASB* 5: 359–96.

———. 1836b, 'Extracts Translated from a Memoir on a Map of Peshawar and the Countries Comprised between the Indus and the Hydaspes.' *JASB* 5: 468–82.

———. 1839, 'Collection of Facts which may be Useful for the Comprehension of Alexander the Great's Exploits on the Western Bank of the Indus.' *JASB* 8: 304 ff.

Cowell, E.B., gen. ed. 1895–1913, *The Jataka.* 6 vols. Cambridge.

Crook, Mordaunt. 1972, *The British Museum.* London.

Cunningham, Alexander. 1834, 'Correction of a Mistake Regarding Some o f the Roman Coins Found in the Tope opened by M. Court.' *JASB* 3: 635–7.

———. 1840a, 'Notes on Captain Hay's Bactrian Coins.' *JASB* 9: 531–44.

———. 1840b, 'Description of, and Deductions from a Consideration of, Some New Bactrian Coins.' *JASB* 9: 867–89.

———. 1840c, 'Notice of Some Counterfeit Bactrian Coins.' *JASB* 9: 393–6.

———. 1841a, 'Abstract Journal of the Route of Lieutenant A. Cunningham, Bengal Engineers, to the Sources of the Punjab Rivers.' *JASB* 10: 105–15.

———. 1841b, 'Description of Some Ancient Coins and Seals from Bactria, the Punjab and India.' *JASB* 10: 147–57.

———. 1841c, 'A Sketch of the Second Silver Plate Found at Badakshan.' *JASB* 10: 570–2.

———. 1842, 'Second Notice of Some New Bactrian Coins.' *JASB* 11: 130–7.

———. 1843, 'An Account of the Discovery of the Ruins of the Buddhist

City of Samkassa—by Lieut. Alex. Cunningham, of the Bengal Engineers, in a Letter to Colonel Sykes, F. R. S.' *JRAS* 7: 241–7.

———. 1843–4. 'The Ancient Coinage of Kashmir. With Chronological and Historical Notes, from the Commencement of the Christian Era to the Conquest of the Country by the Moguls.' *Num. Chron.* 6: 1–38.

———. 1845, 'Notice of Some Unpublished Coins of the Indo-Scythians.' *JASB* 14: 430–41.

———. 1845–6, 'An Attempt to Explain Some of the Monograms Found upon the Grecian Coins of Ariana and India.' *Num. Chron.* 8: 175–97.

———. 1848a, 'Verification of the Itinerary of the Chinese Pilgrim, Hwan Thsang through Afghanistan and India, During the First Half of the Seventh century of the Christian Era.' *JASB* 18: 13–62.

———. 1848b, 'Correspondence of the Commissioners deputed to the Tibetan Frontier, communicated by H.M. Elliot, Secretary to the Government of India, Foreign Department.' *JASB* 17: 89–132.

———. 1848c, 'Journal of a Trip through Kulu and Láhul, to the Chu Mureri Lake in Ladak, During the Months of August and September 1846.' *JASB* 17: 201–30.

———. 1848d, 'An Essay on the Arian Order of Architecture, as Exhibited in the Temples of Kashmir.' *JASB* 17: 241–327.

———. 1848e, 'Memorandum by Capt. A. Cunningham, Detailing the Boundary between the Territories of Maharaja Gulab Singh and British India, as Determined by the Commissioners, P.A. Vans Agnew, Esq. And Capt. A. Cunningham, of *Engineers.*' *JASB* 17: 295–7.

———. 1848f, 'Verification of the Itinerary of Hwan Thsang through Ariana and India, With Reference to Major Anderson's Hypothesis of its Modern Compilation.' *JASB* 17: 476–88.

———. 1848g, 'Proposed Archaeological Investigation.' *JASB* 17, 1848: 535–6.

———. 1850, 'An Attempt to Explain Some of the Monograms upon the Grecian Coins of Ariana and India.' *Journal of the Archaeological Society of Delhi*, 1: 38–40.

———. 1853, *A Few Notes and Experiments on the Stone and Timber of the Gwalior Territory; Showing their Values as Building Materials.* Roorkee.

———. 1854a, *Ladák, Physical, Statistical, and Historical; With Notes of the Surrounding Countries.* London.

———. 1854b, *The Bhilsa Topes or Buddhist Monuments of Central India: Comprising a Brief Historical Sketch of the Rise, Progress and Decline of Buddhism; With an Account of the Opening and Examination of the Various Groups of Topes around Bhilsa.* London. 1997 reprint edn, New Delhi.

———. 1860, 'Memorandum on the Irawadi River, with a Monthly Register of its Rise and Fall from 1856 to 1858, and a Measurement of its Minimum Discharge.' *JASB* 29: 175–83.

———. 1863, 'Remarks on the Bactro-Pali Inscription from Taxila.' *JASB* 32: 139 ff.

———. 1864a, 'Note on the Bactro-Pali Inscription from Taxila.' *JASB* 33: 35–8.

———. 1864b, 'Remarks on the Date of the Pehewa Inscription of Raja Bhoja.' *JASB* 33: 223–9.

———. 1865, 'Coins of the Nine Nâgas, and of two other Dynasties of Narwar and Gwalior.' *JASB* 34: 115–19.

———. 1866, 'Coins of the Indian Prince Sophytes, A Contemporary of Alexander the Great.' *Num. Chron.* (NS) 6: 220–31.

———. 1868–73, 'Coins of Alexander's Successors in the East.' *Num. Chron. (N.S.)* 8–13.

———. 1871a, *Ancient Geography of India*: I. *The Buddhist Period, Including the Campaigns of Alexander, and the Travels of Hwen-Thsang.* London. 1975 reprint edn, Varanasi.

———. 1871b, *Four Reports Made during the Years 1862–63–64–65. ASR,* 1. Simla.

———. 1871c, *Four Reports Made during the Years 1862–63–64–65. ASR,* 2. Simla.

———. 1872, 'Coins of Alexander's Successors in the East.' *Num. Chon. (N.S.)* 12: 157 ff.

———. 1873a, *Report for the year 1871–72. ASR,* 3. Calcutta.

———. 1873b, 'Coins of Alexander's Successors in the East.' *Num. Chron. (N.S.)* 13: 187 ff.

———. 1875, *Report for the Year 1872–73. ASR,* 5. Calcutta.

———. 1877, *Corpus Inscriptionum Indicarum.* Vol 1: *Inscriptions of Aśoka.* Calcutta. 1961 reprint edn, Varanasi.

———. 1879a, *Report of a Tour in the Central Provinces in 1873–74 & 1874–75. ASR,* 9. Calcutta.

———. 1879b, *The Stûpa of Bharhut.* London.

———. 1880a, *Report of Tours in Bundelkhand and Malwa in 1874–75 and 1876–77. ASR,* 10. Calcutta.

———. 1880b, *Report of Tours in the Gangetic Provinces from Badaon to Bihar in 1875–76 & 1877–78. ASR,* 11. Calcutta.

———. 1881, 'Relics from Ancient Persia in Gold, Silver, and Copper.' *JASB* 50: 151–86.

———. 1882a, *Report of a Tour in the Punjab in 1878–79. ASR,* 14. Calcutta.

———. 1882b, *Report of a Tour in Bihar and Bengal in 1879–80 from Patna to Sunargaon. ASR,*15. Calcutta.

———. 1883a, *Reports of Tours in North and South Bihar, 1880–81. ASR,* 16. Calcutta.

———. 1883b, 'Relics from Ancient Persia in Gold, Silver, and Copper.' *JASB* 52: 64–67, 258–60.

———. 1883c, *The Book of Indian Eras.* Calcutta.

———. 1884a, *Report of a Tour in the Central Provinces and Lower Gangetic Doab in 1881–82. ASR,* 17. Calcutta.

———. 1884b, 'Coins of Alexander's Successors in the East (communicated to the Numismatic Society of London).'

———. 1885a, *Report of a Tour in Eastern Rajputana. ASR,* 20. Calcutta.

———. 1885b, *Reports of a Tour in Bundelkhand and Rewa; And of a Tour in Rewa, Bundelkhand, Malwa, and Gwalior, in 1884–85. ASR,* 21. Calcutta.

———. 1888a, 'Coins of the Indo-Scythian King Miaus or Heraus.' *Num. Chron.* 8: 47–58.

———. 1888b, 'Coins of the Indo-Scythians.' *Num. Chron.* 8: 199ff.

———. 1889, 'Coins of the Tochari, Kushans or Yue-ti.' *Num. Chron.* 9: 268–311.

———. 1890, 'Coins of the Sakas or Sacae-Scythians.' *Num. Chron.* 10: 103 ff.

———. 1891, *Coins of Ancient India: from the Earliest Times Down to the Seventh Century A.D.* London. 1971 reprint edn, Varanasi.

———. 1892a, *Mahâbodhi or the Great Buddhist Temple under the Bodhi tree at Buddha-Gaya.* London.

———. 1892b, 'Coins of the Kushans or Great Yue-ti.' *Num. Chron.* 12 (3rd series): 40 ff., 98 ff.

———. 1893a, 'Later Indo-Scythians, Scytho-Sassanians and Little Kushans.' *Num. Chron.* 13 (3rd series): 166–202.

———. 1893b, 'Later Indo-Scythians.' *Numismatic Chronicle* 13 (3rd series): 93–128, 184–95, 166–83.

———. 1894a, 'Later Indo-Scythians, Ephthalites, or White Huns.' *Numismatic Chronicle* 14 (3rd series): 243–93.

———. 1894b, *Coins of Mediaeval India from the Seventh Century Down to the Muhammadan Conquests.* London.

Cunningham, J.D. 1834, 'Description of an Ancient and Remarkable Monument near Bhilsa.' *JASB* 3: 490–4.

Daniel, Glyn.1950, *A Hundred Years of Archaeology.* London.

Das, Sisir Kumar. 1978, *Sahibs and Munshis: An Account of the College of Fort William.* Calcutta. 2001 reprint edn.

Davidson, A. 1788, 'On some Roman Coins found in Nellore.' *Asiatic Researches* 1: 331–2.

Davies, Richard H. 1997, *Lives of Indian Images.* Princeton. 1999 reprint edn, Delhi.

de Beer, G.R. 1953, *Sir Hans Sloane and the British Museum.* London.

de Sieveking, G. 1960, 'Morhana Pahar: Or the Mystery of A.C. Carleyle.' *Man* 60: 98–100.

Dehejia, Vidya. 2000a, 'Fixing a Shadow.' In *India Through the Lens: Photography 1840–1911*, pp. 11–34. By Vidya Dehejia *et al.* Washington D.C.

———. 2000b, 'Maharajas as Photographers.' In *India Through the Lens: Photography 1840–1911*, pp. 226–30. By Vidya Dehejia et. al.. Washington D.C.

Desmond, Ray. 1976, 'Photography in India during the Nineteenth Century.' In *India Office Library and Records: Report for the Year 1974*, pp. 5–36. London.

———. 1982, *The India Museum 1801–1879.* London.

Dirks, Nicholas B. 1994, 'Colonial Histories and Native Informants: Biography of an Archive.' In *Orientalism and the Postcolonial Predicament*, pp. 279–313. Edited by Carol A. Breckenridge and Peter van der Veer. Delhi.

Duncan, J. 1798, 'An Account of the Discovery of Two Urns in the Vicinity of Benaras.' *Asiatick Researches* 5: 131–2.

Edney, Mathew H. 1999, *Mapping an Empire: The Geographical Construction of British India 1765–1843.* New Delhi.

Falconer, John. 2000, 'A Passion for Documentation: Architecture and Ethnography. In *India through the Lens: Photography 1840–1911*, pp. 69–117. By Vidya Dehejia *et al.* Washington D.C.

Falk, Harry. 1995, 'A Neglected Pillar of Asoka.' *South Asian Archaeology* 1: 429–38.

Fausboll, V. ed. 1877–97, *The Jātaka together with its Commentary.* 6 vols. London.

Fell, Edward. 1834, 'Description of an Ancient and Remarkable Monument near Bhilsa.' *JASB* 2: 490–4.

Fergusson, James and Burgess, James. 1880, *The Cave Temples of India.* London. 1968 reprint edn, Delhi.

Fergusson, James. 1867, 'Description of the Amravati Tope in Guntur.' *JRAS* 3: 132–66.

———. 1868, *Tree and Serpent Worship: Or Illustrations of Mythology and Art in India in the First and Fourth Centuries after Christ. From the Sculptures of the Buddhist Topes at Sanchi and Amravati.* London.

———. 1884, *Archaeology in India with Especial Reference to the Works of Babu Rajendralala Mitra.* London. 1974 reprint edn, New Delhi.

Folkert, Kendall W. 1998, 'Jain Religious Life at Ancient Mathura: The Heritage of Late Victorian Interpretation.' In *Mathura: The Cultural Heritage*, pp. 103–12. Edited by Doris Meth Srinivasan. New Delhi.

Führer, A. 1897, *Monograph on Buddha Sakyamuni's Birth-Place in the Nepalese Tarai.* Archaeological Survey of Northern India, vol. 6. Allahabad.

Ghosh, A. 1951, 'Rajgir 1950.' *Ancient India* 7: 66–78.

———. 1953, 'Fifty Years of the Archaeological Survey of India.' *Ancient India* 9: 29–52.

Gopal, S. 1965, *British Policy in India 1858-1905.* London. 1975 reprint edn, Madras.

Greenfield, Jeanettte. 1989, *The Return of the Cultural Treasures.* Cambridge.

Griffin, Lepel. H. 1873, *The Rajas of the Punjab: Being the History of the Principal States in the Punjab and their Political Relations with the British Government.* 2nd edn, London.

———. 1909, *Chiefs and families of Note in the Punjab.* Lahore.

———. 1911, *Ranjit Singh and the Sikh Barrier Between our Growing Empire and Central India.* Oxford.

Guha, Sumit. 1988, 'Lower Strata, Older Races, and Aboriginal Peoples: Racial Anthropology and Mythical History Past and Present.' *The Journal of Asian Studies* 57, 2: 423–41.

Guha-Thakurta, Tapati. 1997, 'The Museumized Relic: Archaeology and the First Museum of Colonial India.' *Indian Economic and Social History Review* 34, 1: 21–51.

———. 1998. 'Tales of the Bharhut Stupa: Archaeology in the Colonial and Nationalist Imaginations.' In G.H.R. Tillotson, ed.: *Paradigms of Indian Architecture: Space and Time in Representations and Design.* Surrey, Centre of South Asian Studies, School of Oriental and African Studies, University of London, Collected Papers on South Asia No. 13, pp. 26–58.

Gupta, Narayani. 1981, *Delhi Between Two Empires 1803–1931.* Delhi.

Harle, J.C. 1986, *The Art and Architecture of the Indian Subcontinent.* London, etc. 1990 reprint edn.

Hopkirk, Peter. 1991, *The Great Game: On Secret Service in High Asia.* Oxford.

Howes, Jennifer. 2002, 'Colin Mackenzie and the Stupa at Amaravati.' *South Asian Studies* 18: 53–65.

Hudson, Kenneth. 1987, *Museums of Influence.* Cambridge.

Huntington, Susan L. 1985, *The Art of Ancient India: Buddhist, Hindu, Jain.* New York, Tokyo.

Imam, Abu. 1964, 'Sir Alexander Cunningham (1814–93): The First Phase of Indian Archaeology.' *JRAS*: 194–207.

———. 1966, *Sir Alexander Cunningham and the Beginnings of Indian Archaeology.* Dacca.

Indraji, Bhagwanlal. 1882, 'Antiquarian Remains at Sopara and Padana.' *JBBRAS* 15: 273–328.

Jeffrey, Robin, ed. 1978, *People, Princes and Paramount Power: Society and Politics in the Indian Princely States.* Delhi.

Jones, William. 1788, *A Discourse on the Institution of a Society for inquiring into the History, Civil and Natural, the Antiquities, Arts, Sciences, and Literature of Asia.* Extract from *Asiatic Researches* 1. Calcutta. 1985 reprint.

Joshi, M.C. 1989, 'Mathura as an Ancient Settlement.' In *Mathura: The Cultural Heritage*, pp. 165–70. Edited by Doris Meth Srinivasan. New Delhi.

Julien, Stanislas. 1853, *Histoire de la Vie de Hiouen-Thsang et de ses voyage dans l'Inde, depuis l'an 629 jusqu'en 645.* Paris.

———. 1857–58, *Mémoires sur les Contrées Occidentales traduits du Sanscrit en Chinois, en l'an 648, par Hiouen-Thsang, et du Chinois en Francais.* 2 vols., Paris.

Kak, Ram Chandra. 1933, *Ancient Monuments of Kashmir.* London.

Keer, Dhananjay. 1963, 'Dr. Bhau Daji lad, G.G.M.C.' *Journal of the Asiatic Society of Bombay NS* 38: 1–19.

Kejariwal, O. P. 1988, *The Asiatic Society of Bengal and the Discovery of India's Past 1794-1838.* Delhi.

Khan, Sayyid Ahmed. 1846, *Asar-al-Sanadid.* (Urdu).

Khan, Shahryar M. 2000, *The Begums of Bhopal: A dynasty of women rulers in Raj India.* London, New York.

Kittoe, M.1847a, 'Notes on the Places in the Provinces of Behar, Supposed to be Those Described by Chy Fa Hian.' *JASB* 16: 953 ff.

———. 1847b, 'Note on the Sculptures of Bodh Gyah.' *JASB* 16: 334 ff.

Knox, Robert. 1992, *Amaravati Buddhist Sculptures from the Great Stupa.* London.

Kopf, David. 1969, *British Orientalism and the Bengal Renaissance: The Dynamics of Indian Modernization.* Berkeley and Los Angeles.

Kuraishi, Mohammad Hamid. 1987, *Rajgir.* New Delhi.

Lafont, Jean-Marie. 2002, *Fauj-i Khas: Maharaja Ranjit Singh and his French Officers.* Amritsar.

Lahiri, Nayanjot. 1999, 'Bodh-Gaya: An Ancient Buddhist Shrine and its Modern History (1891–1904).' In *Case Studies in Archaeology and World Religion.* British Archaeological Reports International Series 755, pp. 33–43. Edited by Timothy Insoll. Oxford.

———. 2003, 'Commemorating and Remembering 1857: The Revolt in Delhi and Its Afterlife.' *World Archaeology*, 35, 1: 35–60.

———. 2004, 'From Ruin to Restoration: The Modern History of Sanchi.' In *Belief in the Past. The Proceedings of the the Manchester Conference on Archaeology and Religion.* British Archaeological Reports Series. 1212, pp. 99–114. Ed. Timothy Insoll. Oxford.

Latif, Syad Muhammad. 1891, *History of the Panjab from the Remotest Antiquity to the Present Time.* Calcutta.

———. 1892, *Lahore its History, Architectural Remains and Antiquities, with an Account of its Modern Institutions, Inhabitants, Their Trade, Customs, etc.* Lahore.

———. 1896, *Agra Historical and Descriptive with an Account of Akbar and His Court and of the Modern City of Agra.* Calcutta.

Lopez Jr., Donald S. ed. 1995, *Curators of the Buddha: The Study of Buddhism under Colonialism.* Chicago.

Low, D.A. 1978, 'Laissez-Faire and Traditional Rulership in Princely India.' In *People, Princes and Paramount Power: Society and Politics in the Indian Princely States*, pp. 373–87. Edited by Robin Jeffrey. Delhi.

Ludden, David. 1994, 'Orientalist Empiricism: Transformations of Colonial Knowledge.' In *Orientalism and the Postcolonial Predicament*, pp. 250–78. Edited by Carol A. Breckenridge and Peter van der Veer. Delhi.

Mackenzie, Colin. 1807, 'Account of Extracts of a Journal.' *Asiatick Researches* 9, 272–8.

———. 1823, 'Ruins of Amravutty, Depauldina and Durnacotta.' *Asiatic Journal and Monthly Register.* 464–78.

Maheshwari, S. 1996, *The Census Administration under the Raj and After.* New Delhi.

Maisey, F.C. 1892, *Sanchi and its Remains: A Full Description of the Ancient Buildings, Sculptures, and Inscriptions at Sanchi near Bhilsa, in Central India with Remarks on the Evidence they Supply as to the Comparatively Modern Date of the Buddhism of Gotama, or Sakya Muni.* London.

Majeed, Javed. 1992, *Ungoverned Imaginings: James Mill's The History of British India and Orientalism.* Oxford.

Majumdar, R.C. 1978, 'Rajendralal Mitra as a National Leader.' In *Rajendralala Mitra (150th Anniversary Lectures)*, pp. 1–23. Asiatic Society, Calcutta.

Mani, B.R. 1997. Delhi. *Threshold of the Orient* (Studies in Archaeological Investigations). New Delhi.

Marshall, G.T. 1837, 'Facsimiles of Ancient Inscriptions.' *JASB* 6: 218–23.

Marshall, John. 1905, *Annual Report of the Director General of Archaeology for the Year 1903–4.* Part I. Calcutta.

———. 1951, *Taxila.* Cambridge.

Marshall, John, and Foucher, A. 1940, *The Monuments of Sanchi.* 3 vols. Calcutta. 1983 reprint edn.

Marshall, P.J. 1968, *Problems of Empire: Britain and India 1757–1813.* London.

———. ed. 1970, *The British Discovery of Hinduism in the Eighteenth Century.* Cambridge.

Masson, Charles. 1842, *Narrative of Various Journeys in Balochistan, Afghanistan and the Panjab, including a Residence in those Countries.* 3 vols. London. 1975 reprint edn. Karachi.

Metcalf, Thomas R. 1989, *An Imperial Vision: Indian Architecture and Britain's Raj.* London, Boston.

———. 1998, *Ideologies of the Raj.* New Cambridge History of India III. 4. New Delhi.

Miller, Edward. 1973, *That Noble Cabinet: A History of the British Museum.* London.

Misra, B.B. 1970, *The Administrative History of India, 1834–1947: General Administration.* Bombay.

———. 1990, *The Unification and Division of India.* Delhi.

Mitra, Debala. 1972, *Excavations at Tilaura-kot and Kondan and Explorations in the Nepalese Tarai.* New Delhi.

Mitra, Dilip Kumar. 1978, 'Rajendralal's Contribution to Languages and Literature.' In *Rajendralala Mitra (150th Anniversary Lectures)*, pp. 70–98. Asiatic Society, Calcutta.

Mitra, Rajendralala. 1875, *A Report on Sanskrit MSS. in Native Libraries.* Calcutta.

———. 1875–80, *The Antiquities of Orissa.* 2 vols. Vol. 1, 1875; vol. 2, 1880; 1961, 1963 reprint edn. Calcutta.

———. 1878, *Buddha Gaya, the Hermitage of Śákya Muni.* Calcutta.

———. 1881, *Indo-Aryans: Contributions Towards the Elucidation of their Ancient and Mediaeval History.* 2 Vols. Calcutta, London.

Mitra, Sisir Kumar. 1973, 'Raja Rajendralal Mitra.' In *Historians and Historiography in Modern India*, pp. 1–14. Edited by S.P. Sen. Calcutta.

Mitter, Jogeshwar, ed. 1892. *Speeches by Raja Rajendralala Mitra.* Calcutta.

Mitter, Partha. 1977, *Much Maligned Monsters: History of European Reactions to Indian Art.* Oxford.

———. 1994, *Art and Nationalsim in Colonialist India 1850-1922.* Cambridge.

Mukharji, P.C. 1899, *Report on the Antiquities in the District of Lalitpur, N.-W. Provinces, India.* Roorkee.

———. 1901, *Report on a Tour of Exploration on the Antiquities in the Tarai, Nepal; The Region of Kapilavastu; During February and March, 1899.* Calcutta. 1969 reprint edn, Delhi, Varanasi.

———. 1902–3, 'Reports Made during the Progress of Excavations at Patna.' *Indian Antiquary,* 31, 1902, pp. 427–41, 495–8; continued in vol. 33, 1903, pp. 76–80.

———. 1903, 'An Independent Hindu View of Buddhist Chronology.' *Indian Antiquary* 32: 227–33.

———. Mukherjee, B.N. 1978, 'Rajendralal Mitra and His Contemporaries.' *In Rajendralala Mitra (150th Anniversary Lectures),* pp. 48–69. Asiatic Society. Calcutta.

Mukherjee, S.N. 1968, *Sir William Jones: A Study in Eighteenth-century British Attitudes to India.* Cambridge.

Müller, F. Max, ed., 1879. *The Sacred Books of the East,* vol. 1. London. 1965 reprint edn, Delhi.

Nath, R. 1979, *Monuments of Delhi: Historical Study.* New Delhi.

Pollock, Sheldon. 1994, 'Deep Orientalism? Notes on Sanksrit and Power Beyond the Raj.' In *Orientalism and the Postcolonial Predicament,* pp. 76-133. Edited by Carol A. Breckenridge and Peter van der Veer. Delhi.

Possehl, G.L. 1990, 'An Archaeological Explorer in Afghanistan: Charles Masson.' *South Asian Studies* 6: 111–24.

Preckel, Claudia. 2000, *Begums of Bhopal.* New Delhi.

Prinsep, 1858, 'On the Coins and Relics discovered by M. le Chevalier Ventura, General in the Service of Maha Raja (sic) Ranjit Singh in the Tope of Manikyala [July 1834].' In Prinsep, James, *Essays on Indian Antiquities,* vol. 1, pp. 90–108. Edited by Edward Thomas. London. 1971 reprint. Varanasi.

———. 1836, 'New Varieties of the Mithraic or Indo-Scythic Series of Coins and their Imitations.' *JASB* 5: 652 ff.

Rajendralala Mitra. 150th Anniversary Lectures. 1978, The Asiatic Society. Calcutta.

Raz, Ram. 1834, *Essay on the Architecture of the Hindus.* London. 1972 reprint edn. Delhi.

Ramaswami, N.S. 1975, *Amaravati: The Art and History of the Stupa and Temple.* Archaeological Series No. 41. Hyderabad.

Rhys Davids, T.W., transl. 1880. *Buddhist Birth Stories.* London.

Rocher, Rosane. 1994, 'British Orientalism in the Eighteenth Century: The Dialectics of Knowledge and Government.' In *Colonialism and the Postcolonial Predicament,* pp. 250–78. Edited by Carol A. Breckenridge and Peter van der Veer. Delhi.

Roy, Anamika. 1994, *Amaravati Stupa: A Critical Comparison of Epigraphic, Architectural and Sculptural Evidence.* 2 vols. New Delhi.

Roy, Sourendranath. 1953, 'Indian Archaeology from Jones to Marshall (1784–1902).' *Ancient India* 9: 4–28.

Sampson, Gary D. 2000, 'Lala Deen Dayal: Between Two Worlds.' In *India Through the Lens: Photography 1840-1911*, pp. 259–91. By Vidya Dehejia *et al.* Washington D.C.

Said, Edward W. 1978, *Orientalism.* London. 1980 reprint edn. London and Henley.

Saraswati, S.K. 1978, 'Raja Rajendralal Mitra.' In *Rajendralala Mitra (150th Anniversary Lectures)*, pp. 34–47. Asiatic Society, Calcutta.

Schwab, Raymond. 1984, *The Oriental Renaissance: Europe's Rediscovery of India and the East 1680–1880.* Translated by Gene Patterson-Black and Victor Reinking. New York.

Sewell, Robert. 1880, *Report on the Amaravati Tope, and Excavations on its Site in 1877.* London.

Shahjahan, H.H. the Nawab, Begum of Bhopal. 1876, *The Táj-ul-Ikbál Tárikh Bhopal; or The History of Bhopal.* Translated by Barstow, C.; Calcutta.

Singh, Upinder. 2001, 'Amaravati: The Dismembering of the Mahācaitya (1797–1886).' *South Asian Studies* 17, 2001: 19–40.

Sinha, N.K. 1995, 'The Armenian Traders in Bengal.' In *Trade and Finance in Colonial India 1750–1860*, pp. 99–106. Edited by A. Siddiqui. Delhi.

Sivaramamurti, C. 1953, 'Museums.' *Ancient India* 9: 233–49.

———. 1977, *Amaravati Sculptures in the Madras Government Museum.* Bulletin of the Madras Government Museum. New Series—General Section, vol. IV. Madras.

Sivaramamurti, C. and Roy, J.K. 1953, 'Museums.' *Ancient India* 9: 233–49.

Smith, V.A. 1887, General Index to the Reports of the Archaeological Survey of India, Volumes I to XXIII. Calcutta.

———. 1906, 'Pygmy Flints.' *Indian Antiquary* 35: 185–95.

Spiers, Edward M. 1980, *The Army and Society, 1815–1947.* Themes in British Social History, gen. ed. J. Stevenson. London and New York.

Srinivasan, Doris Meth, gen. ed. 1998, *Mathura: The Cultural Heritage.* New Delhi.

Srivastava, K.M. 1996, *Excavations at Piprahwa and Ganwaria.* New Delhi.

Sykes, W.H. 1841, 'Notes on the Religious, Moral, and Political State of India before the Mahomedan Invasion, Chiefly Founded on the Travels of the Chinese Buddhist Priest Fa Hian in India, A.D. 399, and on the

Commentaries of Messrs. Remusat, Klaproth, Burnouf, and Landresse.' *JRAS* 6: 450.

Tartakov, Michael Gary. 1994, 'Changing Views of India's Art History.' In *Perceptions of South Asia's Visual Past*, pp. 15–36. Edited by Catherine B. Asher and Thomas R. Metcalf. New Delhi, etc.

Taylor, Philip Meadows. 1851, 'Ancient Remains at the Village of Jiwarji Near Ferozabad on the Bhima.' *JBBRAS* 3: 179–96.

———. 1853, 'Notices of Cromlechs, Cairns and Other Ancient Scytho-Druidical Remains in the Principality of Sorapur.' *JBBRAS* 4, 380–429.

Trautmann, T. 2000, 'Inventing the History of South India.' In *Invoking the Past: The Uses of History in South Asia*, pp. 36–54. Edited by Daud Ali. Delhi.

Trigger, Bruce G. 1984, 'Alternative Archaeologies: Nationalist, Colonialist, Imperialist.' *Man*, NS. 19: 355–70.

———. 1989, *A History of Archaeological Thought*. Cambridge.

———. 1995, 'Romanticism, Nationalism, and Archaeology.' In *Nationalism, Politics, and the Practice of Archaeology*, pp. 263–79. Edited by Philip L. Kohl and Clare Fawcett. Cambridge.

Watters, Thomas. 1904–5, *On Yuan Chwang's Travels in India (A.D. 629–645)*. 2 Vols. London. 1961 reprint edn, Delhi.

Whitteridge, G. 1986, *Charles Masson of Afghanistan*. London.

Wilkins, Charles.1788, 'Translation of a Sanscrit Inscription, Copied from a Stone at Boodha-Gaya by Mr. Wilmot.' *Asiatick Researches* 1: 284.

Willis, Michael. 2000. *Buddhist Reliquaries from Ancient India*. London.

Wilson, David M. 1989, *The British Museum: Purpose and Politics*. London, 1990 2nd impression.

Wilson, H.H. 1839, 'Account of the Doe Kue Ki; or Travels of Fa Hian in India, Translated from the Chinese by Remusat.' *JRAS* 5: 108–40.

———. 1841, *Ariana Antiqua: A Descriptive Account of the Antiquities and Coins of Afghanistan with a Memoir of Buildings called Topes by C. Masson*. London. 1997 reprint edn, New Delhi.

Young, R. 1827, 'An Account of Some Ancient Graves in the Vicinity of Oopulgutt.' *Transactions of the Literary Society of Madras* 1: 26–32.

Index